Books by Arnold Hauser

THE PHILOSOPHY OF ART HISTORY (1958)

THE SOCIAL HISTORY OF ART (1951)

THESE ARE BORZOI BOOKS
PUBLISHED IN NEW YORK BY ALFRED A. KNOPF

THE PHILOSOPHY
OF
ART HISTORY

Arnold Hauser

THE PHILOSOPHY
OF
ART HISTORY

38556

ALFRED A. KNOPF   NEW YORK 1959

L. C. CATALOG CARD NUMBER: 58–10966

© ARNOLD HAUSER, 1958.

THIS IS A BORZOI BOOK, PUBLISHED BY ALFRED A. KNOPF, INC.

FIRST AMERICAN EDITION

Originally published in Germany as PHILOSOPHIE DER KUNSTGESCHICHTE. © *C. H. Beck'sche Verlagsbuchhandlung (Oscar Beck) München 1958.*

Preface

THIS BOOK is concerned with the methodology of
art history, and so with questions about historical
thinking; it enquires what scientific history of art can accomplish, what are its means and its limitations. It contains philosophical reflections on history, but not a philosophy of history
in the sense of a theoretical scheme of world history, nor a
logic of the historical process, nor yet historical prophecy;
there will be no attempt to deduce the process of history from
some higher idea, nor yet to press everything past and future
into a unitary scheme. In this respect it remains faithful to the
principles that guided me in *The Social History of Art* (1951).
However, the point of view and form of exposition will be quite
different. In the former book I adopted the descriptive method
and aimed at complete subordination of my theoretical presuppositions and the regularities I believed I had discovered to
the task of describing and interpreting the historical phenomena. It was left to the reader to take note of and to criticise
the categories in terms of which the interpretation proceeded.
I deliberately avoided providing an introduction in which I
might have informed him directly about my intentions and
method. In a sense, the present work is intended to take the
place of that unwritten Introduction. In it the philosophical
presuppositions of my conception of art history are set forth
explicitly, historical material being employed only to illustrate
fundamental conceptions of a systematic character. This time
it is left to the reader to test these conceptions in the light of
his own experiences with art and his own view of history.

Where he feels a lack of agreement, author or reader may have been at fault, the author if he has lost sight of the concrete historical realities which are his subject, the reader if he has failed to make the effort of abstraction necessary for any systematic enquiry.

My view of the character of the historical process within which art is enmeshed remains unchanged, notably my conviction that the sociological method is as indispensable in the history of art as in the history of the other spiritual creations of mankind. I am still very conscious of the limitations of the sociological method. The leading principle, both of my previous work and of this, may most simply be formulated as follows: everything in history is the achievement of individuals; individuals always find themselves in a certain definite situation in time and place; their behavior is the product both of their inborn capacities and of the situation. That is in truth the kernel of the doctrine of the dialectical character of historical events. The opponents of the method I adopted accused me of being overmuch entangled in the preconceptions of the dialectical theory of history. Readers of the present book will not fail to note the reservations that I have to enter against the classical formulations of this theory; and they will find that the most serious defect I now see in my former book consists in a failure to apply the dialectical method cautiously enough. I had not sufficiently realized when I wrote it that the meaning and function of a stylistic trend are by no means unalterable, that the flexibility of its connection with the various social groups can scarcely be over-emphasized. It is of the essence of all historical development that the first step decides the second, these together the third, and so on. No single step by itself enables one to draw conclusions as to the direction of all subsequent steps; without knowledge of all the previous steps, no single step can be explained, and even with such knowledge it cannot be predicted.

The problems of the present book have occupied me without intermission since the appearance of my *Social History of*

Art; they all revolve round the few points that I have just indicated. That common origin of the problems examined gives the present work its unity. Different sections arose out of various occasions, but I would not let myself be deflected from the end I had in view. The intimate connection between problems that recur in several different chapters, though in different perspectives, has made some repetition of my fundamental theses unavoidable. This defect might have been remedied by pruning, but it seemed preferable to leave some few repetitions rather than risk impairing the completeness and natural flow of thought.

The first two chapters reproduce with little alteration the text of lectures. This fact explains both the briefness of the bibliographical notes, which were added subsequently, and also a certain pithy, programmatic character of the text. They take up problems that are more precisely formulated in later chapters. The chapter on the concept of "art history without names" both is the most elaborate and occupies a central position in the book; in it the philosophical outlook basic for the whole work is most thoroughly discussed. The chapter on psychoanalysis is the contribution of an enthusiastic, professionally uncommitted outsider. The chapter on folk art and popular art is the outcome of long, enthralling study and of that unremitting anxiety about the future in which my generation has grown up. The chapter on the role of convention in the history of art is perhaps the most personal one in the book, and the one in which most evidently the thought both promises and requires further development.

A. H.

Contents

ix

CONTENTS

x

I

Introduction:

The Scope and Limitations

of a Sociology of Art

A WORK OF ART is a challenge; we do not explain it, we adjust ourselves to it. In interpreting it, we draw upon our own aims and endeavors, inform it with a meaning that has its origin in our own ways of life and thought. In a word, any art that really affects us becomes to that extent modern art.

Works of art however are like unattainable heights. We do not go straight toward them, but circle round them. Each generation sees them from a different point of view and with a fresh eye; nor is it to be assumed that a later point of view is more apt than an earlier one. Each aspect comes into sight in its own time, which cannot be anticipated or prolonged; and yet its significance is not lost, for the meaning that a work assumes for a later generation is the result of the whole range of previous interpretations.

We are now living in the day of the sociological interpretation of cultural achievements. This day will not last for ever, and it will not have the last word. It opens up new aspects, achieves new and surprising insights; and yet this point of view evidently has its own limitations and inadequacies. At best perhaps, before its day is over, we may be able to anticipate some of the future criticisms and become aware of its insufficiencies without forgoing the insights that have been and may be gained within these limits.

There are still people who do not feel quite happy when

spiritual phenomena, or, as they prefer to call them, the higher spiritual values, are in any way brought into connection with the struggle for existence, class conflict, competition, prestige, and the like. To deal with them fully would take us too far from our subject; here we can only remark that requiring the spiritual to be preserved from all contact with the material frequently turns out to be a way of defending a position of privilege.

Far more worthy of consideration are those who resist a sociological interpretation of spiritual achievements from a conviction that any significant structure, and above all a work of art, is an independent entity, a closed and complete system in itself, the elements of which are to be entirely explained in terms of interdependence, without any recourse to circumstances of its origin or to its influence. For a work of art undoubtedly has an inner logic of its own, and its particular quality is most clearly seen in the internal structural relations of the various levels of organization and the various motifs distinguishable in it. It is further indisputable that consideration of genetic relationships, that is, of the stages by which the artist moved from one idea or motif to another, not merely introduces a different emphasis, but is also likely to blind us to internal connections and alter the values upon which the aesthetic effect of the work depends. The factors that are most important in the actual production of the work are not equally important in giving it artistic value and effectiveness. Again, the practical aims of the artist, that is, the extraneous purposes that the work of art may be intended to serve, are not always in accord with the inner aesthetic structure that the work reveals. But the exponents of the theory of "art for art's sake"—and that is what is at issue here—are not content with asserting that a work of art is a microcosm and exerts a sovereign power over men; they maintain that any reference to actualities beyond the work must irretrievably destroy its aesthetic illusion. That may be correct, and yet this illusion is not all, to produce it is not the exclusive or the most important aim of

4

artistic endeavor. Even if it be true that we have to loosen our hold upon reality to a certain extent in order to fall under the spell of art, it is no less true that all genuine art leads us by a detour, which may be longer or shorter, back to reality in the end. Great art gives us an interpretation of life which enables us to cope more successfully with the chaotic state of things and to wring from life a better, that is, a more convincing and more reliable, meaning.

The purely formal laws of art are not essentially different from the rules of a game. However complicated, subtle, and ingenious such rules may be, they have little significance in themselves, that is to say, apart from the purpose of winning the game. Considered as mere movements, the maneuvers of football players are unintelligible and, in the long run, boring. For a time one can find a certain pleasure in their speed and suppleness—but how meaningless are these qualities compared with those noted by the expert observer who understands the object of all this running, jumping, and pushing. If we do not know or even want to know the aims that the artist was pursuing through his work—his aims to inform, to convince, to influence people—then we do not get much farther in understanding his art than the ignorant spectator who judges the football simply by the beauty of the players' movements. A work of art is a communication; although it is perfectly true that the successful transmission of this requires an outward form at once effective, attractive, faultless, it is no less true that this form is insignificant apart from the message it communicates.

The work of art has been compared to the opening of a window upon the world. Now, a window can claim the whole of our attention or none. One may, it is said, contemplate the view without concerning oneself in the very least with the quality, structure, or color of the window-pane. By this analogy, the work of art can be described as a mere vehicle for experiences, a transparent window-pane, or a sort of eye-glasses not noticed by the wearer and employed simply as means to an end.

But just as one can concentrate one's attention upon the window-pane and the structure of its glass without taking note of the view beyond, so, it is said, one can treat the work of art as an independent, "opaque" formal structure, complete in itself and in isolation, as it were, from anything external to it.[1] No doubt one can stare at the window-pane as long as one likes; still, a window is made to look out of.

Culture serves to protect society. Spiritual creations, traditions, conventions, and institutions are but ways and means of social organization. Religion, philosophy, science, and art all have their place in the struggle to preserve society. To confine oneself to art, it is first of all a tool of magic, a means of ensuring the livelihood of the primitive horde of hunters. Then it becomes an instrument of animistic religion, used to influence good and bad spirits in the interest of the community. Gradually this is transformed into a magnification of the almighty gods and their earthly representatives, by hymn and panegyric, through statues of gods and kings. Finally, in the form of more or less open propaganda, it is employed in the interests of a close group, a clique, a political party, a social class.[2] Only here and there, in times of relative security or of social estrangement of the artists, it withdraws from the world and makes a show of indifference to practical aims, professing to exist for its own sake and for the sake of beauty.[3] But even then it performs an important social function by providing men with a means of expressing their power and their "conspicuous leisure."[4] Indeed, it achieves much more than that, promoting the interests of a certain social stratum by the mere portrayal and implicit acknowledgment of its moral and aesthetic standards of value. The artist, whose whole livelihood, with all his hopes and prospects, depends upon such a social group, becomes quite

---

[1] José Ortega y Gasset: *La Deshumanización del Arte* (1925), p. 19.
[2] Cf. Arnold Hauser: *The Social History of Art* (1951), I, 23–103.
[3] Ibid., I, 91–4; II, 684, 731–4, 780, 786.
[4] Thorstein Veblen: *The Theory of the Leisure Class* (1899), p. 36.

6

unintentionally and unconsciously the mouthpiece of his customers and patrons.

The discovery of the propaganda value of cultural creations, and of art in particular, was made early in human history and exploited to the full, whereas thousands of years passed before man was ready to acknowledge the ideological character of art in terms of an explicit theory, to express the idea that art pursues practical aims either consciously or unconsciously, is either open or veiled propaganda. The philosophers of the French, and even of the Greek enlightenment, discovered the relativity of cultural standards, and doubts regarding the objectivity and ideality of human valuations were expressed again and again in the course of the centuries; Marx, however, was the first to formulate explicitly the conception that spiritual values are political weapons. He taught that every spiritual creation, every scientific notion, every portrayal of reality derives from a certain particular aspect of truth, viewed from a perspective of social interest, and is accordingly restricted and distorted. But Marx neglected to note that we wage a continual war against such distorting tendencies in our thought, that in spite of the inevitable partialities of our mental outlook, we do possess the power of examining our own thought critically, and so correcting to a certain extent the one-sidedness and error of our views. Every honest attempt to discover the truth and depict things faithfully is a struggle against one's own subjectivity and partiality, one's individual and class interests; one can seek to become aware of these as a source of error, while realizing that they can never be finally excluded. Engels understood this process of pulling oneself out of the mud by one's own bootstraps when he spoke of the "triumph of realism" in Balzac.[5] But no doubt such correcting of our ideological falsification of the truth operates within the limits of what is thinkable and imaginable from our place in the world, not in a vacuum of abstract free-

[5] Letter to Miss Harkness, April 1888, in Karl Marx & Friedrich Engels: *Literature and Art* (1947), pp. 42–3.

7

dom. And the fact that there are such limits of objectivity is the ultimate and decisive justification for a sociology of culture; they stop up the last loophole by which we might hope to escape from the influence of social causation.

Apart from its external limitations, the sociology of art also has internal limitations. All art is socially conditioned, but not everything in art is definable in sociological terms. Above all, artistic excellence is not so definable; it has no sociological equivalent. The same social conditions can give rise to valuable or to utterly valueless works, and such works have nothing in common but tendencies more or less irrelevant from the artistic point of view. All that sociology can do is to account in terms of its actual origin for the outlook on life manifested in a work of art, whereas for an appreciation of its quality everything depends upon the creative handling and the mutual relations of the elements expressing that outlook. Such elements may assume the most diverse aesthetic quality, and again the qualitative criteria may be the same in spite of great diversity of outlook. It is no more than an idle dream, a residue of the ideal of *kalokagathia,* to suppose that social justice and artistic worth in any way coincide, that one can draw any conclusions with regard to the aesthetic success or failure of a work from the social conditions under which it has been produced. The great alliance envisaged by nineteenth-century liberalism between political progress and genuine art, between democratic and artistic feeling, between the interests of humanity in general and universally valid rules of art was a fantasy without any basis in fact. Even the alleged connection between truth of art and truth in politics, the identification of naturalism with socialism, which was from the beginning a basic thesis of socialistic art theory and still is part of its creed, is very dubious.[6] It might be very satisfying to know that social injustice and political oppression were punished with spiritual sterility, but this is not always the case. There have indeed been periods such as that of the Second Empire, in which the predominance of a

[6] Hauser, op. cit., II, 775.

not very sympathetic social type was characterized by bad taste and lack of originality in art; but along with that inferior art much valuable work was being produced as well. Along with Octave Feuillet there was Gustave Flaubert, along with the Bouguereaus and Baudrys, artists of the rank of Delacroix and Courbet. It may, however, be significant that from the social and political point of view Delacroix was no closer to Courbet than to Bouguereau, that the common artistic aims of these two artists did not rest upon any sort of political solidarity.

Still, on the whole one may say that in the Second Empire the *arriviste* bourgeoisie got the artists it deserved. But what is one to say about epochs such as those of the Ancient Orient or the Middle Ages, in which a most severe despotism or a most intolerant spiritual dictatorship, far from preventing the production of the greatest art, created conditions of life under which the artist did not seem to suffer in the least, certainly no more than he now fancies himself to suffer under the compulsions of even a very liberal form of government? Does not this show that the preconditions of quality in art lie beyond the alternatives of political freedom or unfreedom, and that such quality is not to be compassed by sociological methods?

And what of examples that seem to suggest a contrary view: Greek classical art, which had scarcely any connection with the common people and only the very slightest connection with democracy? Or the "democracy" of the Italian Renaissance, which was anything but a democracy in reality? Or cases from our own day which show the attitude of the masses to art?

It is reported that some time ago an English firm published a book of reproductions of paintings of the most various sorts— good and bad, examples of popular and of more refined taste, devotional pictures, illustrations of anecdotes, and genuine pictorial creations all jumbled up together. The purchasers of the book were requested to indicate the pictures they preferred. The result was that, although as book-buyers the persons questioned were more or less cultivated, and although eighty per cent of the reproductions fell within the category of "good art,"

9

thus loading the scales in its favor, not one of the first six pictures getting the most votes belonged to this category.[7]

If we took this kind of response to signify that the great public is definitely opposed to the better sort of art and prefers the worse, we could at any rate formulate a sociological law establishing a relation—though an inverse relation—between aesthetic quality and popularity; but there is no trace of any consistent attitude to aesthetic quality in this case. Undoubtedly there is always a certain tension between quality and popularity, at times—as now with modern art—an open conflict. Art that is worth anything is addressed to those who have attained a certain cultural level, not to the "natural man" of Rousseau; understanding of it depends upon certain educational preconditions, and its popularity is inevitably limited. Uneducated people, on the other hand, do not positively favor bad art over good; they judge success by quite other than aesthetic criteria. They react, not to what is artistically good or bad, but to features that have a reassuring or a disturbing effect upon their course of life; they are ready to accept what is artistically valuable provided that it supplies vital value for them by portraying their wishes, their fantasies, their day-dreams, provided that it calms their anxieties and increases their sense of security. One must not, however, forget that the strange, the unaccustomed, the difficult has, merely as such, a disquieting effect upon an uneducated public.

Thus sociology fails to explain the connections between artistic quality and popularity; and to questions about the material conditions of the creation of works of art it gives answers that are not altogether satisfying. For sociology is subject to certain limitations common to all those disciplines, notably psychology, which employ the genetic method to deal with cultural forms, limitations arising out of that method. It is in fact likely to lose sight, from time to time, of the work of art as such and to consider it a record of something more important than

[7] I have been unable to obtain further information about the work in question.

the work itself. And just as the factors psychologically decisive in the creative process are not always identical with the artistically most important factors in the work, so also the sociologically most significant features of a work or of a school are not always the ones that are aesthetically relevant. From a sociological point of view a second-rate or third-rate artist may occupy a key position in a particular artistic movement. The social history of art does not replace or invalidate art history, or vice versa; each starts from a different set of facts and values. When the social history of art is judged by the standards of art history, the facts begin to seem distorted. To counter this impression, one may point out that even art history adopts standards different from those of simple art criticism, and again from those of immediate aesthetic experience, that there is often a decided tension between historical and aesthetic values. The sociological view of art is to be rejected only if it claims to be the sole legitimate point of view, and if it confuses the sociological importance of a work with aesthetic value.

Apart from this shifting of emphasis, which, though it may confuse is easily compensated for, the sociology of art has in common with other disciplines employing the genetic method a further inadequacy in the eyes of the art-lover: it claims to derive special and unique characteristics of works of art from that which is of quite another order, from something general and artistically indifferent. The worst example of this sort of trespassing is seen in any attempt to show that artistic quality or artistic talent is dependent upon economic conditions. It would be too cheap a retort merely to assert that only a few dogmatic simpletons have proposed to derive spiritual forms directly from economic facts, that the formation of ideologies is a long, complicated, gradual process, far different from that envisaged by vulgar materialism. Complicated, full of interruptions and contradictions the way may be that leads from certain social conditions to the creation of spiritual values, as for instance from Dutch middle-class capitalism to the works of Rembrandt; still, in the end one has to decide whether or not such conditions are relevant. One can put off the decision, conceal one's position, talk of dualism and dialectic, reciprocity and mutual dependence of spirit and matter; but after all one is either an idealist or a realist, and has to face the question of whether genius falls from heaven or fashions itself here on earth.

However one may decide this ultimate question, the translation of economic conditions into ideologies remains a process that can never be completely clarified; at some point or other, it involves a gap or leap. But we should not suppose that only the transition from material conditions to the spiritual involves us in a leap of this sort; all transition from one spiritual form to another, change of style and fashion, collapse of an old tradition and rise of a new, influence of one artist on another, or even a single artist's turns of direction—all these changes are equally discontinuous and inexplicable. Seen from without, every change looks abrupt and remains, strictly speaking, unintelligible. Continuous gradual change is something of which we have only a subjective, inner experience; it cannot be reconstructed from objective data.

The leap from the material to the spiritual is immeasurable, and yet we make this leap within the sphere of social life, even within the sphere of economics. The most primitive economy is a humanly organized economy, not a natural condition; nature once left behind, we do not anywhere encounter the merely material; we may think we are talking about material conditions, but the leap into the realm of spiritual conceptions has already occurred. The distance between natural occurrences and the most primitive economy is thus in a way greater than that from primitive economy to the highest flights of the human spirit, although every stretch of the way is broken by abysses.

One of the most obvious shortcomings of the sociology of art, as of all genetic explanation of spiritual structures, derives from the endeavor to analyze into simple elements an object whose very nature consists in its complexity. No doubt scientific explanation involves simplification, analysis of the complex into such components as occur in other complexes also. Outside the field of art this procedure does not destroy anything really of the essence of the object, but when applied to art, it eliminates the object as presented in its completeness, the only way in which it can be properly presented. If one eliminates or purposely neglects the complexity of the work of art, interweaving motifs, ambiguity of symbols, polyphony of voices, mutual dependence of form and content, unanalyzable fluctuations of cadence and emphasis, then the best of what art offers us is gone. Still, sociology is not alone in incurring this sort of loss, for all scientific treatment of art has to pay for knowledge gained by destroying the immediate, ultimately irretrievable, aesthetic experience. In even the most sensitive and understanding historical analyses of art, that original direct experience has been lost. All this is, of course, no excuse for the special shortcomings to which the sociologist is prone, nor does it liberate him from the duty of correcting the defects of his point of view as best he may, or at least of being aware of them.

The work of art is not only a source of complex personal experience, but also has another kind of complexity, being a nodal point of several different causal lines. It is the outcome of at least three different types of conditions: psychological, sociological and stylistic. As a psychological being, the individual retains not merely the freedom of choosing among the various possibilities permitted by social causation; he is also always creating for himself new possibilities in no way prescribed by his society, even though they may be restricted by the social conditions under which he lives. The creative individual invents new forms of expression, does not find them ready-made. What he takes for granted is of a negative rather than positive character: it is the totality of what cannot be thought, felt, expressed, or understood at that particular historical moment. Undoubtedly, such "blind spots" of an epoch can be established only subsequently; our actual state of affairs always has an anarchical look, as if the individual could do with it just what he fancies. Subsequently one comes to see a social law that has moulded the individual choices in accordance with a unitary trend. In a similar way a stylistic line gradually comes to be recognized, along which particular modes of expression which have seemed to be freely selected fall into place. Indeed, stylistic trends, even more than sociological, have definitely the appearance of being objective regularities that impose themselves upon the individual choices; viewed retrospectively, the individuals seem to be little more than carriers of these anonymous stylistic trends.

But the history of style cannot do away with either psychological or sociological causation. It will never be possible to explain by purely formal, stylistic considerations why a line of artistic development breaks off at a certain point and gives place to a completely different one instead of going on to further progress and expansion—in short, why a change occurred just when it did. The "climax" of a line of development cannot be foretold on the basis of formal criteria; revolution occurs when a certain style is no longer adapted to expressing the spirit of the time, something that depends on psychological and sociological conditions. Change of style, no doubt, occurs in a direction determined from within; but there are always a number of possible directions, and in any case the "maturity" of choice is never fixed in advance or secure from the unforeseeable. Among the circumstances governing the occurrence of the change, social conditions are probably pre-eminent; but it would be a mistake to suppose that social conditions produce the forms in terms by which the artistic revolution expresses itself; these forms are just as much the product of psychological and stylistic as of sociological factors. When one considers social causation, psychology appears as a sort of incipient, abortive sociology; when one regards the psychological motivation, sociology looks like a refusal to trace events to their ultimate origins in the make-up of the human soul. From the stylistic point of view, both psychology and sociology make the same mistake: they derive what is special to art from motives of a heterogenous character, explain artistic forms in terms of something that has nothing to do with "form." Only in descrip-

14

tive analysis is the uniqueness and complexity of the work of art preserved; it is inevitably destroyed by attempts at pragmatic explanation, whether genetic or teleological. In this respect psychology and art history are on the same footing as sociology.

The inadequacy, however, that we often find in the sociologist's view of art is not simply the result of the method of research which sociology shares with psychology and art history. It is also owing to the rather undeveloped language applied by the sociologist to the subtly differentiated world of art, a language vastly inferior to the far more refined and appropriate language of the psychologist and the art historian. The concepts with which the sociologist works are woefully inadequate for dealing with the wealth and subtlety of artistic production. Categories such as "courtly," "bourgeois," "capitalistic," "urban," "conservative," and "liberal" are too narrow and schematic and also too rigid to do justice to the special character of a work of art. Each category comprehends such a variety of artistic views and aims that it does not tell us much that is really relevant. What do we really know about the artistic problems with which Michelangelo had to wrestle, about the individuality of his means and methods, when we have noted merely that he was contemporary with the formulae of the Council of Trent, the new political realism, the birth of modern capitalism and absolutism? When we know all this, we perhaps understand better his restless spirit, the turn that his art took in the direction of mannerism, possibly even in some measure the astounding inarticulateness of his last works. His greatness and the incomparable quality of his aims are no more explained this way than Rembrandt's genius is to be explained by the economic and social conditions that were at once the foundation of his artistic career and his undoing. Here we come up against the definite limits of sociological inquiry.

But if there are such limits, do they really matter? If sociology is unable to penetrate to the ultimate secret of the art of a Rembrandt, are we to dispense entirely with what it can tell us? For example, are we to refuse to probe into the social preconditions of his art, and so of the stylistic pecularities that distinguish it from the art of the contemporary Flemish painters, notably Rubens? That would be to ignore the only means of throwing light upon the otherwise unintelligible fact that two such different types of art as Flemish baroque and Dutch naturalism arose almost simultaneously, in direct geographical contact with one another, on the basis of similar cultural traditions and a long political experience in common, but under markedly different economic and social conditions. Certainly, we have here no explanation of Rubens's greatness or the mystery of Rembrandt. But then, what genetic explanation of this stylistic difference is there other than the sociological one that Rubens produced his works in a courtly-artistocratic society, Rembrandt his in a bourgeois world, with its inclination to inwardness? That Rubens, unlike Rembrandt, went to Italy and absorbed the spirit of Italian baroque is rather a symptom than an explanation in itself. Mannerism was in fashion at the turn of the century in the northern provinces as in the southern, and at first Protestant tendencies were to be found in the South just as much as in the North. But in Flanders, in consequence of the Spanish rule, there was an ostentatious court, an aristocracy accustomed to appear in public, a magnificient Church—all things that did not exist in the sober, protestant Holland that repelled the Spaniards. There, on the contrary, we find a bourgeois capitalism, liberal and without much feeling for prestige, and so ready to let its artists work according to their own fancies, and starve as they pleased. Rembrandt and Rubens are unique and incomparable; not so their styles and their fates. The various turns and changes that we detect in the course of their artistic development and the story of their lives are by no means without parallel, and do not incline us to attribute the difference of type in their art simply to individual disposition and personal genius.

Sociology possesses no philosopher's stone, does not work miracles or solve all problems. Still, it is more than just one departmental discipline among many. As was theology in the Middle Ages, philosophy in the seventeenth century, and economics in the eighteenth, it is a focal discipline in our day, one upon which the entire world-view of the age centers. To recognize the claims of sociology is to decide in favor of a rational ordering of life and for a struggle against prejudices. The idea upon which this cardinal position of sociology is founded is the discovery of the ideological character of thought, a discovery made in several different guises, during the past hundred years, in Nietzsche's and Freud's exposures of self-deception no less than in Marx's historical materialism. To get clear about oneself, to become conscious of the presuppositions of one's own character, thought, and will is the requirement upon which all these different thinkers insist. Sociology endeavors to probe into the preconditions of thought and will which derive from a man's social position. Objections made to such research are mostly due to the fact that correct estimation of these social connections is not a purely theoretical matter; men are inclined to admit them or deny them on ideological grounds. Many of those who will not hear of sociology exaggerate its deficiencies in order that they need not become conscious of their prejudices. Others resist sociological interpretation of everything in the spiritual realm, not wishing to give up the fiction of a timeless validity of thought and a meta-historical destiny for man. Those on the other hand who accept sociology as simply one means toward more perfect knowledge have no reason to minimize either its undeniable limitations or the extent of its unexplored possibilities.

II

The Sociological Approach:
The Concept of Ideology
in the History of Art

T HE CONCEPT OF IDEOLOGY, derived from the notion of "false consciousness," shows striking analogies with the concept of "rationalization" in psychoanalysis. The individual "rationalizes" his attitudes, his thoughts, his feelings, his actions; that is, he is concerned to give them an acceptable interpretation, unobjectionable from the standpoint of social conventions. In a similar way, social groups, speaking through representative individuals, interpret natural and historical events, and above all their own opinions and valuations, in accord with their material interests, desire for power, considerations of prestige, and other social aims. And just as the individual in his motives and aims remains unconscious that he is rationalizing, for the most part the members of a social group also are unaware of the fact that their thought is conditioned by material conditions of life. Otherwise, as Engels says, "the whole ideology would collapse." [1] The analogy with psychoanalysis takes us a step farther. Just as the individual does not need to rationalize the whole of his behavior, a large part of his thoughts, feelings and acts being socially unobjectionable or negligible, so also the cultural products of groups include representations and interpretations of reality which are "harmless" and "objective" because they have no direct connection

[1] Friedrich Engels: *Ludwig Feuerbach and the Outcome of Classical German Philosophy*, in Karl Marx & Friedrich Engels: *Selected Works* (1942), I, 417 ff. Letter to Franz Mehring of July 14, 1893, ibid., pp. 388 ff.

with the interests of the groups concerned and do not collide with the interests of any other groups. Thus, mathematical propositions and theories of natural science are, on the whole, objective, and obey principles that may be considered to be timeless and invariable criteria of truth. But the scope of such objective propositions is relatively narrow, and though one feels a certain reluctance to make the history of mathematics or mechanics an appendage of economic history, there can be no doubt that even a natural science such as medicine shows traces of dependence upon economic and social conditions, so that not merely the emergence of problems, but often also the direction in which the solution of the problems is sought, can be seen to be socially conditioned. On the other hand, the humanistic disciplines too, especially the different branches of historical research, are confronted with a vast number of problems that have nothing, or scarcely anything, to do with an ideological interpretation of the material, problems of which the solution can in the main be judged by objective criteria.

Leaving questions of detail aside, it is obvious that each of the various cultural structures, such as religion, philosophy, science, and art, has its own proper "distance" from its social origin; they form a series with many steps, manifesting progressive "ideological saturation." This series reaches from mathematics, which is almost neutral from the sociological point of view, its particular propositions scarcely allowing one to draw any conclusions as to their date, place, or circumstances of origin, to art, in which hardly a single feature could be considered indifferent from the historical and social point of view. In this series, art stands in the very closest connection with social reality and farthest from the region of what are commonly regarded as timelessly valid ideas. At least it is directed in a far more unreserved and straightforward way to social aims, serves far more manifestly and unmistakably as ideological weapon, as panegyric or propaganda, than objective sciences. That the social tendencies art serves can scarcely ever be seen unconcealed and unsublimated—that is of the essence of the

22

ideological mode of expression, which, if it is to achieve its aims, cannot afford to call a child by its proper name.

In the series that runs from art to the exact science and mathematics, the autonomy of cultural structures grows in inverse proportion to the distance from the immediate experience of the actual living individual, in whose psychic life thought and feeling, contemplation and action, theory and practice are undifferentiated—the individual whom Wilhelm Dilthey, as we know, termed the "whole man." The more nearly the "subject" of the various fields of cultural creation coincides with the concrete real man, the less this subject is regarded as something impersonal and unhistorical, and the more is his thought seen to be socially dependent and ideologically conditioned. Undoubtedly both "consciousness in general" as the correlative of the natural sciences and Dilthey's "whole man" are simply *limiting* concepts and useful only as "ideal types." Abstract, timeless "consciousness in general" is not found in its purity even in a mathematical operation; and the "whole man" free from all trace of specialization is not manifest even in those works of art which have the most universal and immediate appeal—for any work of art requires for its realization a certain degree of one-sidedness and mediation, a restriction upon the role of the whole living individual.

Even in Marx and Engels there is talk of the varying distance between the different cultural structures and their economic substratum; and Engels remarks in a well-known passage of his work on Feuerbach that in the higher ideologies "the interconnection between the ideas and their material condition of existence becomes more and more complicated, more and more obscured by intermediate links." This view of the matter is essentially correct. The content of art, religion, and philosophy is much richer, and their structure far more opaque, than that of the natural sciences and mathematics; it is so even when compared with that of Law and the State, in which economic conditions are expressed more directly, that is, in a less sublimated fashion. But the fact that the property conditions of a certain economic system are expressed more directly in current legal provisions and political institutions than in the contemporaneous trends of philosophy or art does not imply that art and philosophy are more independent than juristic or political thought of the actual conditions of life. In fact, they keep drawing upon immediate, socio-historical reality to a much greater extent than Law with its codified rules or the State with its stereotyped institutions. In the case of art and philosophy, the workings of social causation may be veiled, but they are no less decisive and no less far-reaching than in the other cultural fields.

The problem of ideology, however, takes on a different form in the field of art from that in the sciences, the concept of truth in art being so strikingly different from that of theoretical truth. A work of art is not "correct" or "incorrect" in the way a scientific theory is; it cannot properly speaking be termed either true or false. The concept of changeless, super-historical validity can be applied to art only with very special reservations, and here all talk of "false consciousness," as of correct consciousness, is out of place. In other words: when truth is not what is aimed at, it is idle to speak of conformity to it or evasion of it. Art is partisan through and through, and because a view of reality which did not reflect any particular standpoint would be devoid of all artistic quality, the problem of relativity simply does not arise in art. Every aspect of art is a perspective; only one that involves an inner contradiction can rightly be termed "false."

And yet it would be wrong to deny to art all claim of achieving truth, to deny that it can make a valuable contribution to our knowledge of the world and of man. That works of literature are an abundant source of knowledge requires perhaps no further proof; the most penetrating achievements of psychological insight which we have at our disposal derive from the masters of novel and drama. But there can be no doubt that the visual arts also contribute a good deal toward giving us our bearings in the world. It is, of course, important to point out the difference between scientific knowledge and artistic representation, to emphasize, for instance, that to speak of "stylistic" trends is perfectly legitimate in art, but very questionable in science.[2] The sociologist, however, can only feel uneasy about any too radical separation of art and science. For after all, the world-view of a generation—or, more exactly, of a group that is historically and socially self-contained—is an indivisible whole. Attempts to demarcate the different fields in which this world-view manifests itself may be very promising from the epistemological point of view, but to the sociologist they appear as violent dissections of the reality he studies. To him, philosophy, science, law, custom, and art are different aspects of one unitary attitude to reality: in all these forms men are searching for an answer to the same question, for a solution to one and the same problem of how to live. They are not ultimately concerned with formulating scientific truths, producing works of art, or even laying down moral precepts, but with achieving a workable world-view, a reliable guiding principle for life. Always and everywhere they are bent upon one and the same task, that of subjugating the bewildering strangeness and ambiguity of things.

To point to the share of art in the formation of world-views is not to say that it is continuously tied to practical needs or to deny that a special feature of art is precisely its emancipation from current reality. If anyone is inclined to over-stress the real conditions of artistic production, it may be rightly pointed out that the development of stylistic forms has an inner logic of its own. Art displays a rigorous consistency in its pursuit of the solution of certain formal problems, and within each stylistic period a fairly steady and continuous progress toward that goal can be discerned. It has, however, been asserted that an immanent development of this kind occurs not only in the phases of history which are stylistically unitary and coherent—

[2] Theodor Geiger: *"Kritische Bemerkungen zum Begriffe der Ideologie,"* in *Gegenwartsprobleme der Soziologie* (*A. Vierkandt zum 80. Geburtstag,* 1949), p. 143.

periods, for instance, in which there is steady progress in naturalistic representation or in abstract formalization—but also in the succession of the various styles. From this point of view, the successive styles seem to be related as question and answer, or as thesis and antithesis. For example, the baroque is said to be, not the expression of new socio-historical conditions of life, but the "logical" continuation of the Renaissance—that is, in part the solution of the formal problems set by the works of the Renaissance masters, in part the result of a contradiction, which also arises out of a relationship to those masters. Such a "logic of history," which asserts the inner necessity of each successive step in the development, always has a certain appeal; however, it justifies itself only when applied within the limits of a certain unitary stylistic trend. When one comes to a change of style, it breaks down.

For even supposing that one could admit such an antithetic relation between successive trends to be a general principle of stylistic development, one could never explain by purely formal and intrinsic characteristics why at a certain point of time one trend gives way to a different one. The stimulus to a change of style always comes from without, and is logically contingent. Nor are feeling of satiety and desire for change at all adequate as an explanation of the disappearance of a style. Certainly, desire for change often plays as important a role in the history of art as in the history of fashions; but this requirement can be satisfied, when talent is available, without going outside the potentialities of the current style. In any case, with the ageing of a well-established social culture, there comes both a growing desire for a renewal of the accepted forms, and, often, an increased resistance to every attempt to change them. In general, the emergence of a new public is needed to shake a deeply and firmly rooted tradition of art and bring about a radical change of taste. The dissolution of the rococo is to be accounted for not at all on intrinsic grounds, slick and unexciting as its products had become, but primarily by the new patronage of art in the revolutionary period. Wölfflin held that

the external stimulus is more marked and more clearly dis-
cernible in a reversal of style, than in the ups and downs of an
uninterrupted line of development. In reality, there is no difference of principle between these two phases or kinds of the
one process. External influences are not more decisive, they
are merely more obvious in the case of the interrupted development. A closer look reveals extrinsic factors always at work
whether there is a change of style or not. Social realities—what
Wölfflin called "external conditions" [3]—always play the same
role in influencing the choice of form; for any formulation involves a *choice* of form. At every moment of the development
the question of what one should do, what attitude one should
take to the current possibilities, is an open question that has
to be answered afresh. One says "yes" or "no" to the direction
in which the others are moving and which one has followed
oneself up to now; and acceptance is neither more mechanical
nor less voluntary than rejection. To uphold an established
tradition is often just as much a decision, just as much the result
of a dialectical process full of conflicts and having its internal
and external preconditions, as the decision to change it. The attempt, for instance, to stem a tide flowing in the direction of
ever-greater naturalism does not involve different principles of
motivation from those which govern the contrary desire, to
promote and accelerate this naturalism. One is always faced by
the same questions: is the received style still serviceable as a
guide to life in a changed world? Can it still impress, convince,
and spur to action? Is it still a suitable weapon in the struggle
for life? Does it reveal what should be revealed and veil what
should be veiled?

The artist never puts these questions to himself in so many
words. Seldom does he answer them consciously or directly;
nor are they put to him by any particular agents of society.
Wölfflin's mistake, his lack of sociological sense and his abstract
logical conception of history, are mainly due to his too radical

[3] Heinrich Wölfflin: *Kunstgeschichtliche Grundbegriffe* (1929),
p. 252.

27

differentiation between external influence and inner logic. The error in his way of thinking is typical; a similar failure to understand social causation underlies the common incomprehension of sociological methods and, in particular, the misinterpretation of historical materialism. The essence of the materialistic philosophy of history, with its doctrine of the ideological character of thought, consists in the thesis that spiritual attitudes are from the outset anchored in conditions of production, and move within the range of interests, aims, and prospects characteristic of these; not that they are subsequently, externally, and deliberately adjusted to economic and social conditions. *"Primum vivere, deinde philosophari"* is a truth one does not need any theory of historical materialism or of ideology to recognize. The remarkable thing is that even well-tried thinkers in this field represent the economic dependence of art in terms of a purely external tie. Even such a writer as Max Scheler falls into this way of thinking, when he speaks of the material conditions of artistic creation. "Raphael requires a paintbrush," we read. "His ideas and his visions cannot provide that. He needs politically powerful patrons who commission him to glorify their own ideals; without them he could not give expression to his genius." [4] It is extraordinary that a sociologist of the rank of Scheler should have failed to note that the artist glorifies the "ideals" of potential as well as of actual patrons; that the ineluctable character of ideology—in so far as it really is ineluctable—leads the painter to represent the ideas and aims of the predominant, cultured classes even when he has no patrons—or better, in spite of his not having the right patrons or representing social groups with whom he would feel really in harmony. Failure to recognize this is the more remarkable because Engels in his thesis on the "triumph of realism" and the nature of Balzac's method left no room for doubt as to what is meant by ideology in art.[5] One would naturally think that it

[4] Max Scheler: *Die Wissensformen und die Gesellschaft* (1926).
[5] Engels: Letter to Miss Harkness, in Marx & Engels: *Literature and Art*, pp. 42–3.

would have been realized that the artist does not need to be aware of the social ideas he expresses, that he may, so far as his consciousness goes, feel himself in opposition to the ideas and ideals he portrays, justifies, or even glorifies in his works. Balzac, as is well known, was an enthusiast for absolute monarchy, the Catholic Church, and the French aristocracy; but that did not prevent him from writing the most impressive of apologies for the bourgeoisie.

Art can express social aims in two different ways. Its social content can be clothed in the form of explicit avowal—confessions of belief, express doctrines, direct propaganda—or in that of mere implication, that is, in terms of the outlook tacitly presupposed in works which seem devoid of social reference. It can be frankly tendentious or a vehicle of an unconscious and unacknowledged ideology. The social content of a definite creed or an explicit message is consciously realized by the speaker and consciously accepted or rejected by the hearer; on the other hand, the social motive behind a personal manifesto can be unconscious, and can operate without men being aware of it; it will be the more effective the less it is consciously expressed and the less it is or appears to be consciously aiming to gain approbation. Nakedly tendentious art often repels where veiled ideology encounters no resistence. The plays of Diderot, Lessing, Ibsen, and Shaw are undisguisedly tendentious; the message for which they seek to gain approval does not have to be read between the lines, as must the meaning of Sophocles, Shakespeare, or Corneille; it is not wrapped up in an ideology; but it is convincing only to him who is already half convinced. And in art, the indirect, ideological mode of expression is not only the more effective, it is also the more illuminating from a historical point of view, for in truth a social outlook creates a style only when it cannot find expression directly. The open expression of a social outlook is compatible with the most various stylistic forms, as in that case the content of ideas is simply superimposed upon a given formal structure; no transformation of this content into novel forms of expression is required. With Diderot, Lessing, and Shaw, versions of liberalism are expressed in three different styles, whereas the styles of Sophocles, Shakespeare, and Corneille are the expressions of different social and political situations. In the one case the social attitude maintains a certain abstract independence of the artistic form; in the other it is embodied in a stylistic form appropriate to it. The translation of a social outlook into a style evidently requires quite a different mechanism from that which suffices for its straightforward expression in a political program or a manifesto. The artist as exponent of a style is not merely the mouthpiece of society, and his function as representing a social group cannot be explained in psychological terms alone; it becomes intelligible only through research into the nature of connections that are the theme of historical materialism.

Historical materialism is not a psychological theory; it derives ideologies not from the motives of persons, but from objective conditions that work themselves out often without the consciousness, and not infrequently contrary to the intentions, of the participants. Even to speak of "interests" in this connection is not altogether appropriate, for the thoughts, feelings, and actions of men are by no means always in accord with what, from a psychological point of view, one might designate as their interests. They generally think and act in accord with a class-consciousness for which the maintenance of a certain class is the cardinal, though not always the acknowledged, aim. Men's thinking depends on this consciousness, although the collective unity with which they are at one is not always the social class from which they sprang, and although they are not always aware of their class-situation. The motives, for example, which lead someone to volunteer for a certain war may from a subjective point of view be wholly idealistic; nevertheless, not only can the war be economically conditioned, but also there may be operative, behind the idealistic motives of the volunteer, unconscious factors of a materialistic, interested, and class-determined character. Class-consciousness is not a psychological reality; it materializes only to the extent to which individuals do in fact behave in accord with their class-situation. In so far as class-consciousness does find expression, one may, in the language of the romantics, speak of the higher intentions of the group—or, in the Hegelian jargon, of a sort of "cunning," in this case the cunning of the class-war. Put in less romantic and speculative terms, this is equivalent to saying that men's thought is much more decisively influenced by their social situation than by their illusions or by their conscious reflections on their situation—although current social conditions presumably work only through psychological motivation, or as Engels has it, "everything that sets men in motion must go through their minds." [6]

The most effective argument, at first sight, against the admission of ideological factors in the history of art derives from the observation that the same stylistic traits often do not appear simultaneously in the different arts, that a style may last longer in one branch of art than in another, that one may appear to lag behind the rest instead of keeping in line. Thus in music, until the middle of the eighteenth century, that is, up to Bach's death, we find the baroque style still flourishing, whereas in the visual arts the rococo has already reached its climax. If, however, the argument runs, like social conditions do not produce like results in all provinces of art and culture, then there is evidently no justification for talk of ideological conditioning or of sociological laws of any sort, and movements in art are free from the influence of social causation.

The solution of this apparent difficulty is obvious. In any fairly advanced state of civilization, social conditions are never quite uniform; they do not present us with the same situation in the various fields of art and of culture. In the first half of the eighteenth century, the middle ranks of the bourgeoisie exerted a much greater influence upon painting and literature than upon music. They were a very influential section of the consumers in the fields of literature and painting, whereas in music the taste of Court and Church authorities was still

[6] Engels: *Feuerbach*.

predominant. The institution that in the case of music was to do the work of book publishers and art exhibitions, the commercial organization of concerts for a middle-class public, was still in its infancy. Indeed, a similar tension, caused by the differences of the publics concerned, between the visual arts and literary forms persists throughout the history of Western culture. The circle of customers for painting and sculpture, and of course for architecture, is for obvious reasons a much more restricted one than for literature. That does not imply that stylistic change always starts with literature; literature takes the lead only when the bourgeoisie takes over the leadership in society, and that only comes about with the enlightenment, the French Revolution, and the democratization of the reading public in the eighteenth and nineteenth centuries. It is clear that this preponderant place of literature in the evolution of style, as also that of music at a later date, is brought about by a shift in the art market.

The concept of ideology can be sensibly employed only in relation to a certain social group; to speak of the ideology of a historical epoch, without an attempt to differentiate classes or groups, is sociologically meaningless. Only when we assign ideological phenomena to particular social units do we get beyond a mere registering of historical sequence; only then are we able to work out a concrete, sociologically useful concept of ideology. In a historically advanced period there is no one ideology, but only ideologies—in the same way as there is not just Art, but the various arts, or as there are several relevant artistic trends to be distinguished, corresponding with the various influential social strata. This does not alter the fact that in any historical period one class predominates, but it reminds us that this predominance does not go unchallenged by competitors in the spiritual realm any more than in economics or politics. As a rule, the new forces of production begin to manifest themselves in the form of "new ideas," giving rise to dialectical tensions in the field of thought which often work themselves out in economic organization only at a later date; but this does not invalidate the contention of Marx and Engels that the new ideas are only a sign "that within the old society, the elements of a new one have been created."[7] In fact, we frequently get a situation in which the spiritual tendencies are much more tangled, more pervaded by deep-seated oppositions than the economic; in which, as for example in the age of the enlightenment, the ruling class was already spiritually divided into two hostile camps while economically it still maintained an appearance of unity.

The differing composition of the publics is undoubtedly not the sole explanation of the differing speeds of change found in the different arts. In the various branches of art, the traditional formal rules that prescribe modes of representation and set limits to what may be represented can be more rigorous or less, and so can offer more resistance or less to the influence of contemporary social conditions. In an art-form such as church music, in which production is governed by rather strict traditions and serves precisely defined functions, in which the executants generally belong to a closed professional group, and the demand for novelty is naturally slighter than elsewhere, the speed of change will be relatively slow and the stylistic forms less obviously ideological—unless one treats the very rule of tradition itself as an ideological symptom, as in a sense it is. But for the formation of new ideologies all tradition is a factor of inertia, as both Marx and Engels observe. "The tradition of all the dead generations weighs down the brains of the living," says Marx,[8] and Engels, somewhat more favorably, but still with a certain horror, speaks of tradition as a "great conservative force in all ideological fields."

Tradition owes its existence to the fact that cultural structures outlast the socio-historical conditions of their origin, and can live on, although, as it were, without roots. There exists a remarkable linkage of transitory and enduring factors, whose

---

[7] *Manifesto of the Communist Party.*

[8] Marx: "The Eighteenth Brumaire of Louis Bonaparte," in *Selected Works*, II, 311 ff.

problematic character Marx seems to have noticed first when he came to deal with artistic experience. The passage in the Introduction to the *Critique of Political Economy* in which he speaks of the difficulty of accounting for the effect of the Greek epic upon generations living in a world utterly different from that of Homer is well-known. Here Marx stumbled upon the discrepancy between genesis and validity, without, however, being able to formulate the problem accurately. He was scarcely aware that he was concerned with a peculiarity of all forms of spiritual activity, and thus with the central and most difficult problem of the whole doctrine of ideology: the circumstance that the so-called superstructure has a vitality of its own, that spiritual structures have both the capacity and the tendency to cast loose from their origins and go their own way. In other words, they become the origin of new structures that develop according to inner laws of their own, and also come to have a value of their own which enjoys more than ephemeral validity. This phenomenon by which the cultural structures that were once vital tools and weapons, means for mastering nature and organizing society, gradually become formalized and neutralized, and finally ends in themselves, is no doubt closely akin to the process of "reification" (*Verdinglichung*) discovered and so vividly described by Marx. The spiritual structures, with their independence, autonomy, and immanence, their formal, superhistorical values, confront us as so many "alien natural forces"—as Marx terms the institutions of capitalist society. Even in art, the most human of all human forms of expression, this alien character is felt whenever art is treated as pure form. A work of art, taken as a purely formal product, a mere play of lines or tones, an embodiment of timeless values without relevance to anything historical or social, loses its vital relationship to the artist and its human significance for the person contemplating it. In art, especially in art, the setting up or postulating of supertemporal and superpersonal values has about it something of "fetishism," which Marx held was the essence of "reification." By the setting up of such abstract values and the marking off of distinct mental faculties which goes with it, that unity of the spiritual world which the romantic philosophy of history discerned in the so-called "organic" cultures, with their total world-view and their natural growth, is finally destroyed. Marx himself describes in somewhat romantic terms the dissolution of this natural state, which he makes coincide with the beginning of modern capitalism, as "the end of human innocence." His messianic gospel, with its dominant theme of the "absolute sinfulness" of the capitalist era and its promise of classless society, is certainly a romantic legacy.

In reality, the formalization of spiritual powers and achievements, the invention of "pure science" and "art for art's sake," is no more a creation of modern capitalism than is the commodity character of industrial products. The process begins in the seventh century B.C. in Ionia, and evidently is a concomitant of the Greek colonization.[9] Here we meet not only with a completely novel, unpragmatic conception of science, but equally with a completely new idea of art, which is no longer exclusively magic, incantation, votive offering, or propaganda, but an attempt to realize beauty for its own sake. As out of knowledge directed to purely practical ends there arises "enquiry" that is in some degree purposeless, so out of art as means of winning the favor of gods, spirits, or potentates, there gradually emerges pure, untendentious, disinterested form. This development is undoubtedly an accompaniment of the Greeks' contact with foreign peoples, of their discovery of the variety and relativity of values, which entails the dissolution of their ancient wisdom, that more or less undifferentiated unity in which religion, science, and art are scarcely distinct. The process of formalization and separation of the branches of culture goes along with the contemporary beginnings of monetary economy, and may to some extent be explained by the notion that use of abstract means of exchange promotes in-

[9] Arnold Hauser: *The Social History of Art* (1951), I, 93.

tellectual adaptability and power of abstraction;[1] but all that has not much in common with the rise of modern capitalism.

In spite of the process, almost uninterrupted from that time on, of increasing separation of the cultural fields, with the autonomy of art growing more and more assured, still in no phase of art history, not even in times of the most extreme aestheticism and formalism, do we find the development of art completely independent of the current economic and social conditions. Artistic creations are far more intimately linked with their own time than they are with the idea of art in general or the history of art as a unitary process. The works of different artists do not have any common aim or common standard; one does not continue another or supplement another; each begins at the beginning and attains its goal as best it can. There is not really any progress in art; later works are not necessarily more valuable than earlier; works of art are in fact incomparable. That is what makes truth in art so very different from truth in science; it also explains why the value of the knowledge gained and propagated by art is not at all impaired by its ideological character. The fact that the insights gained by art often so quickly go out of currency and never really secure universal acceptance does not trouble us in the least. We regard them as uncommonly, often indeed uniquely, valuable interpretations of life, not as objectively compulsive, demonstrable, or even, properly speaking, arguable propositions. The artist's communications about reality intend to be and ought to be relevant; they do not have to be true or indisputable. We can be completely overwhelmed by a work of art, and yet quite reconciled to the fact that it leaves other men, who are our spiritual neighbours, unmoved. That there is nothing compulsive about judgments of taste is one of the earliest aesthetic insights, *de gustibus non disputandum* being almost a piece of popular proverbial wisdom. The remarkable thing is that judgments of taste do none the less make a claim, and though not claiming universal validity, do have a normative aspect: the person judg-

[1] Georg Simmel: *Philosophie des Geldes* (1900).

36

ing believes himself to be recognizing an objective value that is in a way binding, at least for him. This complication deserves to be noted, but does not alter the fact that validity in art is utterly different from validity in science, and that there is no contradiction in art's being ideological and at the same time having objective value. ✓

But the problem of relativity of values, which we thus avoid in considering the actual production and enjoyment of art, confronts us when we turn to art history as a science with difficulties almost as great as are encountered in any other field of study. The development of art history does not even manifest that rather small element of continuous progress which can be detected in other branches of historical writing. In the case of art, the historical interpretations and evaluations of one generation not only are not felt to be binding upon the next, but often have to be positively ignored, even fought against, in order that the new generation may gain its own direct access to the works of the past. We enjoy all this variety and many-sidedness of historical interpretation, feel infinitely enriched and enlivened by such constant shifts in the point of view from which sensitive and ingenious art historians investigate and reflect upon the works of the masters; in the end, the question of the validity of all these different interpretations which successive generations put upon the artistic creations of the past obtrudes itself and demands further investigation. It is somewhat disquieting to observe that the ranking of the artists considered important is being continually changed, that for example Raphael or Rubens is being constantly re-appraised, that artists such as El Greco, Breughel, and Tintoretto have had to be rescued from complete oblivion or neglect, that types of art that yesterday were decried as the most frightful aberrations are today acclaimed as the most interesting and stimulating of all, that a Burckhardt wrote with contempt of the baroque and a Wölfflin with contempt of mannerism. Are such interpretations correct or incorrect? Is one more correct than another? Is a later interpretation always more correct than an earlier? Or has the temporal sequence of judgments in this case nothing whatever to do with progress, with any progressive discovery of truth? Is relativism in art history inevitable and unobjectionable? Or have we in the last resort to do with assertions that are not to be distinguished as true or false, but according to some quite different criteria, such as the degree of relevance of the connections pointed out, or the extent of the deepening and enrichment of our aesthetic experience which may result? It certainly seems clear that the course not merely of art, but of art history also—that is, not only of the practice but also of the interpretation of art—is subject to the laws of something like Alfred Weber's "cultural development," which is not a strictly progressive movement, unlike the continuous process of cumulative achievement which he terms "civilization." The judgments of art history can be neither completely objective nor absolutely compelling; for interpretations and evaluations are not so much knowledge, but are ideological desiderata, wishes and ideals that one would like to see realized.

Works or schools of art of the past are interpreted, discovered, appraised, neglected in accord with the point of view and current standards of the present. Each generation judges the artistic endeavors of former ages more or less in the light of its own artistic aims; it regards them with renewed interest and a fresh eye only when they are in line with its own objectives. In this way, around the middle of last century, a generation of middle-class liberals headed by Michelet and Burckhardt discovered or revalued the art of the Renaissance; the generation of the impressionists led on by Wölfflin and Riegl did the same for the baroque; our own generation, with its expressionism and surrealism, cinematography and psychoanalysis, is undertaking the same task for the intellectualistic, problem-ridden, and inwardly disrupted art of mannerism.

The evaluations and revaluations of art history, it is plain, are governed by ideology, not by logic. They relate to the same living conditions, are based upon the same social foundations as are the contemporary artistic tendencies and, like these, express and reveal a definite world-view. The sociology of art history has still to be written; it could make a valuable contribution to the social history of art. It would have to treat such problems as that of the changing significance of classical antiquity over the centuries: its naturalistic-progressivist interpretation by the cultured patricians of the Italian Renaissance, its formalistic-conservative interpretation by the courtly aristocracy of seventeenth-century France, and its rigorously academic interpretation by the bourgeois intelligentsia of the revolutionary period.

No doubt art history, as well as interpreting and evaluating, has a number of other tasks not essentially different from those of factual historical research in general. In this field, the objective truth of its findings is a problem that cannot be ignored. Such tasks are those concerned with the dating and attribution of works, their grouping in a way that correctly reflects the development of schools or of individual personalities, the determination of what can be inferred from them as "documents," regarding social groups and individuals, the discovery of the patron's identity and of the extent of his influence upon the form of the work, the examination of changes in the art market and in the modes of organizing artistic production. All these are questions of which the putting and solution are but little affected by any particular ideology, though even here those aspects and modes of explanation will naturally tend to be preferred which are appropriate to conditions of life at the time. For example, appraisal of current market conditions and of the relationship between artist and patron is never altogether unaffected by the social position and economic prospects of those who carry on the business of art history. Nevertheless, in this sort of question we certainly need not give up hope of finding out "how it actually was."

But the central problem of art history is the interpretation and evaluation of styles, and here it must be questioned whether one should even aim at objectivity and immutability of judgment. Can one, should one, experience and appreciate

39

works of art in a sort of vacuum without any presuppositions? Does not their meaning and value consist in a satisfaction of particular, concrete, ideologically conditioned requirements? Is a work of art not a Utopia, the gratification of a need that finds expression in an ideology? Is it not, in Stendhal's phrase, "a promise of happiness"? What can art signify to one who does not judge it from a position in real life, who is not entangled in life as deeply, as passionately, as dangerously as the artist himself! Art helps only those who seek her help, coming to her with their qualms of conscience, their doubts, and their prejudices. Dumb to the dumb, she can speak only to those who question her.

Analysis of the sociological presuppositions of art history enables us to get a truer view of the problem of ideology, its place in our spiritual life, its importance for the vitality and enlivening power of our thought. Such analysis reminds us that the ideological entanglement of our consciousness also has its good side. It confirms the suspicion that desire to be free of all ideology is just a variant of the old idea of philosophical salvation, which promised the human spirit access to a meta-historical, supernatural, secure world of absolute, eternal values. In a word, it helps us to realize that ideology is not just error, delusion, falsification, but an expression of some requirement, some need, willing, or striving that has wrapped itself in a cloak of seemingly objective, passionless propositions.

Man is a creature full of contradictions: not merely existing, but aware of his existence; not merely aware of his existence, but also willing to change it. History is a dialectical controversy between ideology and the ideal of truth, between willing and knowing, the desire to alter things and the awareness of the inertia of things. We move back and forth endlessly within the space set by the material conditions of our life and by our aims. All talk of an end to the movement, that is, an end of history, whether on Hegelian or on Marxian lines, is pure speculation. For rational thinking, the limits of history coincide with the limitations of man.

40

III

The Psychological Approach:

Psychoanalysis and Art

1. *SUBLIMATION AND SYMBOLIZATION*

FREUD'S FUNDAMENTAL STATEMENTS on art, set forth in a couple of pages of the *Introductory Lectures* start from the proposition that the artist is an introvert who, because of excessive instinctual urges, is unable to come to terms with the demands of practical reality, who turns for satisfaction to the world of fantasy, and there finds a substitute for the direct gratification of his wishes. He achieves the conversion of his unrealistic demands into aims that are realizable, at least spiritually, by what Freud calls a "power of sublimation." This is a kind of defence mechanism, which saves him from punishment or illness, but confines him to a fictitious world in which he has "not far to go to become neurotic," and is, in fact, often as precariously cut off from reality as those who are suffering from nervous or mental disorder. Yet, unlike the neurotic or the insane, the artist finds a way back to reality; that is to say, he is by no means imprisoned in a world of rigid delusion, but retains a certain pliability, which allows him to vary his distance from and maintain contact with the world of facts. Instead, however, of researching farther into this flexibility of self-deception, without which no artistic creativity can be conceived, Freud is concerned, above all, with a way of redemption—the way from mere fantasy to the work of art as vehicle of social integration. The artist creates a world of fulfilment which is more than a private domain of his own mind, one in which others also may participate and find enjoyment. He can per-

43

form this trick simply because most people suffer, to some extent, from the same kind of frustration from which he has sought and found relief in his work. But because those who are not artists produce only meager, unsubstantial, and incommunicable daydreams and long for more effective consolation, and because the artist, with his sense of defeat and his loosening contact with reality, feels just as lonely as these daydreamers, he finds consolation in consoling them. That is to say, just as the audience vicariously participates in the fulfilment realized in the work of art, so he, the artist, through the success of his work, enjoys the gratification of wishes which has hitherto been denied to him; he wins honor, power, fame, and the love of women. Illusion, for him, turns into tangible reality. But Freud here merely asserts what, as the crucial point of his argument, he should perhaps demonstrate in more detail, namely, that the artist knows how to elaborate his fantasies in such a way that they become enjoyable for us, and, unlike ordinary daydreamers, can disguise the fact that these fantasies have originated in respressed wishes, so that we forget that we have to pay a price for them.

Freud's most important addition to these statements is his later emphasis on the substitutive nature of the gratification obtained from a work of art, and his insistence that formal beauty is nothing but an "incitement premium," a bait or a bribe that provides us with no more than a "forepleasure," only prepares the way for the achievement of the real aim of art and the true enjoyment it provides: the release of unconscious psychic tensions. According to Freud, this ultimate, merely latent, part of the effect of a work of art far exceeds the manifest part in significance as well as in intensity. Form and beauty are but by-products in a scheme directed to objectives that have little to do with disinterested pleasure or with art for its own sake. Beauty is not among the artist's direct aims: what he is concerned with is, above all, problems of life; beauty is only a weapon, a means of defence, or an evasive device in his wrestling with reality.

44

Freud's theory reveals many new aspects of art and previously unnoticed relationships, but it contains only one entirely original concept, that of sublimation. The success of the psychoanalytic approach to art depends, to a great extent, on the usefulness of this concept in the interpretation of artistic creativity. The idea of sublimation seems, at first sight, to open up wide new vistas, to be full of momentous implications and unexpected conclusions. A closer examination shows, however, that it purports to be no more than one aspect of psychic conversion in general. As a matter of fact, it contains hardly a single positive feature; the whole definition of it is almost entirely negative. It consists mainly in the diversion of an impulse from its direct but objectionable aim to an indirect and socially more acceptable gratification. We learn that, in the process of artistic creation, a biological urge is being deflected from its normal course, but in the sublimated form of behavior we can recognize only the aim to which this force has been directed; we see nothing of the process of diversion itself, and we learn hardly anything about the way in which the change occurs, that is, about the power that diverts the biological impulse in question from one course to another or the means and methods by which the diversion is performed.

It is not enough to recognize that art is a converted form of libidinal or other instinctual impulses; we ought to know more about the preconditions of successful sublimation, the circumstances that bring it about or prevent it from occurring, in other words, the reasons why certain impulses are sublimated, others repressed, and others satisfied directly. We ought to know whether sublimation is predetermined and preformed by the nature of the impulses themselves or by the artist's whole spiritual make-up, his life-history, the socio-historical conditions in which he finds himself, his cultural heritage, and the conventions connected with the forms in which he expresses himself. If both an expressionist painter and a butcher are sublimated sadists, or if a painter and a charwoman alike are anal erotics, then at least the difference between the sadism that re-

45

sults in expressionism and that which finds satisfaction in killing steers calls for explanation, and we need to learn more about the biological foundations of a proclivity with a range wide enough to include the scrubbing of floors as well as the covering of canvases with painted forms. Above all, as long as we are ignorant of why one and the same impulse results in a sexual act in one case and in artistic activity in another, or as long as a *principium differentiationis* between the mere diversion and the artistic transcription of an impulse is undiscovered, the whole theory of sublimation is irrelevant for art criticism.

A work of art is not simply the product of a transference of power. Sublimation may be a factor in artistic creativity, but it is not identical with actual artistic creation; even if it proved to be one of the inevitable preconditions or preliminary forms of the work of art, which is in any case a questionable hypothesis, the work of art has many other preconditions and prerequisites. Besides the desire to satisfy one's libidinal urges, there is the will to produce, which is not identical with a wish for propagation; there is the aspiration for self-expression, which need not be mere narcissism; there is the endeavor to win public approval, which can never be completely reduced to a desire for love on the part of the artist.

In his earlier definitions of sublimation, Freud tended to obliterate the sensuous quality of art by excessive emphasis upon the direction of impulses to a "higher end." Later, however, this no longer seems to have been the most important feature in his eyes; the subsistence of the libidinal quality of a desire in its sublimated form and the gratification of such a desire in fantasy became far more essential. The meaning of sublimation is, according to Freud's final formula, divesting an impulse of its offensive nature without depriving it thereby of its pleasure-seeking and pleasure-giving quality. Freud achieves, in this way, not only a more congenial appraisal of the artistic experience, but also a more nearly perfect agreement between his theory of art and the rest of his doctrine. Sublimation proves to have many features in common with a neurotic

46

symptom; each represents a compromise in which the pleasure principle is by no means abandoned; the only difference is that neurosis is a defeat of the ego in its conflict with the id, sublimation a victory of the ego, in alliance with the id, over the superego, though certainly not a victory of the superego, which would necessarily lead to repression. Again, though both reaction-formation and sublimation may divert an instinctual drive from its original aim, the occurrence of a reaction-formation presupposes repression, while that of sublimation excludes it. But we must also differentiate here between sublimation and symbolization, for these too are likely to be confused with one another. "Only what is repressed is symbolized; only what is repressed needs to be symbolized," says Ernest Jones.[1] To this we may add: only what is not repressed can be sublimated; only what is not repressed needs to be sublimated. Symbols and sublimations are, nevertheless, the result of the same mental dynamics, the same conflict between instinctual drives and the moral censorship of the ego. Both are forms of disguise and compromise assumed by unacknowledged wishes in order to achieve at least an indirect expression and a roundabout way of gratification.

However similar the dynamic functions of sublimation and of symbolization may be, yet their difference is essential from a formal point of view. Sublimation means a mere transference of attitudes and activities, a mere change of media and settings; if it is connected with a change of structure at all, psychoanalysis has little to tell us about that. Symbolization, on the other hand, produces many original qualities, and psychoanalysis can draw, in its description of symbols, not only on the whole range of art and literary criticism, in which the interpretation of symbols plays such an important part, but also on its own clinical experiences and theoretical conclusions. In the psychoanalytical view, the mind is a symbol-producing agent, and in dreams expresses itself almost exclusively in symbols. We know that many of the technical devices of "dream-work" apply to

[1] Ernest Jones: *Papers on Psycho-Analysis* (1938), p. 158.

the creation of symbolic forms in general, and that overdetermination, in the sense used in the psychoanalytical interpretation of dreams, is a decisive factor in artistic symbols too. A symbol is, in fact, an overdetermined image; its power lies in a multiplicity, a seeming inexhaustibility, of meaning.

[A symbol is a form of indirect representation that does not call a thing by its name but avoids straightforward description in order either to disguise or to reveal it in a more striking way, or even, perhaps, to disguise and reveal it at the same time. A symbol is a characterization of an object which fits into different contexts: First, it fits into a train of thought that is both rational and irrational, an association of ideas that is conscious and unconscious, or at least not always or equally conscious. Then again, it fits into the context of different individual experiences: it may mean one thing to the author and another to the audience, one thing to one member of the audience and something else to another. All this only suggests that a symbol or a symbolic meaning can hardly spring from a single layer or move on a single level of the psyche; it can but be overdetermined and have roots of which neither the artist nor any particular audience is fully aware.] To assure us, however, that symbols are produced, as Dr. Jones maintains, "spontaneously, automatically, and, in a broad sense, unconsciously," [2] is to make a mystification of artistic creativity. The power of a work of art to carry a symbolic meaning has, above all, certain formal preconditions, which can only be brought about with much care and skill. The mind contains no elements of artistic relevance which were not acquired, experienced, or worked out consciously, even if some of the links between their origin and their final forms have later been repressed and forgotten. Symbols may spring from sources of which a man is temporarily unconscious; they are not products of the unconscious.

From the fact that a symbol is more sensuous and therefore more concrete than the symbolized idea, Dr. Jones infers that it represents a more primitive stage in the development of the

[2] Jones: "The Theory of Symbolism," ibid., p. 132.

human mind than abstract, rational, discursive thought.[3] Primitive man, however, as we know, is just as rational as civilized man, perhaps even more so, as he can hardly afford the luxury of being irrational. The psychoanalytical conception of mental development is, in fact, still dependent on Lévy-Bruhl's romantic anthropology, with its "pre-logical" stage of human thought; it clings to the romantic equation of the irrational and the spiritually genuine.

There is, no doubt, in every kind of artistic symbolism an element of mystery and mystification, a tendency to choose a longer, more winding and arduous way instead of a shorter and smoother one; but it can hardly be maintained that the purpose of a symbol is simply to hide and to conceal, and not also to elucidate and to reveal. Every form of art that is more than a joke or a manifestation of insanity attempts to make valid statements about reality. To suggest that symbols are used by the artist merely as a kind of hide-and-seek or as a means for self-expression in conformity with a moral code, is to take a very poor view of what he has to tell us. What seems to be obscure in a symbol is not the underlying idea, but the context of implications dormant in that idea. The idea enters, in the artist's imagination, into relationships so manifold, so complex and involved, that only a few of them become transparent at the same time. The real characteristics of symbolic expression, then, are not obscurity or secretiveness, but ambiguity and variety of possible interpretations, that is to say, a continuous shift in the meaning of the symbols.

That much mental functioning is to be explained as an attempt to disguise the real motives of one's behavior is among the most important discoveries of psychoanalysis; a like attempt also explains certain features of the work of art. The misinterpretation of artistic achievements by psychoanalysis originates, on the one hand, in a propensity to regard the work of art as no more than a kind of puzzle whose meaning can never be comprehended directly; on the other, in a habit of regarding

[3] Jones: ibid., p. 185.

symbols as abstract, rigid, conventional signs, with an explanation that may be looked up, as it were, in a dictionary, a book of reference, or, indeed, a book of dreams. Psychoanalysis is no doubt an extremely valuable method of investigating the psychological origins of artistic symbols, their emotional roots, and the reasons for our perplexed reactions to their half-revealing, half-concealing quality; but unfortunately it treats all art as symbolic and all symbolism as sexual. Art is, however, to a very great extent, mere statement, direct or indirect propaganda, or formal interpretation that may or may not be combined with a symbolic meaning. A theory of art which applies only to an indirect expression of repressed sexual or possibly also aggressive impulses is therefore extremely limited in scope. But psychoanalysis gives no account of and has no means of dealing with artistic forms that are other than the expression of such impulses.

The study of works of art as a vehicle of sexual symbolism has been from the very beginning a favorite side-line of psychoanalytical investigation. It was a rewarding job, which could be performed in a more or less mechanical way, seemingly with no limit set to daring speculations and surprising results. However, as time passed, the effect of surprise diminished, and eventually people got accustomed to and bored with the assertion that any material object could be a symbol of the genitals, that nearly all human relationships might be connected with the Oedipus situation, that art swarmed with mother images, and that heroes apprehended nothing but castration.

In so far as art does consist in expression of unconscious instinctual impulses and unadmitted wishes, it inevitably speaks a symbolical language replete with sexual images; and nobody will deny that excessive libidinal urges, incestuous attachments, infantile erotic experiences and fixations are among the *leitmotivs* of art and literature. Poetry continues the erotic dreams of infancy, and the poet hardly ever succeeds in breaking away from the scenes of his "family romance." But with the growing awareness of the universality of sexual symbolism, the

50

ubiquity of the Oedipus complex, the innumerable variations of the incest-motif, obsession with the mother image and similar emotional patterns, one becomes increasingly conscious not only of the monotony and rigidity of that symbolism, but also of the artistic irrelevance of such hidden meanings whose manifest forms are so much more varied and differentiated than their actual content. One eventually realizes that a hidden meaning of this kind need not be the real meaning of a work of art. If psychoanalysis maintains that "poetry is nothing but an oral outlet" or that "every artist is unconsciously a voyeur," that everything erect in a picture means the penis and everything hollow the female genitals, that the column or the sculptural representation of the erect human body was originally no more than a phallus-symbol and the interior of a building a symbol of the womb, there is, of course, no more definite evidence against than in favor of the correctness of these assertions. However, it is safe to say that the alleged symbolism has little, if anything, to do with the artistic effect or merit of the respective works of art.

What is probably the most famous example of the psychoanalytical interpretation of a work of art, the analysis of *Hamlet* by Ernest Jones, exhibits most clearly the merits and, at the same time, the shortcomings of the method. The riddle of Shakespeare's play, never solved to anyone's complete satisfaction, consists, as everyone knows, in Hamlet's lack of resolution about taking revenge upon his uncle for his father's death. Dr. Jones says that Hamlet cannot kill a murderer for committing a crime that he himself, being erotically fixated on his mother, unconsciously wished to commit. Now, this is certainly not only as good an answer as any to the actual question; it also helps to explain one of the most puzzling features of the play, namely, the awkward and unconventional relationship between Hamlet and his mother, the overheated, stifling and bewildering atmosphere of the scenes between them. The mere fact that we are at last able to exhibit the character of these scenes, still more the enigmatic nature of the Ophelia episode and the neurotic mood of the whole drama, is a result of the psychoanalytical approach. The critics, however, who maintain that the Oedipus situation is not the meaning of the play, are quite right. Nobody who has ever experienced the massive reality of Shakespeare's figures, the convincing quality of the situations in which they find themselves, the vigor and beauty of the language they speak, will admit that the incest-motif is the true meaning, the essence or the real source of the work, or that its artistic success, its unfailing theatrical effect, and the magic of its cadences and images are due to the appeal of the Oedipus situation. But if that appeal, or something of the kind, is not the explanation of its power, then what is?

The psychoanalytical interpretation of *Hamlet* is by no means refuted by the well-known argument that if Shakespeare had anything like the Oedipus complex in mind, he would have told us so. We know that the criterion of a "right" interpretation is independent of the question as to whether the meaning ascribed to a work was intended by the artist or even consciously present to his mind during the process of creation. Psychoanalysis, after having shown in a thousand ways the unconscious origins of spiritual attitudes is no doubt justified in its approach to art, that is to say, in minimizing as it does the relevance of consciousness as a direct source of artistic creativity. But is the Oedipus complex even present in the minds of the audience who enjoy and appreciate the work? The answer is that the audience too may be under the influence of forces of which they are not fully aware. But is the author then responsible for this effect? Is he responsible for it to the same extent as for an effect that proves to have been intentional? We must, to start with, agree that a work of art has always more than one meaning. It may be that none of the various interpretations of *Hamlet* corresponds to the meaning that was consciously predominant in Shakespeare's mind when he conceived the play. But a good many meanings must have been unconsciously present to his thought while he was occupied with the subject of the play. We must realize that there is no greater chance of our hitting upon the implications of a meaning the author was aware of than on the explanation of one that was only latent in his mind. Our interpretation of a work produced in the past is necessarily involved in misunderstandings—misunderstandings of the author's conscious as well as unconscious motives in creation. When we attempt a new kind of interpretation, we often revert from an allegedly conscious to an apparently unconscious motive; we assume that we have become aware of a meaning of which the author himself might not have been aware. We may even go so far as deliberately to interpret a work in a sense that could not have been conceived by its author, and to assume, as has been assumed in connection with Cervantes and his *Don Quixote,* that the author misunderstood his hero and was at a loss in interpreting his own creation.

If, however, a critic maintains that the Oedipus situation is not the real meaning of *Hamlet,* and is not simply implying that it is not the meaning that Shakespeare intended to convey, he then usually wants to say that it is not the play's most relevant meaning. And, indeed, psychoanalytical interpretations are more often irrelevant than inadequate to the specific quality of the artistic experience. Relevance is, however, the peculiar form truth takes in the humanistic and historical disciplines. The occurrence of a historical event has many causes; in every attempt at an interpretation some of them are simply dismissed, others overrated, and every generation makes its own, from a timeless point of view arbitrary, selection of motives in interpreting history. The description of a historical personality or the explanation of a work of art is, therefore, not simply true or untrue, but rather relevant or irrelevant, evident or pointless, offering a new, direct approach to the subject or obstructing such approach. The only valid criterion of a "possible" interpretation is, at any given time, to be found in the spontaneous experience of contemporaries, that is to say, the contemporaries of the interpreter, not those of the author. There is, however, a continuous interaction between direct experience and theoretical interpretation; even a fundamentally spontaneous experience may be partly the result of speculation and of subtle connections among the different provinces of the mind. Thus the psychoanalytical explanation of art itself, irrelevant as it may often seem to the particular quality of our direct artistic experience, is just now entering the sphere of our sensibility and adding new qualities to works of art, which are, as we well know, the creations not merely of individual artists but also of centuries past and centuries to come. The Oedipus complex may not be the meaning of *Hamlet*, yet it is becoming part of its meaning, and, at least for the immediate future, no relevant interpretation of the play is likely to discard the psychoanalytical point of view.

2. *ROMANTICISM AND THE LOSS OF REALITY*

Critics who find fault with the psychoanalytical theory of art are usually most troubled by Freud's anti-formalism and anti-aestheticism. They are not prepared to admit that in man's struggle with life, art is not an end in itself, but only a means to an end, and they cannot quite see the point in Freud's putting the artist in the same category as the neurotic. They recognize, of course, the neurotic features in the artist's spiritual make-up, but they do not realize what must for Freud have been the crucial fact in the whole complex, that the artist and the neurotic manifest the same neglect—and suffer the same loss—of reality. Both art and neurosis are for Freud the expression of a failure in adaptation to the social order. The artist's relationship to the facts of life is, as a result of an inability to control his impulses and to put up with the place assigned to him in society, an extremely disturbed and distorted one. He alienates himself from actuality and withdraws into the unreal sphere of his illness. Frustration is, on these premises, a precondition of the work of art; there is no artistic creation without the feeling of a loss or a wrong, without the experience of being tricked out of life. The concept of art as a compensation for missed opportunities, for lost time and happiness, can in fact, be so strong that every fulfilment in life appears as an abortion of a work of art. *"Chaque femme avec laquelle on couche,"* says Balzac, *"est un roman qu'on n'écrit pas."* Or as Freud himself expresses it, "happy people never make fantasies, only unsatisfied ones." The artist is the very individual who is in disagreement with life; those who find it agreeable have little to tell us about their experiences; they are, as Virginia Woolf says, "wordless."

Don Quixote is the classical, the immortal symbol of the artist at variance with reality. In the same way as he fails to come to terms with the routine of common life, as he loses his sense of practical necessity and creates an imaginary world of his own, so does the artist. Don Quixote's delusion in not even a very exaggerated caricature of the artist's self-deception. All art is, properly speaking, a kind of Donquixotism, an attempt to adjust the world to the claims of an individual who reacts to an intolerable reality with unrealistic ideas. Both the artist and the fool sacrifice the world rather than their own demands or, as they prefer to call them, ideals. A lack of tension between the soul and the objective world, between dreams and facts, inwardness and outward reality, characterizes both the phantoms of Don Quixote and the fantasies of the artist. The way from these fantasies to the work of art consists above all in the recovery of the tension whose loss is the origin of mental disorder as well as of artistic creation. But the artist never enjoys the complete "freedom" of the fool, and art proves, even in this respect, what Freud has called a way back to reality—back to its ease as well as to its fetters.

In the case of the artist then we cannot speak of a total

<hr/>

[4] Sigmund Freud: "The Poet and Day-dreaming," in *Collected Papers,* IV, 176.

loss of reality. This is only appropriate with the insane. The artist's departure from actuality is, in fact, even less radical than that of the neurotic, and a correct description of his relationship to the realities of life can hardly establish more than a dialectical strife between rejection and acceptance, destruction and preservation, violation and imitation, a process in which the two opposite attitudes fuse into one indivisible answer to the challenge of reality.

Both neurosis and art are essentially purposive; they are not only the expression of a failure and resignation in the face of reality, but also a kind of escapism. They represent partly an outcome of, partly a means of withdrawal from, the real. "Every neurosis," says Freud, "has the result, and therefore probably the purpose, of forcing the patient out of real life, of alienating him from actuality."[5] As far as the work of art is concerned, there can be no doubt about the existence of such a purpose. Neurosis and art equally reject reality, but neurosis does not deny it, only tries to forget it; art, on the other hand, tries both to deny and to replace it. The artist's attitude is, therefore, in this respect at least, more akin to insanity than to neurosis.

For psychoanalysis, mental life consists in the conflicts, interactions, and mutual adjustments among instinctual drives and the claims of reality as expressed in social conventions and moral codes. Whenever one of these motive forces gets the upper hand at the expense of the other, a case of disorder and abnormality follows. An uncontrollable instinctual proclivity proves just as dangerous a disposition as an overscrupulous ego with too strict moral claims. In other words, disregard of the demands of actuality by indulgence in the gratification of unadmitted libidinal desires, be it in reality or fantasy, results in a no less dangerous frame of mind than the repression of imperative instinctual urges. The question is, however, whether psychoanalysis is right in assuming that artistic activity, too, originates in an unbalanced relationship to existing conditions,

[5] Freud: "Formulations Regarding the Two Principles in Mental Functioning," ibid., p. 13.

whether art necessarily involves a discomfort with the world and a loss of reality, as neurosis and psychosis do. Proust's words, *"on n'aime que ce qu'on ne possède pas,"* [6] express a typically romantic feeling, and if psychoanalysis gives a similar answer to the question about the nature of our interest in art, we ought to examine, in the first place, whether the evidence supporting such an answer is not too one-sidedly romantic in origin.

Freud's description of art as result of the individual's disturbed relationship to reality is, no doubt, a sweeping statement. Art is not a consistent and unvariable pursuit, and if we are to do justice to its implications, we have to make generous allowances for its particular trends and aims in the different historical or social settings in which it appears. There are long periods in the history of art, and they are by far the greater part of it, in which the only form of artistic activity is the practically purposive and socially useful form, and in which any idea of the artist's alienation from society would seem absurd. Incongruity between the artist's personal claims and the demands of social order, in the sense of Freud's statement, first becomes noticeable with romanticism, and in fact the whole conception of art as a substitutive gratification, a compensation or consolation, is based on the experience of romantic and post-romantic art. Before the age of romanticism, art may have been an expression of fantasies or daydreams, the representation of a world that transcended normal experience; it may have been thought of as an improvement on commonplace reality and the daily routine; but it was not a substitute that one would have been prepared to take in exchange for life. The idea of a flight from reality into a fictitious order of existence, an escape from one delusion into another, as religious- or metaphysical-minded people would describe it, was entirely alien to any period prior to romanticism. This experimentation and flirtation with alternatives, this gambling with divided loyalties, is in fact a result of the romantic approach to life. To the un-

[6] Marcel Proust: *La Prisonnière*, II, 247.

romantic mind, art may be a picture of an ideal existence, a promise of happiness, or a foretaste of salvation, but never a consolation for missed or unattainable opportunities.

The idea of a loss of reality as an inevitable precondition of the creation of works of art has no connection with pre-romantic situations, and, before the rise of romanticism, nobody in his senses would have ventured to put forward such an idea. The very conception of a forfeited life was beyond the mental horizon of the pre-romantic artist. It first appears in relation to the idea that there is a choice between art and life, the work and the world, a stylized and a spontaneous self. As long as art is taken for a form of craftsmanship and the artist for a purveyor of beautiful and useful things, fun and amusement, instruction and information, panegyric and propaganda, there is no danger and, indeed, no chance of his losing contact with reality. As soon, however, as he starts producing works of art for their own sake, he is likely to regard the world, including his own being, as the mere raw material of his creations. *Don Quixote* had, of course, been invented long before romanticism, but it was rediscovered and recreated by the romantics, and the work as we see it today, namely as a representation of the contrast between the idea and reality and the impossibility of realizing the idea in this world of "windmills," is a perfect embodiment of romantic philosophy.

The rejection of common reality is, according to romantic views, on the one hand a concomitant of the creative urge, on the other a precondition of successful artistic creation. In other words, the practice of art is not only a compensation for real life, but is also incompatible with its enjoyment. Art is legend, not a copy of life, the expression and not the possession of reality—*dire* and not *avoir*, as Flaubert called it. You must not be a hero, a saint, a lover, if you want to describe heroism, faith, or love. The real hero, saint, or lover does not even think of giving an account of his condition. Only would-be heroes and saints and unhappy or shy lovers realize and tell us what kind of being a hero or a saint or a lover is or may be.

58

The artist, that is to say the modern, romantic artist, is inevitably a failure, a person who is not really what he would like to be, and who spends his time depicting the man he fails to be, the life he fails to live, the meaning of life he fails to realize.

Since romanticism, there has been an alarming feeling on the part of most artists, among them some of the greatest, that the practice of art means not only irretrievable loss, but also a betrayal of life, of life that should be enjoyed and fully consumed instead of being merely described and analyzed. The fact that the separation of art from life and the renunciation of life as the price of art are, above all, an expression of romantic disillusionment, becomes evident if we realize how these attitudes transform a sense of loss into a cult of resignation. *"On ne peut recréer ce qu'on aime qu'en le renonçant,"* declares Proust, suggesting thereby that only an abandoned, rejected, or destroyed world can be called back to life in the work of art. The romantic reaction to the artist's emancipation from reality is, however, ambivalent: it produces a feeling of triumph as well as of nostalgia, a sense of freedom and independence as well as a yearning after normal, natural, spontaneous life, a desire to live out life simply and directly. The artist's sense of guilt is, therefore, not the origin of his renunciation of life, as has been assumed,[7] but rather a result of his flight from life.

The romantic character of the psychoanalytical theory of art is most clearly revealed by the prominent part assigned to the irrational and intuitive faculties in artistic creativity. These powers, described in turn as inspiration, intuition, inborn talent, devine grace, or the hidden sources of the unconscious, are in fact nothing but the romantic's compensation for forfeited reality and a disturbed or spoiled relationship with his audience. The opponents of romanticism deny, above all, the influence of these powers, and, in their definition of artistic genius, replace inspiration by skill and discrimination. William Morris, for instance, pleading for a return to pre-romantic standards, declares that, as far as art is concerned, "that talk of

[7] Otto Rank: *Art and Artist* (1943), p. 429.

inspiration is sheer nonsense: there is no such thing; art is a matter of craftsmanship."

The idea that art originates in illness, physical deficiency, or nervous delicacy, is equally romantic in character, and so is the assumption that the sources of artistic creativity are to be found in the depth of the mind, in that dark, mysterious, inscrutable region, that unaccountable spontaneity, which the artist seems to share with the primitive and the child. But romantic in origin above all is the doctrine that the work of art is a dream-like structure, wishful, ambiguous, sensuous, almost tangible, and still remote, enigmatic and meaningful, uncanny and fascinating, as nothing but a dream.

There have, of course, always been artists with neurotic proclivities, but they have had different chances of success at different periods in history. They have usually passed for poor cranks, and it is only since romanticism that they have assumed spiritual leadership. For only in periods with a philosophy based on the idea of "art for art's sake" have artists of this kind a chance of becoming the spokesmen of their generation. In periods in which art has a practical function to fulfil, they will come and go, emerge and, for lack of response, disappear again, that is to say, prove ephemeral phenomena without any historical or sociological relevance. The romantic and neurotic frame of mind as a predominant mood dates from a time when literature ceased to be a source of practical guidance and the visual arts a public concern, when the artist had no longer anything "useful" to offer his contemporaries, and lost, with his functions, his footing in society. His sense of "usefulness" resulted in a feeling of exaggerated self-esteem, a deliberate striving for originality, inordinate subjectivism, and an excess of narcissistic claims. He has ever since been in constant revolt against a society that has seemed unwilling to listen to him and unable to understand him. Even his illness was a form of passive resistance, a protest and a defence against the prevailing social order, the powerful, cruel, disgustingly healthy bourgeoisie. Health and happiness have become dull and trivial, malady and misery a title to glory. The "secondary gain" of illness, as psychoanalysis defines it, is unmistakably effective in all these reactions. And thanks to psychoanalysis we realize how much the romantics enjoyed their suffering and unhappiness, how great was the share of self-pity, masochism, and self-punishment in their pessimism. Being hopelessly isolated and lonely, they made the misunderstanding and ill-treatment they met with a matter of pride; they sought obscurity, ambiguity, and extravagance in their work and behavior, regarding themselves as the challengers, while in reality they were among the most helpless victims, of the newly established social order.

Before the days of romanticism, a work of art may have been a protest against some particular institution or abuse of power, a social group or a political movement, but it was never a protest against social reality as a whole, never an indictment of society as such. The feeling that the routine of social life inevitably spells the frustration of the individual is, at the time of romanticism, a new experience, and it has historical and social rather than psychological motives. The enlightenment and the Revolution encouraged the intelligentsia in extravagant hopes: an age of the unrestricted reign of reason and genius seemed near at hand. However, the outcome of the Revolution changed the whole situation. The writers and philosophers, who had been the intellectual leaders of the progressive classes, were now made responsible in turn for the achievements and the failure of the Revolution, that is to say, for having gone too far or not far enough. They were unable, in the subsequent period of political reaction and intellectual eclipse, to maintain their prestige; they saw themselves condemned to absolute ineffectiveness, and felt at bottom utterly superfluous. Their sense of frustration revealed itself in countless attempts to escape. They turned to the past and to Utopia, to the unconscious and the fantastic, the uncanny and the mysterious, to childhood and nature, to dreams and mental extravagances, in a word, to forms of existence and behavior which satisfied their yearning for irresponsibility and their desire to be set free from their

sense of defeat. The writers and philosophers of former generations agreed to be ruled by others because they ruled themselves and believed that life can be ruled. The romantics, on
the other hand, acknowledged no external ties, because they
had lost their faith in any rule, and felt that a society that
denied them all influence on the course of events was less
justified in putting a brake on their instinctual urges than a
politically and intellectually more liberal social system would
have been. For it is a fact that an individual with a feeling
of security and a chance of success will yield more readily to
society's demand that he should renounce excessive claims
than an individual dissatisfied with life, hungry for recognition,
and impatient with society as a whole. Here psychology is, in
fact, dependent on sociology; inner conflicts are dealt with and
solved, above all, according to the individual's position and
function in society. Striving for originality, extravagant self-
esteem, and excessive subjectivism are, from a sociological
point of view, nothing but weapons in a competitive struggle
between individual writers and artists who have lost their old
patrons and begin to feel the risks connected with an unpro-
tected market. The romantic mood is, in many respects, a
neurotic reaction to constant rivalry and the fear of succumbing
in a contest as inevitable as it is relentless. It is, in other words,
a result of a feeling of insecurity and anxiety in a never-end-
ing struggle for material existence, success, influence, and
power—the first distinct manifestation of the neurosis of our
age.

Psychoanalysis is itself a kind of romanticism; it is unthinkable without the romantic frame of mind and the romantic
inheritance. Freud's real spiritual ancestors are among the romantics, and the presuppositions of the psychoanalytical approach to mental phenomena are among the fundamental implications of the romantic outlook on life. Psychoanalysis regards, as did romanticism, the unconscious as the origin, if not
of a higher, at least of a more genuine, more perennial form of

truth. Its principle of "free association," which is not only the foundation of its therapy, but also its criterion of spontaneous mental functioning, is a variant of the "inner voice" of romanticism. The very idea of the convertibility of mental energies and attitudes, on which the whole structure of the psychoanalytical doctrine, with its reaction-formations, defence mechanisms, rationalizations, and sublimations is based, is unthinkable without the experience of romantic frustration and a constant need of compensations in a period that Freud himself has described as that of man's "discomfort with civilization"—although he perhaps did not realize the special limitations of this period, and insisted, in his typical way, on the universally human character of what was in reality a merely historical situation. In any case, psychoanalysis came into being as an answer to the problem of a civilization in which, as a result of the romantic crisis, an individual's life and his work have become two separate provinces, and in which a cleft has been opened between his private self and public performance.

3. *ART AS A MEANS OF SUBSTITUTIVE GRATIFICATION*

Nobody who is aware of the complexity of the artistic experience will be very content with Freud's description of the enjoyment of art as a substitutive gratification, a narcotic or sedative pure and simple. Even non-formalists will prefer a definition that includes the autonomy of the work of art at least as an aspect, and the principle of *l'art pour l'art* as at least a possible approach. For, whatever the practical scope of art may be, it can fulfil no extraneous function without some merit of its own. But Freud is none the less fundamentally right: art is a great comforter and appeaser, although in a much wider

63

sense than that of a "substitutive gratification." Every work of art aims to be an improvement upon life and a compensation for its deficiencies.

Apart from the rather cheap ways in which art beautifies life by concealing its real difficulties or by representing them as more easily soluble than they really are, art possesses a considerable number of means of reconciling us, if only momentarily, with the harshness of existence. It exerts a soothing influence, above all, by introducing sense and order into a chaos that threatens to engulf us, and the world with us. Art reconciles the cruelty of life and a meaningful scheme and releases it thereby from its apparently arbitrary character, taking away its edge, which seems to be directed precisely against us. But art appeases by the mere description, the deliberate and elaborate representation, of all that is disquieting, painful, and often intolerable in reality. It may convince us that our tribulations are the essential price of life, our tribute for participating in what has been called the "highest good." Again, even blasphemous indictment of a power supposed to be responsible for the wickedness of life may relieve the violence of pain if the artist assumes the role of mankind's advocate. The effect of art is, however, soothing and gratifying mainly as a result of the artist's ability to raise his voice against the overwhelming force of destiny, to call his distress by name and describe disaster instead of being paralyzed by it. All this contributes to the effect of the work of art as a triumph over the brutality and meaninglessness of life, an effect that is, however, rather inadequately termed "narcotic"; for we know only too well that art often achieves its deepest influence by intensifying our suffering and making us fully aware of it.

The work of art has, as psychoanalysis rightly asserts, much in common with a daydream. It is, of course, not always a picture of heaven, but is nearly always that of a Utopia. Even the most naturalistic work of art is a pretence or, as it were, a legend about life. There is an element of unreality, something wilful and arbitrary, even about the most faithful representation of nature. Every work of art is a wish-fulfilment, the conquest of a perfectly meaningful, fully conceivable, but normally inaccessible world—a world whose heroes lead a life entirely adequate to their nature, their dispositions and potentialities, and in which, therefore, the real sense of existence is restored and brought to full, unhampered dominion. Art is an escape: it deserts or destroys reality, in order to make it more endurable and manageable; for even the most violent naturalism is less bewildering and alarming than life itself. Art produces a rationalized and humanized picture of the world, providing at least a formulation, if not a solution, of its otherwise inexpressible and often unapproachable problems.

Art creates a better world; a less chaotic, less confusing, more consistent form of existence. Even tragedy is, in this sense, "better" than reality. It suggests a rule of inevitability and consistency in what may appear as mere chaos and disorder. Even tragedy is a Utopia—a fantasy about a world in which unalterable, unmistakable, indisputable moral laws are supreme. It creates a Utopian form of life in which man is at one with his destiny, and in which his feelings, opinions and deeds are no longer a matter of moods and whims. The standards according to which he is judged and judges himself are unequivocal and unquestionable; it is from their stability that his whole life obtains its coherence and significance. Tragedy is formidable, but it is not "sad," not depressing, disconcerting, or degrading. The hero may lose his life, but he never loses himself, never the awareness of what he stands for. The tragic drama is, in a way, the pattern of all art; it abolishes the incongruity between the amount and the often trivial cause of suffering, between motives and their effects, subjective claims and objective aims; it is a perfect answer to the demand that lies at the bottom of the very urge to create works of art.

But how are we to explain our actual enjoyment of a picture of fear and terror, death and destruction, as tragedy presents it? When Freud came to analyze that peculiar indulging in the repetition of traumatic situations which is found in the dreams of war neurotics and the plays of children, he once described this kind of gratification as lying "beyond the pleasure principle." [8] This attitude is based, as he declared, on an urge to face an unresolved problem, an uncontrolled, precarious, threatening situation, again and again. It is an attempt to master an intractable difficulty by repeatedly noting, confronting, and contemplating it. Unpleasant, disquieting, disturbing art such as tragedy is a kind of psychoanalytical treatment; it forces us to admit existing difficulties, conflicts, and dangers, and allows us to gain spiritual independence only by becoming and remaining aware of them, by avoiding all illusion, pretence, or deception about their solution. Aristotle's theory of *catharsis* finds a reinterpretation and reaffirmation through psychoanalysis; and no description of the psychoanalytic technique, its approach to neurosis as well as to art, is more adequate than the definition of it as a cathartic method.

The psychoanalytic explanations of art as a means of sublimation, symbolization, or substitutive gratification have one essential feature in common, namely, the dynamic character of artistic creativity. The new and revolutionary approach of psychoanalysis to the functioning of the mind is as well revealed in this field of research as in any other part of the doctrine. There is no doubt that Freud's most remarkable and fruitful achievement consists in his dynamic conception of the personality, that is to say, his conception of a being continuously at variance with the world and himself, driven from outside and inside, determined by motives often hidden from his consciousness, of which he is often unaware and unsuspecting, and to which he is, in many respects, unequal—a being constantly striving for the gratification of his needs, for protection, escape, and survival. Freud recognized that mental attitudes and activities spring from conflicts and are, as a result of these conflicts, purposive; that there is, in other words, a scheme, a kind of strategy, an agency, at the bottom of our behavior which plans, directs, censors, and often deceives.

[8] Freud: *Beyond the Pleasure Principle* (1950), pp. 9–17.

Psychoanalysis describes the mind as a system of interrelations and interactions, a system ruled by mutual dependence and functional unity. It visualizes the mind in a state of perpetual modification, with factors of varying influence and motives of changing power, in a condition of antagonisms and compromises, conversions and compensations, in dramatic situations expressed in terms of inhibitions, repressions, disguises, and deviations. According to psychoanalytic views, mental life first arises when instinctual drives meet a resistance—the resistance of inhibiting forces. If they were not opposed, they would never assume psychic quality; life would be, and continue to be, merely vegetative. But, once admitted to the mind, the instincts are invincible; with their self-will and cunning, they get the upper hand of the reasonable part of the self, just as Hegel's "cunning of reason" gets the upper hand of the individual's irrational passions and unreasonable activities.

Even instinctual energy, the most elementary psychoanalytic conception is, therefore, dynamic. The division of the mind into a conscious and an unconscious region expresses an altogether dynamic and dialectical idea. Consciousness and the unconscious mind are involved in constant antagonisms; there is an incessant tendency to repress impulses into the unconscious and another to allow unconscious urges to come to light. Repression, the cornerstone of psychoanalysis, is a dynamic conception par excellence. Psychic dynamism is revealed, above all, in thrusting out of consciousness what is felt to be incompatible with the rest of the personality and dangerous to the preservation of the ego as an agent of social order and discipline. The repressed material tends, however, to force its way back into consciousness, and there is, in accordance with these movements, a continuous shifting of the manifest and the latent contents of the mind. The latent factors make themselves felt in and through the manifest elements, and every concrete mental disposition is, in fact, a dialectical synthesis of both. Mental attitudes have a positive and a negative aspect. Psychoanalysis, in its dialectical way of thinking, may go even so far

67

as to maintain that a positive and a negative attitude to the same fact are psychologically equivalent. The antagonisms between the id and the ego, the ego and the superego, the pleasure principle and the reality principle, libido and aggression, sadism and masochism, introversion and extraversion, oral and anal, heterosexual and homosexual, and a good many more antitheses of this kind, are all instances of mental dynamism. Neurosis itself is a dynamic phenomenon, a conflict within the self; so also is art.

Psychoanalysis describes mental processes as taking place through continuous conversions and modifications, vicarious functions and substitutions. Convertibility—that is, the plasticity and variability of impulses—is the very formula of mental dynamics. The greater part of mental life develops in derivative and devious forms: reaction formations, rationalizations, symptoms, symbols, compromises, and compensations. The result of this mobility and exchangeability of trends is an *incognito* of the mind, a life of deceit and self-deceit, a constant recourse to psychological alibis. The affections that people manifest are often mere façades to screen rather than to disclose their minds. They hide a socially or morally objectionable attachment behind apparent aversion, lack of love behind exaggerated care and fondness, lack of self-confidence behind arrogance. Fear is often a disguise of desire, illness a form of defence, suffering a self-inflicted punishment. Nothing remains as unmistakable reality in this deceitful play of attitudes except the dialectic of appetites and the moral check on them, the interaction of instincts and inhibitions, in other words, the mutual outwitting of the two basic forces of the mind. The individual is engaged in an unremitting fight for the satisfaction of his desires, for pleasure, love, security, prestige, and power. The aims pursued in this fight dictate the strategy of behavior and turn every step into a meaningful and purposeful activity. Mental operations are directed by the logic of the unconscious—a "cunning" more irresistible and inevitable than the triumph of Hegel's Reason or of any other abstract philosophic principle.

It is easy to see how much our interpretation of art and literature owes to this psychology of exposure, which, instead of taking spiritual manifestations at their face-value, tries to understand them, above all, as aggressive or defensive maneuvers. Artistic activity appears not only more easily accounted for, but also more meaningful, if explained as a device of mental strategy, a means of conquest or revenge, a form of defence or escape. The fundamental contribution of psychoanalysis to the understanding of art consists, in fact, not so much in its biological definition of the work of art—that is to say, in the revelation of its libidinal origin or the interpretation of its sexual symbolism, as in the conception of artistic activity as part of a universal scheme of rationalization and self-justification, in which concealment of libidinal impulses is by no means the only end and aim. "Rationalization" is in this context certainly a far more adequate, more comprehensive, and more exact description than sublimation or symbolization, with their strictly limited sexual connotation. But psychoanalysis, as a theory of rationalization, may render invaluable services not only to the criticism and the history of art, but also to the historical and social sciences in general; it may provide historical materialism above all with a psychological model, showing how "false consciousness" comes into being, how especially biological facts turn into passions, opinions, beliefs, and doctrines. Historical materialism as a dialectical philosophy of history and psychoanalysis as a dynamic theory of mental processes could go a long way together. They move, in reality, in spite of their distrust of one another, on the same ground, both conceiving man as a physico-spiritual being who is involved in a deadly struggle and has to engage all his faculties and abilities to maintain a state of balance between the opposing powers that govern his life.

But if the deepest insights of psychoanalysis into the functioning of the mind are due to the dynamic quality of this doctrine, some of its worst shortcomings are a result of the fact that it is not dynamic enough. Not only does it view the in-

69

stincts and the whole biological constitution, the so-called "in-eradicable animal nature," of man, as being of a static char-acter; psychoanalysis is also involved in many other undynamic conceptions. There is, to start with, the unchangeable constitu-tion of the repressed impulses and the unvariable state of the whole content of the unconscious, which is mostly imagined as a kind of reservoir. Infantile experiences and fixations are, ac-cording to psychoanalysis, likewise immutable, and exert a per-manent influence on the behavior of the individual. Even the choice of one's form of sexuality belongs to this class of rigid trends and irreversible resolutions. The fixed nature of the char-acter types, above all Jung's distinction between introverts and extraverts, is utterly incompatible with the principles of a dy-namic psychology, for, as psychoanalysis itself implies, a char-acter may change, and a person may be an introvert in one respect and an extravert in another.[9] There are really no perma-nent contents of the mind, no rigid types of character, no con-stant patterns of behavior; there are only varying psychological situations with ever-new factors, new combinations, and contin-uously shifting aspects. Nothing in the mind, in fact, remains unchanged throughout any measurable period of time. Not even at one and the same time is the character of a person a coherent and consistent whole; he may be kind, courageous, or firm in certain relationships and cruel, cowardly, or weak in others; he may be realistic, practical, and remarkably active in certain circumstances, but romantic and quite impractical under dif-ferent conditions.

Much of the psychoanalytical oversimplification of art is a result of insufficiently dynamic thinking. With more flexible conceptions, psychoanalysis would, for instance, emphasize less the recurrence of the Oedipus situation in literature and pay more attention to its differentiation. It would turn from the ubiquity of motifs to their development, from an obsession with the primeval and the perennial to a greater interest in the

[9] O. Fenichel: *The Psychoanalytic Theory of Neurosis* (1946), p. 526.

unique individual case. It could develop into a more comprehensive and less dogmatic theory without necessarily losing its dogmatic power. ⌐

4. PSYCHOLOGISM AND THE AUTONOMY OF SPIRITUAL FORMS

Compared with previous academic methods, psychoanalysis marks an advance as revolutionary for the comprehension of art as for the comprehension of neurosis. It is the first really constructive form of genetic psychology—the first to point to origins really relevant to the quality of a personal attitude or a creative activity. Pre-analytical psychological theories, on the whole, adopted the methods of the natural sciences; they moved within the categories of chemical affinities or mechanical forces, reduced mental phenomena to what were assumed to be their components, and tried to reconstruct consciousness out of a number of constant and interchangeable elements, that is to say, sensations, perceptions, and compulsive reactions. Classical, atomistic psychology depersonalized the human mind and transformed it from a concrete living reality into the sum total of abstract constituent factors. Psychoanalysis, on the other hand, in spite of a certain obviously unavoidable stereotyping of tendencies and processes, regards the mind as the unique, unmistakable, and incomparable expression of a biography. Freud views every mental phenomenon in connection with the whole of the personality, and never breaks up the continuity of actual experience. There are no meaningless or aimless moments in a person's behavior; every manifestation of the mind is symptomatic, that is to say, typical and strictly motivated. Even irrationalisms and irregularities, faulty performances and obsessive acts, inhibitions and phobias, which before Freud were considered the result of merely external and accidental influences, are now recognized as psychically determined phenomena for whose occurrence immanent and intrinsically purposeful, even if unconscious, motives are responsible.

The historical significance of Freud's doctrine consists in its being the first teachable and methodically perfectible psychological theory, with aims which, before the rise of psychoanalysis, had been pursued only by novelists or dramatists in their own hit-or-miss way; it is the first attempt to deal with the human character by means of a method that can be practiced and transmitted as an objective scientific "technique." Psychoanalysis is, in other words, the first systematic way of investigating the personal motivations, obsessions, and passions, even if the psychoanalytic conceptions of mental trends are themselves not always sufficiently flexible. The individual is not born with constant qualities and never develops unchangeable features of character. But even if psychoanalysis is somewhat conservative on this point, its sense of the complex structure and tortuous ways of the human mind is unfailing, and the benefit of its unconventional approach to the interpretation of works of art inestimable. The question however is whether it is a right approach to such a formal organization as a work of art.

As soon as the act of creation is completed, the work emancipates itself from its author in such a way that an awareness of its role in the life of the artist may even be felt as obliterating its intrinsic meaning or inner logic, that is to say, the principles governing its formal organization. The artistic merit of that organization has little or no relation to the usefulness of the work in solving personal problems of its author. The aesthetic significance of a work has no psychological equivalent; the same mental disposition may account for the most qualitatively different products. Psychic conditions and circumstances are mere opportunities; they make the work of art possible, but do not provide the stuff of which it is made. The Oedipus complex, incestuous desires, fixations, regressions, libidinal or aggressive tendencies, are some of the opportunities that may stimulate the artist, but do not suggest to him how to achieve his creation.

A poem is made, as has often been remarked, of words, not of feelings; it follows the logic of language, not that of the emotions. An emotional motif owes its artistic significance to the context of the work into which it enters, and not to the context of experiences from which it emerges. It has its life, as T. S. Eliot observed, "in the poem and not in the history of the poet." [1] The whole content of a work of art may become trite and unsubstantial if taken out of the texture of the work and put back into the continuity of the psychic development, into the "history of the poet." Briefly, the closer we go to the origin of a work of art, the farther we may get from its artistic meaning. A too close relating of the work to the biography of the artist may lead to an abuse of psychology—to psychologism. The life-history of an artist is, at any rate, as definitely determined by his work as his work is determined by his life-history. They are interrelated and condition one another in many ways. The life of the artist is an expression of his talent, as his talent is a product of his life. He experiences, by a kind of anticipation, the material adequate for his works, that is to say, he makes of his life what he is able to represent and interpret as an artist.[2] The problem of the dialectical relationship between work and personality therefore receives only an abortive solution if exaggerated stress is laid on biography.

Reducing the work of art to the history of its author is, however, only one variant of that evolutionism which considers the first stage in a process the real origin of its outcome. Even if we admit that biographical facts, such as the experiences described by psychoanalysis, are the starting-point of the artist's creation, we can still maintain that the decisive step in creating a work of art as a unique, unmistakable, incommensurable spiritual achievement occurs somewhere on the way be-

[1] T. S. Eliot: "Tradition and the Individual Talent," in *Selected Essays* (1932), p. 22.
[2] Cf. Rank, op. cit., p. 384.

73

tween that point of departure and the final shaping of the work. It is a fallacy of biological thinking to regard the first phase of a process as the principle, germ, and essence of whatever the issue of the process may be. The result of a development is often only a by-product of the tendencies present at the outset. Every genetic, and as such every psychological, explanation is likely to neglect the significance of the deviations and modifications of an initial tendency occurring in the course of development. The most essential characteristics of a work of art are by no means identical with the most original or the predominant factors in the act of creation. Artistic merit or aesthetic character prove to be accidental from a genetic point of view, be it physiological, psychological, or even sociological. Those abilities and experiences, on the other hand, which, according to psychology in general and psychoanalysis in particular, account for the origin of the work of art, are, at least within certain historical periods, present in numerous human attitudes, and are equally responsible for artistic and non-artistic, or for artistically successful and unsuccessful, achievements. It is mere psychologism to consider the work of art a "document" or record of mental tendencies and experiences. Documentary facts may be indispensable for the comprehension of its formation, but they do not refer to its formal structure. Art is nearly always expression, but is never only expression. Apart from its practical functions, which are vast and varied, it contains an infinity of traditional and conventional elements that may be fully appropriated by the artist, but do not spring from his own subjective needs or personal aims. The assumption that every single step in the creation of a work of art has an aesthetic function or meaning, or an objective "meaning" at all, is but an attempt to create the semblance of inevitability where chance and choice prevail.

Freud once said, in reply to a question of the French surrealist André Breton, that a dream does not mean anything apart from knowledge of the dreamer's personality, his conflicts, symptoms, and past experiences. A work of art, on the other hand, may mean a great deal without conveying any information of this kind about its author. In one of his last writings, Freud himself acknowledged that "the creative power of an author does not always follow his good will," and that "a work grows as it chooses and sometimes confronts its author as an independent, alien creation."[3] Here we have, indeed, evidence that he had more than just an inkling of the non-psychological factors in the organization of the work of art.

The structural approach to the interpretation of art does not, however, invalidate the genetic point of view. It is just as legitimate to explain the work as an endeavor of the artist to express himself as to consider it a self-contained, impersonal system. One can concentrate on its symbolism as well as on the interdependence and interaction of its elements. Every feature of a work of art is determined in a twofold way: by the effect at which it aims and by the experience from which it springs. It is, in fact, "overdetermined." It appears as the expression of an individual eager to unbosom himself and, at the same time, as a message intended for other individuals. It is, however, not only determined by the mind of the person who wishes to express himself or to impart a message, but also by that person's awareness that he is expressing himself or imparting a message, that is to say, by awareness of the available means and the inevitable preconditions of an intelligible mode of expression. Many of the components of a work of art can be explained on the lines of what is called an "art history without names" or by an art criticism that ignores the person of the artist, but others are simply incomprehensible if disconnected from the facts of their origin. They do not fit into the consistent whole of a formally integrated work; they seem, in contrast to the other elements, accidental and arbitrary, however strict the genetic motivation that determines their presence. Again, there are motifs in a work of art which seem accidental and incomprehensible even from a psychological point of view—in the old, academic sense of the word. They emerge without any

[3] Freud: *Moses and Monotheism* (1939), p. 164.

75

evident reason, and do not reveal any direct connection, structural or psychological, with the rest of the work. They do not
cohere with the body of the thoughts and feelings which, judging by the work as a whole, must have been present in the
consciousness of the artist. The only hope of finding an explanation for their occurrence lies in psychoanalysis as a doctrine
of the connections between the conscious and the unconscious
processes of the mind.

The psychoanalytic theory of art moves on strictly psychological lines; it is not interested in, and has no direct approach
to, what we understand by the autonomous meaning or "inner
logic" of the work of art. The exploration of formal structure is
not within its scope and competence, and Freud considers the
enjoyment of artistic form, which he cannot and does not try
to explain, meaningless in itself, that is to say, merely a kind of
allurement or, as he calls it, a "forepleasure" to whet the appe-
tite of the audience. Psychoanalysis is a psychology of purposive subjective attitudes, not of objective forms of expression. It
is a theory of mental functioning, not of objectivations that owe
their meaning and effect partly to factors beyond the influence
of the individual artist. Psychoanalysis never leaves the uninterrupted flow of mental life, never relinquishes the psychic
apparatus of the mind, and, significantly, never breaks contact
with the biological foundation of that apparatus: the instincts,
the bodily needs, and the pursuit of "pleasure." Physiological
constitution and instinctual organization belong, according to
psychoanalysis, to the indispensable preconditions of the mental as well as the physical forms of life. The biological reality
of instincts plays, in Freud's theory, a part similar to that of
the economic reality of production in historical materialism.
Psychoanalysis is, like the Marxist philosophy of history, a materialistic and positivistic doctrine; it rests on biology as Marxism rests on economics. The mind is linked with the body,
and with the world through the body, and the instincts are, as
Freud asserts, nothing but "the demand made upon the mind

76

in consequence of its connection with the body." [4] Psychoanalysis is perfectly right: "the natural man is always with us"; it forgets, however, that, as there are no purely mental manifestations, so there are no human activities that could be explained on a purely biological plane.[5] We never see, in reality, unmixed, uninfected, universally human instincts, but only historically differentiated variants of them. "Natural" instinctual behavior, on a human level, is an abstraction as bold and unwarranted as absolute, unrestricted, perfectly independent spiritual power.

5. PSYCHOANALYSIS, SOCIOLOGY, AND HISTORY

Psychoanalysis has often been blamed for neglecting the sociological point of view and considering man as a merely biological, that is to say essentially asocial, being. In reality, however, it considers man as ahistorical and takes his present state for the human condition pure and simple. Many of the basic conceptions of psychoanalysis do represent social categories, and have no exact meaning if divorced from their social background. The family, above all, in which the whole of the child's future life is being shaped, forms a social group, and the connections between its members are social relationships. The system to which the "reality principle" refers is society, and the inexorable facts that frustrate, cripple, annihilate the pleasure-seeking individual are social conventions and institutions. Finally, the superego is nothing but the representative of society, the summary of its cultural achievements in the form of claims,

[4] Freud: "Instincts and Their Vicissitudes," in *Collected Papers*, IV, 64.
[5] Cf. F. H. Bartlett: "The Limitations of Freud," *Science and Society* (1939), III/1, p. 73.

commands, moral laws, threats, and sanctions. All these relationships, however, in the statements of psychoanalysis, are di-
vested of their economic aspect and suffer from a lack of historical definition. "Family" is to psychoanalysis always the same
monogamous, patriarchal, precariously balanced, and radically
menaced institution, irrespective of the facts that modify its
character in the course of time. Social reality means always the
same set of prohibitions, the same check on pleasure. And the
superego appears in the shape of a mythical demon beyond
space and time, an apocalyptic figure outside the bounds of history.

It is incorrect, therefore, to say that psychoanalysis pays
no attention to the social setting of the individual. It is just,
however, to insist on the fact that it regards even social phenomena, such as war or dictatorship, as a product of instinctual
impulses, and explains a social structure so extremely complex
and historically intricate as capitalism by the simple and homogeneous proclivity to anal eroticism. The sociological conceptions of psychoanalysis are blurred, above all, by the fact
that they represent even social groups and social behavior as
magnified individuals or mythologized individual attitudes.
Categories such as the "collective mind" or "collective memory," not to mention Jung's "collective unconscious," originate
in an unscrupulous direct application of the principles of the
psychology of the individual to the psychology of groups. The
root of these misconceptions is to be found, above all, in the
fact that Freud includes sociology and history in psychology,
and maintains that there are, strictly speaking, only two sets of
scientific disciplines, psychology, pure and applied, and the
natural sciences.[6]

Freud emphasises that different people behave in different ways even under the same economic conditions. This may
be so; but they often behave in a very similar way, in spite of
their different psychological constitutions, under the same
economic conditions and produce uniform social attitudes, such

[6] Freud: *New Introductory Lectures* (1933).

78

as class-consciousness, the spiritual climate of an epoch, consistent political, religious, or artistic movements. The whole question revolves around the familiar fact of interaction between biological constitution and environment, nature and nurture, psychology and sociology, of which pairs evidently neither constituent can be ignored. Every manifestation of life is the outcome of a set of constitutional dispositions and a set of environmental conditions. The social process consists in the gradual adjustment of instinctual constitutions to economic conditions and the institutions in which these conditions express themselves. This adjustment, however, can take place only by means of a psychic apparatus. Psychology, at any given historical moment, may itself be a result of social development; the individual, with his biological constitution and psychic disposition, is, nevertheless, the only exponent of social developments. The instincts, instinctual urges, biological needs belong to the "basis" of ideologies, and Freud justly insists that psychoanalysis is "but a superstructure," a system built on an organic, biological foundation. The trouble here again, as in many other cases, originates not so much in the statement itself as in its implications, not in starting from the instincts, but in assuming that they are also responsible for spiritual structures in which the original impulses are thickly overlaid, deflected, or superseded by non-instinctual motives.

More recent psychoanalysts assert that Freud did not consider the instincts immutable, but they cannot deny that he maintained their "conservative nature," [7] and imagined their transformation to be so slow that they retained a practically invariable, ahistorical character. But the conflicts between instinctual drives and cultural demands are, as everybody knows, historically determined. "Love," that is to say, all its implications, what is fair and right in love, and what is considered an offence against public morality, changes with time. Yet Freud never speaks in such connections of anything except typical, historically indifferent, attitudes, overlooking the fact that not

[7] Ibid.

79

only are repressions and frustrations a result of social development, but also that certain allegedly instinctual needs and appetites, above all aggressive and narcissistic tendencies, actually are socially and historically conditioned. It is not enough to know, however, that different social conditions bring about different kinds of frustration. We must also realize that members of different societies react in different ways to the same kind of frustration. Aggression itself is to some extent a result of frustration, that is to say, not a pure instinctual impulse, but a derivative, and therefore by no means as direct and simple as an instinct.

Although the argument about the primacy of psychology or sociology cannot be decided in a comprehensive and conclusive way, there are features, such as the relationship between repression and social institutions, which reveal the full strength of the social point of view. It is not institutions, social conventions, moral standards, customs, laws, *etc.*, that are, as psychoanalysis implies, a product of repression; on the contrary, repressions are a result of existing institutions. First comes an established rule, which may be the expression of economic, political, or other interests, and then a prohibition. Where there are no conventions, there are no prohibitions or inhibitions either. There is simply no reason for prohibiting what does not menace the continuance of an established order. Moral or civil laws presuppose the existence of an authority; dependence precedes attachment, and precedes resistance, revolt, and aggression as well. The biological and psychological apparatus of man is, however, the instrument on which history plays its tunes—an instrument that has not only its limitations but also its own possibilities, its own unmistakable tone and timbre.

Freud's unhistorical way of thinking is most evident in his theory of the repetition of phylogenetic trends in the development of the individual. Repetition is itself an essentially unhistorical conception, and Freud's repetition-compulsion as an endeavor to restore an earlier stage of development is mere metaphysics into the bargain. His later writings contain, notoriously enough, many other philosophical escapades of this kind. He discovers contents in dreams which, on his view, cannot originate in the dreamer's own experiences, but are, as he puts it, an archaic heritage, like that preserved in the oldest legends and folkways of mankind.[8] He claims that "in the history of the human species something happened similar to the events in the life of the individual,"[9] and that the individual only recapitulates the phases in the development of the race. The Oedipus complex, for example, is nothing but the ontogenetic repetition of a prehistoric situation occurring in the patriarchal horde and leading to what he describes as the "primal parricide." Freud assumes that certain psychic attitudes, which had been conscious in primitive man, being his solutions of a given difficulty, as, for instance, his resistance to incestual desires, become unconscious when inherited and transformed into automatic reactions. He even refers to a "memory of the race," and connects, among other things, the dread of castration with a mythical faculty whose implications are not very different from those of Jung's "collective unconscious." Moreover, he asserts not only that "society has a superego as well as the individual,"[1] but also assumes the possibility of a racial neurosis.[2] All these propositions have one feature in common: they originate in the assumption of a group soul or a collective mind. Social groups have, however, as we know, no collective faculties, no common instincts, appetites, inhibitions, dreams, memories, or creative urges: only individuals can desire, repress, dream, remember, think, feel, or express themselves in an articulate way. A social group is not an enlarged or condensed individual; it consists of single individuals, and has no reality apart from their existence.

It would seem that the unhistorical character of the psy-

---

[8] Freud: *An Outline of Psychoanalysis* (1941).
[9] Freud: *Moses and Monotheism*, p. 126.
[1] Freud: *Civilization and Its Discontents* (1930).
[2] A. Kardiner: *The Individual and His Society* (1949), pp. 381–2.

81

choanalytic conceptions is, above all, a result of their origin in natural science. Freud tried, at least in his earlier period, to keep as close as possible to quantitative principles, and his whole thinking developed in spatial rather than temporal categories. The mind as he imagines it is a structure consisting of compartments, not an integrated organism developing in phases. The only important example in his work of the investigation of the mind from the point of view of growth and development is the description of the stages of infantile sexuality. But even there a quantitative conception of the unfolding impetus is maintained. According to Freud, mental life consists, above all, in conversions of measurable and mathematically divisible energies. His theory of the convertibility of mental tendencies leads him to a kind of mental economics. The basic assumption is that the psyche has at its disposal only a limited fund of mental power, and that the amount of energy used up in one area diminishes the amount of energy available in another. Thus, for instance, narcissistic libido and object-love hold a balance,[3] or fixation and regression complement each other.[4] But, properly speaking, the whole of the psychoanalytical theory of neurosis, or of any other mode in which a displacement of mental power takes place, is based on an economic principle: the mind breaks down and mental bankruptcy occurs when a substitutive gratification is not sufficient to make up for the lack of direct satisfaction of an unacceptable demand. Neurosis is, according to psychoanalytical conceptions, a phenomenon of mental economy even in the sense that for every pleasure achieved by indulging in a symptom, a corresponding amount of pain has to be paid. Or, to look at it from another angle, the neurotic person imposes on himself the pains of illness, in order to avoid other pains, subjectively less endurable, but objectively equally severe. An economic conception of mental functioning is also responsible for the view that power in one field of human activity is bought at the price of

[3] Freud: "On Narcissism," in Collected Papers, IV.
[4] Fenichel, op. cit., p. 57.

a weakness or inability in another; that Hephaistus is lame, Homer blind, Philoctetes suffering from his wound, and that they have their abilities as a compensation for their deformities and incapacities; it is not for nothing that poets and artists are sick or degenerate, that suffering is the price of greatness, and that there is no success without sacrifice.[5]

Physical energy and mental power, which here appear interchangeable, belong in reality to two completely different orders. Spiritual power, operative in any more or less complex psychic activity, is not measurable. It is an unwarranted, purely mechanistic view of the mind to hold that it disposes of a constant amount of energy, and that its power is subject to a law similar to that of the conservation of energy in physics. Such an assumption is just as untenable as the proposition that the spiritual capacity of a person diminishes with an excessive consumption of mental energy. There is, of course, the phenomenon of fatigue and exhaustion, but we know equally that intensity of awareness and power of concentration may grow with the growth of the tasks set the mind and accepted by it. Spiritual power often increases with expenditure. The quality of the single components in a mental achievement of higher order depends on so many different factors that the attempt to trace it back to its origin must prove futile. Only on the level of very elementary mental activities is it suitable to speak of a correlation of quantity and quality. A quantitative assessment is inadequate to any not merely reactive psychic manifestation. Freud returns, in fact, to the mechanistic views of the old, pre-analytical psychology, when he explains aesthetic pleasure, as well as the enjoyment of wit, by the experience of saving mental energy.[6] This is certainly one of those propositions in which the revolutionary power of his thought is least perceptible. Unfortunately, it is not quite incidental to his basic conception of art.

[5] Edmund Wilson: *The Wound and the Bow* (1929).
[6] Freud: *Wit and Its Relation to the Unconscious* (1916).

6. PROBLEMS OF ART ANSWERABLE AND UNANSWERABLE BY PSYCHOANALYSIS

Freud was, of course, not aware of the limitations of his theory of art consequent on the unhistorical nature of his method, but he knew as well as anybody that there were problems, answers to which are essential to a satisfactory interpretation of the work of art, which psychoanalysis could not hope to solve. He mentions these problems occasionally, in a rather unsystematic way, under four different headings. The first of them refers to a limitation peculiar to psychoanalysis; the others are concerned with difficulties that psychoanalysis shares with psychology in general. Freud affirms repeatedly, and without qualification, that the explanation of the "nature of the artistic gift" lies beyond the scope of his doctrine (*Autobiography*), and that "psychoanalysis must lay down its arms before the problem of the artist" (*Dostoevsky and Parricide*). In relation to this specific problem, the position of psychology, in the more comprehensive sense of the word, is not so hopeless as that of psychoanalysis with its bias in favor of the unconscious mind. But even if general psychology can contribute in a useful way to the explanation of the artist's spiritual make-up and establish at least some of the mental preconditions of artistic talent, it is, in respect of the rest of Freud's unanswerable problems, above all that of the "nature of beauty," just as much at a loss as psychoanalysis itself. And if Freud declares that "psychoanalysis has less to say about beauty than about most other things," then psychology in general has not much more to say about it, risking the use of its genetic method to destroy the specific nature of beauty. The same holds true for the criteria of "artistic quality," which Freud readily admits cannot be tackled by psychoanalysis

(*Short Outline of Psychoanalysis*). Psychology may, at best, explain why people accept certain artistic values, but the scale of values, that is to say, the criteria of what constitutes good art and distinguishes it from less good or inferior art, is not a problem of psychology. Finally, Freud relinquishes the solution of the problems connected with "artistic technique," and admits that the "means by which the artist works" are unattainable by the scrutiny of the psychoanalyst (*Autobiography*). Artistic technique is, in fact, inaccessible to the psychologist altogether, being determined by what is called the "inner logic" of the work of art and by tradition, that is to say, the accumulated experiences of generations, the rules that have proved helpful in handling motifs, materials, and instruments, rather than by the particular mental constitution of the individual artist.

But if psychoanalysis cannot answer the question about the preconditions and criteria of artistic activity, it can very well answer that of the function of art in the life of those who produce or enjoy it. The reasons why a person has become an artist, why he gave way to the urge of creation as a solution to his problems, why his difficulties and conflicts called for a solution by art, and art alone, are by no means obvious; they have to be found out, and psychoanalysis may be a very helpful, perhaps indispensable, way of doing this.

The romantics were incorrigible myth-makers: art is certainly not the mother tongue of mankind. It is, in fact, a highly artificial language, a strange, equivocal, unspontaneous way of expression. Normal people see no reason to make use of it. To write poetry or to paint pictures for the enjoyment of others and for reward may be a harmless or even commendable occupation; to produce works of art, however, as a habit or an obsession is, to say the least, a queer business. Why should a normal person pretend that life is different from what it really is? To do so, he must be at variance with the world and feel alienated or bewildered in some way.

Freud's answer to the question was, as we saw, that the

artist's instinctual urges are stronger than those of other people, that he reacts in a more impatient way on the demand to renounce the satisfaction of his desires, and that his need for a substitutive gratification is therefore more imperative. He claims more power, a more complete mastery of life, and a greater amount of love, attention and success than people in general. He turns away from the daily routine of life, and finds in a fictitious world the reward that reality denies him. His flight into fiction, however, is by no means in accord with a "normal," safe and sound, conduct of life; his evasion is, on the contrary, just what makes of him a permanently menaced introvert, and brings him into so close a contact with the neurotic. Thomas Mann declared that a "decent and normal person does not write, act or compose" (*Tonio Kröger*), and this, in spite of his admiration for the great masters, must have been Freud's opinion too. Instead of "decent and normal," he would have said, perhaps, that it is the "moderate or uninhibited" people who do not write poetry or compose music, but he certainly disapproved in a way of those who did write or compose. He knew that the romantics have just invented the legend of the exultant and buoyant genius with the kiss of the Muse on his brow, and that the artist, loud and arrogant as he often is, never feels quite safe or settled in this world.

The function of the work of art in the life of the artist is varied and manifold: it may be the resolution of an unbearable tension, or a means of creating tension in an otherwise dull and frustrated existence; it may become a part of the artist's being, more important and precious than life itself, a source of pride, self-exaltation, and self-complacency, or again an eternal self-reproach, a dreadful evidence of failure; it may be a substitute for a woman, for family and friends, or an enemy, an insatiable vampire that drains one's forces, sucks one's blood and brains, tricks one out of one's own life, youth, and happiness. The creation of works of art may be a defence against the fear of losing control over life or oneself, but may also be a form of surrender and self-effacement. Every work of art, at least of post-romantic

art, is, in a sense, a fight against chaos. The artist may be successful or not in his struggle against darkness and disorder, but
there is certainly no incentive to creation where there is no
menace to the continuance of an established world or a settled
outlook on life. Artistic creativity may be, in the end, a means
of the integration as well as the disintegration of the self; it
may be a vehicle for the restoration of one's lost peace of mind,
but also an escape from oneself—a way of splitting up one's
personality by identification, by experimenting with various
ego-ideals incorporated in the characters of a work of art. Most
of these aspects of the function of art in the life of those who
produce it were simply inconceivable before Freud's method
was available, and one cannot hope to do justice to art's complexity without turning to psychoanalysis for guidance.

This applies also to the study of the motives for the acceptance or rejection of a work of art by the public. As everyone knows, these motives are mostly far from adequate; the
commonest thing is an inappropriate, that is to say, non-
aesthetically determined approach to artistic creations. We are
therefore, in analyzing artistic experiences, to refer to the practical function of art in people's lives, and to be prepared to
meet with different evaluations according to the different degrees of success it has in fulfilling such a function. The most
common reasons for a non-aesthetic approach to art are social;
there are, however, also psychologically or biologically rather
than socially determined motives that produce an "inadequate reaction" to works of art. People may find a work unen-
joyable or even repulsive, because their anxiety or sense of
guilt is increased by it; because the work reactivates some of
their painfully repressed desires and bring back to their consciousness unresolved or unrealized contradictions dormant in
their minds; finally, because the artist emphasizes rather than
conceals the fact that the world lies in ruins around them, and
that they themselves may not be quite innocent of the destruction. People feel, on the other hand, attracted and delighted by
works of art that show the world at peace, safe and sound, in-

87

tact and incorruptible; works that help to solve their problems or allow them to appear as soluble and therefore harmless. They describe such works as perfectly beautiful and imperishable. The fact is that, in accounting for their artistic appreciation, they rationalize their likes or dislikes in the same way as they rationalize the motives for their opinions and emotions in general. To put it briefly, people, as a rule, like works of art that enhance their feeling of security and diminish their fear of life; they dislike, on the other hand, those which touch sore spots in their past or present. One needs a high degree of artistic awareness and discrimination—a frame of mind which is not typical of a spontaneous, "naïve" reaction—to emancipate oneself, in enjoying works of art, from such practical and personal points of view.

7. ART, THE UNCONSCIOUS MIND, ILLNESS, AND THE DREAMS

To a very large extent, the creation of the work of art takes place in the full light of consciousness, under the permanent control of the artist, who more often than not starts with a deliberately chosen motif, and remains on the whole aware of what is happening in the course of its elaboration. The study of this process, as a conscious and purposive mental operation, does not call for or admit of a psychoanalytical approach; it is not a proper subject for depth psychology. Everything, however, that can be described as a flash of thought or a suddenly emerging idea, what the French call a *trouvaille* and the Germans an *Einfall*, which the artist himself feels to be a windfall or a gift rather than the result of his own conscious effort and deliberate choice, is inexplicable by a psychology restricted to the exploration of conscious mental phenomena. This and only this part of the process of artistic creation justifies and rewards

88

the psychoanalytical approach. It springs, as a spontaneous, involuntary, and apparently unpremeditated activity, from hidden sources of the mind, sources unknown and unfathomable by the artist himself, the unnoticed presence of which is characterized by Freud's conception of the unconscious. The significance of psychoanalysis as a theory of art depends on the importance of the material coming from these sources.

Psychoanalysis is, to define it briefly, a theory of the working of unconscious motives in mental life. Freud himself describes his doctrine as a "particularly onesided scientific discipline concerned with the unconscious"; [7] and in comparing the transformation of the unconscious contents of the mind into conscious elements with the act of cognition in Kant's epistemology,[8] he even seems to consider the unconscious as a kind of "thing in itself" and to attribute to it as it were the dignity of a metaphysical principle. According to psychoanalytical views, only the unconscious is continuous in mental life; [9] consciousness, on the other hand, consists of more or less incoherent fragments whose connections with one another and the mind as a whole lie beyond the limits of conscious experience. In line with these propositions, the introduction of psychoanalytic methods into the exploration of art is called for, above all, by the fact that the production as well as the enjoyment of the work of art is a more or less discontinuous process full of gaps, incongruities, and riddles. As had been rightly suggested, "an unconscious origin of single elements of a work of art should be taken into consideration only if the composition produces an incoherent effect"; [1] and, as we may add, a psychoanalytical interpretation of a work of art should not be attempted unless an unconscious origin can be assumed for one or more of its components.

Some of Freud's most competent and influential followers

[7] Freud: *The Problem of Lay-Analysis* (1927).
[8] Freud: "The Unconscious," in *Collected Papers*, IV, 104.
[9] Cf. I. Hermann: *Die psychoanalytische Methode* (1934), p. 4.
[1] W. Born: "Unconscious Processes in Artistic Creation," *Journal of Clinical Psychopathology* (1945), VII/2, p. 267.

89

are, however, by no means content with the establishment of mutual dependence or a dialectical interaction between conscious faculties and unconscious impulses in spiritual activity; they maintain rather that the unconscious has to free itself from the control of consciousness in order to become productive. "The living motive force comes from beyond, from the unconscious," says Dr. Jones, "the conscious mind merely interposes obstacles in its path." [2] The truth is, however, that no work of art imposes itself as a whole on its author, and indeed no independent part of a work is conceivable without the collaboration of the conscious, rational, and critical faculties of the artist. The production of a real work of art requires the presence of a sound and cautious mind with roots in a living cultural tradition and command of a stock of practicable devices, a capacity to learn and to assimilate, a readiness to experiment, to delete, and to start again. Unconscious impulses, unrealized inclinations, ambitions originating in unadmitted and repressed desires, may produce a mental tension leading to the work of art as their expression or solution; the power of expression cannot, however, be explained by a mere impulse or tension. An urge to creation is one thing, the ability to achieve it quite another. Freud was on this point better advised than most of his disciples.

Conscious and unconscious tendencies are, in the creation of the work of art, not merely inseparable: the work itself is a result of their irreducible duality. Freud, as is known, characterizes artistic talent as "flexibility of repression," that is to say, as due to the fact that for the consciousness of the artist the unconscious is more easily accessible, and that from his unconscious there is a more direct way to consciousness than is the case with most people. In examining the course of artistic production, a constant variation of level of consciousness is recognizable, the act of creation being, from a psychological point of

[2] Jones: "Psychoanalysis and Sociology," in *Social Aspects of Psychoanalysis* (1924), p. 27.

view, often no more than an oscillation between unconscious impulses and their gradual realization. The spontaneous and the unconscious on the one side, and the conventional and the conscious on the other, roughly correspond; we must not forget, however, that what is felt to be spontaneous may be prepared for in a more or less conscious way, and what appears to be conventional may be an unconscious defence mechanism against dangerous instinctual urges. But the spontaneous and the conventional elements in a work of art correspond even less frequently to the articulate and the inarticulate elements, and are by no means simply the result of a primary and a secondary elaboration. It is not satisfactory to speak of two altogether distinct phases of artistic creation, that is to say, to assume a stage of compulsive inspiration and another of conscious endeavor. There is no inspiration without vestiges of a previous organization, and no artistic organization without uncontrollable and unaccountable moments of inspiration. The description of the process as an appropriation of material first attempted by an unconscious approach and then revised and improved upon by a conscious manipulation is utterly false. The ego does not simply edit a somewhat confused, but in itself complete text, provided by the id. The contributions of the conscious and the unconscious mind to the artistic creation are on no level divorced from one another. A continuous shift of focus, not a progress from one stage to another, characterizes the successive steps of production. Even the first idea of a work of art may be consciously and deliberately conceived; on the other hand, even the last touch on the work may involve unconscious elements: lucky findings, unexpected connections, gratuitous solutions.

The dichotomy of unconscious creativity and conscious and rational, but merely regulative, organization introduces a totally inadequate set of alternatives into the philosophy of art; for "regulation," as part of the artist's activity, may be just as creative as "invention" is rational. The whole conception of artistic creativity as a fluid and more or less chaotic state of mind, "out of which emerge definite form-ideas," [3] still reflects the ro· mantic view of productive chaos. Unfathomable irrationality is here once again the real origin of artistic creation, and the "inarticulate qualities," that is, the "imponderables" of romantic aesthetics, are still regarded as the most genuine and most valuable features of the work of art. To differentiate between the articulate and the inarticulate elements of artistic forms is, nevertheless, a rewarding task, provided that one avoids categorizing these in a too mechanical way. The melody in a piece of music, for instance, may be to a far greater extent the result of an unconscious, undeliberate, spontaneous spiritual attitude than some of the "inarticulate" features of its elaboration or delivery—features that are often shrewdly calculated, in spite of their apparently improvised character.

Any benefit from applying the category of the unconscious to the interpretation of art depends on our success in finding a method that helps us to detect the principles of an artistic technique different from the conscious and purposive elaboration of a formal scheme. The problem is, in other words, to find a clue to the unconscious motivation of certain artistic forms, such as images, metaphors, or symbols, for which the evidence of conscious motivation is lacking. It is easily conceivable that a mechanism similar to "free association," as practiced in psychoanalytic therapy, is operative in artistic creation, and that it reveals some of the basic principles of spontaneous invention. A suddenly emerging creative idea is, on a merely psychological level, not very different from the associations produced in an analytical interview. Freud, no doubt, had this affinity in mind when he declared that although psychoanalysis can hardly answer the problem of artistic talent, it can certainly throw light on the working of the artist's imagination.[4] Evidence for the share of compulsive associations in the pro-

[3] A. Ehrenzweig: "Unconscious Form-Creation in Art," *British Journal of Medical Psychology* (1948), XXI/3, p. 192.
[4] Freud: *An Outline of Psychoanalysis* (1941).

duction of a work of art is, however, often unavailable. In most cases the artist cannot be interviewed about the order of emergence of his ideas. It has been suggested therefore that we should examine the connection of ideas or images as they appear in the finished works themselves, and try to draw conclusions from their proximity.[5] In doing so, however, one must consider that the order of their actual emergence is seldom preserved in the final pattern of the work. Only if one and the same sequence of motifs recurs in quite different compositional contexts, and if a certain combination of images or ideas amounts to a kind of obsession, can we attribute their association to an unconscious urge rather than to a particular artistic aim.

The fact that creation may originate in the unconscious does not, however, mean that it is pure spontaneity. Intuition, inspiration, improvisation bring to light nothing but forgotten experience and buried knowledge; and a suddenly emerging vision, an unaccountable flash of thought, or an apparently spontaneous invention is often simply the result of long, though unconscious, unrealized or obliterated preparation. Indeed: "*Le hasard ne favorise que les esprits préparés.*" It is, nevertheless, possible to make a program or largely stereotyped procedure of this sort of production, to pretend that one is acting under an irresistible coercion or a spell when composing poetry or painting pictures. No one will be surprised to discover that romanticism invented the device of "automatic writing" or that surrealism developed it further by simply imitating the psychoanalytical technique of "free association." Nothing, however, could be less spontaneous and have less to do with the unconscious mind than the carrying out of such a sophisticated program.

The presence of unconscious material in the formation of the work of art is, in spite of all these qualifications, unmistakable, and a legitimate objection to the usual psychoanalytic in-

[5] Kenneth Burke: "Freud and the Analysis of Poetry," *American Journal of Sociology* (1939), XLV, 283.

93

terpretation of art can be based only on the fact that, in relation to the richness and the complexity of a real work of art, this material is rather poor, undifferentiated, and monotonous. If psychoanalysts never stop repeating that writers and artists are concerned, above all, with repressed sexual wishes, the Oedipus complex, the dread of castration, sadistic, masochistic, or narcissistic trends, then perhaps the unconscious mind, as psychoanalysis interprets it, does not contain much more than this. But psychoanalysis may not grasp the whole range of unconscious motivations. It is a fact, and, by the way, one of the most significant points of contact between historical materialism and psychoanalysis, that a writer—here Balzac is the classical example—does not always represent the interests of that social class which he intends, and which he believes he is defending or protecting. What Engels understands by the "triumph of realism" may rather induce the artist to follow, instead of the ideological fallacies of his abstract thought, the unconscious direction of his genius, which represents the facts of life in a more adequate and, in the sense of historical materialism, more "concrete" way than his social theories or political convictions. With an eye to unconscious impulses of this kind, psychological investigation could substantially enrich our knowledge of the process of artistic creation and modify some of the results of psychoanalysis in this field of research. But be that as it may, it is an unsubstantiated supposition that whatever the mind brings forth in a spontaneous and irrational way necessarily originates in a deeper and more vital region of the psyche than what is produced by a conscious and rationally controlled effort; just as it is no more than a romantic myth that intuition and emotion move closer to timeless, universally human, and spiritually comprehensive ideals than does rational discursive thought. In reality, the unconscious represents just as imperfectly as consciousness the unity and integrity of the mind. The former is poorer but by no means better integrated than the latter. The unconscious mind of different people shows just as varied a picture as their historical past or their social backgrounds, their education or predilections, in a word, their consciousness. It is by no means one and the same kind of unconscious tendencies that are revealed in Negro sculpture, a child's drawing, the scribbles of a madman, and a painting by Van Gogh. The conscious and the unconscious mind are not two water-tight compartments, not even two rooms connected by a door with a doorkeeper, as Freud liked to describe them, but rather two communicating vessels whose liquid contents constantly mix by a kind of osmosis.

Moreover, the dreams, fantasies, or delusions of a savage, a child, or a neurotic person are just as different from the mental attitudes of a civilized normal adult as are their conscious thoughts or unconscious feelings. The deranged mind of a primitive person is quite unlike that of a genius. If you smash a complicated piece of clockwork, you get, as a famous psychiatrist put it, destroyed complicated clockwork, not simple clockwork. Illness does not of itself equalize different kinds of people; not even the same kind of illness does. An artist is never simply a lunatic or a neurotic, or even a mere introvert. But if it is true that he has "not far to go to become neurotic," and if the ancient myth of the sick artist has some foundation, at least to the extent that there is a certain "rigidity" in the artist's reactions, which would be a minimum condition for neurosis, then the interpretation of the work of art by a psychoanalytic approach could gain much in scope, in spite of occasional overrating of the significance of illness in spiritual achievement.

Since the day of romanticism there has always been, at least among the artists and poets themselves, a tendency to insist on sickness as a distinguishing feature of genius. When the former representatives of public opinion suddenly found themselves barred from the general competition for riches and power, they sought to invest their disability for fight and contest with the insignia of the elite and exempt. "Poetry may be an illness of man," said Heine, "as the pearl is a disease of the oyster." He seemed to emphasize the words illness and disease, but what he really meant to do was to display the pearl.

"Every artist is a neurotic," declares Stekel with amazing simplicity; if this is no more than the daydream of a psychiatrist, Proust's dictum that "everything great in the world comes from neurotics" is certainly more than the lament of a poet; it is a claim to exterritoriality. But are artists really more neurotic than other people? Are their restlessness, irritability, and moodiness exceptional? Are the sudden changes from exultant self-confidence to hopeless doubt, from perfect harmony and the feeling of unshakable security to the most desperate anxiety experiences that they share with none but the insane? Are these not, to some extent, features common to the reactions of people whose existence and whose material and moral success in life depend on the issue of an unbridled and unpredictable competition? Are not all in whose life chance, good or bad luck, incalculable and apparently uncontrollable success play a decisive part, that is to say, all gamblers and speculators, conjurers and champions, good and bad actors, real artists and unreconciled failures, to the same extent neurotics? And is not here, once again, the historical and social situation the real cause of the disease? It is, in any case, only the modern, romantic and post-romantic, artist, not the artist in general, who appears more closely akin to the mentally deranged than the other competitors for public favor. The real problem, however, does not consist in the connection of art and genuine illness, which is a highly differentiated, fluctuating, and singular relationship; and the question to be answered is not whether and to what extent the artist may be described as a psychopathic or neurotic person, but if the artist really is sick, how great a part illness plays in artistic activity.

The whole matter of art and illness is, however, only part of a larger complex of problems in which the relationship of artistic talent to such extrinsic conditions as childhood, a primitive, unsophisticated, or uncivilized state of mind, estrangement and isolation from the community of normal and useful people, is the subject of inquiry. The answer to all these problems can only be the same. The artist may be a neurotic, and the child, the savage, or the lunatic may produce things with unmistakable artistic qualities, but art is never the product of neurosis, insanity, or a primitive state of mind. André Malraux's remark, that the child is controlled by his talent without controlling it,[6] also applies, *mutatis mutandis*, to other cases. The real artist, on the other hand, is the master and not the slave of his ability. He may be ill, but his gift has no direct connection with his good or bad health. Illness may intensify or modify the use of his capacities, but it is no more responsible for his creative power than, say, an experience of love, which provides him with new material, but never with the means of its representation.

Mental disorder cannot be considered relevant to the creation of art if its emergence fails to produce a change in style or a new orientation in the artist's outlook on life; that is to say, unless some new fashion in conceiving or representing his motifs is clearly assignable to the outbreak of illness. Perhaps the only unquestionable case of such a coincidence is, however, that of Van Gogh, and even with him a causal relationship between violent expressionism and derangement of mind is by no means established. The attempt to equate artistic power with the abilities of a neurotic or psychotic person, a child, or a primitive, is therefore no more than an effort to make a complicated mechanism more comprehensible by taking it to pieces. But if we disintegrate a complex thing and reduce it to its constituent elements, we lose the very quality we have been trying to put a finger on: its complexity. A complex structure is not a mere sum total of simple facts; its complexity is present, to some extent, in all its components. The attempt to approach artistic creativity with an eye on the performance of children, primitive men, or the mentally deranged is based on the assumption that there is, in spiritual

[6] André Malraux: *Les Voix du silence* (1953), p. 283.

97

matters, a way from the simple to the complex, or at any rate a way back from the complex to the simple. A genius, sane or insane, is an extremely complicated psychological phenomenon, and the ability of a madman, if it is real artistic power, is just as complicated and has just as little to do with madness as the gift of a balanced mind has to do with sanity. The child and the primitive, on the other hand, are utterly simple beside a mature and experienced artist even in their most successful artistic achievements; on their level, the complexity in question does not occur at all.

The difference between a neurotic person and an artist—who may, but need not, be neurotic—consists, above all, in the fact that the latter produces works of art instead of neurotic symptoms as a solution of his inner conflicts or as an outlet for his repressed desires. The neurotic knows "no satisfaction without suffering" (Franz Alexander); the artist, on the other hand, extracts from his very suffering a kind of gratification, thanks to his ability to tell us, in the famous phrase of Goethe, "how he suffers." The artist escapes illness by what Freud calls his capacity for sublimation. Art is for him a substitute for neurosis or an escape from mental aberration. Thus artistic talent, far from being an illness, is a protection against illness, even if not always an adequate protection. We may, therefore, speak of a flight into art, as we speak of a flight into illness, neurosis, or psychosis. And thus we come back, after all, to the old, familiar truth, that art is a refuge of those who are unable to cope with reality or are not willing to handle it; that art is, in a word, the realm of the Blue Flower, the old romantic land of the gentle and the delicate—if it is not a Utopia—a refuge of rebels.

The affinity between the dream and artistic creation belongs to the most familiar propositions of the psychoanalytic theory of art. The idea itself is, of course, not original; it is part of the romantic heritage, and it retains certain characteristics of its origin. But in psychoanalytic interpretation of the work of art it shifts from the level of a poetic whim to that of a scientific hypothesis and offers reasonably solid ground for systematic investigation. The most conspicuous and, from a psychological point of view, most fundamental feature that the dream and the work of art have in common is their meaningful character and their share in maintaining the balance of psychic life. They both represent substitutive gratifications of unadmitted wishes and indicate compromises between repressed impulses and the claims of the censoring ego. Their effect consists in reducing mental tension and in creating a *modus vivendi* where neither a yielding to impulse nor a complete repression of it could easily be sustained. Both in the dream and in the work of art the ego is involved in a bitter fight against dark and dangerous powers, but in both cases it maintains its mastery and prevents inroads of the unconscious on the individual's direction of life.

Apart from these general psycho-dynamic features, Freud establishes the existence of a number of technical devices that are characteristic of the dream-work as well as of the work of art and seem to provide the best foundation for a psychoanalytic approach to art criticism. Indirect representation, symbolization, displacement, condensation, overdetermination, primary and secondary elaboration, and a differentiation of manifest and latent meanings are the most pregnant of these devices. But, furthermore, Freud enriches the picture by a variety of revealing sidelights, as, for instance, his well-known remark that the dream is witty because it finds the direct way to the expression of its thoughts blocked.[7]

The application of this and similar approaches to the criticism of art discloses extremely important formal principles of artistic representation, and at the same time shows that even the happiest artistic expedients and the most brilliant *tours de force* are often no more than makeshifts and the result of accidental difficulties.

However, the real significance of the features that the work of art shares with dreams and, for that matter, with day-

[7] Freud: *The Interpretation of Dreams* (1933).

dreams, fantasies, and neurotic or psychotic symptoms, consists far less in the evidence they present for pathological or other extra-aesthetic qualities of artistic creativity than in the fact that the mind appears in all these manifestations as the same unrealistic or, as it has been suggested, "poetry-making" organ.[8] Seen from this point of view, the whole of the psychoanalytical interview presents itself in a new light, and makes us wonder how much of what the patient imparts to the analyst as his recollections, associations, or other direct experiences, is genuine, that is to say, based on facts, real happenings, genuine biographical situations. Does he not partly invent the history of his illness, his conflicts and symptoms? But even if he does really invent them, can his cheating impair the value of his communications in the eyes of the analyst? A symptom remains to some extent a symptom in spite of being invented. But if so, then an undisguised invention also, such as the work of art, may both retain its own independent character, and at the same time fulfil the function of a symptom. In other words: a work of art may be a deceit, a pretence, an escape, a sedative, a form of substitutive gratification, and still remain a work of art, a structure with a meaning, a unity, and a totality of its own. The aesthetic quality of a work of art is by no means destroyed by the non-artistic nature of its origin or the extra-artistic objective that its author may have in view in creating it.

At least one of the many points of difference between a dream and a work of art should, however, be kept in mind. Aesthetic illusion is a form of conscious self-deception, a "willing suspension of disbelief," as Coleridge described it. Its flexibility and its governable nature, the varying degree of awareness which accompanies the experience of being deceived by it, makes a return from art to reality possible at any time. But in dreams, daydreams, and neurotic and, above all, psychotic delusions, such a flexibility of attitude is beyond the power of the persons involved. The secret of artistic effect lies, in contrast to mere delusion, in a "right" distance to both reality and

[8] Lionel Trilling: *The Liberal Imagination* (1951), p. 52.

fantasy. An "underdistance" to the world of artistic illusion, to use a word that has become popular,[9] would obstruct the way back to reality; an "overdistance," on the other hand, would never allow us to emancipate ourselves from the standards of real life. Aestheticism loses life through art and for the sake of art, in the same way as dreams, daydreams, or delusions lose the solid ground of reality by indulging in unrealistic and socially destructive wishes. A total lack of imagination, on the other hand, has this in common with a too strict realism and rationalism, or with a too relentless domination of the ego over the id, that it prevents real artistic experience altogether, and loses art through life and for the sake of a socially sound and useful life.

8. *IMAGES AND THEIR AMBIGUITY*

The ultimate aim of the psychoanalytic exploration of art is to bring to light the implicit motifs underlying the explicit contents of the work of art. Images, above all in poetry, have, apart from their manifest motifs, often a hidden meaning, not immediately realized, even though this meaning may be from the outset very impressive. They are the result of a partly unconscious act of invention, and work more or less unnoticed on the reader's mind. They owe their complexity to the very fact that their meaning is not perfectly or not immediately clear, and that it cannot be grasped save step by step and, as it were, by chance, through anticipations and revisions, guessing and wondering. A poet may choose one word or image instead of another without exactly knowing why; he may choose a certain form of expression which carries a meaning perhaps not present to his conscious mind, but, nevertheless, decisive for the

[9] E. Bullogh: "Psychical Distance," *British Journal of Psych.,* V (1912).

success of his work. Artists tell us that they have occasionally contemplated the deletion of certain details in one or another of their works, being unable to realize at once the connection of these parts with the rest of the work in question, only to discover later that the reasons for preserving them were after all very sound, and that they obeyed, in fact, a kind of unconscious logic in inventing them. This shows very well that an artist may put more into his work than he is aware of, and draw on sources to whose origin psychoanalysis often indicates the shortest way.

Ambiguity is the most familiar form of complexity, and in modern poetry the most usual. We call an expression or an image ambiguous if it conveys more than one meaning by means of one statement, and if two or more meanings of a statement, not coherent in themselves, combine to express a complex but unitary experience or a more or less richly differentiated though not disintegrated mind. Ambiguity may originate in the most varied circumstances, but it is above all, a result of a latent meaning prevented, for some reason or other, from expressing itself directly. Its artistic attraction consists in the presence of an unknown, unrealized, but none the less most effective, factor of an impenetrable and therefore apparently inexhaustible source of excitement. There is an element of ambiguity in every genuine poetical image. The two objects compared in a simile or connected with one another in a metaphor resemble a third object rather than each other. Their "common denominator," which is the real, although unconscious, link between them, often reveals quite clearly a repressed force at work in the writer's mind. A simile or a metaphor may, therefore, be entirely nonsensical from a logical point of view and still completely satisfactory and self-evident as a piece of poetry. Baudelaire's *"Vous êtes un beau ciel d'automne"* makes no sense unless it conveys the vision of a woman stretched out on a couch at full length, indolently, voluptuously, irresistibly—a situation that the poet might never have enjoyed in reality.

No kind of explanation of poetical ambiguity seems more

rewarding than the method practiced by psychoanalysis in interpreting dreams, that is, the method of inferring from manifest to latent contents; and no conception more adequate to the nature of poetical images than that of "condensation" or "overdetermination" in the sense of Freud's analysis of dreams. It has been pointed out that most of what seems vague and indeterminate in art is, in fact, "overdetermined," and that overdetermination, as psychoanalysis defines it, is "central to the understanding of poetry." [1] Freud himself seems to have been fully aware of the implications of this parallelism between the images in a dream and those in a poem. He says explicitly that, just as a neurotic symptom or a dream, so "every genuine poetical creation must have proceeded from more than one impulse in the mind of the poet, and must admit of more than one interpretation." [2] We must not forget, however, that the ambiguity of artistic form is not merely a result of the artist's divided mind, but also a product of a continuous reinterpretation, which every new generation has to attempt if it wants to find a direct approach to the works created by its ancestors. The variety of interpretations grows as historical development proceeds, and the work of art becomes the more complex, and often the more ambiguous, the older it is.

Psychoanalysis has to be content, as we saw, with the interpretation of those factors of the artistic experience which cannot be accounted for by a psychology restricted to the expression of the conscious mind, which cannot be taken at their face value. But even the meaning of the manifest and explicit statements in a work of art is more or less lost for us as soon as we move away from the artist in time and no longer feel or think in the terms of his outlook on life. We do not properly know what the artist of a past period meant to say, even if he happened to express himself without inhibitions, mental reservations, or a bent to secrecy; there is, therefore, hardly any fundamental difference for us between manifest and latent mean-

[1] Ernst Kris: *Explorations in Art* (1952), p. 254.
[2] Freud: *The Interpretation of Dreams* (1933).

ings as far as a work of the past is concerned. Every interpretation of such a work is, to some extent, a misinterpretation. But
if we misunderstand a work of art, it is not because we "project
an articulate structure" into the work, where the artist himself
was inarticulate, but because our inarticulate experiences are
just as different from his inarticulate ways of expression as our
articulate thoughts and feelings from the articulate forms of
his art. Ambiguity and inarticulateness in a work of art are, incidentally, not at all identical. Inarticulateness may be the origin of ambiguity; the most complex forms of ambiguity are,
however, the result of an exaggerated care for articulation
rather than of a lack of concern about being articulate.

But ambiguity is itself a historically determined psychic
phenomenon, and by no means timeless or historically indifferent. Before the age of mannerism, that is, before the end of
the High Renaissance, it was never a very important means of
artistic representation; with the Marinists, the Gongorists, the
Elizabethan dramatists, and the Metaphysical poets, however,
who are all addicted to the devices of ambiguity and conceit,
a new, previously inconceivable predilection for complexity
becomes the literary fashion, and incongruity is felt to be the
adequate expression of a spiritual crisis that seems to shake the
very foundations of Western culture. It is highly symptomatic
that in the artistic production of this critical period conflicts
between sensuality and spirituality, that is to say, antagonisms
calling for a psychoanalytic interpretation, are the main origin
of the ambiguous forms of expression. Ambiguity is, in fact,
just as is a neurotic symptom or a dream, the expression of a
spiritual tension in which one engages and remains, not for fun,
but because none of the conflicting tendencies present in the
ambiguous experience appears acceptable. Shakespeare, for example, as has been pointed out, often deliberately refuses to
choose between two different meanings of an image and maintains ambiguity as the most faithful and most inevitable expression of his frame of mind.[3]

[3] William Empson: *Seven Types of Ambiguity* (1947).

104

A new and certainly more adequate approach to the phenomenon of mannerism than any previous explanation, an approach, by the way, which would hardly have been possible without the lesson learned from psychoanalysis, has showed in a perfectly convincing way that art is not only a form of exposure, but also one of disguise, that works of art are created not only as forms of self-revelation and communication, but also as a means of concealment, self-deception, and deceit, or, at most, of confessing but half the truth. Freud once remarked of the works of Goethe that they were all used by him as "a means of self-concealment," by which he obviously meant to qualify the poet's own dictum, that his works were "the fragments of a great confession." Freud's statement applies to artistic expression in general, even if we maintain that the decisive difference between artistic images and the symbols occurring in dreams, neurotic symptoms, or faulty performances consists in the fact that the artist seeks, above all, expression and explanation, whereas the neurotic, the dreamer, and the "absent-minded" person seek an alibi and a disguise.

Psychoanalysis has taught us better to comprehend not only that obscurity and ambiguity have an artistic value of their own, but also some of the reasons why, as Coleridge formulated it, "poetry gives more pleasure when only generally and not perfectly understood." Modern poetry is an expression of the mind in motion, a representation of its dynamic nature, its conflicts, and its persistence in conflict. Ambiguity, obscurity, difficulty, elliptic modes of expression, rejection of the easy and agreeable, are all means of sustaining the dynamism of mental life and of avoiding the over-simplification of depicting it as if it were static. But mental dynamism, again, is a historical phenomenon, as indeed all forms of artistic expression, ambiguous or unambiguous, are essentially historical in character. There is no evidence whatsoever for the assumption that symbols, because of their ambiguity, are the residues of an archaic way of thinking, or that they belong to the common spiritual property of mankind. In postulating a ubiquity of symbolic

105

forms, psychoanalysis restricts its attention to a few primitive examples and neglects the fact that new symbols are incessantly being created, and that even if neurotic symbols can be described—though with some reservation—as stagnant or conservative, artistic symbols are, on the other hand, in a state of constant flux and differentiation. It is, at all events, a fallacy to pretend that because both art and neurosis express themselves in a way that conceals as much as it reveals, the symbols of an artist are of the same kind as those of a neurotic person. The latter are and remain neurotic symptoms, that is to say, rigid formulas with a fixed and strictly defined function in the mental life of the sick person, whereas the symbols used by an artist show an extremely flexible and variable structure.

9. PSYCHOANALYSIS AND ART HISTORY

The psychoanalytic approach to art criticism or the biography of artists needs no vindication, but a question of a somewhat different order remains to be answered: can psychoanalysis be of any use to the history of art? Style is not a psychological conception, nor the development of styles a process that can be explained in psychological terms. The similarity of aims and means in stylistically related works or movements lies beyond the choice of the individual; and although it amounts to no more than a result of particular attempts to solve personal problems, style represents a superpersonal trend to which the single individual has to adjust himself. He is, as agent of a stylistic development, never completely independent or unrestricted, even if he is destined to change the direction of a given artistic tendency. The real meaning of the Romanesque or the Gothic, the Renaissance or the baroque, cannot be realized if we try to understand these trends merely as expressions of psychological attitudes or pretend simply to deduce them from the artistic aims of individual artists. The definition of a style never corresponds with the frame of mind of a particular person, however articulate or creative. If a style were no more than the expression of a personal idiosyncrasy, one could hardly account for the fact that at any given time it dominates the work of so many psychologically different people.

A psychology of style is, nevertheless, conceivable, for, although the direction of stylistic developments is fundamentally a superindividual phenomenon, the strategy by which a style follows its own direction, often without being approved or even realized by its exponents, makes use of individuals as its instruments. A style cannot be conceived or expressed in works of art save through psychological operations. It is more than a formal structure; it has a characterological meaning. Formalism and naturalism, impressionism and expressionism reveal, apart from their historical, technical, or formal implications, different ways of dealing with facts, different attitudes toward the realities of life; they are symptoms of personal predilections or aversions. In the founders of a new stylistic movement, such motivations are often of the greatest consequence, although in the later representatives of the same movements they may lose much of their importance. But however strong or weak the personal motives for the artist's participation in a stylistic movement, however relevant or irrelevant his personal attitude to the stylistic character of his work, every problem presents itself to him in the form of a psychological dilemma, just as every solution seems to him the result of a personal choice. For no rifle goes off without someone pressing the trigger.

Whatever, therefore, the individual artist's eventual attitude proves to be, he has to make up his mind and fight out the antagonism of the given stylistic possibilities for himself. André Gide's dictum, "the struggle between classicism and romanticism takes place within every mind also," applies to any radical change in style. And this struggle is, in every case, a process subject to the laws of psychology. In other words: the superpersonal quality of a style is not produced by a supernatural, transcendental power; the only agent in human affairs is man, the only psychological agency the individual. Yet the individual creates, in following the voice of his own instincts, passions, and interests, certain ideas and values that transcend his capacities and become to some extent his masters. If we translate Hegel's "cunning of reason," that is to say, the device by which superpersonal spiritual values are achieved by means of personal attitudes and abilities, into psychological terms, we are confronted with a mechanism similar to the working of Freud's unconscious. Here, as there, the individual is prompted to think or to act by motives unknown and often inconceivable to himself, is prompted to serve purposes that transcend his consciousness. We must not, of course, overstrain the analogy, but we may hope that the study of the unconscious mind will allow us to deal with performances as Hegel's "cunning of reason" claimed to, but in a scientifically more verifiable way.

Since the beginnings of dialectical thinking in the historical sciences, art critics have distinguished two basic types of artistic approach and have attempted to reduce all formal or stylistic endeavors to these alternatives. The differentiation between classicism and romanticism, idealism and realism, an objective and a subjective approach, belongs to the earliest formulations of the problem. Schiller spoke of a *naïve* and a *sentimental* frame of mind, Nietzsche of an *Apollonian* and a *Dionysian* art, Worringer of *abstraction* and *empathy*. We ourselves are in the habit of speaking of stylization and naturalism, geometrism and expressionism, tectonic and atectonic structures. All these concepts, however, revolve around one and the same antagonism. The same alternatives of surrender or violence to reality, of absorption in or a withdrawal from the world, of its preservation or destruction, always recur in the continuous alternation of naturalistic and formalistic tendencies. The permanent recurrence of this pattern suggests that the alternatives of mental process, discovered by psychoanalysis, may have some bearing on the changes of style. The relationship between formalistic or classicistic and regulating or domineering trends on the one hand, and between naturalistic or imitative and life-preserving or life-enhancing endeavors on the other, is obvious. Naturalism and classicism, or, for that matter, impressionism and abstractionism, are related to one another as libido and aggression, extraversion and introversion, masochism and sadism. In the two continuously alternating forms of stylistic approach, reality is either accepted or rejected, imitated or distorted, experienced as a reassuring or a menacing principle; the ego submits to the world or imposes on it the rules of a higher order, the features of an ideal existence.

The real problem consists, however, in the ways in which one or another of these trends becomes predominant in spite of the psychologically different characters of its representatives. To account for the prevalence of a stylistic tendency throughout the whole of a generation or a historical epoch, one has to assume that certain socio-historical situations favor certain psychological responses or, in other words, that at different times there are different chances that a particular psychological approach to reality will be successful and will win general approval.

Psychoanalysis may be successful in interpreting the work of art as a personal document, or even in explaining an artistic style as the ascendency of a particular psychological disposition over one or two generations, but it has no grasp of the essential formal features of a style; it tries therefore to detect stylistic character from accessories, from unobvious yet revealing details rather than from essentials. Being a kind of psychology of exposure, it follows up clues rather than plain and direct forms of expression and expects the artist to give himself away, more or less as a neurotic patient does, neglecting, however, the fundamental difference, that the meaning of a style is not a puzzle, but a guide. In accord with the spirit of his detective work, Freud was deeply impressed by Morelli's method in art history as an attempt to establish the identity of stylistic trends above all from those features of a work of art which had least to do with the artist's conscious and deliberate ways of expression. That is to say, the fashion in which a painter has drawn an ear or formed a finger, the character of his handwriting, of which he might not even have been aware, was, Morelli claimed, more revealing than the features by which he meant to express himself most clearly. "It seems to me," Freud remarked with obvious satisfaction, "that his method of inquiry is closely related to the technique of psychoanalysis. It, too, is accustomed to divine secret and concealed things from unconsidered or unnoticed details, from the rubbish-heap, as it were, of our observations." [4]

10. DESTRUCTION AND RESTITUTION THROUGH ART

The antagonism of artistic styles received a stricter definition and, to some extent, a deflection from its original meaning from a group of British analysts, who explained the rejection of or the submission to reality in art by destructive or restitutory tendencies. In translating the opposition of formalistic and anti-formalistic stylistic trends into the terms of psychoanalysis, one identifies almost instinctively the naturalistic, formally liberal approach with libidinal urges, and the more rigoristic, classical tendency with aggressive ones. According to the destruction-restitution theory, however, all art, classical as well as anti-classical, is connected in a way with aggressive or sadistic impulses, the only difference being that in the former, harmony and unity are achieved by restoring life and reality, which remain deformed and distorted in the latter. In other words, the advocates of this theory discover vestiges of destruction everywhere in art and pretend to find eventual peace and order only in those forms in which one would recognize mainly the expression of a regulating, domineering, life-restricting tendency.

[4] Freud: "The Moses of Michelangelo," in *Collected Papers*, IV, 271.

Every work of art is more or less a criticism of life, an attempt to deliver it from its shapelessness, to make it more consistent and unequivocal, if not more perfect. Without the feeling that the world is, as Van Gogh said, "a sketch that didn't come off," there would be perhaps no urge to artistic creation at all. But no work of art is entirely negative in its relation to reality. In the artist even the most violent rejection of the world accompanies an obsession with all that is real, living, breathing; and art is in a sense the result of this ambivalent attitude. A work of art is never the expression of a merely contemplative mood; it is always an answer to a challenge. And whether or not one shares the view that all art consists in an aggression against the wholeness of the world and in a subsequent attempt to restore it from its ruins, that our need for beauty springs from the pain caused by our destructive impulses, there can be no doubt that art is, above all, a means to conquer chaos, to prevail over the inconceivable, the unfathomable, the inhuman in the world. If there is a universally valid psychological explanation for the urge to create works of art, it cannot start from anything but this attempt to recover lost or buried provinces of conscious life. And if anything may be considered progress in the course of art, it consists in our advancing farther and farther in the conquest of chaos and rescuing more and more territory from its grip.

Art is a means of taking possession of things by violence as well as out of care or desire for their preservation. The cave paintings of the Old Stone Age are in this respect typical: they depict in order to kill and possess. And in quite a similar way to that of the palaeolithic hunters, children's drawings are, as has been pointed out,[5] a means of magic rather than disinterested representation. To the child, drawing means gaining power over the figures represented, a way of doing good or evil. To have realized that art is, on the one hand, an outlet for aggressive impulses, the expression of a narcissistic hostility to

[5] John Rickman: "On the Nature of Ugliness," *International Journal of Psychoanalysis*, XXI/3 (1940).

the world, an urge to distort and destroy, and on the other a remedy against life's imperfect, fragmentary nature, a protest against its darkness and dullness, its lack of meaning and purpose, is the great merit of the theory which, although overstraining its point, has called attention to the element of destruction in artistic creativity.

With the romantic conception of art as the mother tongue of mankind, one often finds combined another, equally romantic, view that regards art as an expression of sheer love and devotion, and the artist as an unselfish servant of the principle of life and nature, or a magnanimous friend of his fellow-men. Psychoanalysis has denounced both views as mere illusions. As there is nothing naïve and natural about art, so there is nothing harmless or generous about the artist. Art is often no more than a means of revenge or compensation for a wrong suffered by the artist. If there is sympathy or piety in him, it is mainly a result of his anxiety and his sense of guilt for the destruction of a world that he conceives as a kind of mother and invests with mother-images. The identification of the mother with nature is probably as old as mankind, and its explanation is obvious. The expression of a sense of guilt in art, however, is a discovery of psychoanalysis, and the element of a guilt toward the mother in the artist's relationship to nature is a remarkable contribution of the destruction-restitution theory.

John Rickman refers in a very illuminating way to the connection between people's responses to mutilated works of art, such as ancient statues, and their own destructive impulses or anxieties at having caused destruction.[6] The historical point of view is neglected here, however, as in psychoanalytic writings in general, for otherwise the author could hardly have failed to notice that the enjoyment of or the aversion to fragmentary works of art is, above all, a historical phenomenon, varying with cultural background. The delight in ruins, torsos, unfinished sketches, so characteristic of the second half of the eighteenth century and the subsequent period, is a symptom

[6] Ibid., pp. 4–5.

of the romantic mood, which has now taken hold of the Western world. It is only within this frame of mind that the whole psychic mechanism of frustration, retaliation, compensation, a sense of guilt, and anxiety for restitution, as psychoanalysis describes it, becomes operative and creative in art; it is only from that time on that a torso is felt to be more suggestive and expressive than an unmutilated work of art.

It is since romanticism that art has become a quest for a home that the artist believes he possessed in his childhood, and which assumes in his eyes the character of a Paradise lost through his own fault. His sense of guilt, as a conflict between his libidinal and destructive impulses,[7] becomes one of the strongest motive forces behind his work. And art is thenceforth not only an expression of guilt, but also a means of alleviating guilt and anxiety; it assumes the cathartic function of a confession, of utterance as the price of absolution, of naming as a means of magic. The idea that art can relieve anxiety is very old; Aristotle's catharsis is its most familiar formulation. But with romanticism artistic creation becomes an instrument of self-punishment into the bargain. Samuel Palmer reports a conversation between himself and William Blake, who was just working on his Dante illustrations. Blake said to him that he began them with fear and trembling. Palmer answered: "O! I have enough of fear and trembling." "Then," said Blake, "you'll do."[8] Nobody at an earlier time would have felt "fear and trembling" in producing a work of art; it had been, as William Morris said, "a matter of craftsmanship." But Ibsen is even more explicit in this matter than any poet or artist before him:

> *Living means—fighting dark forces,*
> *Spectres in us contained,*
> *Writing means—sitting in judgment*
> *Over one's ego arraigned.*[9]

[7] Freud: *Civilization and Its Discontents* (1930).
[8] A. Gilchrist: *Life of William Blake* (1942), p. 390.
[9] Translation by Helen Burlin.

Since the romantic movement, artistic creation has become a kind of reconstruction, a recovery of what the artist feels he has lost of his spiritual heritage, of what seems to him to be buried under the wreckage of the past. The real significance of the art of Proust, from a historical point of view, consists in the fact that this salvaging of the past forms the very subject of his work, which proves, partly as a result of this fact, an inexhaustible storehouse of material in support of the psychoanalytic conception of art. It is, above all, a classical example of what, in accordance with psychoanalysis, we understand by loss of reality and the way that leads back to it. To Proust, artistic creation means essentially striving to recover lost time, and to redeem that past which reveals reality in a far more faithful and direct way than the present. The artist's striving for the past is, in fact, a striving for the real. The present is always "lost time," a losing of ourselves and those who belong to us; art, on the other hand, is a re-creation, in Proust's sense the only possible re-creation of a disintegrating world around us and within us. One must, indeed, have lost the world in order to possess it, for, as far as the artist is concerned, there is no other but an indirect way to outward reality. Proust's conception of existence is the epitome of an introvert's philosophy. The subject of his novel is the history of a vocation, the artist's vocation, for the discovery of a way to the past and, therewith, to the real meaning of existence is identical with becoming an artist.

Proust reclaimed his dead or lost world from the unconscious by a method similar to that of psychoanalysis: by digging deep into the hard ground of memory. Artistic creation meant to him just as desperate an attempt to elicit an answer from the twilight (*"faire sortir une réponse de la pénombre"*) as the unearthing of the unconscious motives of illness means to the analyst and his patient. And he conceived the repression of essential reality into the unconscious—to anticipate a terminology foreign to him—to be the result of a great fault, a deadly sin, which he called the "cessation of the heart."

Proust made his great discovery, that one's true life and real being have to be recovered from the unconscious, that consciousness reflects this life and this being in a distorted, deceptive, or, as psychoanalysis calls it, "rationalized," form, and that we realize the true motives of our reactions and habits only by mistrusting the evidence of the conscious and rational mind—Proust discovered all this without the aid of Freud's teaching, although by no means without the heritage of romantic thought. But we ourselves could hardly appreciate the whole bearing of his philosophy without our apprenticeship in psychoanalysis, without knowing and viewing in a right perspective the fact that the artist's way to his work leads through a loss of reality, and that his way back to reality is a result of his work. It is therefore more or less immaterial whether the direct statements of psychoanalysis on art are fully acceptable or not; even a completely negative answer to this question could hardly change the fact that our indebtedness to Freud for a better understanding of art, and especially of modern, romantic, and post-romantic, art, is immeasurable.

The whole of Proust's work is an expression of a sense of guilt and of anxiety. He feels guilty because of his mother fixation, his Oedipus complex, his homosexuality, his inability to do regular work (at least as long as his parents are alive), his introversion, his fundamental indifference to the world, his lack of love (knowing that his grief on account of others is not what he calls *"une véritable chagrin"*), his way of destroying his beloved ones, the world around him, his own life and self. His aim and work as an artist are no more than an attempt to get rid of this sense of guilt, to survive spiritually, to prevent a complete disintegration of his moral being. Proust is perfectly aware of these dangers, anguishes, and attempts at self-preservation, but behind the anxieties that he is aware of there is a sense of guilt which he himself can hardly realize. Only in connection with the death of his grandmother and the disappearance of Albertine does he get an inkling of his "professional" indifference to whatever may happen to other people, of his not being really interested in anything but the study of his "heart," the description and exhibition of his own feelings, his frivolous experimentation with the most crucial and dangerous situations in life, his treatment of life as a kind of laboratory or training ground for spiritual acrobatics, in a word, his taking life as the mere raw material of his work. The guilt feeling, however, which he seems to be unable to realize at all, is his artist's bad conscience for leading, after all, an idle existence, for enjoying his work while others toil and drudge, for the privilege of an exterritoriality in the midst of people whose life consists of nothing but responsibilities, for living, in spite of all frustration and misery, a life of pleasure, for being, in a word, an unsocial creature. All this is there, the unrealized as well as the realized anxieties, the unconscious as well as the conscious sense of guilt, and not only in Proust's own life, but even in the novel, which gives away its cautious and self-conscious author without mercy or reserve. And all this makes of one of the most fascinating works ever written a cold, cruel, tortured, and torturing manifestation of the mind. The author could not escape from writing, instead of a surpassing apology for art, an irrefutable indictment of the artist. And he has written, without suspecting it, a brilliant vindication of psychoanalysis. For, although he was an expert and a master of psychology, he could not help being the dupe of his unconscious mind.

IV

The Philosophical Implications

of Art History:

"Art History without Names"

1. *WÖLFFLIN AND HISTORICISM*

IN THE WEST ever since the time of romanticism the idea of remaining anonymous has maintained its attraction. This is a feature of an individualistic age. To the Middle Ages there was nothing particularly desirable about anonymity; one put up with it, but was not eager for it; one wanted to be known—it was a coveted distinction—though one which the clergy on the whole reserved for their fellow clerks, especially where works of art were concerned.[1] Anonymity is a defence mechanism required by the socially rootless individual left to his own devices and wanting to repudiate responsibility for his freedom and for setting his own standards. In a community with deeply rooted cultural traditions and definite conventions, that is, with objective, impersonal standards, it has no place.

In the age of romanticism we find for the first time a self-contradictory, ambivalent attitude toward individuality. In no previous generation was the artist so determined that his productions should be personal, unmistakable, incomparable; but never before did he show so little confidence in himself as an emancipated, self-determining individual. This ambivalent attitude is best illustrated in the historicist philosophy, the doctrine that uncovers and stresses the unique and unrepeatable character of all historical events, but none the less asserts that everything historical is the manifestation of some superhuman

[1] Cf. Arnold Hauser: *The Social History of Art* (1951), pp. 179 ff.

and timeless principle. In this view, the individuals who build this world of time are just the servants of a world-architect who is "cunning" enough so to play upon their impulses and interests as to give them a sense of freedom and creativity, whereas all the time they are only carrying out menial tasks for him.

Historicism is really a counter-revolutionary philosophy that would like to make the licence of the emancipated individual responsible for the consequences of the Revolution without abandoning individualism itself—recognized as the one lasting achievement of the age of enlightenment and Revolution. It adopts the mystifying method of referring every historical event to some superindividual—ideal, divine, or primeval—origin, but combines with this an individualizing treatment that asserts not simply the uniqueness, but also the absolute incomparability of historical structures, and so concludes that every historical achievement, and thus every art-style, must be measured only against its own acknowledged standards.

Philosophy of history during the nineteenth century is confined between the poles of this attitude, which finds its extremest expression in the leading art historians of the turn of the century. With his doctrine of the "artistic intention" (*Kunstwollen*), maintaining the absolute uniqueness and incomparability of artistic achievements, Alois Riegl represents the one pole, whereas Heinrich Wölfflin, with his thesis of an "art history without names" and his depreciation of the artist's individuality as a factor in history, represents the other. As two of the last great exponents of the ideas of the Historical School, they belong together and have much in common in spite of the fundamental contrast between their doctrines.

The proposition that art history should disregard names is based on the assumption that artistic aims and stylistic trends are altogether the product of an epoch. Wölfflin's own formula is that "not everything is possible at all times." [2] By this he means not only that the artist is always implicated in a

[2] Heinrich Wölfflin: *Klassische Kunst* (1904), 3rd ed., p. 249. *Kunstgeschichtliche Grundbegriffe* (1929) 7th ed., p. ix.

certain historical situation, but additionally that he cannot ever transgress the given limitations of his epoch. The artist, we are told, has available certain "optical" possibilities, which are a kind of vocabulary and grammar of artistic communication, and to which he is essentially restricted.[3] He can enrich and revitalize this language of art-forms, but he can never evade or overleap the actual state of the problems with which he is faced. According to Wölfflin, "visual forms" and schemes of representation have a history of their own and maintain their supremacy over any individual or national tastes that the artist may have. He holds it a serious error to suppose that subjective attitudes and aims are constantly changing, the artist's means of expression being, as it were, a store of tools which is at all times complete and available to be drawn on at will.[4] On the contrary, nature is seen through spectacles whose tint and sharpness of focus is continually altering and giving different, more or less true views of things. Everyone comes to reality with a certain optical set, with his seeing organized in a particular way; and so the history of art is not a history of man's imitation of nature, but rather a history of artistic optics, *i.e.*, of the physiological and psychological conditions of any given approach to nature.[5] In this sense we must understand his assertion that one always sees in terms of "given colors and harmonies," and that the evolution of coloring is not the result of "more intensive observation of nature."[6] In other words, art does not depend on a will to express something or on the content of what is expressed; the available means of expression are decisive for the form that the work of art takes.

Thus this "art history without names" makes the basic theoretical assumption that the history of "seeing" develops according to an inner logic, according to immanent laws of its own, independently of external influences, which latter are taken

---

[3] *Kunstgeschichtliche Grundbegriffe,* p. 12.
[4] Ibid., pp. 13–14.
[5] Ibid., p. 249.
[6] Wölfflin: *Gedanken zur Kunstgeschichte* (1947), 4th ed., p. 10.

to include not merely the social environment, but also the individual psychic constitution of the artist. This type of immanent causation is basic to Wölfflin's anonymous art history; it is just this which enables him to transform the history of the artists' personal aims and motives into a history of impersonal forms and problems and to give a historical account of these which is strictly logical and unbroken. Wölfflin was not desirous, however, of representing the history of art as a mechanical process, and asserted, perhaps not quite consistently with his principles, that "art can always achieve what it wants," and that people only neglect what does not interest them or fails to please them.[7] In this he largely agrees with Riegl, as also in rejecting as a cause of historical development the aim to achieve a more and more accurate reproduction of nature. For Wölfflin, however, increasing demand for imitative skill is replaced as the primary motive force by an equally rigid principle, that of decorative form.[8]

What Wölfflin wants is to find a formula of development, and so he emphasizes that "even supposing one always sees things in the way one wants to see them, this does not exclude the possibility that there is some law governing the changes in the mode of seeing."[9] In fact, the real aim and purpose of his "anonymous art history" is to free the history of art from all appearance of the accidental and the arbitrary, and to display it as a manifestation of rigorous laws and inner necessity.[1] These features are to be seen above all in the supposedly irreversible sequence of the styles: in a "logic" that requires a plastic-linear style to be followed by a painterly, a tectonic style by an atectonic. According to this logic, the development of art moves ceaselessly between certain contrasts, follows the waxing and waning of certain antithetic "basic concepts"— Wölfflin's name for his categories of "seeing." His formula reflects in essentials the self-movement of some higher super-

[8] Ibid., pp. 17–18.
[9] Ibid., p. 19.
[1] Cf. Wölfflin: *Renaissance und Barock* (1907), 2nd ed., p. 52.

individual principle, such as we find in Hegel's philosophy of history. The schematic sequence of styles repeats itself of necessity, and its periodic recurrence is a consequence of the inherent causation and the inner logic of the evolution. Wölfflin's well-known view of the parallelism by which "baroque styles" follow upon "classical styles" in a regular wave-like rhythm is the most striking instance of this theory.

According to Wölfflin, the visual arts of a given epoch manifest the same stylistic character in all their forms; architecture, sculpture, and painting have the same "optical denominator" and are conditioned by the same "optical schema." [2] This uniformity is simply one example of the inner necessity with which the logic of development imposes itself on the artists. But the common style manifested in optical forms is without any influence upon the non-visual arts. Were artistic activity directed toward expression and dominated by the will to express, then—Wölfflin argues—all the arts and art-forms of an epoch would manifest the same style; but that is obviously not the case. The fact that similar stylistic characteristics in the different arts are not necessarily contemporary is one more proof, according to him, that the evolution of styles is not conditioned by external circumstances, but governed by an immanent system of laws which is different for the different arts.

But Wölfflin does not succeed in showing that the evolution of art really is completely free from the pressure of "external circumstances." For if periodicity is to be our supreme principle in the history of art, we must suppose that the course of development, each time it has run through the allegedly normal "progressive phase" from the severe to the free style, or from the simple to the complex, takes a "jump backwards" to the start, *i.e.*, begins again in a "rigoristic," "archaic," or "classical" mode. But such reversals cannot be explained by reference to immanent laws of complication or differentiation. Wölfflin here feels himself obliged to concede a more important

[2] *Kunstgeschichtliche Grundbegriffe,* pp. 13–14.

role to environmental conditions, which have nothing directly to do with art, than he does when dealing with the rectilinear and seemingly automatic progress of styles. None the less, his theory remains rooted in a mechanistic conception of history, in essentials derived from Comte's *histoire sans noms;* [3] even in the case of the abrupt break in style, he does not allow the individual any real freedom. His ideal of rigorous scientific method, aiming to establish universal laws, really requires a "history of art without artists," just as the scientific and political ideals of the nineteenth-century historians and philosophers demanded that general history should be without heroes or revolutionaries—without, as they put it, "psychologically incalculable" or "politically irresponsible" persons. In this taste for anonymity the positivist and socialist historians are in complete agreement with the historians of an idealistic and conservative outlook, except that the former pursue the phantom of a collective soul whereas the latter develop such fictions as "consciousness in general" (*Bewusstsein überhaupt*), the abstract "categorical imperative" and the "universal ideal of beauty"—the characteristic ideology of an élite. The impersonal subject of Wölfflin's "art history without names" is in a way just an appendage of this abstract and fictitious consciousness.

Under the pressure of the numerous and, in some cases, severe criticisms to which his doctrine was subjected in the various quarters, Wölfflin attempted to revise his conception of "art history without names." He loosened the rigid limits he had set to the powers of the creative individual and admitted that factors of content might have a rather more important influence upon the origination of a style. But the idea of the evolution of art as an autonomous and immanently determined process remained the basis of his whole theory and the unquestioned assumption of his method. While allowing that a form can only be the form of a certain content, he stuck to the principle that "any given content can only be realized within

[3] Auguste Comte: *Cours de philosophie positive,* Leçon LII, éd. Littré (1877), V, 14.

the medium of a certain formal conception (*Formvorstellung*)," that the sensory apparatus, not the object sensed is the primary factor.[4] Wölfflin concludes with the assurance that his theory "does not impair the value of the individual."[5] But he leaves us in no doubt that his main interest and his ultimate preference is for those objective impersonal necessities which the history of art revealed to him. To the end, he found satisfaction in the reflection that the artist moves within a field of possibilities that are—fortunately for him—restricted, and in the thought that there is a spiritual creative principle that leads and guides the artist, who is never able to break it or distort it. The idea of an autonomous evolution of forms, through which the artist's modes of expression are enriched and diversified, of art as evidently obeying an inviolable inner law, retained its fascination for him. In spite of all the doubts that he encountered and felt, his final judgment was that "there is only a loose link between art and culture in general" and that, after all is said, "art has its own life and its own history."[6]

Wölfflin's philosophy of art history contains much that is not only absolutely convincing, but also forms part of the implicit assumptions of every serious history of art. No one would really maintain against Wölfflin that the various phases of artistic development succeed one another without rhyme or reason. Obviously every artist takes up the threads, in the form of a predominant tradition, a certain level of technique, and a certain set of problems and subjects which are to the fore at the time. No doubt, we know well enough that impersonal trends are not to be taken as something superhuman and valid in themselves, but are simply to be explained by reference to the social conditions of artistic endeavor, to the expressive and communicative function of the work of art, to the master-pupil relationship of artists, and to the mutual influence of the various rival schools. None the less, they act as an objective factor,

[4] Wölfflin: *Gedanken zur Kunstgeschichte,* pp. 10–11.
[5] Ibid., p. 13.
[6] Ibid., p. 24.

conditioning the artists' work in a way well expressed by the phrase that "not everything is possible at all times."

To form a proper estimate of Wölfflin's theory, we should consider that in art, besides the factors rooted in social reality or determined by the desire for self-expression, there is the whole apparatus of the craft, of instruments that are gradually and progressively perfected, as in any other technique. This apparatus has its own history, which *is* on the whole one of continuous progress attributable to immanent causation. Though the production of these instruments is not altogether independent of the general conditions of life, and is subject to interruptions and regressions, it is still quite reasonable to speak of an autonomous development here. Were the history of art nothing more or less than the history of a craft, one could more readily dispense with the naming of names and with the discrimination between different personalities. But even the formal and representational elements in art manifest certain intrinsic developmental trends independent of the circumstances and aims of the particular artist; such trends, however, are dominant only for a period and may at any time be reversed. For example, we find a continual endeavor to intensify the effects that the available means of expression allow, and again a general tendency to introduce some break or change of style by way of a violent reaction—though the new style may have been in preparation and latent in old forms for a long while before it suddenly comes to light.

If, as is so often the case, one finds the many variously tempered and variously gifted artists of an age all engaged in mastering the same problems, one easily gets the impression that art-forms and art-styles in the course of time detach themselves from their origin and proceed to work out their own inherent potentialities. The individual artists seem to be merely executing some superindividual commission, merely destined to do what they have to do. But the supposition that what they are doing is bound to be done, inevitably, if not by Peter then by Paul, cannot be sustained, and is in fact one of the

myths of romantic history-writing; it is far more likely that
Paul couldn't do anything in just the way Peter does it. Now,
however great the part played by individual talent and the
personal aims of the artist in the origination of a work of art
or a style, it is clear enough that every work is rooted in the
general trend of development and the way prepared for it by
previous works. The turn toward modern naturalism taken by
the brothers Van Eyck was not a purely individual move, any
more than Leonardo's turn toward classicism; Michelangelo's
growing distaste for the ideals of the High Renaissance was
"in the air," as was Caravaggio's rejection of the refinements of
mannerism. If artists really produced their works in absolute
freedom, without any presuppositions, if they did not, on the
contrary, always find at hand definite standards of truth and
good taste, a whole set of formal tasks and subjects, a minimum
obligatory level of technical skill, and a certain prevailing
measure of sensitivity, then there could be no talk about artistic
development or about styles of art at all. The very concept of
"style" as a sort of adjustment of personal talents to generally
valid aims, the very fact that individual inclinations and aims
are canalized as if into a single stream—this in itself leads one
to think of something like an "art history without names."
When Wölfflin declares that if we go into any of the larger
historically arranged galleries, we can convince ourselves how
well "the great masters fit into the general trend of development," [7] he is calling our attention to the point of view from
which the concepts of "style" and of "anonymous art history"
overlap, and from which it may seem as if *any* history of styles
aimed to be "anonymous art history."

The trends the artist finds at hand are certainly exposed to
continuous external influences; in fact, they are always unstable, likely to be upset in one direction or another. However,
because solutions once discovered have a certain inertia, they
to some extent resist external influences and set certain limits,
albeit flexible ones, to what can be accomplished at a given

[7] Ibid., p. 14.

127

moment. This gives rise to a tension between two sets of causal factors, one more variable than the other, the one inherent in the art-forms, the other coming from external circumstances. This tension cannot be completely abolished on the lines of either an idealist or a materialist philosophy, by way either of a history of ideas or of an economic and social history. "One only sees what one is looking for, but one looks only for what one can see," [8] says Wölfflin, pointing to the circular causation that characterizes every advanced phase of history. What has already been achieved is constitutive of, inevitably moulds, what is to be achieved. And whereas the inner logic of development cannot of itself bring forth any new forms, every novelty requiring some stimulus from without, yet this logic can at certain times definitely exclude the possibility of certain products. And so one may speak of the evolution of art being negatively, but not positively, conditioned by the inner nature of the available forms.

We may go farther and admit that even Wölfflin's restriction of the role played by the factor of expression is in great measure understandable and justified. In medieval, in fact in all pre-romantic, music, we can as a rule hardly discover whether it expresses religious or worldly emotions; and in painting, Christian motives and ideas are expressed in ancient pagan forms hundreds of years after the birth of Christ. For example, around A.D. 800 the *Libri Carolini* complain that representations of the Mother of God can with difficulty be distinguished from pictures of Venus. Still, the assertion that the role of expression in art is necessarily a secondary one is as little justified as the assertion that current trends manifest only an impersonal necessity by which the individual artist is carried along as by some independent and uncontrollable stream. In these cases, all we have is a consciously or unconsciously accepted convention, an explicit or implicit consensus, not any "higher" ideal principle—whether in the Platonic or the Hege-

[8] *Kunstgeschichtliche Grundbegriffe*, p. 248.

lian sense—which, so to say, realizes itself over the heads of the individuals.

Equally untenable is the view that the sequence of styles, whose mutual relation can often be described as one of question and answer, thesis and antithesis, crest and trough of a wave, discloses an inevitable and unalterable rhythm because of the essential structure of art, or of the human psyche, still less tenable that it realizes and expresses a teleology of history. The view that there is any uniform, periodic sequence of typical styles is itself a pure fiction. Not only are the wavelengths of the periodic movement always changing, but also the intermediate links between each rise and fall, thesis and antithesis, problem and solution, or whatever one likes to call it, vary so much in respect of number, influence, and effectiveness that the attempt to find a general formula of the periodicity can lead only to a forced over-simplification of the facts. Greek classical and Hellenistic, Romanesque and Gothic, Renaissance and baroque styles can be said to follow one another in roughly the same sort of pattern, but the interval between opposite poles is in one case a matter of centuries, in another of decades or even of years. Again, in one case the antithesis is reached only by means of series of transitional styles whereas in another it is seen to be latent in the thesis itself. Often the new style is just a further development and logical consequence of the old, but equally often it represents the utter rejection of all previous standards and values. Supposing, then, that we could detect a pattern of antithesis in stylistic change, we should still be far from any universal formula for changes of style, for the varying duration of the phases would still remain incalculable. Merely to assert that on the expiration of one stylistic period a contrasting period begins tells us nothing; for one style is not taken to have expired until the contrasting style is already in the ascendant. The ever-different variations in the process of intensification, decadence, and change which we observe between the con-

129

trasting poles simply do not fit into any formula. Were the change of style "logically" conditioned, we should find the maturity of one style going hand in hand with the infancy of the next. This is by no means always the case. There are numerous examples of a style outliving its proper span, lingering on unfruitfully, becoming ossified and academic, producing nothing but sequels, in a word, refusing to yield to the alleged law of antithetic development.

The doctrine of the irreversibility of the distinct phases in the development of art is perhaps the most impressive, but not the most convincing, part of Wölfflin's conception of an "art history without names." The idea is untenable, because the trend that one observes depends upon the point at which one begins to observe. If, for example, one starts with Giotto, the course of events shows a tendency to complication and can be described as a turn from the tectonic to the atectonic, the terms in which Wölfflin describes the change from the Renaissance to the baroque. If, however, in the attempt to discover periods one starts with fifteenth-century naturalism, as is equally appropriate to the matter in hand, the tendency is evidently towards simplification, clarification, and serenity. Again, when one considers that the oldest known works of art, the palaeolithic paintings, are naturalistic, unconventional, and highly dynamic, yet are followed by the stiff, severe, and static geometric style of the neolithic age, there seems to be hardly any justification for Wölfflin's alleged irreversibility of phases always going from formalism toward dissolution of forms. We know that even within the same stylistic period, e.g., the Carolingian, a more complicated, more painterly, more "baroque" trend preceded a more severe, more classical, more archaic one.[9]

No doubt, there is a close connection between different stages of development, and any one is largely conditioned by the previous one; but the artist—and this is the essential point

[9] Cf. Meyer Schapiro: "Style," in *Anthropology Today*, ed. A. L. Kroeber (1953), p. 297.

for our present purpose—always has more than one possibility open to him. His selection of one particular problem out of several acute at the time, one solution out of several, one trend of taste—and there are always two or three such trends at any one time, as there are always several educational strata —can hardly be explained by any inner logic, but becomes intelligible only in the light of circumstances beyond the field of art.

Wölfflin's later qualification of his original assertion of immanence, his distinction between progressive movements and "rebounds" that break and reverse the continuity, is far from being adequate as an account of the place of art in life. He maintains that when there is a reversal of trend, "this is more obviously due to external circumstance" than in the "normal" case of continuous development—in other words, that in principle a distinction can be made between some artistic developments that are immanent and self-explanatory and others that are susceptible to external influences. But this thesis rests on a wholly uncritical conception of the relationship between cultural patterns and actual living conditions. Because of the intimate contact and mutual dependence of the two, we cannot suppose that conditions of life influence art only at a few points and in certain special situations. If the artist really is a psychic and social being, then he is such at all times and in all circumstances. And if so, for any step he takes, any decision he makes, any form he selects, both inner and outer conditions can be found, unless he sets himself in conscious opposition to them. At all times and in all respects, life faces the individual with novel problems, with open questions that have to be answered in terms of the given situation and the available means. Whatever one does, whether one takes up an active or passive attitude, whether one carries on a well-established line or chooses a new line, whether one upholds the taste of the previous generation or seeks to discover new values, one accepts a possibility and rejects other possibilities, one takes one's stand. To maintain a given course is just as much a vital

131

decision, rooted in life as a whole, as to alter course. You can swim with the stream or against it; if you let yourself go with the stream, this means that you have implicitly opted for passivity and conformity. It is thus quite false to suppose, for example, that toward the end of the eighteenth century rococo art began to yield to external influences, suddenly ceased to be motivated by inward, purely formal considerations. If an artist remained true to the ideals of rococo rather than make an abrupt break with the aesthetic standards of the *ancien régime* and turn to the revolutionary classicism, we need not refer to a different psychological mechanism to explain this, but merely to different standards or aims. Every step in the evolution of art requires an alogical decision, unaccountable in terms of any self-contained system and going beyond the aesthetic sphere— an act of will which chooses among the available possibilities. Art is form and expression conditioned in part internally, in part externally, at no time simply going its own way, at no time quite at the mercy of external circumstances.

Wölfflin's view that in the history of art increased external pressure always induces a retrograde movement shows that for him any influence of a non-formal character signifies an interruption and a disturbance of the normal course of evolution. This view evidently derives from the conceptions of the romantic philosophy of organism, and points to one of the most important, though not necessarily direct or fully realized, sources of his idea of anonymous art history. Organic development, as Wölfflin conceives artistic development to be, is an immanent process, essentially insusceptible to influences and interruptions from without. For the concept of organism, as for Wölfflin's concept of art, the decisive mark is the appearance of gradual growth, of spontaneous, plantlike, self-induced development. In both cases the thought is of an original, prevailing urge more powerful than foreign influences or individual caprices, which might impair the essential structure of growth were it not that nature is wiser than mere understanding can conceive and is able to triumph over the inordinate desires of the individual and the vagaries of chance.

The employment of the concept of organism to describe historical structures is one of the spiritual weapons of that philosophy of history by means of which the age of Restoration and romanticism, starting with Burke, endeavored to discredit reformist aims and the conquests of the Revolution and to reinstate tradition in conformity with the aims and interests of the "historic classes." The kernel of the organismic doctrine is the thesis that if an evolution is to bring forth valuable and vital forms, it must always remain in contact with the past, must seek to unfold the new from the old, and to "surpass" (*aufheben*) the old, in Hegel's sense of the word, going beyond it and yet preserving it. From this postulate derives the conservative concept of nation and national culture as a spiritual community of successive generations. Here everything revolves around the idea of conservation through change. Nothing betrays the conservative and sophistical character of the doctrine so evidently as the proposition, first hinted at by Burke and later explicitly formulated by August Wilhelm Rehberg (1757–1836), that any change in the existing form of government which might result from a plebiscite would be necessarily unlawful because in relation to the numbers of past and future generations the living can never be anything but a minority.[1] According to this philosophy, what in politics was stigmatized as arbitrariness or caprice, in the other spheres of culture was called betrayal of the national genius that had brought forth the great historic achievements of the nation.

Just as on these assumptions the customs, laws, myths, and sagas of a nation are not simply invented or mechanically "produced," but germinate and "grow" in accord with the inner constitution and instincts of the people, so also on the assumptions of "anonymous art history" styles of art are not thought

[1] Gunnar Rexius: *"Studien zur Staatslehre der historischen Schule,"* *Historische Zeitschrift*, CVII, 513.

out and intentionally brought to light by individual artists, but are imposed by an "organic" principle spanning the lives of many individuals and generations. Wölfflin comes gradually to elucidate the nature of this principle, and finally defines it as the principle of artistic "seeing," by which he then proceeds to account for the whole history of art. In his early essay on the *Psychology of Architecture,* the connection of his idea of an endogenous and anonymous history of art with the organismic philosophy is more directly and more openly expressed than in his later works. "That stylistic forms cannot be introduced by individuals at pleasure," we find stated there, "that on the contrary, they arise out of the national feeling—a current equivalent for *Volksgeist*—is now so universally recognized as to need no further discussion." [2] Wölfflin's conception of historical development has a number of features in common with the concept of organic growth. Thus his style-forms are not thought of as mere aggregates, but are pre-eminently structural unities. Homogeneity, not heterogeneity, of their components and interdependence rather than independence of functions are striking characteristics of these structures. With them, as in the organism, the whole is in the Aristotelian sense "prior" to the parts, or, in other words, the universal prior to the singular, the typical style prior to the particular works and to the aims of the individual artists. Thus, the style is no more a mere sum of its constituents than the plant a sum of its parts or the life of an organism a composite of its functions.

The basic insight from which organismic doctrines in historical and social philosophy derive is presumably the recognition that a social group does not consist simply of a collection of individuals, that the individual's behavior is different in a group from what it is when he feels himself isolated, and that the members of a group develop common characteristics and consequently react similarly to particular stimuli. These are facts that nobody doubts, and they belong to that part of the

[2] Wölfflin: *Prolegomena zu einer Psychologie der Architektur* (1886), p. 49.

organismic doctrine which is scientifically well founded. What is illegitimate is only the hypostasizing of the uniform attitudes of a group into an autonomous psychic force or a psychological subject supposed to have a capacity for thought and action more or less independently of the members of the group, in the way in which the Historical School conceives the *Volksgeist* or the social-psychologists (*Völkerpsychologen*) conceive the "group mind." The concept of the group mind as a unitary and independent psychic entity is to some extent a consequence of the application of the concept of organism to social bodies. The collective behavior of the group is then seen, not for what it really is, namely, the manifestation of the mutual adaptation of various temperaments, specific aims, and particular interests, but as the real carrier of the distinctive marks of the group, and it is then judged according to the psychological principles that are applied to the individual. [3] But the group mind, if this concept is to have any satisfactory scientific meaning, cannot designate an originating cause, but only a resultant, not a unitary and original agent, but merely the effect produced by a set of completed actions that on account of their mutual adaptation easily lead us to personify it. It is just a collective concept, which as such must never be supposed to be "prior," but only "posterior" to the components that it unites. The group mind consists exclusively of traits that the individual members display in the course of their co-operative and co-ordinated action; the alleged subject manifesting this mutual adaptation is no more a psychological than it is a biological reality. There are then collective attitudes, mutually adapted actions and reactions, but there is no real substratum other than the individuals to which these phenomena might be ascribed. If there is such a thing as collective spiritual wealth, there is certainly no superindividual unitary subject responsible for its creation.

[3] Cf. Max Weber: *"Roscher und Knies und die logischen Probleme der historischen Nationalökonomie," Gesammelte Aufsätze zur Wissenschaftslehre* (1922), pp. 9–10.

But the extension of the concept of organism to social groups is illegitimate, if only for the reason that within an organism there can be no oppositions or conflicts except in a metaphorical sense of the word, whereas a social group by its very nature is always involved in conflicts of interest and competitive struggles. However complicated the vital processes of a natural organism may be, however intricate the mutual conditioning of its various functions, an organism "some of whose parts would like to change places with other parts" is, as it has been well said, unthinkable. [4] The organismic doctrine, with its emphasis on inner equilibrium and the co-operation of all parts of the whole, is a quietistic philosophy, an ideology of appeasement, which will not recognize social conflicts, class-war, and revolution, and so portrays them as unnatural and unhealthy excrescences. The poetical, moralizing language in which the organismic doctrine was cloaked, its rhetorical insistence on bowing to historic reality and accepting the legacy of history, fascinated the romantic temper of the nineteenth century. People yielded themselves up eagerly to the claims of the past so as not to have to take notice of the present, with its unromantic problems and troubles. Their prejudice in favor of anything that seemed "organic" meant a sympathy for dark, unconscious instincts and blind indiscriminate submission to traditions, conventions, and institutions; it was their inclination to passivity, conformity, and fatalism, expressed in these ways, which accounts for the great influence of the organismic doctrine. The concept of "anonymous art history," and indeed the thesis of the autonomy of the spiritual, developed this tendency toward conformity and fatalism into a thoroughgoing, because completely unconscious, ideology.

Organismic ideas permeated the work of Wölfflin and Riegl through the medium of historicist philosophy. Historicism, in abandoning the rationalism of the enlightenment, also abandoned its optimism, that is to say, its faith in the moral

[4] Josef Popper-Lynkeus: *Die allgemeine Nährpflicht als Lösung der sozialen Frage* (1923), 2nd ed., p. 72.

136

and intellectual perfection that would result from the reign of reason. The naïveté of that expectation was evident; the path of history certainly does not lead upwards in all respects. But in no sphere of culture is there less justification for talk of steady progress and ever greater achievement than in art, so that Riegl and Wölfflin, in attacking aesthetic absolutism, might seem to have been battering at an open door. However, for men to grasp this aspect of art, which had been so completely concealed by eighteenth-century optimism about the future, the historicists' work in devaluing the idea of progress was needed. Even when dealing with abstract aesthetic values, Wölfflin and Riegl make no use of the idea of progress as a heuristic principle, but seek to substitute for it other more concrete concepts. They employ all the time purely historical concepts and avoid basing their theories upon any philosophy of art. They pay strict attention to the sense of Ranke's saying: "Imagine aristocracy in all its aspects, you will never be able to imagine Sparta." [5]

Again, the inner contradictions characteristic of historicism are also to be found in the theories of Riegl and Wölfflin— above all its ambivalent attitude to the problem of the individual. The replacement of generalization by an individualizing method has often been taken to be the essence of historicism.[6] But the theories of the Historical School, while stressing the singularity of all historical events and the role of the individual in creating cultural values, none the less depreciate the individual in favor of a superindividual creative principle, which, according to the doctrine of *Volksgeist* and the Hegelian philosophy, rules the whole realm of the spirit. The particular is explained as a mere effulgence of a higher power, of a stronger, purer light. Wölfflin's "anonymous art history" is in a way just a variant of this emanatistic doctrine, which makes concrete history a reflection or a realization or an articulation of a universal metaphysical principle, of an other-worldly idea, or

[5] Ranke: *Das politische Gespräch.*
[6] Friedrich Meinecke: *Die Entstehung des Historismus* (1936).

137

of a superhuman power.[7] The essence of any emanatistic theory of history lies in the principle that a "world-spirit" is inherent in historical events, which in this way are pre-established and pre-formed. The process of history is thus represented as a process from potentiality to actuality. The immanent character of the evolution of art, the recurrence of the same stylistic types, the inner logic of "visual forms," the notion of species and branches of art, each furnished from the start with fixed standards and clear and final solutions—all these concepts are the result of emanatistic thought in the history of art. In fact, it is Hegel's idea of the "cunning of reason" which is applied here, usually in a somewhat veiled and derivative form. The doctrine of *Volksgeist* started from the reflection that in a cultural community, arrangements come into being which were never willed or foreseen by the individual members of the group concerned; this idea was taken up and further developed into Hegel's "cunning of reason." However, the representatives of the *Volksgeist* theory in the end assert no more than that structures such as the Greek epic, Roman law, Catholic dogma, and the English constitution are the work of centuries and of many generations, that no one can come forward as their author and claim any special property rights in them. But Hegel goes farther and maintains that cultural structures have a much deeper source, that their immediate authors, *i.e.*, the *Volksgeister* ("national geniuses"), as well as the individuals, are merely mouthpieces of the world-spirit, which employs them and all other particular forces that emerge in the course of history as means for its own higher ends. The problem that the "cunning of reason" concept claims to solve is the remarkable phenomenon that the private motives and subjective choices of individuals create something that transcends the individuals and attains a measure of objective validity. In art history, this phenomenon takes the form of the artist, with his individual

[7] Cf. Emil Lask: *Fichtes Idealismus und die Geschichte* (1902), pp. 56 ff.; M. Weber: *Gesammelte Aufsätze zur Wissenschaftslehre*, pp. 9–10; Hauser: *Social History of Art*, II, 659 ff.

gifts and his personal aims, submitting to the general canons of a style valid for a whole epoch or for a whole educational stratum. For the origination of a style, though not contrary to the aims of the individual artist, is not explicitly willed, is *incidental* to his aims and purposes; it is a "collective form" by no means included in his conscious intentions. If Hegel's "cunning of reason" is a wholly unsatisfactory answer to the question before us, at least it formulates the problem sharply, makes us intensely aware of the paradox of such a phenomenon as that of a style. This powerful effect of Hegel's thought is still present in Wölfflin's "anonymous art history"; and though his conception is not entirely acceptable, it has proved fruitful by focusing our attention with the utmost intensity upon the difficulties implicit in the concept of a style.

2. THE "BASIC CONCEPTS OF ART HISTORY" AND THE CATEGORIES OF HISTORICAL THINKING

Wölfflin describes the transition from the Renaissance to the baroque by means of five pairs of concepts. Each pair may be said, on the whole, to disclose different aspects of the same development from the severe and simple to the freer and more complex. He calls them "basic concepts" because he maintains that they are not just applicable to the particular period, the analysis of which suggested them, but prove their value again and again in interpreting the course of the history of art. The discovery of these basic concepts proves to Wölfflin that his idea of an "art history without names" is justified, for the finding of such general principles of development confirms his belief that some superindividual forms underlie the artistic endeavors of the different stylistic periods.

Wölfflin's aim is to describe certain historical examples of change of style by means of formulas that shall be as simple and comprehensive as possible. He certainly thinks that such formulas are illustrated time and again in the course of history, but he does not suppose that these historical similarities have any common *a priori* origin, whether in some immutable constitution of the human spirit or in some necessary and inescapable presuppositions of artistic perception. Critics who complain that Wölfflin has not produced any *"a priori* categories" fail to understand both what he was about and the real meaning of such concepts as these. In Kant's critical philosophy, the apriority of space, time, or causality means that, for us, all phenomena must manifest the forms of co-existence, succession, causation, and certain other similar relations; objects of experience are unthinkable except in terms of these categories, which set both the presuppositions and the limits of all knowledge. But Wölfflin's "basic concepts" make none of these claims. However often we may actually find cases illustrating them, there is nothing universal about them; they derive from particular experiences, particular works of art, or particular styles, and hold only for certain restricted periods. Though Wölfflin speaks of the various forms of "seeing," he is not thinking of any timeless and universal faculty of man as such, nor yet of some essential form of the aesthetic attitude which would determine all artistic creation. He is not interested in finding a framework into which the historical events can be fitted; he is not seeking universal aesthetic principles, but "laws" of periodicity in history.

It may be granted that the mere fact of these "basic concepts" having been inductively derived from certain particular historical phenomena is not a coercive argument against their having timeless validity or some *a priori* origin in the nature of artistic perception as such. Even the Kantian transcendental forms of knowledge become manifest to us only in particular experiences; but in their case, experience leads us to recognize principles or categories that characterize experience without being derived from it or being specific to any particular experiences. But Wölfflin's "basic concepts," like all aesthetic categories, are not merely suggested to us by our experience of individual historical events, but are logically delimited by these events. It is true that with his eagerness for anonymity and periodicity, Wölfflin gets perilously near to implying the "consciousness in general" of science; but he never really forgets that the individuality of forms of art is of their very essence—in this respect they are quite unlike the categories of knowledge, which manifest their real meaning only in so far as one disregards individual differences of experience. The concept of time or of causation in the natural sciences does not presuppose the occurrence of any particular phenomenon; rather the fact that one *can* experience the phenomenon results from one's presumption of these concepts. The case is quite otherwise with the basic concepts of art history: linear or painterly representation, plane or recession, closed or open form, clearness or unclearness of arrangement, additive or integrative organization of motifs—all these concepts are meaningless unless one refers to concrete occurrences, to particular experiences of one's own, or to the actual intentions of artists. Take away the individual features of a work of art and nothing remains that one could call artistic.

Those critics of Wölfflin who want to base art history upon a system of *a priori* categories, maintain—naturally enough from their point of view, though without adequate reason—that Wölfflin's categories are not really "basic." [8] Nor are they in that sense; but they are not intended to be. Wölfflin never expected the whole wealth of artistic styles to be deductible from a few supreme formal principles; he was always aware that the historical variations of artistic endeavor are inexhaustible and not to be established by way of a logical system. Just as for the Historical School, positive law never can be deduced from natural law, so for Wölfflin his "basic con-

---

[8] Erwin Panofsky: *"Der Begriff des Kunstwollens," Zeitschrift für Aesthetik*, XIV (1920), 330–1; *"Ueber das Verhältnis der Kunstgeschichte zur Kunsttheorie,"* ibid., XVIII (1924–5), 130–1. Edgar Wind: *"Zur Systematik der künstlerischen Probleme,"* ibid., p. 481.

cepts" can never be fitted into a system of aesthetics. Adapting Ranke, he might have said: "Imagine the visual arts in all their aspects, you will never be able to imagine the baroque"; or, "Imagine the baroque with all its possibilities, you will never be able to guess Caravaggio, Rubens, or Rembrandt." The fact is that the aspects and possibilities of the baroque style just *are* Caravaggio, Rubens, and Rembrandt. Whence could one derive these "possibilities" unless from the vocabulary of the masters themselves? In the aesthetic experience we do not—if we are to speak in terms of the Kantian philosophy—become aware of any concepts except as they arise from the works themselves. General stylistic tendencies of the epoch may overlay the conscious aims of a particular artist, but they are in no wise principles which could be called *a priori*, inevitable, or superhistorical. The only universal assertions that can be made about art are that it is "art" or that it is "beautiful" or that one cannot *know* what it is. With any attempt at a more definite explanation one leaves the sphere of the unconditional and timeless for the realm of the relative and the historical.

If, however, it is suggested that we are to understand by the *a priori* nature of art not some transcendental ground, but rather some ideal "meaning" that a work of art may be said to express independently of its actual embodiment and the contingent circumstances of its origin—then let this pretentious assumption not blind us to the fact that "the meaning that the work has from all eternity and to all eternity" is just a tautology, and that what we are really talking about is a certain aspect or a certain selection of concrete and ephemeral features.

Even such a merely formal, that is, logically consistent system of the "basic artistic concepts" as Wölfflin's neo-Kantian critics advocate, a coherent and comprehensive account of the highest formal principles of art, is an impossibility. Not only is prediction of the artistic future impossible, but to give a complete and exhaustive description of what has already been accomplished is also impossible. From no point of view do the creations of art manifest a single common root or make a

142

logical series or a logical whole; there is no necessity about
their occurrence, whether we look for it in their historical
succession or in a sociological cross-section of history. For example, from the concept of the "painterly" we cannot derive
the variants of this particular mode of seeing and representing
—neither those contemporary within a certain style nor those
which occur successively in different periods. Still less can
there be "one single grand original problem" within which, as
it has been maintained, all legitimate artistic categories are
comprehended.[9]

As regards the past, an exhaustive exposition of the problems of art would depend on whether in defining the supposed
"original problem" of art one could really get at the earliest
form in which the supposed task presented itself—for it is
questionable whether the earlier forms can always be reconstructed from the later forms, even if these later forms in-
corporate the earlier ones, and that is also a problem. And as
regards the present, a systematic exposition of basic concepts
would imply that there is a certain homogeneity of aim in the
art of any particular period—which Wölfflin would by no
means allow. "To demand," he says, "that such concepts be
derived from one supreme principle is, I think, unjustified. A
certain mode of seeing can have its roots in different circumstances."[1] That is to say that the five basic concepts of the
baroque may have their origin in separate sets of circumstances,
so that we should not jump to the conclusion that they indicate
a unitary world-view or are the outcome of a unique historical
tradition—even though in a general way they contribute toward
a unitary mode of seeing. As a matter of fact, painterliness,
recession, and relative lack of clarity are closely linked in the
baroque, just as are linearity, the planar style, and closed form
in the Renaissance, but there is neither necessity nor "logical
consequence"[2] about the mutual relations of these traits. In the

[9] E. Panofsky: *"Ueber das Verhältnis der Kunstgeschichte,"* p. 130.
[1] Wölfflin: *Gedanken zur Kunstgeschichte,* p. 19.
[2] Panofsky: *"Ueber das Verhältnis der Kunstgeschichte,"* pp. 158 ff.

baroque, the painterly and the unclear go with a tendency toward unification and subordination of the work's different elements to a dominant principle; whereas in other styles, *e.g.,* impressionism, the two former characteristics can be found along with a preference for manifold motifs and additive composition. And as for the future, any complete enumeration of all the possible artistic problems would either require clairvoyant powers or would imply that art is forever restricted to going over and over the problems already known and solved, in which case the task of art history would be rather a modest one.

The antithetic relation found to hold among the "basic concepts" proves, it was suggested, that a conceptual system can be constructed, that art-forms always represent solutions of a problem, and that such a problem always manifests itself in the guise of possible alternatives. Thus each antithesis and its solution reveal the inner nature of the historical process, though the advocates of this view did not always realize that here they were simply following Hegel. But while Wölfflin's basic concepts are certainly antithetical, their connection is not systematic, but merely historical; the second member of each pair does not derive logically from the first—it merely represents a later stage in the course of events. For a Hegelian that is all one, but for Wölfflin it makes a vast difference. However, Wölfflin is so far in agreement with his "systematizing" critics that he too describes the history of art in terms of alternatives and treats it as a history of problems and their solution. But here he seems to overlook the fact that some changes in the development of art occur without any "problem," and that in any case a solution is often a choice among more than two possibilities. His antithetical formulation of the basic concepts, bringing out the different stylistic traits with the utmost possible sharpness, is well suited to the educative purpose of his work, but it may be that he has gone too far in his *schematic* description of the material. For to suggest that there are only two solutions is usually to over-simplify. For example, plasticity of form represents a third possible mode of representation along with linearity and painterliness; plasticity is not just a variant of linearity. Again, as modes of organizing space, limited depth is to be distinguished from unlimited depth, and both from planar representation. And this again may spring from the simple desire to decorate a given surface, but it may also express the radical rejection of space in accord with an other-worldly outlook. Then again, the forms of recession become in the course of time even more markedly differentiated than those of the plane; there are great differences in this respect among Early Netherlandish painting, the Italian Renaissance, mannerism, baroque, naturalism, and impressionism. In Ambrogio Lorenzetti's townscapes the organization of space is as strikingly different from that of Giotto as it is from the Quattrocento perspective. The homogeneous representation of depth in the Renaissance, the heterogeneous structure of space in the work of the mannerists, and the baroque masters' dynamic conception of space are so many different solutions of the problem. And although not all these possibilities were available at any one time, it certainly cannot be maintained that at such an advanced stage of development as that of the baroque the problem of space was reducible to the mere choice between Wölfflin's two alternatives.

Now, however Wölfflin may at times seek to justify the antithetical character of his "basic concepts," what he has in mind is merely a typology, not a system of visual and stylistic forms. He aims no doubt to assemble a set of formal principles which shall be as complete as possible, but it need not be either complete or homogeneous to be of practical value. In setting up a typology of this sort, Wölfflin is pursuing the same aims as Riegl; and both remind one of Dilthey and his efforts to discover the basic types of European world-view.[3]

As a matter of fact, the idea of a historical typology of art originates with Gottfried Semper. "As it is with the works of nature," he writes, "so also the works of our hands are connected

[3] Cf. Hans Sedlmayr: Introduction to Riegl, *Gesammelte Aufsätze* (1929), p. XX.

145

with one another by a few basic ideas; and these find their simplest expression in certain original forms and types. . . . It should be an important task to single out some of these basic types of artistic form and to follow them through progressive stages up to their highest point of development. Such a method, analogous to that of Baron Cuvier, were it applied to art, would at least help us to make a clear survey of the facts, and might perhaps even provide a basis for a theory of styles and a sort of map of possibilities or chart for discovery." [4] This parallel to Riegl's and Wölfflin's method is the more illuminating because it discloses the origin of this idea of cultural typology and shows to what extent it was modeled upon the procedure of the natural sciences. In fact, it has recently been maintained that Dilthey's reduction of world-views to certain basic types is in effect a "de-historization" of the historical events. [5]

Any cultural typology tends to impose a timeless order upon the historical facts, and Wölfflin is exposed to this error just as much as Riegl, Dilthey, or writers under the influence of neo-Kantianism or of Husserl's phenomenology, except that he falls into the trap much less often. The main difference between the two attitudes lies in Wölfflin's marking off his basic concepts largely by psychological or physiological considerations, whereas the idealists despise psychology no less than physiology, and subject both psychological and historical realities to the claims of a higher realm of "validity."

"Visual forms," it has been correctly remarked, as purely optical, physiologically conditioned, non-emotive instrumentalities of perception, have nothing to do with the criteria of a style or with motives for stylistic change. Visual forms as such are neither linear nor painterly, neither planar nor recessive, for the criteria of these distinctions lie beyond the sphere of pure optics. "Seeing" considered as a power formative of style

---

[4] Gottfried Semper: *"Entwicklung eines Systems der vergleichenden Stillehre," Kleine Schriften* (1884), p. 261.

[5] Hans Freyer: *"Diltheys System der Geisteswissenschaften,"* W. *Goetz-Festschrift* (1927), pp. 492, 497 ff.

is not a simple function of the eye; it includes also an expressive
factor arising out of spiritual attitudes that interpret and shape
reality.[6] Wölfflin himself therefore never describes it as if it
were a mere physiological activity; but still he never admitted
that personal self-expression was a factor in the creation of
style. He recognized indeed that his basic concepts "denote
such deep-seated spiritual-sensuous opposites that they can
hardly be characterized otherwise than as forms of expression";
on the other hand, he emphasizes that they are only "schemata
which can be employed in the most various ways according to
one's mood, and which, even if they are not without a certain
aspect of intentionality, have little to do with what is generally
called 'expression' in art history." His position at this point as
elsewhere was undecided. "No doubt the concepts have a
spiritual aspect," he would concede, but he persisted in stating
that they were concerned with "those products of an artist's
work which can only properly be assessed by the eye."[7]
Wölfflin then, in setting out his basic concepts, runs the risk of
stopping short of the expressive, thus failing to cross the thresh-
old from the physical to the artistic; but others, by over-
spiritualizing aesthetic concepts, especially by attributing to
them "pure validity," all too easily *go beyond* the limits of the
expressive into a realm outside the artistic. Their alleged universal categories of art, which are to be independent of all
concrete experience, all psychological actuality, and all historical time, however they may be formulated, can have no
bearing upon the modes of expression and are quite as irrelevant artistically as are the purely optical forms of "seeing"
which, in Wölfflin's words, can be grasped only by the eye.

What then, from a methodological point of view, are
Wölfflin's basic concepts, if they are neither *a priori*, timelessly
valid categories, nor systematic principles, and yet not purely
descriptive individual concepts either? They can best be de-

[6] Panofsky: *"Das Problem des Stils in der bildenden Kunst,"
Zeitschrift für Aesthetik,* X (1915), 462 ff.
[7] Wölfflin: *Gedanken zur Kunstgeschichte,* pp. 21–2.

fined as "classificatory concepts." [8] To reject this description on the ground that the establishment of an antithesis goes beyond mere registration and classification means that one has taken too narrow a view of classification.[9] Historical classifications depend upon *ordering* concepts deriving from some presumed idea about the goal of development—presumed, although requiring to be confirmed or corrected again and again. Thus, even Wölfflin's basic concepts go far beyond a mere description of the material, that is, beyond the bounds of a purely empirical art history. As all historical selection and grouping does, they effect a simplification and stylization of the given material and presuppose a special kind of concept-formation without which the object to be investigated would be inaccessible. An individual baroque picture is neither "painterly" nor "recessive"; it only becomes so when it is brought together with other baroque pictures and contrasted with Renaissance works.

Wölfflin's basic concepts are not, however, derived, as such "classificatory concepts" have been said to be,[1] from the methodology of natural science. They resemble rather the concept-formations of grammar. Grammar consists, on the one hand, of the designation and identification of various forms of expression, and, on the other hand, of the comprehension of the given linguistic structures, so far as possible, under simple and exemplary formulas. Especially in Wölfflin's case, it seems appropriate to recognize alongside the "linguistic history" of art a "grammar" of the artistic means of expression, that is, a discipline that does set up laws, but laws valid only so far as the course of development shows them to be, laws whose rules are read off from historical examples and not imposed upon usage. Wölfflin's doctrine evidently derives from the insight that any art history presupposes certain concepts without which, faced with the boundless wealth of artistic production, it would be

[8] B. Schweitzer: *"Der Begriff des Plastischen," Zeitschrift für Aesthetik,* XIII (1918), 259 ff.
[9] Wind: loc. cit.
[1] Schweitzer: loc. cit.

helpless either to draw distinctions and recognize identities, or
to make a selection of what is important. Such presupposed
methodological concepts, however, neither correspond to the
principles that have been designated as *a priori* categories of
artistic creation, nor are altogether identical with Wölfflin's
basic concepts—for the latter, though not claiming to be constitutive forms of art in the Kantian sense, move uneasily on
the frontier between the philosophy and the history of art.

Epistemological reflection has long familiarized Western
thought with the idea that not merely objective but also subjective preconditions of knowledge must be reckoned with in
the natural sciences, which do not simply mirror reality. In the
historical sciences, on the other hand, we are far from having
reached the same stage of epistemological reflection, of getting
beyond "naïve realism"; the methodological preconditions of
historical knowledge are still insufficiently clarified, and the
boundary between reproduction and reconstruction of the historical realities is still indefinite. The factual material of historical research is no more than an inarticulate collection of
traditions, institutions, and records, whose scientific value is
quite indeterminate. Of the actual doings, feelings, and happenings in the past, any knowledge that the historian may
have is at second-hand. Even those products of history—fore-
most the works of art and literature—which have a meaning
and value in themselves taken in relation to the living stream
of history are no more than documents, *i.e.*, indirect evidence
of what took place, and so susceptible of various interpretations. They are historical structures coming into being and
passing away, gaining recognition and losing it again; and yet
they are also significant objects whose value for those who
recognize them seems to be something unconditional and timeless. From them we can neither discover the objective meaning
of the historical events they portray nor yet infer with any
certainty the precise meaning and value these works had for
their contemporaries. We do not even understand what kind of
validity the value we attribute to them may really have. For

we do not apprehend them directly, but by means of our own categories of thinking and feeling, and it is essential to be clear about the nature of these categories, if we are to form a proper judgment of the distance that separates us from the art of past generations.

Artists, poets, and philosophers are fond of talking with the utmost conviction and enthusiasm about the ahistorical or metahistorical essence of art. E. M. Forster's remark that history evolves, art stands still, evidently has no more than rhetorical value; for nothing evolves so strikingly as art, and there is nothing whose historical function changes so utterly and so quickly as that of a work of art. Still, this takes us no nearer to the real problem of the historical treatment of works of art. Art may be a historical product through and through, and yet art history might have at its disposal certain points of view, concepts, and standards derived not from its subject-matter, but from a certain attitude to it or from a particular method of forming concepts. The origin and disappearance of states is no doubt a historical phenomenon, but it may quite properly be asked how far the historian's outlook and the questions he puts have moulded the structure of these con-cepts—in any case, that can be a subject of critical inquiry. As a matter of fact, it is possible to treat these phenomena in an unhistorical way, *e.g.*, from the point of view of system-atic sociology or natural law, and even to maintain that the idea of "state" has been unduly historicized, as Platonizing and neo-Kantian philosophers would contend. In a similar way, one may allow that art is an essentially historical phenomenon, and yet hold that its complexities are treated by the art historian in a one-sided and over-simplifying manner or, at least, that he is employing concepts that do not fully cover the actual features of the works themselves.

One thing is certain: neither the original artist in the act of creation nor the receptive spectator at the moment of his aesthetic experience is at all aware of the historical connections in which he is implicated. The artist is conscious only of his contemporary world, and produces for it, while the person who enjoys a work of art with naïve and spontaneous enjoyment is conscious of it alone and completely absorbed in the experience. The art historian's point of view, for example that of Riegl, with his theory of the equal value of all styles and tastes, is as utterly foreign to the one as to the other. Immediate experience in art, though free from any cognizance of other stylistic possibilities, is always characterized by sympathies and aversions and by apprehension, even if unconscious, of positive or negative quality. The relativism of the art historian, measuring all achievements by their own artistic standards, neutralizes the spontaneous impression of value and quality given by the object. In taking note of this fact, one must however also recognize that—equally with the historical point of view—the *aesthetic* point of view, for which the work of art is pure "disinterested" form, is far removed from the naïve, personal, and practical quality of direct artistic experience. In relation to that, the standpoint of the philosopher of art is equally unnatural and arbitrary; indeed, the idea of "a work of art" that possesses all the essential aesthetic attributes is the most farfetched abstraction in this whole field; it is a product of what Malraux calls the "Museum," an airless room from which life has been shut out. In reality, there are just images of saints in churches, monuments in squares and cemeteries, portraits in private houses and public halls, unaware of one another and having nothing to do with one another. Only by way of the concepts of art criticism or art history do they turn into comparable, compatible, comprehensible examples of one unitary human activity.

The mere selection of what is historically relevant, the sifting of the essential from the inessential in the artistic production of the time, the bringing together of the works considered important is a spontaneous, creative act of thought; it is the result of having a point of view, which is not prescribed by the matter in hand, but which we bring with us to its investigation. This selection is often found to differ from genera-

151

tion to generation, even from one historian to another, for it depends just as much upon current judgments of the available works of art as upon the works themselves. It anticipates a great part of the judgments of the art historian and contains in germ principles of interpretation which he carries out. The notion that we start by making a collection and a review of the material is illusory. It is not a matter of first selecting and then interpreting and valuing the facts; the reality is that we register only those facts which we have already ordered in a historically meaningful series, those facts whose progressive emergence we understand—facts, in other words, which have become a problem for us and are accepted as relevant. At least this is true with the qualification that presumed interpretations ought to be constantly subjected to revision and correction by further research into sources, and that they are as a matter of fact revised whenever tension arises between the facts and their explanation. In practice, research into sources is inseparable from historical criticism, exposition of the material from its interpretation. Only reflection upon historical methodology may enable us to distinguish the different factors in what is one single endeavor.

Eduard Meyer has maintained that the criterion of historical importance is "effectiveness." "The historic is that which is effective," he wrote,[2] a view that shows very clearly how relative are the standards upon which the historian's selection depends. For "effective" means what one regards as effective. Only if a fact in its particular context seems remarkable or problematic, if one is led to ask oneself how it came about, does one begin trying to account for its existence and to discover other facts from which it might have resulted. In a sense, everything that ever happened was in some way "effective." This is not what sets the problem; what sets it is the relevance of effects, and that depends on the spectator's historical position and point of view. Each new point of view is heralded by a

[2] Eduard Meyer: *Zur Theorie und Methodik der Geschichte* (1902), p. 36.

certain feeling of discontent with the usual explanation of some facts whose special effectiveness has suddenly been discovered. But however important such a discovery may be, it is senseless to be constantly complaining about how many features of the actual events history-writing leaves out of account. That the historical sources, for example, make no mention of "the violets that were trampled upon at the capture of Liège," as has been lamented,[3] is certainly no great loss for historical science. On the other hand, the circumstance that we have so little to say about the illnesses and the material cares of the artists, that generally speaking we know so little about their childhood, their family life, their reading, and their intellectual interests may have the most far-reaching consequences. Even in the case of so recent an artist as Courbet we do not know enough to get anything like a satisfactory picture of the psychological background of his work. And now art history comes and subjects this most inadequate material to a further censorship, selecting from it according to the cultural and social standpoint of the particular historian.

But if the discovery of the important factors in a historical complex depends on having a preconceived idea, then one is bound to ask both how we get such an idea—which after all must be supposed to be a result of what we already know about history—and what the criterion of its truth could be. The answer is simple enough, even though philosophy was not quick in finding it. The principle one follows corresponds in essentials to the Napoleonic dictum *"On s'engage, puis on voit."* One begins with a more or less arbitrary assumption conditioned by one's historical situation, that is, with an intention or an act of will and a hypothesis appropriate to it; then one follows up the course thus marked out or one modifies it according as the facts that emerge agree with it or not.[4] No

[3] Theodor Lessing: *Geschichte als Sinngebung des Sinnlosen* (1921), 3rd ed., p. 15.
[4] Cf. Georg Simmel: *Die Probleme der Geschichtsphilosophie* (1907), p. 20.

doubt, the dialectical structure of the undertaking gets more and more complicated at every step, for what "new facts emerge" depends in part upon the preconceived idea, upon the provisional review and the original choice of course. One is continually driven from the one point of view to the other without ever reaching a final solution. This interdependence of the two factors in knowledge is of course no peculiarity of the historical studies; it marks our wrestling with reality by way of all forms of knowing and willing.

The spontaneous character of the historian's point of view shows itself not merely in the selection, but also in the ordering, of his material. The conception of groups and schools, of influences and resistances, of history as a process impelled by the driving force of internal oppositions—such are the manifold forms and means of concept-formation whereby the living, but by themselves inapprehensible, historical events are incorporated into an intelligible, but always more or less distorting, picture. No history-writing can describe events "exactly as they happened"; Ranke's effort to maintain the immediacy of historical facts was bound in the end to fail. As a corrective to philosophical generalizations in history, his principle was uncommonly useful; but if taken as a maxim to be literally obeyed, it contradicts the very nature of history. Not only a philosophy of history, but even the most unspeculative piece of special historical research can be achieved solely at the price of to some extent letting go of the immediate palpable facts. The birth of history as a systematic study means the end of history as a living process. The mere idea of progress "mediatizes"— to use Ranke's expression—the historical events, but without this idea, at least in its more general and less evaluative form, viz., the concept of history as a *process*, no meaningful historical account can be given of anything. A work of art is a microcosm whose totality is indescribable by the historian; to treat it as a result of influences, traditions, and institutions, a manifestation of trends, tastes, and fashions, is to strip it of that individuality and independence which we think essential marks of artistic experience. Max Weber pointed out that Eduard Meyer's definition of the historical as the effective "mediatizes" the historical occurrences just as much as any other and may lead to one's overlooking the truly creative forces in history through concern with often quite irrelevant questions about "successors." [5] This line of thought proves especially fruitful when applied to art history—a discipline that "mediatizes" its subject-matter before ever it gets to questions about efficacy and succession. For it a work by Rubens is primarily "a baroque picture," and the Antwerp *Descent from the Cross* perhaps "a Rubens," but never something utterly individual, without presuppositions or sequels.

Works that always appear separate and complete in themselves for the aesthetic experience are apprehended by the art historian as items in a more or less continuous succession. Only in relation to works that have gone before and that come after, as stages in an artistic trend, as steps or stopping-places on the way towards a goal, can works of art acquire historical meaning and reality. For example, much in the art of modern times can be grasped historically only if regarded as a step in a process of freeing visual perception from the dominance of conceptual patterns, if treated as a phase in the development that leads to the "pure visuality" of the impressionists. But as for the *aesthetic* apprehension of the individual works, the line of development leading from the brothers Van Eyck to Monet or Cézanne is quite irrelevant to it, and the particular artists who had a share in this development, however consciously they may have pursued their own individual aims, cannot—so long as this line of development was incomplete—have had the very least idea of the "goal" of their doings. The historical connection among the various works of art and among the individual artists of the West is indeed a living, but largely hidden force which only becomes an apprehensible and analyzible matter of experience through the endeavors of art history. Its interpretation of

[5] Weber: *"Untersuchungen über die kulturwissenschaftliche Logik,"* *Gesammelte Aufsätze* (1922).

the phenomena imputes to them a tendency that only gradually takes shape, and of which the participants, at a time when the supposed goal is still in the future, cannot possibly be aware.

Generally speaking, the principle of continuity in history is emphasized or denied according to one's cultural interests or social standpoint. Ortega y Gasset, for example, takes a completely atomistic point of view, declaring that the idea of "everything being connected with everything else" is "an audacious exaggeration of the mystics." [6] Tolstoy takes a similar view, but formulates it in the individualistic language of the creative artist. "Don't talk to me of the development of the novel," he said in conversation with a French guest, "don't tell me that Stendhal explains Balzac, and Balzac Flaubert. All that is vain imagination of the critics. . . . Geniuses don't derive from one another, they are independent." [7] Such utterances, quite apart from any party-political interests of the writers, manifest what may be called a "liberal" outlook, a protest against any idea that the trend of history is determined in advance. When, on the other hand, thinkers like Schelling and the representatives of organismic philosophy emphasize the principle of continuity in history, it is evidently because they feel any breach in the stable enjoyment of historic rights as an unwelcome disturbance likely to cast doubt upon the validity of traditional standards. [8]

There is a kinship between the concepts of historical continuity and organic growth: both are connected with the ideological aim of securing a measure of autonomy for the "higher" values and excluding material motives as explanations in history, such motives being designated ephemeral and ultimately irrevelant.

The problem of continuity in history can be examined from two different points of view at once. One can maintain, for example with Georg Simmel, that the real course of history

---

[6] Ortega y Gasset: "The Concept of the Generation," in *The Modern Theme* (1931), p. 13.
[7] The conversation took place in 1901.
[8] Cf. Georg Lukács: *Der junge Hegel* (1948), p. 558.

is continuous, whereas the picture that the historian paints of the events inevitably consists of a number of discontinuous partial pictures that can never join on to one another completely.[9] Or one can maintain the very opposite, that historical events are in themselves discontinuous, full of gaps, and without any direction, and that only the historian's description and interpretation effects a meaningful order in the chaos of events. The fact is that the course of history seems continuous when compared with the analysis of it into elements, motifs, and strata which any scientific treatment is obliged to undertake. On the other hand, when compared with the continuum of living experience and the unbroken flow of psychic life, the course of history, consisting, as it does, of acts and external relations among the agents, seems discontinuous, for real continuity, in which individual phases follow and interpenetrate without any perceptible interruptions, is found only in man's inner, psychic life. The process of history consists of continuous and discontinuous elements; for a stretch of its course, events are intimately linked, and then the thread snaps, and a gap in the development occurs. Put in another way, the stream of the events takes an underground course and allows some other current to come to the surface. In the face of this variable structure of the course of history, both the strictly continuous and the radically discontinuous accounts of historical events seem rather arbitrary. What really happens always has both these features: sometimes it runs on continuously; at other times it jumps. The thread itself never really breaks except in the case of the annihilation of a whole culture, which is very rare. One thread is, no doubt, always entangled with other threads, spiritual development with economic, history of art with social history and the history of science, technology, fashion, *etc.* The continuity of a style is never without gaps; in fact, it is interrupted by each new advance, though as long as any of the achievements of that particular style persist, it

[9] Simmel: *"Das Problem der historischen Zeit,"* Zur Philosophie der Kunst (1922), pp. 163 ff.

157

cannot be said to have been lost. Greco-Roman culture was not annihilated by the Christian; rather it became amalgamated with it; but even before the rise of Christianity, it went through such shocks and such changes that to treat the history of its art, as for example Winckelmann aimed to do, as that of an unbroken steady progress is to indulge in a plain fiction.

Even in the most favorable cases, art history achieves a façade of uninterrupted continuity only by an extraordinary simplification of the real course of events. This is done by assuming *one* predominant trend, *one* main line of development, and making everything depend on that. But in fact there are at all times several trends, several lines along which the development of art takes place. The art historian abstracts from this complex state of affairs, and must do so in order to get a somewhat more homogeneous and more manageable survey of the facts, but he should keep in mind that, though he presents us with a sequence of comparable and similarly directed phenomena, in reality there is a variegated mixture of particular endeavors, often at cross purposes and incompatible with one another.

The development of art in any period of advanced culture takes place at various levels, in various strata and directions corresponding to the prevalent social tastes, traditions, and values. And this stratified character of its evolution is by no means due only to different generations being active alongside one another, but is also due to the various classes and educational strata competing and colliding with one another and imposing on the artist tasks that correspond to their special interests and needs. The decision as to which of the various concurrent and competing tendencies is to be considered preeminent usually derives from a preconceived idea of history with its roots in the point of view of the particular observer. It is thus an open question which of the various tendencies manifested in Italy at the time of Raphael's death is to be considered the most typical and the most relevant. The classical, the mannerist, and the early baroque styles persisted and flourished side by side; none of them could be called anti-quated, none premature. The classicism of the Renaissance was still achieving works magnificent in themselves and progressive in point of style; the early baroque expresses just as real spirit-ual needs as mannerism. Different claims are made by different age-groups, different social and spiritual milieux, different cul-tural centers; these derive from special local circumstances, special traditions of artistic training, and changing external influences. None of these tendencies corresponds completely with the ideas of any particular master; none of them exhausts the stylistic potentialities that can be discovered in the works thus classified. The complexity of the spiritual situation and the tangle of interests and influences are not fully manifested in any one of the contemporary styles of that epoch.

No art history can present as many facets or speak with as many voices as the facts of history do; none can exhaust the wealth of possibilities open to the artist even at a relatively primitive stage of culture. Ernst Heidrich in one of his meth-odological essays remarks that the whole of the art history-writing of the Renaissance, even that of Vasari and Karel van Mander, "directly connecting, as it does, antiquity and the Renaissance, to the complete exclusion of the Middle Ages, is no more than one gigantic fiction." [1] This observation is per-fectly correct; it need only be added that all art history works with fictions of that sort. Romanticism, discovering the im-portance of the neglected Middle Ages, in its turn leaves out of account other periods and trends. Thus, every portrayal falls short of the manifold nature of historical reality; each is a projection of a many-dimensional, boundless, inexhaustible reality upon a plane surface on which the artistic relation-ships are relatively simple. This translation of the artistic structure of a period into the one-dimensional is to be con-demned only when it leaves out not simply those factors which were out of sight for the particular observer, but also those of

[1] Ernst Heidrich: *Beiträge zur Geschichte und Methodologie der Kunstgeschichte* (1917), p. 15.

which he was bound to be aware and was in fact aware, which however he deliberately passed over for the sake of presenting a more agreeable, clearer, or more original scheme of things. Thus, for example, Paul Frankl's exposition of Romanesque architecture owes its simplicity and its imposing character to its neglect of one tendency which, as Rudolf Kautzsch showed, characterized Romanesque architecture from the first, though it does not emerge clearly until we get to the Cluniac style of building. For the sake of his formula, Frankl lays down that the whole Romanesque period exhibits one uniform additive static style (*Seinsstil*), whereas the fact is that two different stylistic tendencies, one static and one dynamic, run alongside one another and amalgamate.[2]

Like Rudolf Kautzsch, Henri Focillon also emphasizes the stratified character, or as he calls it, the polyphony of a style, which should be read like a score. The fact that some features of a style are contemporary with one another in no wise means, in his view, that they are of the same age or the same kind. We should rather envisage the process of history as consisting all the time of a conflict among the timely, the premature and the superseded. The art history of a given epoch is faced not merely with individual works that reflect the temper of various different times, but also with elements in the works which are very dissimilar from the stylistic point of view. We find ephemeral and enduring stylistic tendencies, the survival of some traits that have already become obsolete, and the anticipation of others whose day is yet to come, short-period aims and long-period traditions.[3]

Art history is concerned in the main with trends and movements in the field of art; yet the only artistic reality is the work of art. All concepts are risky abstractions if they go beyond the single, individual, concrete object of an aesthetic

---

[2] Rudolf Kautzsch: "P. Frankl, *Die frühmittelalterl. u. roman. Baukunst*," *Kritische Berichte zur kunstgeschichtlichen Literatur*, I–II (1927–8).

[3] Henri Focillon: *Vie des formes* (1947), 3rd ed., pp. 82–3.

experience in order to embrace a number of different works. They replace the particular and unique creation by a category, which does not correspond to any aesthetic, *i.e.*, directly experienced, reality. Konrad Fiedler contended that there is no such thing as "Art"—there is only visual art as the form of "pure visuality," poetry as the art of language, *etc.* But he did not follow this new and fruitful idea to its end, for the fact is that as directly experienced aesthetic realities there are no such things as "arts" either—these also are mere abstractions, universals, *flatus vocis.* A nominalist type of logic is the only one that does justice to the aesthetic experience. And so, following this nominalist line of thought, Wilhelm Pinder goes so far as to declare that not merely the *Zeitgeist,* but also his own concept of a "generation" is after all only an abstraction. In this view of the matter, the personality of the artist seems to be the only psychological reality answering to the work of art. But now, this "personality" as creator of a certain *oeuvre, i.e.,* as a mere substratum of a set of works, is also an abstraction, for this life-work in its unity and totality can never be the object of a definite concrete experience. The *oeuvre* of an artist is just one of those collective names or collective concepts which are indeed indispensable tools of the art historian, but which unfortunately remove him from the actual work of art.

The greatest danger for art history, and one to which it has been constantly exposed ever since Riegl's historicism laid the foundation of its modern methodology, is that it should become a mere history of forms and problems. Let it once yield to this danger, and not only the individual works and the personalities of the artists, but also the historical situation, with the particular conditions of life obtaining, come to seem more or less irrelevant. Its whole attention is directed upon formal and technical problems, in the solution of which whole generations may be involved, and which seem to emerge not only in a definite order of direction, but also with a certain inner necessity. Any achievement, each stylistic form, each work of art, is treated simply as the solution of a task to be reconstructed: as the known answer to an as yet unknown problem. Art history if treated as a history of problems represents the evolution of styles as consisting simply of questions to be decided, of threatening crises, of inevitable conflicts and ineluctable changes. It transforms the aggregate of co-existent and successive works and tastes into a dramatic struggle between will and reality, into a continuous wrestling with nature, into a series of difficulties that arise out of one another and go on without end. The work of art becomes just an illustration of problems of form. This, it seems, is all the artists are there for, and their works have a degree of meaning and importance according as they are substrata or residues of an evolution directed toward the performance of more and more complicated tasks.

These problems and tasks are real enough; they are neither inventions nor methodological fictions, and any scientific art history must trace them and work them out. There are a living active tradition and a common stock of artistic problems, just as there is a common effort, now conscious, now unconscious, to master them. The works of art, however, are not brought into being in order to solve these problems; the problems turn up in the course of creating works to answer questions having little connection with formal and technical problems—questions of world-outlook, of the conduct of life, of faith and knowledge. But in whatever context these problems turn up, there is neither any stock of knowledge about them that is always available to the artist nor any deliberate concern with them which is always occupying his mind. Art history may treat the creations of art as solutions of problems, *i.e.*, as the outcome of continuous endeavors carried on consistently over long periods, but the individual artist neither aims to do something better than perhaps his predecessors did nor to make things easier for his successors. As has been well said, "that each age provides building material for the next is not to say that each age *wants* to provide building material for the next."[4] There is no task assigned by providence or overriding historical

[4] Günther Müller: *Die höfische Kultur der Barockzeit* (1929).

duty in respect of formal or technical problems which an artist or a generation of artists has to accomplish or wants to accomplish. For Titian the *Danae* was the picture of a beautiful woman, for Monet the *Gare Saint-Lazare* was the rendering of an impression or a mood. The most powerful effect that a work of art can produce, and probably the one that gets nearest to the intentions of the artist, comes from the re-living of that beauty or that mood. It is only for the art historian that Titian's *Danae* becomes the Renaissance solution of the problem of the female nude, and the *Gare Saint-Lazare* the impressionistic solution of the problem of light and space. The appropriateness of treating a work of art as just a "solution of a problem" may be doubted, if only because the supposed problem as a rule gets its meaning from the works it is intended to explain. Before Monet there was no problem of light in the same sense as there was after the *Gare Saint-Lazare*. In art, problems come into being along with their solution, so that in it there are, strictly speaking, no unsolved problems. The setting of the problem entails its solution, and includes—in their essentials—the elements of artistic achievement, productive experience, and creative vision. The "problem" anticipates the work; only the artist can set himself the problem; the art historian can only reconstruct it.

The assertion that a "problem" as expression of latent antithesis and inner conflict is the precondition of any progress in the evolution of art [5] could be justified only if every new style was a choice between two opposite possibilities and represented a solution essentially opposed to the one predominating up to that time. Yet the rococo, for example, can by no means be regarded as the opposite of the baroque, nor the baroque as the simple antithesis of the Renaissance. The notion of Romanesque and Gothic, Medieval and Renaissance, Renaissance and baroque, classicism and romanticism, romanticism and naturalism being opposites belongs to the apparatus of art history, not to art itself. Certainly, the polarity of styles is fundamental for

[5] Wind: loc. cit., pp. 440 ff.

the concept-formation of art history and philosophy of art; it emerges with the birth of modern art criticism, which arose out of the conflict between classicism and romanticism. Since the beginning of last century it has seemed as if styles could not be apprehended except as antithetical to one another. Schiller speaks of "naïve and sentimental" styles, Goethe of "realistic and idealistic" or "antique and modern" styles; for the romantics the styles are "the Greek and the Christian," for Nietzsche "the Apollonian and the Dionysian," for Riegl "the haptic and the optic" or "the objectivistic and the subjectivistic," for Wickhoff "the isolating and the continuous," for Wölfflin "the linear and the painterly"; for Worringer the polar factors are "abstraction or empathy," for others again "remoteness or nearness to nature," "concentration or differentiation," "regularity or freedom," "the tectonic or the atectonic," "the centripetal or the centrifugal," the static or the dynamic," "the successive or the simultaneous," "the geometrical or the organic," *etc.*

Now, whether the successive styles do really fit into this schema of polarity depends on where one, contemplating the line of development, chooses to place the accents and the caesuras. Because some of the factors making up the course of history are continuous and other discontinuous, periodization is not a matter of noting, but rather of interpreting, facts. For example, according to the way one divides up Italian art of the sixteenth century into phases and periods, it can appear as a series of gentle transitions or as a dialectical contest with sharp contrasts and violent crises. The conception of the course of art as a process consisting in the origination, change, and decline of styles is in the main the result of how one places and displaces caesuras. On this depends whether one regards the late antique as the death of pagan or the birth of Christian art; whether in late Gothic one sees the dissolution of the medieval or the beginning of a new, modern tendency in art; whether one treats the rococo as a mere symptom of decadence or as a style with its own positive values, such as that intimacy of motifs which is so characteristic of the nineteenth century; whether *pointillisme* appears as the last stage of impressionism or the beginning of post-impressionist, stylized painting. The best-known examples of a reinterpretation and revaluation of styles consequent upon a new periodization of history are Riegl's analysis of late Roman art and Dvořák's explanation of the naturalistic elements in the painting of the brothers Van Eyck. But any new point of view that alters the accepted historical connections of the styles creates a possibility of making revaluations of that kind.

Riegl's thesis that in principle all styles are of equal value is the logical consequence of recognizing that the meaning and value of works of art alter with the standpoint of the observer. But this thesis represents merely the attitude of the historian. In reality there are two different kinds of appraisal of a work of art, and its aesthetic value may in certain circumstances have nothing whatever to do with its historical significance. A work of art may be extremely important from a historical point of view, may be the origin of a fruitful line of development and call into being a creative movement rich in valuable works without itself being excellent or aesthetically in any way remarkable. Second- or third-class works often play a decisive role in the history of art and of literature; on the other hand, there have been very great masters—Bach and Raphael are examples—who were not revolutionary artists and who, historically speaking, do not hold such a key-position as many of their inferiors. Incidentally, artists of the second rank are often more faithful and more adequate representatives of their age than the great masters, whose artistic aims were more personal and spontaneous. The discrepancy between aesthetic and historical values is so far-reaching that the course of art history would not be essentially different were it to ignore altogether many of the greatest artists; for example, without Rembrandt the history of Dutch painting would remain essentially the same. It would of course be immeasurably poorer —it would have lost its peak—but it would not have lost the direction leading to that peak.

That the trend, of artistic production is relatively independent of the existence of the great masters seems to reinforce the thesis of "anonymous art history." But in fact it only signifies that the continuity of evolution is often better represented and better maintained by the lesser personalities than by the overwhelming genius, and that the concept of style is determined rather by the average or median of the production than by its peaks. It does not signify either that the grand achievements are dependent upon inferior products, nor yet that works of genius originate according to different laws from those governing works that display mere talent. The great masters are usually lonelier, more isolated in the midst of their own kind, than the lesser men, who form more of a compact group, but they are not for that mere puppets nor is the fate of art decided over their head. Talented men like Perugino, Fra Bartolommeo, and Pontormo in painting, or Richardson, Chateaubriand, and Sir Walter Scott in literature are from an evolutionary point of view more important than the geniuses who follow them; they are not "anonymous" supers in the drama, and they do not really fit into the concept of "anonymous art history" any better than the geniuses do.

3. LOGICAL AND AESTHETIC VALIDITY

Along with the notions of the "historical" and the "organic," the conception of the "valid," current in Wölfflin's time, was evidently one of the major influences on the birth of his "anonymous art history," even though he himself was perhaps not altogether aware of it. Just as all history-writing and art criticism of the early nineteenth century had been colored by the ideas of the Historical School, so in the first decades of the present century, Continental philosophy, both academic and amateur, was permeated by the conceptions of the theory of validity. Then it was the unique individuality of works of art, now it was the nature of their superindividual validity which formed a regular subject of philosophical discussion. These two streams of thought flow together, in line with the historical doctrines of neo-Kantianism, to shape Wölfflin's philosophy of art history, which thus sums up a whole century of thought on this subject.

The basic idea of this theory of validity was not novel; every antinominalist philosophy has always taken its stand upon the superpersonal and supertemporal nature of truth, and even historicism tended to view history as something superindividual, as an emanation of spirit. The theory of validity was distinguished from earlier doctrines only through being the child of a more violent reaction against scientific positivism and, in consequence, in assuming a more radical character than most of the other idealistic philosophies that have followed upon Plato's reaction to the Sophists. The independent quality of spiritual structures was rediscovered, and this had far-reaching effects. The rules of logic appeared to express this autonomy of the spiritual realm in its purest form, and so logic was taken as the model of a law-abiding order to be found in the various fields of culture. This belief in the exemplary position of logic now became the source of the most arrant misconceptions, and from it derive some of the fallacies upon which the doctrine of "anonymous art history" is based. In order fully to understand Wölfflin's mistake, one must be clear about the unsuitability of logic as a model for art history, must recognize that "validity" in science is utterly different from any meaning that this concept may have in art.

The theory of validity starts from the recognition that true statements are marked by a certain objectivity and that the claim they make to our assent is founded upon the statements' objective content, which differs from their "subjectively intended meaning." Hegel was evidently thinking of this sort of objectivity when he warned his readers against supposing that ideas are only in people's heads. Any product of man, whether it be tool or significant pattern, primitive implement or the most elaborate work of reasoning or of art, differs from a natural object in that one can detect in it an *intention;* and one can separate the content of this intention or "intended meaning" of the given structure from its accidental form, from the circumstances of its origin, even from the personality that produced it, in order to give a correct conceptual description of it. By this intended meaning, which may never be completely realized by any particular psychic act or acts, the theory of validity envisages something both compelling and exemplary which presents itself to the subject as an aim, ideal, or directive. When we take anything to be true, good, or beautiful, it is said, we expect our judgment to be accepted by anybody, irrespective of his personal inclinations. We assume that the meaning of the statement is necessarily the same each time that it is understood or thought, and that the person judging, in so far as he has done so "correctly," always envisages the same ideal object. In this way the idea of validity is taken to be absolutely distinct from the concept of approval or preference, the latter being always historically, psychologically, or in some other manner empirically conditioned. Validity is a kind of value, and entails the concept of a claim or demand.

From this objective and normative character of values, the theory of validity tacitly infers their timelessness; as values appear to be superindividual, they come to be represented by it as superhistorical. The perfect, in Nietzsche's phrase, "cannot have had a beginning"; it must have an existence beyond the bounds of time. According to the theory of validity, intended meaning is that configuration or pattern of a certain logical judgment, a certain moral imperative, or a certain art-form which must be supposed to have been there before anybody actually thought or experienced that particular pattern. It is a law of thought or law of form, which maintains an identity of its own, which is given as independent of the act of thinking or experiencing, and set as a task or goal for the subject who performs the mental act. Spiritual values persist and are valid even if no one recognizes them, confirms them, or thinks of them.

The distinction between genesis and validity is certainly one of the most important discoveries of modern philosophy. It finds expression in the principle of the irrelevance of circumstances of origin to the meaning of intellectual structures; or in the assertion that no intellectual creation, no cultural achievment or institution, is to be explained in terms of motives—neither by the personal aims of the originators nor by the needs of the social group in which they originate. All psychology, in this view, circles around some significant structure and endeavors to grasp its meaning, which task, however, it always performs incompletely; it is faced by an immutable—in fact, an inaccessible—objectivity with which it is in a state of permanent tension. This remarkable state of affairs is often portrayed in extremely impressive language: neither the presuppositions of a statement nor the events leading up to it tell one anything whatever about its truth. The circumstances of a discovery are not expressed in the results of the process. There is only an incidental connection between Newton and the law of gravity, and nothing we might discover about Pythagoras could make any difference to the meaning of his theorem. All traces of the struggle to achieve an intellectual creation are obliterated in the final product. The contents of consciousness have to pass through psychological processes, but they do not have their origin in the realm of psychology. The latter is rather a sort of melting-pot in which they lose their proper structure and take on a shape valid only for the particular subject experiencing them.

Now, the origin of a statement may have nothing to do with its objective meaning or claim to our assent. The truth of a scientific thesis may in the main be independent of the circumstances of its discovery, of whether that was the outcome of experiences with an emotional tinge or of a coldly factual interest, or of whether or not the discoverer had practical aims in view; indeed, it may to a certain extent be independent of the significance that the discoverer himself attached to it and the interpretation he set upon it. When, however, we come to consider structures unlike the theorems of mathematics or the laws of natural science, the assumption that knowledge of circumstances of origin can contribute nothing to their understanding is utterly false. Even in the case of certain scientific statements, and above all in the case of historical statements, it may very well be maintained that the social and psychological circumstances of their enunciation are relevant not only to an understanding of their meaning, but also to a proper appraisal of their value. As for moral maxims, religious precepts, or legal rules, their meaning may be completely falsified and distorted if they are considered out of their historical context. Yet, even with these structures one *can* still speak of an ahistorical meaning, which may be extracted from the process of formulation, enunciation, and recognition and elucidated by itself.

The philosophy of validity confuses objectivity with timelessness. A significant structure, a value, or a standard may well be objective in the sense of being separable from the causal conditions of its origin and yet be historically conditioned; it may originate in certain special circumstances and change with them, *i.e.*, lose its validity or become altogether meaningless and insubstantial. Still, whether or not we attribute to these allegedly "valid" patterns some superhistorical, timeless, and eternal mode of being, whether we regard their discovery as accidental and their abandonment as irrelevant, or, on the contrary, treat them as mere hypostasizing of empirical psychic contents, the philosophy of validity does bring out a fundamental distinction between two different sorts of contents of consciousness. Whenever we ascribe to an intellectual structure objective meaning or value, whenever we expect or demand that others look at it the same way as we do, we are dealing with something that may indeed be derived from empirical conditions, but can never be reduced entirely to them. Whether we discover or invent this structure or pattern, we think of it as having a meaning that must for others have the same reference and the same validity that we ourselves ascribe to it. This meaning, in its objectivity and with its reproducible pattern, is *toto genere* different from any subjective and ephemeral contents of consciousness, fluctuating emotions and moods that come and go without committing one to anything.

However, the trait of validity adds nothing to the positive features of a statement; to hypostasize this as a quality is merely to duplicate the content of the statement, to ascribe to it, along with its real, concrete, psychologically and historically apprehensible form, an unreal, superpsychological, and superhistorical existence and subsistence. Validity just means that some connections of meaning can be thought of apart from their actual substratum, and in this way connections that would be more or less obscured by a psychological and historical approach can be viewed in a pure form. In general, the only achievement of the theory of validity has been to make a precise distinction between the objective and the subjective factors in spiritual structures. The only novelty about it has been the rigor with which the analysis of these structures have been pursued and the light that has been focused upon complexes of meaning, once these have been distinguished from subjective experiencing. Yet, one easily falls into the old philosophical mysticism at this point if one is inclined to convert meaningful complexes into objects of intellectual intuition and supposes that one has found a proof of a supernatural or supertemporal origin of truths and values. For the objective criteria of truth are *inter*personal, not *super*-personal. Valid formulas or valid rules are in large part current conventions, but even propositions, correct by more than just convention, need not for that reason be timelessly true.

Although we cannot allow that all statements are true only relatively and in their historical context—that would be to reject any laws of logic and to render scientific thought impossible—still, there is no doubt that rules and methods of thought have in fact undergone far-reaching changes. In science, statements of universal validity are anchored in a logical system that governs the whole of our rational thinking; in morality, unconditional demands are linked up with the character of entire civilizations; in art, laws of form can be discovered which remain valid over entire stylistic periods. But the validity of all these is the result of human—though by no means arbitrary—decision. It is never given by a superhuman, supernatural revelation. Neither metaphysical absolutism nor psychological relativism give a satisfactory account of what validity means. Valid truths and acknowledged values are neither emanations from a Platonic world of Forms nor yet notions simply invented by individuals and alterable at will; they are human, yet their origin is not altogether spontaneous nor their being altogether ephemeral. The origination, recognition, and abandonment of them is indeed linked with historical conditions; but the individual who acknowledges or formulates them is conscious of submitting to superindividual standards. They are the result of numerous attempts, each conditioned by its situation, to master the real: reality keeps setting men similar tasks over and over again, but the attempts to cope with them vary according to the demands of the historical moment. The impression of continuity in the series of attempts, of a cumulation of effects which keeps culture in being, is in the main attributable to a constancy of material conditions and a conservatism of the basic human drives.

The question now arises of how far and in what sense one should speak of an aesthetic validity analogous to logical validity. There does seem to be a certain objectivity about our relation to a work of art, in that when enjoying and appraising it aesthetically, we are conscious of being confronted by an objective structure that imposes upon us one kind of attitude rather than another and provides criteria for its proper appreciation. A work of art appears to us to possess a certain meaning of its own and to require a certain interpretation, even though as a matter of fact it is not always felt, interpreted, and appraised in the same way. In other words, the meaning of a work of art sets a problem that admits indeed of various solutions, but is concerned with an objective state of things. To this the experiencing subject feels himself to be in a tension similar to that which the scientist feels toward the facts he is seeking to describe and explain. Because of this concern with an objective state of things, statements about works of art are made with the conviction that they should be acceptable to anybody. In this way, they make upon us a sort of claim resembling that of logical validity, for they too express something that has to be recognized. Yet they are not at all simple statements of fact, but are just as much judgments of value—and that in a double sense. In the first place, a genuine work of art, by contrast with other aesthetically valueless products, is reckoned to be successful, truthful, or "good" in respect of the aim, ideas, and methods involved in the particular case. The second kind of validity ascribed to aesthetic judgment is more problematic, for now the aesthetic value is held to depend on whether the artist has taken account of superpersonal principles of form, of universal rules and norms, and the rank of his work to depend on the measure of success with which he has fulfilled these requirements. But this shows a complete misunderstanding of the nature of art, and comes from an ill-considered employment of the logical concept of validity in aesthetics.

If one is to use the term "validity" at all in speaking about art, it can only be in connection with values already realized, not as implying that there are absolute, eternal, self-subsistent values that claim to be realized or "have a chance of being realized" by the artist. The artist may feel a kind of obligation to comply with certain formal principles, but such feeling expresses no more than that he has inposed a certain rule on himself; the rule serves to objectify his personal feelings, whereas a person contemplating the work is really faced with something objective. The theory of "aesthetic validity" as the epitome of aesthetic values subsisting eternally in independence of the abilities and inclinations of the artist realizing them is evidently an adaptation of the *logical* theory of validity, according to which truth is independent of the individual who discovers and formulates it, and is regarded as an autonomous, unoriginated order of laws and norms. Theories of art based on this notion of validity can see in the work of art no more than an exemplification of, or variation upon, an ideal exemplar; they treat it as if "fallen from heaven," and as if its creator were a mere intermediary. And fictitious though this notion is, it does have its use for the proper understanding of the work of art, which must, if it is to be elucidated satisfactorily, first be apprehended apart from all external relations as a formal structure complete in itself. But the assumption of some valid formal principles is at bottom just a working hypothesis; aesthetic "laws" are valid only in so far as we presuppose certain psychological wants. Works of art never derive their effectiveness or their value from some conformity to abstract norms supposedly independent of the spectator's personality, but solely from the fact that they satisfy actual, concrete, variable, historically and psychologically conditioned requirements. Apart from such requirements, we could not explain how a certain value or a certain standard gains recognition in the field of art. When wants and requirements change, no standard can retain its previously accepted status; what is "valid" can in fact only be reconstructed *a posteriori* from wants that were acknowledged and are felt to have been satisfied.

In science there is a radical distinction, perhaps even an insuperable gulf, between the validity of laws and the discovery and formulation of these laws, but in art there can be no question of any such cleavage between idea and execution, value and its realization, valid norms and their historical embodiment: each of these pairs is an indissoluble unity. The work of art itself *is* the aesthetic value; and that value is in no way apprehensible apart from the work of art. One may well ask whether there is any sense at all in speaking of "value-in-itself" apart from the value of particular works, in talking of "beauty" in the abstract, or of universal aesthetic "form." An artist may indeed have the feeling that his work does not fully achieve a complete realization of his vision, but this vision becomes objective only in the actual work, and the artist can experience it, think about it, and discuss it only in terms of the work. Artistic values are historical realities, existing only from the moment when they are embodied; the artist does not "discover" them, he "creates" them, he does not find them there, pre-existent, waiting to be apprehended. He does not participate in any metaphysical entities that are anywhere or in any way given. In a word, nothing in the field of art can properly be described as approximation to an Idea. If the artist has a sense of having fallen short of his idea, that only indicates a lack of clearness and definiteness in his idea.

Only when we turn to the spectator do we find a tension between the work and his grasp of it which resembles that between a significant complex and its apprehension by the scientist. The attitude of aesthetic receptiveness leaves the object of the experience more or less unaffected; it is in fact no more than an attempt to identify oneself as closely as possible with the intention of the artist. This intention is the objective value that has to be apprehended. Even so, aesthetic appraisal is a specific phenomenon, in many ways radically different from the recognition of logical validity. Above all, the relation between historicity and timelessness is different in both cases. Scientific enquiry is guided by more or less constant aims, and to a very great extent science maintains, in the acquisition of knowledge, logical consistency among its propositions. Its achievements form, on the whole, a linear, progressive series conditioned less by contemporary historical events than by the direction in which the previous results seem to point, by the solutions of past problems and the gaps felt to lie between them. Strictly speaking, the sciences, and certainly the formal sciences of logic and mathematics, do not have a "history" in the sense of a development determined by the external conditions and accidents of life; in their case one feels inclined to speak more of a history of errors and misconceptions than of the historical character of valid knowledge and truth. We presuppose that in order to know, to discover, truth man must free himself from the bonds of historical circumstance and penetrate into a sphere of timeless and spaceless abstractions. If so, there can at most be a history of discovery, but not a history of truth or of scientific standards in general. The results of scientific enquiry may indeed be formulated in various, historically conditioned fashions, but it is only in the Hegelian philosophy that the history of such formulations has bearing upon the extent to which objective truth is realized.

Now, in art, where the history of aesthetic values is identical with the history of their formulations, the problem of historical evolution is a totally different one. It revolves round the fact that a work created in a certain, definite, unrepeatable historical situation can be valued and be an object of appreciation in other situations too. This is essentially the problem that Marx, in the Introduction to the *Critique of Political Economy,* outlines as follows:

"Is Achilles conceivable in an era of powder and lead? Or for that matter the *Iliad* at all in these days of printing-press and press-jacks? Do not song and legend and the Muse necessarily lose their meaning in the age of the Press?

"But the difficulty is not that Greek art and epic are connected with certain forms of social development, but rather that they still give us aesthetic satisfaction today, that in a sense they act as a norm and an unattainable paragon."

We are confronted here with a strange contradiction, not at first glance explicable: the historicity of origin of works of art is coupled with a constancy of effect. The persistence of a work of art as source of ever-new experiences, although it does not signify a timeless validity as Marx himself seems to have thought, does at least imply a sort of practical emancipation from the conditions of its origin. The philosophers who take the idea of validity as their clue would formulate the problem to this effect: how does a timeless value "come to be

176

in history?" But what one ought to ask is how a historical structure like a work of art comes to acquire a "validity" that is superhistorical, or at any rate transcends the historical situation. However the question is formulated, it is concerned with the contrast between historic actuality and aesthetic standards, a problem difficult enough, but not nearly so vexed as the corresponding problem in the field of logic. To concede that real historical factors of a sociological or psychological nature play a decisive role in the shaping of scientific thought involves one in difficulties that simply do not arise in the case of art. If we take existing, *i.e.*, accidental and variable, conditions to be decisive for the conclusions reached by thought, we thereby undermine the validity of "thought in general" and must allow that our own conclusion is equally relative and questionable. Whereas if we take the creations of art and their "validity" to be conditioned by circumstances that change with time, we fall into no such contradictions. It is even of the essence of art that various attitudes and aims can co-exist. The acknowledged value of a certain type of work by no means excludes some completely different type from having value; the situational determination and consequent relativity of aesthetic judgments does not entail that these must be completely subjective. Works of art do not contradict one another, however different they may be, and critical judgments are symptomatic rather than true or false.

The inadequacy of the concept of "anonymous art history" is intimately connected with this failure to recognize the difference between logical validity and aesthetic value. Wölfflin supposed that because the manner in which the knowing subject arrived at the knowledge formulated in a statement is irrelevant to its logical truth, so the author and circumstances of its origin are equally irrelevant to the work of art. In his view, artistic form is not freely and spontaneously invented, but prescribed or set as a task; it is a possibility unconditionally realizable and to be realized by the artist and his generation. As for Husserl the laws of logic, so for Wölfflin the forms of style are ideal structures that can be considered apart from the individual personality. He may not separate them so sharply from current reality as the phenomenologists separate logical truths from psychological reality, but he is just as definite as the phenomenologists are about objective laws realizing themselves in particular acts of experience; he treats the individual with his specific powers, inclinations, and needs as a mere carrier of superindividual trends bound to be realized.

The asserted autonomy of these tendencies—the "immanence" of artistic evolution which is the very essence of Wölfflin's theory—is but an application of the concept of validity to the field of history. This idea of inner causation in art is no more acceptable than we found the idea of "aesthetic validity" to be. It is based upon the correct observation that the evolution of art manifests trends that are to some extent objective and offer a certain resistance to mere individual caprice. No one who takes account of the remarkable way in which cultural achievements become automatized can ignore the force with which certain trends in culture impose themselves,[6] or can deny that the history of art, like the histories of other cultural achievements, has to a great extent to do with endogenous causation. We should however recognize that this causation assumes the form of *bifurcations*, the consequences of a given situation running in two possible directions or more. "An inner dialectic," says Dilthey, "drives us from one position to another . . . The difficulties inherent in one position do drive men to go beyond it; but it is not correct to assert, with the Hegelians, that they positively lead on to the following position. They can be resolved in various different ways, according to our principle of multiplicity of effects."[7]

---

[6] Simmel: *Die Probleme der Geschichtsphilos.* (1907), pp. 17–20; *"Ueber das Wesen der Sozialpsychologie," Archiv für Sozialwissenschaften* (1908), XXVI, 286–7; *Grundfragen der Soziologie* (1917), pp. 22–3; *"Der Begriff der Tragödie der Kultur," Philosophische Kultur* (1919), 2nd ed., p. 223.

[7] Wilhelm Dilthey: *"Die Funktion der Anthropologie in der Kultur des 16. u. 17. Jahrhundert," Gesammelte Schriften,* II (1914), 458.

This bifurcation of the available ways seriously limits the applicability of the principle of inner causation; and external influences, especially individual motives for choosing one alternative rather than another, now emerge prominently as decisive for the course of history. Individual freedom within cultural tradition is never an absolutely spontaneous or arbitrary choice of what to attempt, but is a free decision as to which fork to take of a dividing road. The varying extent of this freedom in the different fields of culture reflects the limits with which the principle of validity can be taken to hold in each. The more rational the character of a specific field of culture, and the more it is appropriate for the application of rigorous logical principles, the more evolution within that field will be self-contained and unaffected by external conditions. Thus, the sciences develop in a more consistent and continuous way than law or custom; and tradition and convention play a much more important role in law and custom than they do in art. And in art itself the various technical procedures and skills develop in a more strictly logical and continuous manner than the emotional and irrational factors. The manipulation of the materials and tools of art has in fact a history of its own which is to a certain extent independent of artistic intentions; but if, on the other hand, we propose an autonomous history of the creative intentions by themselves, it is evident that this would involve a breaking down of the living source of history and a disrupting of the intimate connections among the various forms of human existence. The life of man in history exhibits, in the mutual dependence of its various manifestations, the nearest approximation we know toward the unity of the living organism; and strange to say, it is the organismic doctrine, insisting on exclusively inherent causation within each partial unity, each specific manifestation of the human spirit, which is most ruthless in tearing at those connections.

J. Huizinga has well shown why the concept of immanent causation, in biology extremely fruitful and even indispensable, is nearly useless in history. Biology, he points out, is bound to

179

treat the organism, a carrier of inherent tendencies, to a certain extent in independence of its environment; whereas all that we call "history" begins and ends with the relation of man to his environment. "The Frenchman" as a historical and socio-logical concept manifests itself only as the result of the mutual relations of all the individuals comprised under this concept, whereas the biological concept "mouse" can be adequately il-lustrated in any individual mouse. A phenomenon such as Na-poleon, he writes, can only be considered historically in so far as he is viewed in connection with the world in which he lived; as a historical figure, he cannot be thought of independently of that world. So, whereas biology can for certain researches quite properly abstract from outside influences, history must seek to attribute everything that happens, *i.e.*, every contact of man with his fellows and with nature, to external causes.[8] To repre-sent historical events as if they were immanently caused proc-esses, the result of internal drives like the vital functions of an organism, is, Huizinga maintains, to de-historicize history, for this way of looking at things deprives history of that element of the unforeseeable and the incalculable which is its very stuff. History gets converted into a species of demonstration under laboratory conditions, that is, its material is reduced to a state in which a number of its most typical features, *viz.*, those con-nected with its own specific conception of time, have been limited.

By the standard of *historical* time, immanent processes such as biological growth and logical or mathematical operations, take place timelessly. The medium in which they take place is the abstract, mechanistic, purely quantitative time of classical cosmology and physics. This is a kind of neutral, strictly con-tinuous, and uniform container that sets limits to its contents without affecting their nature in any way. This conception of time as uniform and homogeneous entails the thought of a simple sequence of isolable events, roughly in the manner in which a line can be thought as a sequence of infinitely many

[8] J. Huizinga: *Wege der Kulturgeschichte* (1930), pp. 27–8.

points. But the historical conception of time as a fabric of unique, never recurrent events, as a medium within which the destiny of a nation, an individual, or a task is worked out, has obviously nothing in common with such modes of thought. The conception that mere lapse of time can be creative, fruitful, maturing, or, on the contrary, devastating and disintegrating in its effect is incompatible with the time-concept of physical and biological science. Another difference lies in the way time signifies, for the historian, a continuous flowing of the future into the present and the past, whereby the present is always viewed as a meeting-point of past and future, a point at which everything manifests a Janus-character. The historical concept of time is characterized above all by the features by which Bergson marked off his conception of "duration." In his view, any point in time is rather like a phase of a melody; every phase contains in a way everything that has gone before and all that has been achieved so far, but each new phase and each new note modifies the sense of all the other phases and notes in the melody.

A historiography that is governed by the notion of logical validity, that conceives history as an inherently conditioned, straight-line process toward a definite goal, is not able to do justice to the many-sided aspect of historical time, nor to achieve a proper understanding of the reinterpretations that past and anticipated future are continually undergoing in the light of the present.

Georg Simmel's description of the way in which different cultural achievements become autonomous shows how closely the ideas of autonomy and immanence are bound up with the anti-psychological bias of the doctrine of validity. Simmel maintains that one specific feature of cultural history is the gradual elimination of "consciousness" through the mechanization of attitudes and performances that were originally conscious. The products of culture, he holds, can be originated only by conscious beings, but once these products exist, they confront the individual as objective, self-subsistent, and self-imposing entities. Simmel adduces as an example an observation made by Marx: "If we find slavery giving place to feudalism, and this again to work for wages, the explanation of these changes is not to be looked for in the quasi-logical consequences of the relevant economic techniques . . . In these cases consciousness is completely eliminated." [9] Now the "elimination of consciousness" signifies in this connection a shift toward immanent causation and the acceptance of superindividual principles. When Simmel later declares that although human will and what it can accomplish are subject to a certain inner logic of things, "no state of affairs is brought about by its own logic, but only by social and psychic forces," [1] it is not at all clear how one can envisage the working of this double motivation in practice. The difficulty lies, as Engels recognized, in having to explain how these alleged unconscious, extra-psychological motives "go through the heads" of the men concerned. Marx's solution is as little satisfying as Hegel's. Freud finds an answer to the question, but one that fits only the limited slice of life which interests him. A more satisfactory answer could be reached solely by way of an analysis of social education and adaptation, tradition and convention, competition and imitation, an analysis that would also throw more light upon the singular compound of freedom and non-freedom evinced in the higher collective activities of man.

"In the history of painting the influence of one picture upon another is much more effective as a stylistic factor than anything deriving directly from the observation of nature." So Wölfflin declares, and his appreciation of the part played by tradition and convention in art is perfectly correct. "It is an amateurish notion," he continues, "to imagine that any artist has ever been able to look at nature without any preconceptions. The concept of representation which he has taken over, and the manner in which this concept goes on working in his mind is of greater importance than anything he may have derived from direct

[9] Simmel: *Die Probleme der Geschichtsphilosophie,* pp. 19–20.
[1] Simmel: *Grundfragen der Soziologie,* pp. 22–3.

observation." [2] The passage shows that Wölfflin, despite his dependence upon the idea of validity, does not take such an abstract view of the superindividual principles as the philosophical authorities he recognized. Here he comes very near to as realistic a view of history as that of Paul Lacombe, with his distinction of *événements* and *institution* as the unique and the persistent, the ephemeral and the exemplary, in the development in art. "For me," says this French author, "an 'institution' or 'institutional' is anything about an action, a performance, or a product recalling features that have already occurred in another action, performance, or product. In short, wherever there is similarity, there is something institutional." [3] And again: "When Racine, La Fontaine, Boileau, and so on express the same opinion concerning Homer or some other ancient author, that is institutional . . . The rule of taste which forbade the men of that time to introduce the word "cow" into a poem is the symptom of an institution . . . and so is the rule that prescribed that a murdered tyrant in tragedy should not be given the mortal blow on the stage, but die behind the scenes." [4] Lacombe contends, and in this context Wölfflin would have agreed with him, that what is individual, singular, and unique cannot become a subject of science, which is only concerned with noting similarities with a view to the formulation of laws. [5] Lacombe, however, in spite of this recognition of the generalizing character of science, lays much more stress than Wölfflin on the part played in history by the individual. If, he says, you study an author—as you must—in relation to his public, you will not fail to recognize the influences that have contributed to the formation of his talent; but equally you are bound to notice the influence that he as an individual has exerted. The existence of a certain individual thus appears as an "event" manifesting features of pre-existing and subsequent "institu-

[2] Wölfflin: *Kunstgeschichtliche Grundbegriffe*, p. 249.
[3] P. Lacombe: *Introduction à l'histoire littéraire* (1898), p. 29.
[4] Ibid., pp. 29–30.
[5] Ibid., p. 32.

tions." Throughout history, the institutional and typical is everywhere enlivened by the individual and accidental. But the art historian, by bringing the various works into relation with one another, thereby straightway transforms them from singular phenomena into parts of an objective and persistent context. So any art history, to use Lacombe's words, treats an "event," *i.e.*, a particular work, as carrier of an "institution," *i.e.*, as susceptible of continuation and imitation; the work loses its accidental character, emerges from its isolation and becomes typical. Wölfflin in particular arrives at his notions of "anonymous art history" and immanent causation chiefly by dint of stressing all the persistent, continuous, institutional factors in the historical process while thrusting into the background anything that is singular and untypical.

The greatest gain accruing to the history of art and literature from this definition of their formal principles and stylistic trends as *institutional* phenomena lies in the fact that the concept of "style" thereby loses its abstract character without losing its interpersonal significance or its superindividual authority. For Lacombe, institutions such as a college, a guild, feudalism, the city as social and political form, but equally such phenomena as Western culture, the romantic movement, the form of the drama, and the dramatic unities are not mere collections of particulars under general concepts formed by abstraction from everything singular and concrete. For institutions are also in their own way concrete and singular, though they are not, to be sure, linked with such short stretches of time as the nonrecurring particulars are, but they are in no case supertemporal or ahistoric. They become the framework of collective attitudes, not by a process of eliminating everything individual, but by enabling various individual lines of action to take place at the same time without thwarting one another. In art, the invention of a technical device or the discovery of a *motif*, for example, the discarding of frontality in Greek sculpture in favor of a more dynamic mode of representation, the discovery of the love-motif in drama, the application of the idea of the

184

vassal's homage to love, the introduction of central perspective into painting or of the three unities into tragedy—these were all originally so many "events," that is, achievements of particular individuals at certain times and in particular historical situations. But as soon as a discovery or an invention of this kind becomes an example or rule to be followed, it becomes a common possession; it is no longer simply the expression of a singular experience or of a personal attitude, but takes on the function of a formula, a convention, a scheme, in other words, an achievement the artist can take advantage of in order to make himself understood without himself having to traverse the long, vexatious road to discovering it, developing it, and exploring the problems of its application.

When one treats stylistic forms as institutional structures, the idea of their continuous development and inherent causality may appear more justifiable than it did from the point of view of pure validity. For it is clear enough that such structures, though in their origin by no means independent of external conditions, may persist for a time in independence of anything external. "Men fail to change their vocabulary every time they change their customs," writes a shrewd historian, having the remarkable inertia and toughness of institutional forms in mind.[6] It is in consequence of this inertia that the forms of art too outlive the conditions of their origin and outlive their original meaning; they become in a way neutral vehicles of expression that can be handed on and taken over, and come in the end to convey something more and something different from what was orginally intended. In this connection, nothing is more symptomatic of the immanent causality and automatic character of cultural development than the fact that the causal relation between psychic needs and institutions is constantly shifting and even being reversed. For the institution is often older than the psychological attitude that explains and motivates it; often the significance or the sentiment attached to it is no more than a *post facto* rationalization. In considering such discrepancy

[6] Marc Bloch: *The Historian's Craft* (1954), p. 34.

between the nature of an institution and the justifications given for its existence, one should bear in mind that the consequences of any event are incalculable and that their significance keeps changing as time goes on. There are, therefore, often several different reasons why the function an institution actually fulfils may be out of all proportion to the often irrational and ephemeral motives that set it going. Ritual, as is well known, generally precedes the beliefs connected with it; symbols are usually older than the meaning attributed to them; customs are almost always more primitive than the morality they embody. And similarly Wölfflin may very well have come to the conclusion that stylistic forms are structures for which the artistically extraneous motives that gave them birth are irrelevant or no longer relevant, so that like institutions in general they have a dynamism and a direction of their own. From this point of view, he is quite logical in taking account of external influences as conditioning development only when a style, like some institution, is breaking down. What he seems to have overlooked is that institutions, in spite of their inertia, need some external support—in the form of an actual willingness to support them—if they are to survive.

Henri Focillon shows by a concrete example how intimately in the history of art internal and external factors—the logic of development and extraneous influences—interpenetrate, and may even work in opposite directions within the same artistic phenomenon. [7] He mentions that some authors ascribe the origins of the flamboyant style to the English influence that made itself felt in France during the Hundred Years War, but remarks that others maintain, and quite correctly, that the "flaming line," the basic form of this style, is to be found in the French architecture of the thirteenth century. It is, however, important to note, as he emphasizes, that before the late Gothic this form was generally eliminated, evidently because it was felt to be incompatible with the predominant tectonic principle of the classical period of French Gothic. The foreign

[7] Focillon: *Vie des formes*, pp. 87–8.

influence could not make itself felt until an inward readiness to accept it had matured. The new style did not come in as a direct continuation of the hitherto repressed tendency, nor yet as the result of a revolutionary change of taste breaking in abruptly from outside, but was rather a reconciliation of intrinsic and extrinsic factors, the impulses characteristic of French Gothic with those of the foreign influence. The situation is complicated, as Focillon observes, by the fact that in English Gothic the features that anticipate the future development are bound up with conservative tendencies, so that one does not find a straightforward logical unfolding of style in England either. In short, whenever art history comes to a real change, it can point to some lines of immanent causation, but can never show that the change was caused by intrinsic factors exclusively. From these possibilities of choice no ineluctable necessities open out.

From the fact that one possibility was chosen Wölfflin infers the inevitability of that choice, but he never takes the principle of an intrinsic logic of development in the extreme and radical sense of Riegl, who considers each form of style a simple reconciliation of "latent opposites," whereas Wölfflin to some extent explains it as satisfying a psychological need. [8] Although Wölfflin, and not Riegl, coined the slogan "anonymous art history" and took as his program the exposition of the intrinsic development of styles in art, apodictic expressions like "it follows quite simply from . . ." or "it could not have happened otherwise" are not nearly so common in his work as in Riegl's. Wölfflin could never have brought himself to write such a sentence as the following: "The character of the period from Constantine to Theodosius can be constructed *a priori* from a mere observation of the art of the early Empire." [9] Although Riegl here is certainly not using the term *a priori* in the strict sense of the Kantian epistemology, and though his account of the historical events is in itself correct, his treatment of each

[8] Wind: loc. cit., p. 443.
[9] Alois Riegl: *Die spätrömische Kunstindustrie* (1926), p. 126.

artistic complex as if it were a bud unfolding according to biological laws falsifies the course of history, which is irreducible to any scheme, as a historian like Wölfflin recognizes. Even Wölfflin skates rather too boldly over some of the irregularities of the events as they occurred, but he certainly cannot be accused of giving history "the gait of a sleep-walker," a phrase that has been used about the impression made on us by Riegl's work.

4. HISTORICAL NECESSITY AND INDIVIDUAL FREEDOM

It is a widely accepted opinion that the task of science is to predict phenomena about whose occurrence there is no possible doubt. The calculability of an eclipse of the sun, for example, is generally taken as a model to which any proceedings that are to count as scientific must conform. This ideal of science is what chiefly stimulates attempts to discover in the historical process constantly recurring manifestations of the same universal laws. For the thesis that history moves always in a certain direction and according to a certain scheme is, after all, equivalent to asserting that future events are predictable. But whereas the natural sciences, on the basis of noting sequences, have been able to arrive at reliable predictions, the historian employing this method achieves no more than a few dubious prophecies. The upholders of the supposed inner logic of the evolution of art are also inclined to make predictions. Strictly speaking, the doctrine only asserts that each phase of the development is conditioned by the previous one, that everything novel is dependent upon something that preceded it, and that the events take a course marked out in advance by something intrinsic to them. But the doctrine takes an excessively speculative turn when it does not merely ascribe to history an intrinsically consistent direction, insusceptible to diversion, but also goes on to claim to have found a pre-existing rule, a formula applicable over and over again, by which the course of events is shaped.

The theories of periodicity, of rhythm, of cycles in history, of recurrent types, morphological stages, or dialectical steps, the notions of historic destiny, continuous progress, or inevitable decline are all variants upon the same philosophical mysticism, the belief that the course of history can be schematized and constructed. But in reality there is neither an underlying plan nor a logical sense in events. Historical events have ascertainable subjective causes and are the result of particular aims of persons, but in themselves they are accidental and aimless; there are no historical laws in any objective sense. The course of history is alterable and can always be diverted. "For history," says Eduard Meyer, "everything in nature or human life which is matter of causal law is simply taken for granted. For example, the effect of natural forces . . . and similarly the conditions of human thought, sensation, and volition . . . The same would be true of any other laws of historical life, if there were any; the moment they were discovered they would cease to belong to history; they could never be the subject of historical enquiry, but only its presuppositions. The objective of history is everywhere the discovery and portrayal of individual happenings . . ."[1] Only where we get beyond the reign of law, and where chance or personal initiative, or, as philosophical idealists say, "freedom of the personality" comes in, do we have to do with the experiencing and enduring of human existence. If Wölfflin's "basic concepts" were taken to be no more than typical visual and representational forms which recur more or less automatically from time to time, they could not be reckoned as "historical" categories any more than if they signified some strictly physiological preconditions of artistic vision. Art functions within a conceptual stratum that lies above that of physiological conditions, but below that of

[1] Meyer: *Zur Theorie und Methodik der Geschichte*, p. 29.

general historical patterns. By contrast with both these sorts of conditions, it exemplifies the principle of freedom. At most, art may be said to be governed or conditioned by the ways of life and means of expression that the current traditions and conventions provide, but these set the starting-point, not the goal, of artistic endeavor.

However, we must allow that in history "freedom" and "necessity" are not simple alternatives that can be readily separated. Any event that has already occurred, any completed action or achievement fulfilled, gives an impression of being necessary because its course is then fixed and cannot be altered. Whereas any decision not yet taken or intention not yet carried out has an appearance of being subject to chance. An actual occurrence is inevitable in the sense of having resulted from real conditions, forming a chain of links that are not interchangeable. But while the process of motivation is still uncompleted, new conditions can turn up which in relation to those previously operative have an appearance of being accidental and capricious, but later on, if they prove effective, take on an appearance of necessity. There is no better illustration of the peculiar compound of chance and necessity in history than the well-known example of a number of balls set in motion and knocking against one another. Each ball moves along its path with causal necessity according to the impact it has received. But the circumstance that it is struck by another ball is on a different plane from the type of causal law which governs its motion; and in relation to the original motion this circumstance appears to be accidental, though the path of the second ball is itself also necessary in terms of causal law. The accidental character of the clash is a consequence of its being a resultant of the interplay of *several* causal lines; and so it is with history. The explanation of Leonardo da Vinci's art, for example, is to be found, on the one hand, in the stylistic change leading from the Quattrocento to the High Renaissance, but, on the other hand, no less in the circumstance that at the time this change was taking place there happened to be an artist of the rank of Leonardo. Both of these facts are not without their real conditions and so may be said to be in a sense inevitable, but their coincidence depends on incalculably many chances. Even historical determinism admits accidental factors along with necessary factors in history, but unlike the opposite doctrine of spontaneous evolution, it treats the origination of the various causal lines as accidental and their interplay as necessary. Hegel, for example, calls empirical causality a merely external, "accidental necessity," reserving the concept of higher, rational necessity for the laws manifest in the interplay of various causal lines. "A tile falls from a roof," he writes, "and kills a man. Here the falling, the coincidence may occur or not occur, is accidental. In such cases of extrinsic necessity, only the result is necessary; the circumstances are accidental." [2]

Examples of the decisive role of chance in history are numerous and familiar. How trifling often are the circumstances through which battles are lost or won, how irrelevant seem the causes of the success or failure of an assassination, how "senseless" yet how fateful the early death of Masaccio, Raphael, or Watteau, and how remarkably "lucky" that Leonardo, Michelangelo, and Titian attained such a ripe old age. In all these cases, the importance of the consequences stands in the sharpest contrast with the accidental character of the cause; any talk of logic or purposiveness of history seems out of place. Of course, the objections of the determinists to this line of thought are familiar. A battle or an assassination, it is said, is no more than a symptom of a crisis and an attempt at its solution; when the solution is actually found, the purpose of the lost battle or unsuccessful assassination is attained in another way. The tasks that confronted an artist who died young come to be solved by another artist. There are no frustrated possibilities in history. But nothing of all this can be proved, and so the net result for science of the whole controversy is extremely slight. One can never know how many of the possibilities of a given situation remained unrealized, or whether those that

[2] G. W. F. Hegel: *Werke* (1832–45), XII, 15.

were not realized failed because the time was not ripe for their solution or because of merely accidental obstacles. Who can say to what extent Raphael's ideas in art were lost to the world for ever in consequence of his early death? The fact that the direction his art took in its beginnings was in a way marked out for him in advance does not imply that he was obliged to continue beyond any particular point along the path he had taken or that his path, once interrupted by death, could be taken up by anyone else.

As any historical event has an infinite number of determinants, a thoroughgoing causal explanation of history is an infinitely remote possibility. In consequence, the only possible answer in practice to the question it poses—though in principle this must be always treated as a provisional answer—is to declare its accidental character. The accidental character of historical events does not however mean that any kind of happenings is beyond the range of empirical causality, nor yet that within the framework of causal laws "anything can happen at any time." It simply means that the intrinsic logic of historical change has a purely negative influence upon the shaping of events. In other words, even though the "logic of history" excludes some possibilities in advance, positive decisions are explicable by motives not in any direct relation to that logic. "Accident" is often enough just the expression of embarrassment at our inability *so far* to discover the causes of a phenomenon; what today appears accidental, may be seen tomorrow as causally determined and necessary. But even if one day the whole history of mankind could be exhibited as an uninterrupted series of causal happenings, it would still not have the necessity of a logical deduction. With all the causal necessity thus detected in it, it would still remain logically contingent and justify a distinction between the "logically necessary" and the "contingently necessary." The application of the concepts of logic and logical necessity to history would still remain as inappropriate as ever. Even in this limiting case, phrases like the objective trends of evolution, the autonomy of the different cul-

tural achievements, the priority of prevalent style to the particular work of art, and all other assertions about the element
of "necessity" in history could still be understood only as desig-
nating resultants; how these things come about eludes our observation. As Engels says, we only see the individual factors
in history, the particular wills that engage and clash with one
another like the components of a parallelogram of forces; but
how the resultant emerges we do not see, and thus we easily
get the impression that some higher superpersonal force is at
work. It is an inescapable fact that in human society there is
always someone who wants to obstruct what another wills,
and that what actually comes about is something that no one
has willed or foreseen.[3]

It is evident that in the social structures of history generally, but especially those, like the styles of art, which manifest a
common spiritual character, we are concerned with results
whose origin and make-up is unknown and undiscoverable.
They are collective attitudes that realize what nobody actually
"intended" and more than anyone could have intended. The
Last Supper, the *Disputà,* the Sistine Chapel ceiling were intended, not the "High Renaissance." This latter is none the
less a phenomenon that one can discuss without falling into
mysticism or conceptual realism. Collective cultural tendencies
take on a mystical air only if one sees in them a hidden purposiveness and regards them as serving the purposes of the
world-spirit, expressing the logic of the economic relationships,
satisfying the urges of the unconscious, and so on; or again, if
one sees in their vicissitudes a rhythm, the constant repetition
of a formula, the periodicity of a wavelike movement, as the
various exponents of cultural cycles do.

Talk of such a rhythm is especially inappropriate in the
history of art, for any artistic tendency is in a way the result
of what has gone before, and this creates at any time a unique
situation in the historical process as a whole. The results of one

[3] Engels to Block, September 21, 1890. Cf. *Ludwig Feuerbach and
the Outcome of Classical German Philosophy,* in *Selected Works,* I, 417 ff.

stage of development become the starting-point for the next stage, each stage presupposing the experiences and achievements of the previous one, and so becoming totally different from a period in which these experiences and achievements were unknown. Greco-Roman or late-Gothic "baroque" cannot be set up as parallels to the baroque of the seventeenth century or of romanticism: the earlier "baroque" traits are elements in the later and play their part as historical raw material in the later periods. Rubens is one of the presuppositions of the art of Delacroix; but the latter does not merely start at a point beyond the limits of Rubens's art, but also breaks up Rubens's synthesis into its elements and employs these for his own purposes. Artistic styles cannot be repeated in the form they originally took; for since their first appearance they have never ceased persisting and exerting influence, playing their part in the development, and changing in the process. Delacroix can no longer see the world with the eyes of Rubens, because Rubens's way of seeing is only one factor in the make-up of his world-view, and Delacroix's aims represent a further stage of Rubens's artistic intentions. The only conceivable way—and that is a mere construction—in which a style could recur would be if two different cultures existed without any contact whatever; within the same cultural tradition there can only be further development, never simple repetition or the resumption of a stylistic tendency.

Notions about periodicity and cycles of culture are among the oldest products of philosophical thought about history. Myths of the Great Year are of immemorial antiquity, and the idea of the cycle of constitutions, as is well known, goes back to the Greeks. The eighteenth-century writer Vico speaks of the Ages of Gods, Heroes, and Men, Goethe of "spiritual epochs," Friedrich Schlegel of morphological stages in Greek literature. Hegel and Marx distinguish three, others two, recurrent stages of evolution.[4] The periodic recurrence of styles in the history of

[4] Cf. E. Rothacker: *Logik und Systematik der Geisteswissenschaften* (1948), p. 101.

art was talked of long before Wölfflin, and indeed the fact that
there are such things as species of the baroque was no discovery
of Wölfflin or Riegl, but of Nietzsche. [5] Riegl was, however,
the first who, on noting a similarity, *e.g.*, between Imperial
Roman and seventeenth-century portrait painting, attributed
this to a "higher law" governing those periods, and termed the
sort of universal history which brings together such widely
separated phenomena "the culminating point of art-historical
research." [6] Since his time this "higher law" has never ceased to
occupy the fancy of art historians. For wherever anything seems
to repeat itself, one quite properly looks for a rule. The art
historians' mistake lay not in their conclusions, but in their
philosophical presumption about the nature of history, the presumption that the stylistic analogies they discovered were true
parallelisms. And as for their designation of the method of comparative analysis of styles as the "culminating point of research,"
one is bound to remark that such analyses, by sharpening our
observation, at best provide a useful introduction to art history;
but when one tries to answer the main problems, the problems
of stylistic change and origins, they leave one hopelessly in the
lurch. Riegl hastens to add: "The more certain the results
provided by specialist research, the less chance of doubt about
the conclusion of universal history." [7] In fact, however, the
more advanced the condition of special research, the less appropriate it proves as a basis for universalistic constructions. The
more we know about the current conditions and the actual temporal relationships obtaining for any artistic production, the less
we feel inclined to talk of parallelism between styles. That
which in the art of different periods looks like recurrence of
the same stylistic principle is precisely the element that in a
historical treatment can most safely be ignored. For the most indubitable mark of progress in historical research is the achieve-

[5] Friedrich Nietzsche: *Menschliches, Allzumenschliches*, II, 144.
[6] Riegl: *"Kunstgeschichte als Universalgeschichte"* (1898), in *Gesammelte Aufsätze* (1929), p. 7.
[7] Ibid.

ment of an ever more precise differentiation between phenomena. Historical research at its height will aim to exhibit connections among contemporaneous things, but it will not attach
much importance to parallels between different epochs.

To contrast history with natural science as the sciences of
the "individual" and of the "general" respectively is a dangerous
simplification. It may well be that the individual plays a far
bigger part in the historian's picture of reality—though not in
the course of events themselves—than in the outlook of natural
science. But in itself everything is unique and distinguished
more or less sharply from everything else. The natural sciences
ignore more of the individual features of reality than historical
sciences because the former are more interested in processes
that will recur tomorrow or the day after than in what occurred yesterday or the day before. But even so, the historical
method is not altogether an individualizing method; it too aims
to establish connections among the objects of its research, to
bring these into a causal relation with one another, and to
relate various phenomena under a common concept, for example, that of a style or trend. History, too, sacrifices an immense amount of the complexity and fine gradations of its material. To preserve the utter individuality of every phenomenon
would permit no more than a description, at best, at the
cost of any sort of synthesis, but in fact any systematic research
aims to establish some common characteristics of a multiplicity
of objects, so that it may not be necessary to revert to the individual case every time that some question about the group
crops up. When we coin a concept like the "baroque," we
ipso facto leave out of account a great many traits of the works
of art referred to by this concept. And such a concept at our
disposal not only makes it easier to find the way through the
boundless complexity of the historical phenomena, each particular work thereby becoming either an instance or a modification of a type, but also provides us with a standard by which
to compare the various works and judge the representative
significance of each for history. But all this has to be paid for

by partially losing sight of the concrete features of the works, and such loss is tolerable only within certain limits. Once the works lose their historical character and come to be treated as mere illustrations of universal aesthetic categories, those limits have been decidedly overstepped; this is notably the case with art-historical syntheses of the sort that treats all the so-called "baroque styles" as one unitary species of artistic endeavor.

The only visible agent in history is the individual. One can indeed treat society as the proper matrix of historical events and make the social importance of these the criterion of their relevance for history. One cannot however plausibly maintain that the social group is the carrier of historical action in the sense in which an acting, thinking, feeling, and working human being is, nor deny that the functions of thinking and working belong to the individual alone. It is as little plausible to maintain that the individual always acts, thinks, or works spontaneously, on his own initiative. What conditions the behavior of the individual is not all on the psychological plane, and not everything that is accomplished through him is done on his own behalf. He always finds himself in a certain historical and social situation and behaves in accord with its requirements, often without realizing or intending this. Class situations and class interests are an objective, institutional structure, not a subjectively varying mental condition. The individual speaks on behalf of and acts for the sake of the group he belongs to; he is its mouthpiece and does not express only his private interests and aspirations. The real question is how far he is a product of his group—that is, how much of his behavior which one might explain psychologically must be explained sociologically and how much of the common attitude that he manifests is due to personal initiative.

Collective cultural forms, and notably the styles of art, are obviously not in their entirety the creation of particular individuals. As Ernst Gall remarks when speaking of the Gothic, they are not "invented," not produced all at once or according to plan. Rather, Engels's analogy of the parallelogram of forces

197

is appropriate; they are the by-product of acts and attitudes originally directed toward other goals. They must, however, have started from one particular creative idea, inspiration, or vision, which only an individual could have, even if this origin may now be undiscoverable. However impersonal or widely accepted as means of expression and standard of value a style may be, the first step in its formation is none the less a psychological act, something that cannot be attributed to an impersonal group.

Institutions, forms of thought and style, are products of social evolution, and that in two ways. Not only is everything that follows upon that first spontaneous act the result of cumulative mutual adaptation of individual aims and achievements, but even the first step, original and personal as it must have been, was taken in the light of social presuppositions. The individual was subject to the rule of habitually accepted modes of thought and generally approved modes of conduct before he could take that step, or indeed any autonomous action. He speaks the social language before he has found an idiom of his own, and indeed this latter is never more than a variant of the other. None the less, current, living, spoken language is always the product of interaction between the traditional language of the group and the linguistic creations of the various individuals. Without this ever-renewed and ever-changing personal contribution, the common inheritance would in the end be exhausted or become a lifeless aggregation.

Thus it is not sufficient to admit the existence of the individual: one must recognize him as the source of inexhaustible, ever-fresh spontaneity if one is to see him in the proper light. When Hegel declares that the "universal" has got to be realized by the "particular," Engels that social forces must work themselves out psychologically, they are both envisaging an individual hag-ridden by anonymous forces, one who is the indifferent and on the whole unchangeable substratum of historical processes. For just as in Hegel the "world-spirit" employs the individual as a mere instrument, so in Marxism the effect of the productive forces and the outcome of the class-war are independent of psychological motivation and personal aims, while the critical situations arise not out of relations among individuals, but between "economic subjects" such as workman and capitalist or buyer and seller. The individual as such is ultimately irrelevant for Marx, as for Hegel.

This now idealistic, now materialistic, opposition to individualism falsifies the character of historical change, but the opposite point of view, which treats everything going beyond the individual and the particular case, any general spiritual direction or persistent social structure, as insignificant abstractions, falsifies it no less. To reverse the Marxist thesis and assert that ideologies are the product of men and not men of ideologies is to simplify the actual situation. [8] Men do indeed create ideologies, but not without certain preconceptions. It is precisely in the creation of ideologies that the extraneous, superindividual, and interpersonal elements in thought are most strikingly manifest. Men do not make up ideologies at will; mental structures so worked out would be not ideologies, but mere fancies or poetical images. The seeming contradiction in the conception of man as both maker of ideologies—subject for psychology—and made by ideologies—subject for sociology— is not an insoluble one; it simply expresses his double nature as both an individual and a social being. The criticism to which he may subject the ideologies is not incompatible with ideological conditioning of his thought; nor does the social origin of his thought prevent him from setting himself in opposition to, and remaining in continuous tension with, the society whose spiritual offspring he is.

One of Riegl's followers asserts—not quite consistently with the teaching of his master—that "had the historian an unlimited power of penetrating into the facts, we could follow

---

[8] Erich Fromm: *"Die Entwicklung des Christusdogmas,"* *Imago* (1930), p. 367.

everything that happens in art back to an individual act of creation." [9] Ready as we may be to do justice to the creative role of the individual, we cannot accept this formulation. For if one is going to speak of unknown and unlimited depths of penetration, then there does not seem any reason for exponents of the collectivist view not to declare in their turn that, if one were to penetrate "deep enough," one would find nothing but impersonal, superindividual, intersubjective forces. The argument from the individual to the social can be carried on to an endless regress, just as can the argument from the social to the individual; in each direction there remains a final, unanalyzable remainder that is unknowable from the opponent's point of view. For though the novel and the unique aspects of a work of art make the notion of individuality indispensable, yet the individual is always to some extent a product of the social milieu in which he has his roots. The individual and the social group, spontaneity and convention, psychical constitution and external influences, nature and nurture, are all pairs of correlatives, each inseparable from and irreducible to the other. A certain species of plant may bear a certain sort of fruit, given certain conditions such as a certain quantity of rain and sunshine; in other climatic conditions the fruit turns out differently; another species of the same plant-family does not bear that sort of fruit under any conditions, whatever the amount of rain or sunshine. Each kind of fruit is the product of two totally independent sets of conditions, an inner constitution and external stimulation. By itself the biological classification of the plant no more explains the character of the fruit than does the nature of the environment in which it grows. In the same way, neither the individuality and special talent of the artist by itself, nor the institutions and traditions of his social milieu by themselves suffice to provide an adequate explanation of the peculiar character of a work of art. Not everything is possible at all times; also, that which is possible cannot be achieved

[9] Hermann Tietze: *Die Methode der Kunstgeschichte* (1913), p. 42.

by just anybody; there is need of the right kind of talent at the right time and the right place.

Yet even this account is a simplification of the true state of things. Individual and society, inner life and environment, originality and tradition, interpenetrate at the birth of a work of art in a far more complicated fashion than such talk of a duality of conditions would indicate. In reality, it is not just a question of how far the creative process was due to the one or the other of these factors, which of them was predominant, and whether the relation among them was a constant or a shifting one. The whole concept of a self-existent society and of a separate individual freely associating himself with it is false and misleading. We cannot think of personal and superpersonal forces as independent; individual and society are not to be thought of except in a mutual relation. Where there is no society, there are no individuals, whether in a logical, psychological, or historical sense. An individually feeling, thinking, acting, producing, creative personality only emerges by re-action; it embodies the answer to a question or the response to a challenge. An artist is formed only in the course of grappling with the task that has been set him and which he undertakes to solve. In the solution of that task his individuality realizes itself step by step; it was not there before, and can be portrayed only in connection with a certain situation that the concrete task has brought about. Without the soil of Italy and the world of the Renaissance, without Florence and Rome, without the Papal court and its commissions, without Perugino as teacher and Michelangelo as rival, there could have been no Raphael; there would have been a son of Giovanni Santi, but he would not have been the man we know as the creator of the *Stanze*-frescoes or of the *Arazzi*. No doubt, we can also say that without Raphael, the Renaissance would not have been the Renaissance or Rome Rome. It is not the case that Raphael was inspired by and caught up in the flood of the Renaissance that had been prepared for by the Florentines and Umbrians of the Quattrocento and was then being realized by the material and spiritual resources of Florence and Rome; nor is it the case that Raphael's genius either spontaneously created the High Renaissance or participated with a generation of exceptionally talented men in its creation. The fact is that the Renaissance and the artistic individuality of Raphael come into being all at once and inseparably. Not only is the performance, that is, the work of Raphael, Leonardo, and Michelangelo, the result of certain tasks, but the tasks themselves take on a definite shape only when the possible solutions are seen.

But just as the individuality as a whole must be analyzed into a series of questions and answers, challenges and responses, possibilities offering themselves in various forms and to be turned to account in various ways, so each particular feature of a spiritual tendency, each component of an artist's talent, must be viewed as something dialectically formed and analyzable into conflicting elements. Not only does the personality as a whole come into being through a direct contact and a continuous encounter with its environment, but also each manifestation of the personality is doubly conditioned, individually and socially. Every human being starts life with a few extremely primitive drives; all his more specifiable aims, his more specific capacities, the tasks he sets himself or accepts, and the way in which he copes with them—all that is the result of a tension that develops between himself and the world, and is renewed from day to day. A creature of drives becomes a "man" by becoming a social being; that he takes his moral birth from society does not, however, prevent him from entering into a dialectical relation, one of quarrels and reconciliations, with it.

The role of individuality in art is a phenomenon of complicated structure; it also, like most aspects of artistic creation, takes different historical shapes, and so is not a problem that admits of a single unequivocal answer. Just as in art no universal propositions can be laid down with regard to the relations of form and content, technique and expression, tradition and originality, so nothing can be said about individual and society in general, that is, without regard to particular historical conditions. In the course of history, the role of the individual as a creative power and a source of stylistic changes is continually altering; it may be enormous, or it may be rather slight. Since the Renaissance it has been constantly on the increase, and with the romantic era it took on previously inconceivable proportions. So anyone who studies the matter in the light of this last phase of evolution must come to different conclusions from such as might be based upon the study of the monuments of the Ancient Orient, or even of the Middle Ages. Extreme individualism is a social phenomenon, but individuality plays a large part in artistic creation even when there is a very complete renunciation of personal ambitions. Even to ages with absolutely no conception of individualism, individuality is nothing strange.

Although in the course of history, individual and social factors are ever-present, one finds in historical thought and writing a continual shifting of sympathies from individualism to determinism and vice versa, and that in a way which often runs counter to the prevailing trend of events. For example, since the end of the nineteenth century, in spite of the predominantly individualistic temper of the whole post-romantic era, historical writing and the philosophy of history have become more and more estranged from the type of world-view which revolves about the individual. The notion of "anonymous art history" is only one of many symptoms of this change, and Wölfflin has allies and sympathizers in all fields of historical research. Even Bernhard Berenson, pursuing as he does his own special scientific interests and purposes, proves to be of Wölfflin's party. Above all, the method by which, on purely stylistic grounds, he postulates and proceeds to construct new artistic personalities—for example, attributing a whole series of works formerly ascribed to Botticelli, Ghirlandajo, and Filippo or Filippino Lippi to a new, fictitious artist, "Amico

203

di Sandro" [1]—shows that he believes, if not in "art history without names," at any rate in "artists without biographies." Even more significant for the change that has taken place in history-writing is the theory put forward by Benedetto Croce, stimulated by Berenson's methodological discoveries. Croce makes a distinction of principle between the "aesthetic personality" and the "biographical personality" of the artist, and claims that the art critic and the art historian are only concerned with the former. "As a matter of fact," he writes, "in extreme cases, one and the same artistic personality may be divided among several biographical individuals, and again two or more artistic personalities may succeed one another or alternate with one another in the same individual." [2] Clearly, this "aesthetic personality" of Croce's is a mere construction, no more than a "subject" coordinated with a certain group of works of art, more or less after the fashion of the impersonal subject of logic. By the same method, one could just as well construct a subject to correspond to Wölfflin's "visual forms" without in any way violating his principle of anonymity.

In the sense of Nietzsche's dictum about the "irritability and rancor" of philosophers toward the sensual, Wölfflin's generation was eminently a generation of "philosophers." Its anti-individualism is anyhow in fundamental accord with those "ascetic ideals" for which philosophers, in Nietzsche's view, show such "predilection and cordiality." Its obsession with impersonal and superpersonal forces in history is so remarkable that one naturally asks oneself in the sense of Nietzsche: why does anyone need anti-individualistic ideals? What is the need for this whole apparatus of objectivity at any price, absolute values, unconditional validity, a legend of the timelessly human, of the timelessly good and beautiful, laws without a lawgiver, art without artists, art history without names or personal sponta-

[1] Bernhard Berenson: *The Study and Criticism of Italian Art* (1901), pp. 46 ff.
[2] Benedetto Croce: *"Zur Theorie und Kritik der Geschichte der bildenden Kunst," Wiener Jahrbuch für Kunstgeschichte,* IV (XVIII) (1926), p. 21.

neity? The answer was found long ago, and took various
forms. All this is needed, we are told, because man suffers
from anxiety, anxiety about himself, dread of the responsibility
that goes with freedom and self-determination. "It is so com-
fortable," said Kant, "not to be an adult." [3] That the "longing
for objectivity" is a state of mind in which "man demeans
himself into being a slave" is actually an assertion of Hegel, who
if anyone might be taken to speak for the "philosophical"
party.[4] Rejecting the privilege of being his own lawgiver, man
believes in eternal, superhuman, heaven-sent laws because he
would like to think that he finds these unalterably there, and
would like to participate in the inviolability of a revelation
that he but discovers and passes on to others. The calming
effect that may be had from ideas of universal validity, timelessness, and necessity comes from a sense of greater security.
It is restful to assume that in all the chaos of life, its continual
changes and chances, there is something upon which one can
lean and rely. It reconciles one with life to believe that with all
one's frailty, one has a share in some higher values, becoming
a steward and a possessor of these values directly one acknowledges their authority. But the most encouraging thing of all is
the illusion that in one's own soul, if one only knows how to
listen, a divine power speaks, and speaks unequivocally.

The alternative between accepting individual freedom
and accepting superindividual necessity is not always so clearly
seen; often it is colored by ambivalent emotions, so that there is
a fluctuation between extremes. As regards the present, perhaps
no other phenomenon of our culture exhibits its social contradictions, especially the contradiction of having a repressive class-
structure in an age of liberalism, so plainly as the views
commonly held about the authority and the limits of personality. On the one hand there is a philosophical absolutism that
denies the individual any independent value or enduring influence, seeing in him the source of all shortcomings and the

[3] Immanuel Kant: *Was heisst Aufklärung?*
[4] Hegel: *Philosophie des Rechts*, 141, Appendix.

origin of all delusions, but on the other a so-called "philosophy of life" is also current which is inclined in its turn to pay unlimited, even exaggerated, homage to the value of personal energy and spontaneity. These two different ideological attitudes evidently have their origin in the antinomies of free competition. The satisfaction accompanying a belief in absolute, supertemporal, and superhuman values is disintegrated by a torturing feeling that so ephemeral, transitory, fallible, continually deluded an individual as man cannot be anything enduring or certain, cannot have any real significance or substance. Out of this feeling of their nothingness which has been instilled into people, the protests that begin to be heard against depreciation of individuality are just the ideological counterpart of their readiness for action, to which their economic and social nothingness inclines them. Individualism as expression of this protest is an unmistakable product of the age of the enlightenment; later, the spiritual situation became complicated, through socialism diverging from its origins in the enlightenment and developing an anti-individualistic philosophy of history while its opponents developed a myth of individuality to glorify the "great man." Still, as long as the two attitudes are clear and the two camps clearly separate, we know where we are; both are symptoms of the estrangement of the individual from society, and each seeks to remedy this estrangement in a way that suits its own interests and purposes, the one party by insisting on the value of authority, the other by leveling differences. The situation gets confused and men's minds become clouded only when there is a shilly-shallying between the two points of view and men cannot make up their mind whether to come out in favor of the individual or not. Nothing is more typical of this state of mind than the current pseudo-historical literature written for a half-educated and politically half-hearted public; such literature shuffles about, undecided and ignorant, between idealizations of historical necessity and of personal freedom, between dramatizations of "historic destiny" and the legend of the "strong man" who defies the "iron laws" of history and is the natural leader. In such a situation any compromise must be suspect; but there still remains, as the only task worth attempting, the need to distinguish precisely the historical roles of the individual and the superindividual, and to do justice to them both without slipping into a mystical conception of either or, as so generally happens, of both.

5. *STYLE AND ITS CHANGES*

In no other field of spiritual activity does the individual, with his own particular aims and powers, play so important and striking a part as he plays in art. Nor is there any other field in which we have such well-tried means and methods for tracing general tendencies and describing collective factors in the development. The circumstance that so many works of the visual arts have survived without the names of their authors or any information regarding their date caused historians relatively early to look for signs of their place in the order of development, and on that basis to seek for some indications regarding their origin. Thus the conception of style came to be soonest and most systematically developed in connection with the visual arts; and art history, once in possession of that concept, became in a way the model for all research in the sphere of cultural history. In speaking of "styles of thought" or "styles of economic organization," and picturing these as currents buoying up and carrying along even the independent-minded and the obstinate, writers were employing, although as a rule unconsciously, a mode of thought which originated in the history of art and gradually spread to other fields.

The concept of "style" is central and fundamental to art history. Without it, we could at best have a history of artists, in the sense of an account of the various masters working contemporaneously or successively, together with a catalogue of their certain and their doubtful works. We could have no history of the common trends and generally accepted forms that link the works of an epoch, a nation, or a region and enable us to speak of art as manifesting development or expressing a movement. Above all, style is the basic concept of art history because its fundamental problem can be formulated only in terms of this concept. The concept of style derives from the paradoxical fact that the endeavors of several artists working separately and often independently are found to exhibit a common direction, that their individual aims are unconsciously subordinated to an impersonal, superindividual trend, and— seemingly insoluble contradiction of art history—that an artist, by giving free rein to his own impulses, produces something that goes beyond what he actually intended. Style is the ideal unity of a whole that consists in a lot of concrete and disparate elements. But the clearest proof that the concept of style and that of art history are co-ordinate lies in the fact that the criteria of stylistic quality and the criteria of what is relevant for art history are the same. To be able to answer the question of what it is that confers upon a certain line in art production the dignity of a "style" is also to answer another question, the question of which facts in the field of art are objects for the history of art. The genius entirely left to himself and owing nothing to anyone but himself or, again, the utterly isolated, microcosmic works of art, as these have been represented by academic aesthetics with its unhistorical idea of eternal and universal values, these—could they really exist—would neither exhibit any stylistic features nor be the objects of art history. What is timeless must be style-less.

The most elementary criterion for the presence of a style lies in an agreement in respect of a number of artistically significant traits among the works of a certain limited cultural area or period. This mark of agreement holds also for those cases in which we find several competing integrative tendencies alongside one another. A second criterion consists in a certain

fairly wide diffusion of the common traits, a quantitative principle corresponding to Eduard Meyer's "effectiveness." Some
trends in art, however, exert an important influence only later,
thus earning a place in history which they did not originally
have. In addition, it is usual to adduce an aesthetic criterion of
style, making this consist in the particularly clear and definite
use of a common formal language and in an almost instinctive
certainty of touch in the employment of the available means.
What is meant is a sense for an acceptable standard of work
which influences the artist at times when his own powers of
invention or discrimination desert him. But a standard of this
kind, which is not so much upheld by the individual as serving
to uphold him, can be regarded by art history, with its
empirical outlook, merely as the residue of some convention,
which must have arisen out of the contributions of individuals
in the process of achieving general acceptance.

The questionable character of the concept of style and the
consequent troubles for a theory of art history arise in the main
from the fact that a style has to be thought of as something
general, thought in abstraction from the individual artist and
the individual work, but yet not as a "higher," Platonic, or
Hegelian idea, exemplar, model, standard of value, or norm.
Style is neither a genetic nor a teleological concept; it is
neither set before the artist nor accepted by him as a goal. It
is neither a species-concept under which particular phenomena
are subsumed nor yet a logical category from which other
concepts could be derived. It is rather a dynamic relational
concept with continually varying content, so that it might almost be said to take on a new sense with each new work. And
yet, as said above, it by no means implies anything like Hegel's
progressively self-realizing and self-revealing world-spirit. The
concept has nothing to do with the purposiveness of a world-
plan or with participation of individuals in a supernatural
reality. A style is no more than the result of many conscious
and purposive achievements; it cannot itself be said to have

been consciously or deliberately originated; it is not part of the consciousness for any of the individuals whose products are the substrata of its being.

The dual nature of a style, entailing as it does a definite directive, yet not one of which the individuals affected are necessarily aware or which they necessarily follow, leads historians inclined to idealism to see in this concept the veritable key to the understanding of art, whereas positivists deny it any kind of reality or relevance, declaring art-styles, like all other historical wholes, to be mere abstractions. Neither school of thought does justice to the real character of structures such as capitalism, the enlightenment, the Renaissance, visuality in painting, or the form of classical tragedy, for neither takes full account of their insubstantiality, on the one hand, and, on the other, of their special sort of significance and degree of independence. For a proper appreciation of them, one must recognize that these "structures" are neither concrete nor yet constructions. Positivism overlooks the fact that a certain appropriate, although not unvarying, type of rationality is at work in each field of culture; idealism fails to recognize that the structural principles underlying such historical unities are not the motive forces of history, but configurations whose influence derives from the essentially institutional basis of culture. Historical structures such as tradition, convention, level of technique, prevailing artistic effects, current rules of taste, or topical subjects set objective, rational, superpersonal goals and bounds to the irrational spontaneity of psychological functioning, and in co-operation with this latter produce what we call a "style."

A style is a structure that cannot be derived from the qualities of the works that "carry" it, whether by addition or by abstraction. The Renaissance style is at once more and less than what has actually been expressed in the works of the Renaissance masters. It is something like a musical theme of which only variations are known. The theme, if one tried to reconstruct it, would be neither a sum of the variations, nor a selection of motifs from them, nor yet an abstract compendium of all the identical features found in the variations. A sum can never include more, an abstract always includes less, than the total aggregate from which it is derived. A musical theme, on the other hand, may perhaps contain hardly a single actual element of any of the variations, and yet may exhibit the particular musical thought with a clarity not to be found in any of the variations. It is indeed possible to construct several different themes for a given series of variations, but that does not alter the fact that each series has its own musical structure. The structure is there, whether or not we are particularly successful in formulating it. Not merely the variations, but also the various attempts to formulate the theme itself—corresponding in our analogy to various definitions of the Renaissance style—only circle around a structure without apprehending it completely or finally.

The phenomenon of a structure that persists when every single *concrete* component of it is altered, was, as is well known, first observed and described by the *Gestalt* psychologists. Their results are in the main applicable also to the analysis of the concept of style, which is evidently the concept of a *Gestalt,* or configuration. As the *Gestalt* psychologists, from whom this musical illustration derives, pointed out, we recognize a familiar melody even when played in a key in which we never heard it played before. The question that then arises is by what do we recognize it when all the notes are completely changed. Everything that can strictly speaking be heard is altered, and yet the melody, which surely consists of nothing audible but the notes, which are now utterly different, has remained the same. We grasp it as a complex, a "structure," a sequence of intervals which is indeed expressed through the notes, but not in the notes. This structure is no less real than the actual sounding notes, although nothing of it is actually sensed; we certainly experience it directly and do not just infer it. Now, in art-style one is faced by a very similar phenomenon. Beyond any doubt or equivocation "there is" a Renaissance style, although it "is" in a very different way from *e.g.*, the works of Leonardo or Raphael. What, on the other hand, there "is not" is the beauty, or the ideality, or the common palette of these works; *these* really are mere abstractions which do not add to the content of the concepts they comprehend.

Considerations of *Gestalt* theory also focus a sharper light upon the obvious, but seldom discussed analogy between styles and languages. In both cases we have to do with modifications of a basic form that does *not* exist. There are styles but there is no "style," just as there are languages but there is no "language." That is to say, there is no more a stylistically neutral art than there is a mode of linguistic expression bearing no traces of any historical epoch or ethnic group. As in language, so in art, there are only "dialects"; an art devoid of style is as unthinkable as a world-language unaltered and "uncorrupted" in daily use. "Style" as such is an abstraction, as Esperanto is an artefact, but the particular styles are no more abstractions than are the English, German, and French languages with their grammatical systems, characteristic word-formation, and idiomatic expressions.

The concept of *Gestalt* exhibits unmistakable analogies with the concept of organism in the romantic philosophy of history; each signifies a whole given, in the Aristotelian and Husserlian sense, as "prior" to the parts. The conception of style as a *Gestalt* and the conception of it as an "organic" structure have at any rate this in common: they both purport to designate not a sum of characteristics, but a directly given unity and essential identity of these characteristics. Droysen's definition of historical method, according to which "the particular is to be understood through the whole and the whole through the particulars,"[5] nowhere shows its worth more signally than in art history. But some of the theses of the doctrine of organism are by no means applicable to the concept of style. For example, the assumption that a style finds expression in the entire artistic production of an epoch or a region,

[5] J. G. Droysen: *Grundriss der Historik* (1858), p. 9.

in great works and slight, in the monumental and in the minutest detail of decoration, everywhere with the same intensity and completeness, is untenable. In fact, some styles are more "organic," more homogeneous than others. Just as the individual artist does not always express himself with the same concentration or vigor, so the characteristics of a style are not equally clearly or typically expressed in all instances of a species. The nature of a style is not that of a schema to be applied again and again, but rather that of a pattern not to be found entire in any concrete instance. It should be regarded as an ideal case, not completely corresponding to any particular case, or as a type not exhaustively realized in any individual. In this respect the concept of style has a number of features in common with Max Weber's "ideal type"—among others those which distinguish it from a logical category on the one hand and from a metaphysical idea on the other. "Capitalism" or "the medieval town," to take two of Weber's own examples, are ideal types, in that they do not designate the "essence" of actually occurring phenomena, but a clarified and exaggerated model of these. Their "ideality" consists in the fact that they exhibit certain components of these phenomena in a "pure state," as it were. A style too, as Max Weber says of his ideal type, is a kind of "Utopia"; [6] the reality, that is, the particular work of art, never actually attains to it. It is neither a claim to be met nor an ideal to be realized, nor a problem to be solved, but rather a mean that one must keep in view in order to see any given concrete instance in the right proportions. According to Weber, his ideal type is an "ideal limiting concept," "against which the reality is *measured* and *compared* in order to bring out more clearly certain important constituents of its empirical content." [7] The chief historical function of the concept of style is just this: it serves as a standard for judging the extent to which

[6] Weber: *"Die 'Objektivität' sozialwissenschaftlicher und sozial-politischer Erkenntnis," Gesammelte Aufsätze zur Wissenschaftslehre,* p. 191.
[7] Ibid., p. 195.

a particular work is representative of its time or of a certain aspect of its time and the closeness of its connection with other works of the same time or the same general type.

However, between Weber's ideal type and the concept of style in art history there is at any rate one important difference. The ideal types are merely auxiliary concepts, *i.e.*, heuristic constructions without any kind of reality, and we cannot ascribe any sort of reality to them without, as Weber puts it, falling into conceptual realism. But the styles are not auxiliary concepts, labels, chapter-headings for the historian, but historical facts, which though never so accessible to the senses as the feelings and conceptions expressed in the works of art, show that they are real primarily because the artist is always in a state of greater or less tension with them. For an artist of the fifteenth century, the Renaissance is something objective and concrete, making itself felt in all sorts of ways whether he has at all a clear conception of it as a stylistic movement or whether he is just carried along by it, consciously accepts it, or consciously resists it. "The" medieval town, on the other hand, never existed, there were only particular medieval towns to which the ideal type of medieval town stands in much the same relation as the concept of "style" to the various concrete styles, not in the relation of the Renaissance style to the particular works of the Renaissance masters. "The" medieval town is just a construction, a Utopia, not a reality to be experienced or the object of any psychological process. The example of "capitalism" is rather more complicated because the word can signify either an ideal type or an actually occurring style of economic organization; in the one case it designates an "ideal" remote from reality, in the other an existent form, a system of institutions and modes of behavior, all of which have their history and neither are values nor represent standards of value.

According to Weber, ideal types can be framed for the most varied objects of experience, for spiritual movements as well as for institutions, for historical and systematic conceptions, for collective and also for individual phenomena. In a certain sense, one can speak of the ideal type of Julius Caesar or Napoleon, intending thereby an ideal of personality realizable in varying degrees. But whatever the advantages of this way of looking at things in sociology or psychology, it does not appear particularly fruitful when applied to the concept of style in art history—as, for example, by Riegl, whose concept of "artistic intention" in a way anticipates Weber's "ideal type" in its dual—collective and individual—aspect. As is well known, Riegl speaks of the "artistic intention" of seventeenth-century Dutch painting, but equally of the "intention" of the group portrait, the "intention" of the various Dutch towns, schools, and masters, even the "intention" of an individual work. His aim in thus distinguishing the formal structure from the concrete object is clear enough; the question is whether such an extension of the concept of style, whereby the idea of development is left out of sight, is advantageous or not.

Riegl's concept of style in many respects shows that he is still under the influence of the romantic philosophy of organism. The chief feature of the "artistic intention" of a certain time consists in the fact that its formal principle imposes itself with equal force and immediacy in all the artistic manifestations of an epoch, the most pompous and the meanest alike. Riegl stresses the unity of stylistic character, the consistency and necessity of development which he assumes must be found within a given unitary phase of art history.[8] But this alleged stylistic uniformity of a historical epoch is pure fiction; for in fact the art of any epoch not only divides up by schools, generations, social classes, educational strata, and other groups with common interests, but even within these often shows irreconcilable contrasts. Riegl himself, when he comes to such objects as the Vafio cups, finds himself obliged to speak in this connection of "anachronistic features."[9]

[8] Riegl: *Stilfragen* (1893), pp. 20, 24. *Die spätrömische Kunstindustrie* (1901), p. 138 n. Cf. Max Dvořák: "Alois Riegl," *Mitteilungen der k.k. Zentralkommission für Denkmalpflege,* Vol. III (1905), No. 4, p. 271.

[9] Riegl: *Gesammelte Aufsätze,* p. 57.

For Riegl, the circumstances in which a style originates exhibit the same uniformity as its products. In both respects his view is conditioned by the spiritualistic philosophy that expressed a reaction against the current naturalistic outlook of his time. He attacks Gottfried Semper as representative of that outlook, and develops his own theory of "artistic intention" in the course of a polemic against Semper's materialism and pragmatism. For Semper, art is nothing but a by-product of handicraft, the current style-forms arising more or less mechanically from the qualities of the material, the technique of working it up, and the use to be made of the product. Riegl's definition of style as an act of "will" (Kunst*wollen*) is the almost inevitable consequence of his rejection of any theory making the producer's "abilities" and "necessities," along with his technique and material, the formative cause of styles. Riegl's central thesis—that the artist at all times could make what he wanted to make, instead of just having to make what lay in his power to make—expresses an idealistic rather than a specifically voluntaristic outlook. His terminology, indeed, is not altogether happy. His designation of the artistic impulse as a "willing" is not, as some critics have affirmed, so unsatisfactory because it is too psychological, but because it restricts too narrowly the psychical process that he wished to emphasize. Riegl's chief concern is, on the one hand, to stress the spiritual sovereignty of the artist in relation to his material conditions and, on the other, to lay down the principle that there are innumerable legitimate ways in which the human spirit may express itself, so that every style is to be judged by its own proper standards of beauty and truth. The ideas are closely connected, for if each age is sovereign in respect to the means it employs, then its achievements must be judged according to the aims then current, and all comparative evaluation of the works of different ages is evidently senseless and misleading. If every style can accomplish what it wants to accomplish, then any apparent lack of skill is really a case of not-wanting, and every work of art sets its own standard of

216

value and is its own justification. Thus every stage in the evolution of art is equally valuable and indispensable, or, in Ranke's phrase, "in direct relation with God" (*unmittelbar zu Gott*). The analogy is an illuminating one, for like Ranke's dictum, the theory of artistic intention is meant as a protest against the "mediatizing of an epoch through a subsequent epoch." [1] Riegl, too, only wants to prevent people from looking at one epoch simply as a stage on the way to the next and thus falling into the notion that one style is superseded by another. To such lengths does he go in his rejection of all differences of value between the styles that he is ready to eliminate from art history all questions of artistic quality and to declare that the best art historian is a man "who has no taste of his own." Absurd as this point of view is in itself, it represents, as Max Dvořák rightly observes, "a victory over the aestheticizing type of art history," a triumph of the historical outlook over a much narrower one.

The doctrine of the equal value and incommensurability of all styles starts with the thesis that in the history of art there is neither progress nor decline, that one must get rid of the "periods of florescence" and "periods of decay" so characteristic of the older type of art history. This does not mean simply, as has been supposed,[2] that in art every innovation is a gain—for to set all styles upon the same level is as incompatible with the idea of progress as with that of regress. It simply asserts that each step in the evolution has a unique function and an irreplaceable value of its own. An apparent degeneration is, according to Riegl, often the very harbinger of a new artistic intention and the surest sign that the birth of a new style is imminent. Thus, for example, the disappearance of the free-standing figure from the sculpture of the fifth century of our era, which used to be taken as an obvious sign of decay,

[1] O. Hintze in *Zeitschrift für die gesamte Staatswissenschaft* (1926), LXXXI, 56.
[2] O. Pächt in *Kritische Berichte zur kunstgeschichtlichen Literatur* (1937), Vol. VI, No. 3–4, p. 6.

is the symptom of a new requirement destined to be satisfied by a shift from the classical haptic values towards the optic values upon which modern art rests. The most fruitful part of Riegl's work consists in revaluations of this kind; and the fact that so much of modern art-historical literature is devoted to the rehabilitation of the so-called ages of decline is in great part to be ascribed to Riegl's influence. In such revaluations and reinterpretations the circumstances of the historian's own time no doubt play a decisive part. The rehabilitation of late Roman art by Riegl and Wickhoff would have been impossible apart from the crisis of the classical-romantic period and the modern decadence movement with its preference for "silver ages." So Wölfflin's justification of the baroque would have been impossible without the dynamic vision of impressionism, Dvořák's re-discovery of mannerism impossible apart from the existence of expressionism and surrealism. Indeed, perhaps the whole theory of "artistic intention" and its variants and derivatives was just the outcome of a time that had experienced too many and too abrupt changes to have any confidence in the unconditionality of its own standards of value.

It was certainly worth while to remind us that no good purpose is served by looking for something in a work of art that the artist would not or could not put into it because it was beyond what he could think or experience and incompatible with the requirements, views, and feelings of his public. No danger for the art historian is so great as the temptation to compare the works of an older, more primitive art with those of a later, historically more advanced, epoch on the assumption that the artists were all the time pursuing the same aims, the later ones more successfully than the earlier. Yet, the correct principle, that we should not expect of an artist or generation of artists achievements lying outside the range of what was historically possible to them, does not imply that there can be no difference of value among the modes of conception and representation proper to the different epochs. Whether one feels any such difference when comparing two styles like the Ren-

aissance and the baroque may be doubted, but that for example the classicism of the Renaissance and that of around 1800
are on two different planes of artistic importance is indubitable.
And in the same way, from the correct insight that a work is
best judged by the historian according to the principles of its
own stylistic ideals, it by no means follows that no tension
ever exists between what an artist intends and what he can
accomplish. In reality, not only do we often see incompetent
individual works, but it is possible for all the known examples
of a style, *e.g.*, the works of early Christian painting, to fall far
short of what their creators are likely to have intended.

Plausible as it may seem, it is simply not true that the
artist as representative of a style can do anything he wants to
do, or—according to one interpretation of Riegl's thesis—that
he cannot even will anything except what he is able to achieve.
In line with the theory of "artistic intention," it has been
asserted, for example, that Polygnotus did not paint naturalistic
landscapes because he did not want to, not at all because he
could not.[3] All proof of this assertion is lacking; and just as
good arguments can be given for the contrary point of view.
One attempt to mediate between the two views holds that
Polygnotus "neither wanted to nor could paint a naturalistic
landscape, because that mode of representation would have
contradicted the immanent intention of fifth-century Greek
art."[4] Now, perhaps in that particular case both ability and will
were lacking, but there certainly are other cases in which, for
example, an artist cannot cope with the naturalistic intention
that inspires him, and others in which a naturalistic type of
skill persists and sets a standard of skill, although an antinaturalistic style is already making itself felt. And why adduce
such a difficult and vague conception as "the immanent intention of fifth-century Greek art" when it is simply a case of
conditions in which both the tradition of skill necessary for

[3] G. Rodenwaldt in *Zeitschrift für Aesthetik*, XI, 123.
[4] Panofsky: *"Der Begriff des Kunstwollens," Zeitschrift für Aesthetik*,
XIV, 330.

"being able" and the conventional basis for "wanting" to produce a naturalistic landscape were lacking. There may well have been some isolated personal attempts of the most various kinds then, as there always are; but for the formation of a style there must be some general practice of art to which the individual can attach himself or a consensus of taste upon which he can rely. Only in this sense can we accept the term "immanent intention" in art history. One should be the more cautious because it is just as easy to envelop a whole period as an individual in a heroizing, mystical aura. Assertions such as the following: "The individual artist can fail, but the artistic intention of the age is bound to be fulfilled"[5] or "No doubt, there are various kinds of clumsiness; but they are not to be regarded as attempts to be skilful . . . There are clumsy artists, but there are no clumsy styles"[6] derive from the same mythologizing impulse that holds the genius infallible and works of art immortal.

Wölfflin asserted, here in full agreement with Riegl, that "art has always been able to accomplish what it wanted";[7] but what he, and Riegl as well, was really concerned to do was not to personify and heroize particular ages, but rather to spiritualize and idealize the entire course of history by emphasizing the necessity with which the process of history accomplishes itself. For Riegl and Wölfflin no gap could exist between wanting and being able—for their historicist outlook any period of artistic development must be just as essential and purposeful as any other. Again, all stylistic periods must be of equal value, for otherwise there would be a deficiency in the meaningfulness and necessity that expresses itself in all phenomena of historical existence. The treatment of art history as a history of problems is another consequence of the view that in the historical process an inevitable evolution according to intrinsically meaningful laws finds its expression. What hap-

[5] H. Tietze: op. cit., p. 14.
[6] André Malraux: *Les Voix du silence*, p. 130.
[7] Wölfflin: *Kunstgeschichtliche Grundbegriffe*, p. 249.

pened had to happen, and so it seems to have been the solution of problems already set by what went before. Wölfflin's principle of immanent causation can be discerned in Riegl, and even his depersonalizing of artistic development, which with the idea of "anonymous" art history has become a program, is anticipated when Riegl represented changes of style as reconciliations of "latent conflicts." For Riegl and Wölfflin, the history of forms and the history of problems are interchangeable concepts, as in both they see the manifestation of the same impersonal, ineluctably self-realizing principle. In their eyes the history of art is the history of such problems as the representation of space, the organization of groups, and the transformation of a plastic-linear into a painterly representation; this is because they consider that there is a stricter logical relation among the various phases in such cases of purely formal change than there is among the phases of evolution of any of the other factors in art. That the formalistic point of view should come to be the predominant one in art history, so that from the turn of the century art history was taken to be primarily the history of forms, would have been inconceivable but for the rise of impressionism and the theory of "art for art's sake." Even Dvořák saw in formal problems the ultimate motive force behind all development in art. But in the end he underwent a reaction against so one-sided a view, and this reaction led him later to employ and develop in a more and more thoroughgoing fashion the method of the history of ideas (*Geistesgeschichte*), partly as the result of the impression made on him by Ernst Heidrich's criticism of Riegl's principles.[8] In Dvořák's work, the "strange timelessness" that in Riegl pervades the world of art gradually gives way to a different mode of portrayal, one more appropriate to the historical nature of the material. There are indeed still some remnants of the old belief in historical necessity, and Dvořák seems not to have

---

[8] Ernst Heidrich: Review of Jantzen's *Niederländisches Architekturbild* in *Beiträge zur Geschichte und Methodologie der Kunstwissenschaft* (1917).

taken much notice of Heidrich's conclusion, his assertion about the "thousand and one accidents" of history.

In contrast with Riegl, Dvořák emphasizes the strict continuity of the evolutionary process, founding his whole philosophy of art history upon this concept, which is certainly a fruitful one, though tending to result in rather too drastic generalizations. In any case, he achieves a more flexible view of the course of artistic development than Riegl's, and one less impaired by logical preconceptions.[9] The evolution of art appears to him to be essentially a continual struggle, carried on with ever-increasing technical skill, to master the problems of representing nature—so that for him the history of art actually is reduced to a history of naturalism.[1] The fruitfulness of this strictly evolutionary method showed itself in Dvořák's researches into the art of the brothers Van Eyck.[2] These researches were, in fact, the first successful attempt to solve the "riddle" of their art by putting it in its proper place in the continuous stylistic development of the West and to grasp the history of Western art as a unity by breaking down the barriers that had been erected between medieval idealism and modern naturalism. For, however various the results of the development may be when considered in detail, it retains, for Dvořák, the character of a continuous progress.

For Riegl, on the contrary, there is nothing constant or consistent even about "nature"; his doctrine of the uniqueness and absolute value of each epoch taken by itself is as little compatible with steady progress in the reproduction of nature as with the steady pursuit of any other unchangeable goal. "Every art-style," he writes, "aims at the faithful reproduction of

[9] Dvořák: *"Les Aliscans,"* in *Beiträge zur Kunstgeschichte Franz Wickhoff gewidmet.* Also in *Gesammelte Aufsätze zur Kunstegeschichte* (1929).

[1] Dvořák: Review of Cohn-Wiener's *Die Entwicklungsgeschichte der Stile* in *Kunstgeschichtliche Anzeigen* (1910), No. 2, pp. 32–4.

[2] Dvořák: *"Die Illuminatoren des Johann von Neumarkt,"* in *Jahrbuch der kunsthistorischen Sammlungen des Allerhöchsten Kaiserhauses,* XXII (1901). *"Die Rätsel der Kunst der Brüder van Eyck,"* Ibid. (1904; 2nd ed., 1925).

nature and nothing else; but each has its own mode of apprehending nature." [3] Thus nature also takes on a historical character; not only do the means of representing it change, but
the tasks it presents to the artist change also. It is therefore
senseless to speak of naturalistic and unnaturalistic styles;
for there can be no question of getting closer to or farther
away from nature, but only of adopting one or another conception of nature. Art history is thus concerned not with various
phases in the attempt to reproduce nature, but with various
conceptions of what is natural. Whereas for Riegl the successive
emergence of these conceptions and their mutual relations
indicate no sort of progress or continuity, Dvořák sees in every
instance in which we speak of artistic development a progressive mastery of the real and an ever-mounting stock of naturalistic achievements. The picture which this point of view discloses
is clear and unambiguous. The naturalism of the early Renaissance is seen to be the direct continuation of the endeavors of
the late Gothic. The High Renaissance, again, in spite of its
idealism and stylizing tendency, represents a tremendous
advance in the reproduction of nature; Raphael's and Michelangelo's figures are not only more sublime, but also "more
correctly drawn," than those of Filippo Lippi or Signorelli. The
baroque triumphs over numberless difficulties in the reproduction of nature which no previous style could manage, among
them the more suggestive representation of spatial depth, the
effects of light, expression of psychological nuances, dramatic
concentration, the problems of depicting landscapes and in-
teriors. The eighteenth century attained the zenith of the
whole Renaissance period in the effortlessness and virtuosity of
its portrayal of nature. Even the works of the classicist David,
and still less those of Géricault or Delacroix, do not betoken a
relapse in respect to the observation of nature. The naturalistic
triumphs of Courbet, Daumier, and the impressionists bring us
to the summit. Thereafter the crisis of naturalism sets in, one of
the great breaks in the history of art, a fact certainly not

[3] Riegl: *Die spätrömische Kunstindustrie*, p. 212.

ignored by Dvořák or toned down in the interests of his theory. On the contrary, it led him to take the crises in the history of art, above all the early Christian and the manneristic periods, as the main subject of his later researches, and to revise his doctrine of the unbroken continuity of artistic evolution.[4]

Dvořák's theory of this evolution as a continuous and cumulative aggregation of achievements is at any rate a great improvement upon the theory of historical cycles, for it clearly shows that the position with respect to the problems of art never is and never can be the same at two different times in history. Its axiom of the indestructible and imperishable nature of all that happens, of the unbroken continuance and influence of all that is achieved, is indeed truer to the nature of history than the doctrine of inevitable cyclical recurrence; but this theory is no less than Riegl's a stylization of the facts. History is no more a continuous flow without gaps or breaks than it is a patchwork of bits and pieces or the scene of regular periodic change. And though Dvořák in the end modified his thesis of unbroken continuity, he still overlooked the fact that the sequence of history is being constantly interrupted without ever coming to a standstill. It is not sufficient to note that within a culture the threads of tradition are never quite broken; one should also recognize that tradition never propagates itself without friction, that it is never entirely free from disturbances and interruptions. At every moment it is threatened by more or less perceptible crises, more or less serious catastrophes. The history of culture is the scene of continual, but irregular and inconstant, change. Or more precisely, in the web of culture there are always both continuous and discontinuous threads; some break off while others remain unbroken. A simultaneous breaking of all threads would signify a cultural catastrophe of which the history of the West offers no example. Equally, there is no example of all threads remaining unbroken, even over a

[4] Dvořák: Review of Marie Gothein's *Geschichte der Gartenkunst* in *Gesammelte Aufsätze* (1929).

very short time. The religious life of a period may be shaken by the most violent crises while art and literature go quietly on in the old forms. In one form of art, say painting, a radical change may take place, while in another, say music, the old style is still bringing forth a wealth of achievement. Even within the same category of art there may be a revolution with respect to some of the means of expression while others continue to be employed in the traditional way. New subjects and problems may be handled in worn-out literary forms, new forms tried out upon familiar and even thoroughly exhausted topics. The historic life of culture and art consists in the taking up and dropping of various lines in the tradition, in the lead passing from one voice to another in a concert that sounds sometimes more harmonious, sometimes less. This is approximately what we should mean when we speak of continuity and discontinuity in history, for we must think of a continuity of the whole compatible with manifold discontinuities in the parts.

Dvořák in the latest phase of his work came closer to Riegl not only through the modifications he made in his doctrine of historical continuity, but also by maintaining, with ever-greater emphasis, the fundamental unity of all spiritual manifestations of an epoch. "The idea that the men of a single generation might manifest different feelings and intentions in, say, poetry, religion and art, is absurd"—so runs a characteristic passage in his lectures of 1918–1920 on the History of Italian Art in the Age of the Renaissance.[5] But such spiritual monism is just as dogmatic as the materialistic monism based on the idea that the economic conditions of production are constitutive—and constitutive to the same extent—of all the human activities of an age. By recognizing that the motivation for a change of style belongs to general cultural history, he freed himself from the dogma of the self-sufficiency of the aesthetic sphere; but he could not bring himself to give up the doctrine

[5] M. Dvořák: *Geschichte der italienische Kunst im Zeitalter der Renaissance,* II (1929), 113.

of the self-sufficiency and unity of the spiritual. Nothing was farther from his thought than that the inner consistency of the spirit of an age might perhaps be a fiction, that a cross-section through the stream of events might present as much differentiation as a longitudinal section. However, he did become ever more keenly aware of the manifold nature of the differences that emerge in the subsequent phases of history, coming finally to the important discovery that what changes as time goes on is not only art forms and styles, but also the very conception of art itself. Not only does the Renaissance, for example, approach art with requirements, standards, and tastes different from those of the Middle Ages; art signifies for it, also, something different from what it signified to the centuries when life centered upon faith and the Church. Art now becomes a new, autonomous region of the spiritual cosmos, a middle kingdom that cannot be incorporated into either the empirical or the supernatural realm, and within which the artist may henceforth move freely and feel that he is a law to himself. This idea too reminds one of Riegl: just as Riegl had transformed the concept of "nature" into something historical and relative, so Dvořák makes the concept of "art" at once historical and dynamic, and ends by asserting that, instead of the history of art moving within a framework of timeless aesthetic categories, these categories develop and alter in history.

Every art historian frames his conception of style with his eye upon the problem of breaks, changes, and fresh starts. Every writer is in the end confronted by the same question: why does the continuous development, the progressive differentiation and intensification, of a style-form come to an end at a certain point in time? Why do events then take a new turn, and men begin searching for new standards of beauty and truth? Why does the old formula no longer satisfy? If one is not content with the answer given by the doctrine that all such changes are immanently caused, and looks for a psychological or sociological explanation of the changes in question, then one will probably light first upon some form or other of the exhaustion theory.[6] But the explanation of so complex a phenomenon as a change of style by the employment of such concepts as satiation, nervous fatigue, and increasingly violent stimulation to counter this fatigue, is not much more satisfactory than the recourse to an inner logic of evolution. For the exhaustion theory, in spite of its kernel of truth, exhibits all the defects of the psychologistic method, which makes the different psychological functions operate in such water-tight compartments that nothing of the real unity and identity of personal life seems to be left. This theory ignores the fact that the sense of form, which, if continuously subjected to the same stimulus becomes, in the end, insensitive, does not have a separate existence, but is only part of a single operative whole and can quite well be re-awakened and re-vitalized by what is going on elsewhere in the psyche. Antiquated art-forms often change their function and arouse new interest that saves them from oblivion. The retention of frontality throughout the art of the Ancient Orient, of central perspective throughout the whole period of the Renaissance, of chiaroscuro throughout the otherwise very varied painting of the seventeenth century, shows how untiring a pleasure was taken in the same kind of thing throughout long periods in which a conservative type of art was practiced.

The exhaustion theory is also based on a logical error. As has been correctly observed,[7] it attributes a phenomenon of individual psychology to a superindividual subject of historical events, by treating the cumulative effect of impressions that can cause fatigue in an individual as if this were a process that went on for generations. It simply treats the successive generations as a psychological unity and assumes that they will behave just like a single organized and conscious being—assumes, in fact, a continuity of experience which only obtains in the experience of a single individual. In any case, the exhaustion

---

[6] Cf. Adolf Göller: *Zur Aesthetik der Architektur* (1887). Fr. Carstanjen: *"Entwicklungsfaktoren der niederländischen Frührenaissance," Vierteljahrsschrift der Wissenschaftlichen Philosophie* (1896), XX, 11 ff. Carl Lange: *Sinnesgenüsse und Kunstgenuss* (1903), p. 25.

[7] W. Wundt: *Völkerpsychologie,* III (1904), 2nd ed., pp. 267 ff.

theory can only claim to have discovered a negative factor; at best, it offers an explanation for the decline of a style, but none, as has been asserted,[8] for the character of the style that follows.

Even were one ready to discount these deficiencies of detail, the exhaustion theory must be rejected as an explanation of stylistic change. A change of style is not just a change of taste, and in any case the phenomenon of a change of taste cannot be understood as a mere result of fatigue. There is no inevitable connection between fatigue and change of taste, nor between change of taste and change of style. To produce results, a change of taste must ordinarily express a change in the social make-up of the consumers of art: a change of style implies new aesthetic standards and the availability of artists capable of realizing these. The mere fact that people are getting tired of old forms is not decisive; it is a symptom rather than a cause. Fatigue does not bring about the birth of a new style or even the end of an old one; there can well be fatigue without change of style, and equally there can be change of style without fatigue. Desire for novelty is not necessarily a sign of fatigue; every work of art is a fresh manifestation of the constant struggle to express something original and get away from the familiar and commonplace. The well-worn forms of a style may be inspired with new life or drag out an unprofitable course, according to the availability or absence of competent artists. Whether the hold of traditional forms is becoming tighter or looser does not at all depend on the length of time these forms have been employed; as time goes on, men are just as likely to feel a need to cling to them as to alter them. In a deeply rooted social culture like the rococo, well-established art-forms lose nothing of their power or attractiveness with age. For any radical change of taste or style, the rise of some social stratum with new artistic interests is the main

[8] Wölfflin: *Renaissance und Barock* (1907), 2nd ed. pp. 52 ff. Kautzsch: *Der Begriff der Entwicklung in der Kunstgeschichte* (1917), pp. 7–8.

requirement; the varying speed of change of style, when the so-called "dynamic" cultures are contrasted with the "static," has relatively little to do with the persistence of a certain type of aesthetic experience, habituation, fatigue, or need for change. Fatigue is a secondary phenomenon originating in personal attitudes of a general character, and is in the main socially conditioned.

The phenomenon of fashion in clothes most clearly reveals the close connection of psychological motives and sociological conditions which governs changes such as those of style and taste. In any change of fashion, loss of interest in the old and desire for the novel undoubtedly play a great part, a far greater part than they play in the case of changes of style, for here profound spiritual interests and loyalty to emotionally significant forms often effectively counteract the desire for change. Yet, even in the case of fashion, fatigue is by no means the decisive, let alone the only, cause of change. Clothes, as we know, are one of the means by which the upper social classes seek to distinguish themselves externally from the lower. The lower classes try to imitate them by copying the fashion, but before they reach the front, the leading classes change the line of what is fashionable, so that the distance between the classes stays as it was. The more unconventional, urbanized, and progressive-minded the society, the more frequently this process repeats itself; in peasant societies, in which tradition is stronger than the urge to rise, change of fashion is almost imperceptible. The same motive of competition which determines changes of fashion plays a principal, though not so obvious, part in bringing about changes of style. In art, the conditions of change are not so easily envisaged because here the impulse of change generally comes not from a social class clearly demarcated by birth, position, or wealth, but from a far more intricately organized cultural élite. However, it is an unquestionable fact that, in much the same way in which certain classes seek to mark themselves off as leaders of fashion, a group of cultured men, of dilettanti and cognoscenti, supports

229

and propagates types of art which, because of their novelty and the difficulties it occasions, cannot be enjoyed or even understood by most people. The less advanced then try to catch up with the élite, but in contrast with a mere fashion, which loses all value when it becomes widespread, a type of art becomes a "style" and gains historical importance in proportion as it becomes widely accepted.

Attempts suggestive of new style-forms are almost always there; the question is to what extent they are taken up and developed farther, which of the various stylistic possibilities that any epoch carries in germ are to come to fruition. A great variety of tendencies turns up in the course of time, but most of them come to nothing; the crucial fact for the history of style is not that a possible type of art should have been discovered, but that it should have been maintained. The beginnings of a movement such as romanticism simply cannot be ascertained. From time to time romantic features turn up in literature as early as Racine, and even this statement ignores earlier cases going as far back as Hellenistic times. For all that, romanticism as a historically definite style only asserts itself under the influence of the French Revolution. Unless it can find some point of attachment, any attempt at a new type of art is an event of a somewhat private and ephermeral character. But what is it that brings about this link between the tentative and the established? "The rib of the vault is as it were the first swallow; when is the summer [of the Gothic] going to begin?," asks Paul Frankl.[9] Or even more explicit: "The Gothic grew grain by grain, but could the first man to deposit the first proto-Gothic grain have had any idea of the 'heap'—of the Gothic as a whole?"[1] Those who deny any sort of reality to stylistic structures, declaring them to be mere abstractions, are bound in logic to maintain that this is not a real problem, that

[9] Paul Frankl: *"Der Beginn der Gotik,"* in *Wölfflin-Festschrift* (1924), p. 117.
[1] Frankl: *"Meinungen über Herkunft und Wesen der Gotik,"* in Timmling: *Kunstgeschichte und Kunstwissenschaft* (1923), p. 18.

there are just "grains," and that there is nowhere and never anything like a "heap." But they overlook the fact that the heap is something more than the sum of the grains, and that at some point or other it ceases to be just an aggregate of grains. To drop the simile, a style is something that is never contained in the initiatives suggestive of the style, and the "attachment" or "establishment," which makes of a certain initiative the beginning of a style, takes place at some indefinable point at which quantity turns into novel quality.

Research into the beginnings of the Gothic posed the problem of stylistic change from another angle. What was it that first set in motion the change to the Gothic—a technical invention, as Gottfried Semper maintains, or a new artistic intention, as Riegl will have it? Was a rational motive or a desire for illusionistic effects the decisive factor for the introduction of the new style? Which came first, cross-vaulting or the idea of vertical composition? Did the builders of the Gothic cathedrals get their "vertical" conception from the means that had become available for its realization, or did a new vision of height, the Gothic sense of exaltation, wring from the craftsmen the means needed for the translation of this vision into stone and glass?[2] The rational, technical invention may have been induced by an irrational, previously inarticulate vision, or the vision may have been suggested and to some extent anticipated by the technical invention; either is possible. For the same artistic idea that as a "vision" is something irrational and private to the individual finds through the solution of the technical problem its rational, communicable, and socially acceptable expression. But whether a style starts with a mental act of a rational or of an irrational kind, whether its origin is practical or ideal—such questions cannot be answered any more than can that other question as to where the individual's

[2] Cf. Ernst Gall: *Niederrheinische und normannische Architektur im Zeitalter der Frühgotik* (1915); *Die gotische Baukunst in Frankreich und Deutschland,* I (1925). Victor Sabouret: "*Les voûtes nervurées: rôle décoratif des nervures,*" in *Le Génie civil* (1928). Pol Abraham: *Viollet-le-Duc et le rationalisme médiéval* (1934), pp. 144, 146.

role stops and that of society begins. We shall not go wrong if we regard the process of style-formation as a dialectic movement between the poles of the technical and the visionary, the rational and the irrational, social requirements and individual impulses; in this respect the origination of a style is not essentially different from the origination of a single work.

A work of art is no mere embodiment of an artistic vision or a translation into sensuous forms of something ideal already fully meaningful and complete in itself. The vehicles of representation, as Konrad Fiedler pointed out, are never simply indifferent, inert means mechanically applied; they themselves are productive factors in the creative process, fertilizing and stimulating the powers of invention.[3] In a word, the execution of the artist's idea in the given medium is not a matter of secondary importance; on the contrary, it is strictly identical with the conception of the work in terms of sensuous forms; its execution is its creation. The artist may start with a somewhat indefinite and undifferentiated notion of what has to be accomplished; some vague idea in his mind sets him to making the first strokes, which are usually very tentative and hesitant, sets him to feeling his way slowly forward upon a course of high adventure whose outcome remains undecided until the very last step. The second stroke is already conditioned by a combination of two diverse factors; the original, indefinite, embryonic idea and the first experimental beginning made with its embodiment, that first manipulation of the available material. This second stroke and every further stroke is something that was not and could not have been foreseen: the embodiment of an original, vaguely floating vision in terms of a reality strange to it. Strange to it are the stone, the pigments, the words, strange the chisel, brush, and other tools, strange the cadence of sentences, strange even the particular skills of the artist, which activate his ideas indeed, but also restrict and

[3] Konrad Fiedler: *Schriften über Kunst*, I (1913), 59–60, 275; II, 168–71.

dilute them. The origination of a work involves mutual adaptation of means and end, continuous reformulation of the one out of regard for the other, elaboration of each in entire dependence upon the other; but the same is true of the artistic idea and the artistic technique themselves, for even these are distinguishable only in theory.

The process of creation in which each completed act conditions the next is thus a dialectical interplay among elements that have already achieved form and others that are about to achieve it; Fiedler describes the process as the reciprocal subordination and furtherance by turns of idea and technique, or of eye and hand. "Even in the most elementary attempts to represent anything," he writes, "the hand is not carrying out something that the eye has done before; rather, something novel is emerging, and the hand takes over what the eye initiates, and carries it farther." [4] Or more explicitly: "There is a very widespread error that in our ordinary views of things some mental sketches are contained, which only need to be clothed in material to become works of art. It ought to be realized that anything deserving the name of an artistic representation cannot possibly originate otherwise than in the very process of giving it form. It must be insisted that the hand does not carry out something that has been ready formed by the mind, but that the work of the hand is only a further stage in one indivisible unitary process. There is indeed an invisible preparation of it in the mind, but it can go no further toward that higher stage of completion except through actual physical manipulation. For let us suppose that men were born with mental and spiritual faculties complete, but without hands; this would not involve an impoverishment of their representations, in the sense in which this word was used above, but it would make any artistic representations impossible . . ." [5] Here the link with Lessing's idea of a Raphael

[4] Ibid., I, 275.
[5] Ibid., II, 168.

"without hands," which may very likely have been the origin of Fiedler's train of thought, is obvious. Lessing, with his concept of a painter who could not only have artistic ideas without being able to carry them out, but whose ideas would not suffer any marked loss of artistic value if they were not carried out, is upholding a strictly classicist, that is, a pre-historicist and pre-dialectical point of view. He still holds to the Platonizing conception, according to which the work of art finds its purest and completest form in the artist's idea, while the idea can gain nothing and may lose much by its realization. In contrast to so unrealistic a view, Fiedler stresses both the sensuous and material character and the historical individuality of the work of art. For when the work is seen as product of the interaction of idea and technique, vision and manipulation, problem and talent, it manifests both the special character of its time and its own historical uniqueness.

Bergson seems to be merely continuing Fiedler's line of thought—which must have been unknown to him—when, in laying the foundation of his own theory of art, he develops the following thesis: "The completed portrait is conditioned by the physiognomy of the model, the nature of the artist, the colors . . . But no one, not even the artist himself, could glimpse in advance how the portrait would turn out; for to foresee this would be to anticipate the final form before it exists." [6] Bergson here formulates even more sharply than Fiedler the conception that in art an idea only comes into being along with its realization, that either it is unthinkable apart from its concrete form or else when it is thought the act of creation must be judged to be already complete. Whichever the formulation, the methodological importance of this thesis is evident. It provides a key to an understanding of the origin and change of cultural structures generally, and explains in particular the dialectic of artistic production and the continuous modification of artistic trends. Just as the idea of a work of art originates *pari passu*

[6] Henri Bergson: *L'Évolution créatrice* (1907), p. 7.

with the work itself, so a style comes gradually into being and develops as the result of a dialectic between the works that are in progress at the moment and those which already exist and are influential. And just as the true meaning and the success or failure of a work of art remains, until the last finishing touch has been given, an open question and the goal of doubtful struggle, so we can hardly tell whither a style will lead until it has finished its course and spoken its last word. The mutual relations of its constitutive elements are balanced in an equilibrium as unstable, variable, at all times reversible, as that given by the interplay of the different components of the individual work of art. Past and present, tradition and innovation, common form and individual intention have meaning and importance in a style only when taken together; the meaning of one factor changes along with the meaning of the other.

The first move toward the creation or the transformation of a mode of artistic expression may perhaps come from a mere urge of the artist to make some personal self-revelation; the moment he writes a sentence, makes a stroke of the brush, or strikes a chord, he becomes subject to the rules of a tradition, of a convention; he accepts a system of objective laws of form and criteria of taste. Yet he does not simply allow himself to be conditioned and constricted by this system; he extends it, modifies it, and hands it on to his successors in the form of a personal variant of his own. But what happens is actually far more complicated. For the creative artist, the current style-forms, the tradition of technique, the current conventions of taste, immediately take on the meaning that he attributes to them; they present a different aspect to each individual who confronts them with creative aims and powers. There is no more a ready-made, unambiguous, entirely objective tradition than there is a convention of taste which has the same significance for all and sundry in all possible contexts. Equally, there are neither artistic impulses nor individual aims but such as mark themselves off against the foil of some general stylistic trend and find their expression in and through a state of tension toward something else felt as alien.

6. *UNDERSTANDING AND MISUNDERSTANDING*

From the standpoint of methodological enquiry, it may seem as if a great gulf were fixed between art history and the actual practice of art, for the fields of these two activities are surely different. But does this gulf between the two really exist? Can it be true that for the practice of art "not everything is possible at all times," whereas art history is governed by the principle that all the various historic styles are of equal value, *i.e.*, have an equal claim to recognition and an equal chance of adequate appraisal? In a word, can it be that for art history, though not for art, everything *is* possible at all times? Have the various stylistic trends really the same chance, at any given time, of attracting attention, of becoming a central topic of interest, or even of barely being looked at with a fresh eye and an unprejudiced mind? It has been presumed that there is a difference of principle between the limited stylistic possibilities open to the practicing artist and the art historian's powers of interpreting characteristics of the different styles; but this is simply due to the assumption, whether conscious or not, that art is historically conditioned, whereas the scientific examination of art is *un*conditioned, historically and psychologically. The fact is that the art historian also is confined within limits set by the artistic aims of his time; his concepts of form and categories of value are bound up with the modes of seeing and the criteria of taste of a certain age. At any rate, this is true of any discoveries or revaluations he may be able to make. It may be that an already accepted interpretation or valuation can sometimes hold its own even against the stream of current artistic endeavor, especially in a scientific age, although such a discrepancy is bound to lame that power of empathy which is one of the essential conditions of any successful work in art history. But an important revaluation, such as the recent revaluation of the baroque or of mannerism, cannot come about without some reorientation of the modes of seeing and producing among the artists themselves.

Whereas the course of natural science always shows a far-reaching autonomy, even an automatism, the course of art history is closely dependent upon the current practice of art. This is because it relies upon "understanding," a cultural concept that, unlike that of scientific "explanation," implies a certain emotional tone and a direct relation to life. Dilthey saw the special difficulty—and the special attraction—of history-writing in the circumstance that the historian seeks to grasp his object in all its vital connections and tries from sensible signs to infer an "inner," supersensible meaning. [7] This difficulty is not one that we encounter only in the case of the work of art; the simplest of personal expressions such as a phrase in a letter or a casual remark may set a problem unlike anything confronting us in the material world. Such expressions have meaning and value only when taken as part of a psychic whole; their meaning and value depend upon the spiritual context in which they occur. In other words, to explain a natural phenomenon, we simply require to elucidate its causation; but we can understand a personal utterance, whether it be a simple gesture or a subtly organized art-form, only by identifying ourselves with the subject of the utterance. This inner relationship does not merely control, it may even be said to constitute, the meaning of an emotionally charged expression. In consequence, a work of art can take on a new meaning with each new interpretation, whereas a scientific proposition can have only *one* correct explanation. "Where there is no community, there is nothing from which understanding can make a start," says Schleiermacher, and this definition is taken over

[7] Dilthey: *Gesammelte Schriften*, V, 318.

in principle by Droysen and Dilthey.[8] They do not even discard the irrational character of the concept, which derives from its romantic origin and is by no means essential to it. The process of "understanding" implies, indeed, that all historical interpretation is personal interpretation and based upon inner experience, but not the occurrence of any *unio mystica*.

The question is, what consequences arise from the fact that one draws upon one's own opportunities of outer and inner experience in interpreting history—that is, to what extent are current views in history conditioned, disturbed, or distorted by this fact? For understanding by means of the personal aims and the personal point of view of the historian evidently runs the risk of being a misunderstanding. But the answer to such questions is not at all simple. A scientific proposition can be completely understood or completely misunderstood, but a psychic manifestation, such as an emotional utterance or a piece of self-expression, can neither be completely understood, nor yet—supposing it gives rise to some spontaneous reaction or other—be completely misunderstood. No state of mind can be completely reconstructed from external signs, and every expressive utterance is in some sense "responsible" for the reaction it calls forth. To the negative state or utter incomprehension with which some theoretical proposition may be received, there corresponds in the case of the work of art an utter absence of any immediate effect, a blankness or vacuity, not a misapprehension of the meaning of the utterance, but a failure to apprehend that it *has* a meaning.

Even Goethe had the feeling of having helped to create *Hamlet*, and Friedrich Schlegel undoubtedly felt the same sort of thing with regard to *Don Quixote*. However, Dilthey was the first to claim "to understand the artist better than he understood himself," [9] and Unamuno the first to take credit for having read into *Don Quixote* a meaning that Cervantes could not

---

[8] Droysen: loc. cit.; Dilthey: *Gesammelte Schriften*, VII, 191.
[9] Dilthey: *"Die Entstehung der Hermeneutik,"* *Philosophische Abhandlungen Chr. Sigwart gewidmet* (1900), p. 202.

possibly have thought of.[1] Meanwhile it has come to be generally recognized that the artist need not, that in fact he often cannot or will not, know all there is to be known about his work. If one supposes that the artist best understands his own work, that his conscious intention is the only available key to an understanding of it, then one must certainly admit that later observers have often been guilty of astonishing misunderstandings, and have even sometimes seemed unwilling to accept the "authentic" interpretation. The observer always experiences a certain feeling of strangeness, and even though this diminishes as he gets better acquainted with the work, it nevertheless always remains strong enough to prevent him from ever quite forgetting the radical difference between this work of a past age and contemporary art. The former is a part of culture, the latter of life. And though the bridging of the gulf between them is one of the most important tasks of art history, it is never accomplished with more than moderate success. That this is so is evident, not only from the tension that still remains between knowing about art and genuine feeling for it, but also from the fact that the results of research are being constantly revised without any certainty of real improvement. Art history indeed is always treating its subject-matter from novel angles, but these do not necessarily offer a more comprehensive or more illuminating view than the previous ones. Have we today any better understanding of Raphael, a clearer, more integrated, more direct apprehension of his personality, than the people of a century or of two or three centuries ago, now that he is no longer the radiant figure he was for his contemporaries, for the generation of Poussin and Lebrun, or even for that of Ingres? His art has become for us the epitome of classical pictorial composition, just as we now value Greek tragedy simply as the perfection of dramatic form and can enjoy the *Divine Comedy* only as a somewhat artificial, if magnificent, fiction. The psychology of Shakespeare's characters overwhelms us, but does not always convince us. The

[1] Miguel de Unamuno: *Vida de Don Quijote y Sancho* (1914).

239

peculiarities of the medieval organization of space, the anatomy or the central perspective of the Quattrocento, the monotonous coloring of many of the greatest works of the Renaissance—these are features that we must at times positively ignore if we are to have an unmixed enjoyment of the art of those times. Then, with all these limitations, all these shifts of viewpoint and accent, have we any right to claim an adequate understanding of the works in question? Are they the same works about which people have been talking for centuries? One thing seems certain: neither Aeschylus, nor Cervantes, nor Shakespeare, nor yet Giotto or Raphael, would have agreed with our interpretation of their works. Often we attain to an "understanding" of the cultural achievements of the past only by tearing some motif out of its original setting and putting it in the context of our own world-view. It is much the same with art as with philosophy; when we find ourselves agreeing with a previous thinker, it is, as has been remarked, usually the case that he meant something different; in his system each thought had a different function and so a different meaning from what it would have in the context of our ideas.[2]

Art history can properly claim that sooner or later such misinterpretations are revealed as such, and that they can be reduced to a minimum. The fact remains that it can never completely eliminate them, and that to come to grips with its subject it must be forever trying out fresh historical perspectives. In a word, application to the past of the logical categories and visual forms of the present is indispensable to any historical interpretation. Certainly, there are numberless errors and misinterpretations that we can clear up; to a considerable extent we can determine what the individual artists had in mind; by elucidating the connections of a given work with other manifestations of the period we can replace mere random speculations about its possible meaning by propositions that can be rationally discussed and verified. All this is possible, but

[2] Karl Mannheim: *"Historismus," Archiv für Sozialwissenschaft und Sozialpolitik* (1924), LII, 35.

the question remains whether one can ever be sure of reaching a final conviction as to how the work was really intended to be understood and experienced. If we try to approach the work without any preconceptions at all, are we not acting just like Kant's dove, which, feeling the resistance of the air, got the idea that it would fly better in a vacuum? The resistance we meet wherever we come into contact with reality is one of the constitutive conditions of our spiritual life; our achievements originate in this resistence and derive their form from the very limitations within which we are set. The flight of art history is limited, not only by the fact that the meaning of the art of bygone ages has been lost, but equally by the specifically determined world-view of the art historian; yet that alone enables him to see anything. In fact, it was precisely because this world-view was discovered that the original meaning got lost! Just as flight is not possible in a vacuum, so works of art cannot be understood without a world-view, that is, experienced for what they are and are intended to be, the expressions of a certain world-view.

The idea that works of art change with time, lose their roots and die off, that posterity has to breathe into them a new and alien life to awaken them from this seeming death, was perhaps not discovered, but was at any rate powerfully and impressively worked out by André Malraux. Works of art, he maintained, are always being transformed from objects manifestly fulfilling a vital function into dead museum pieces. The "museum" is the cemetery of art, a place of mummies and ghosts. The voice with which the sculptures of the Parthenon spoke to their contemporaries is for ever stilled; the facial expression of the Smiling Angel of Rheims is frozen in a grimace, and whenever it comes to life again, it says something different. No doubt, they have become "immortal," those maidens of the Parthenon and that Angel of Rheims; art history has turned them into a myth, and what we now possess is mythologized works of art instead of the living works.

No great subtlety is required to perceive the inadequacy

of this view; at the very least it is evident that we must be able to recognize different grades of understanding if we are going to talk of misunderstanding. Did we understand Gothic art no better than the art of the Ancient Orient, were we no better informed about the artistic aims of the Greeks than about those of the Sioux Indians, we could have no inkling that art can be misunderstood. And unless we had in fact been able again and again to show up aberrations and dead-ends of interpretation, we should be unable to feel any tension between a judgment that is simply the product of its place and time and that of a critical historian, between the simple abandonment to the pleasures of art and the contemplation ready to account for its response. This tension cannot ever be entirely eliminated, a fact that Malraux's critics were not the first to discover. In exactly the same way, it was realized, long before Malraux and the critics of modern historicism came on the scene, that history can only be the history of some ahistorical substratum, or, again, that through all the variants of a given mode of spiritual activity, be it scientific or artistic, an identical spiritual capacity is expressed. Did the human spirit undergo absolute changes in the course of history, historical structures would be utterly inaccessible and unintelligible to us.[3] But our situation by no means implies that each change in our historical standpoint consists simply in our taking an interest in a different set of things, never in our taking a different view of the same set of things.[4] The different judgments about classical antiquity, Raphael, Shakespeare, or Rubens are obviously not to be explained by the mere fact that from time to time men fastened upon different parts or aspects of their work—and yet this shift of interest is also an indicator of something relative, no less than revaluations of the same features are. We need not, on the whole, be so terrified of falling into relativism in this matter of the revaluation of historical achievements by different generations. As Karl Mannheim has pointed out, a man has a

[3] F. A. Hayek: *The Counter-Revolution of Science* (1952), p. 78.
[4] Ibid., p. 70.

different view of his parents' character at each stage of his life, say, at ten, twenty, thirty, and forty; yet no one concludes that they have no character in any objective sense or that if they have, it is unknowable; but rather we conclude that at each age one can only understand what is intelligible to one's own particular phase of development. Likewise, the historical perspective shifts, but that is no reason to deny all scientific value to history.[5] That certainly does not mean that any and every interpretation of the past is possible and acceptable without more ado. Mannheim himself offers two types of criteria by which the interpretations of art history can be discussed. An explanation of a work of art must, on the one hand, be free from contradiction and must fit every perceptible feature of the work in the interpretation; on the other hand, it must be compatible with the historical circumstances of origin in so far as these can be ascertained from documents or by other objective methods. All interpretations of a work of art must be in accord with these two requirements, however much they may differ in other respects.

Malraux, with his thesis of inevitable misunderstanding of the art of past ages, finds himself in a rather easily assailable position. This is, however, one of the cases where error is almost more illuminating and more fruitful than its opposite; it is especially so by contrast with that kind of orthodoxy which refuses to see that in the case of art-historical interpretations there is a difficulty of principle which can never be completely overcome.

The past in itself is inapprehensible and formless; it takes on meaning and form only when related to a certain present. Thus, every present has a different past, and so history has to be continually re-written, the creations of art re-interpreted, the works of world literature re-translated. And so the assertion that any understanding of the past is in a way a misunderstanding is not entirely senseless. The standpoint from which we

---

[5] Mannheim: *Beiträge zur Theorie der Weltanschauungsinterpretation* (1923), p. 27.

contemplate history does not lie outside history; our contemplation of the past is itself a product of history. From this queer situation, which makes one think of the snake biting its own tail, the most difficult problems of the philosophy of history derive. For it is not only the case, as Droysen points out, that the object of our historical experience is, not the past itself, but what still survives of the past, that every actual occurrence presents itself to the inquiring historian as saturated with the past;[6] even more important is the fact that for historical inquiries we just cannot choose any standpoint other than that of the present. The meaning of history is a teleological concept; one is always compelled to ask: "meaning"—for whom? "meaning"—in what context? When the current situation changes, it is not only our pictures of the present and of the future that change with it, but our pictures of the past as well. Every culture has its own ancestors, its own heroes; to each a different way leads, a way that becomes visible only when the goal has been reached. The rise of modern expressionism and surrealism both discovered mannerism and rendered it an integral and definable component of our history. Certainly, its products were already there, but they seemed to have occurred without rhyme and reason, and to have remained without posterity; they were without the crucial characteristics that designate "historical" existence. Of a sudden the picture altered—our picture not only of the works we designate "mannerist," but also of the significance of the classical works that carried in themselves the seeds of mannerism or provoked that kind of reaction by their tensionless harmony and regularity. So, if Renaissance art looks different today from what it looked like in Burckhardt's time,[7] the explanation of this changed aspect lies in the fact of its relation to mannerism and the baroque having lately become visible.

Max Weber's remark that history would "suffer a serious shrinkage" if one took this teleological principle seriously is

[6] Droysen: op cit., p. 7.
[7] Wilhelm Pinder: *Das Problem der Generation* (1926), p. 14.

plausible only at first sight.[8] The historian does indeed take note of numerous events that have no inner relationship to his own time, and does not by any means exclude all matters to which his age has lost the key. However, one should not claim that such mere taking note of and keeping track of events is "history" properly speaking. Although even before the rise of modern expressionism we were aware of the existence of Pontormo, Parmigianino, and El Greco, to the extent that their names were to be found in histories of art, still it was not true to say that an account of their art was an organic component of art history. They were dead, buried and forgotten, not simply because of an unfavorable judgment upon their productions, but also because men had no inner relation to them, because for the centuries from the beginning of the baroque to the end of impressionism they meant and could mean but little. They did not mean much even negatively. How different was the case of the classicists' rejection of Rubens! That expressed a vital and fruitful opposition, was and remained an impulse making for progress.

The past is the product of the present, because, for one, each new historical situation is the outcome of a different line of development and so has its own preconditions, and for another because the various effects bring to light different features and different aspects of the same historic events. In this sense we may speak with Nietzsche of the "retroactive power" of the present. "We can have no idea," he writes, "what sort of things are going to become history one day. Perhaps the past is still largely undiscovered; it still needs so many retroactive forces for its discovery." [9] But Nietzsche's idea is exaggerated by Bergson, who asserts that the present, besides revealing hidden aspects of the past, actually brings forth from it something that never was—that the present does not only discover, it actually creates the past. If, for example, we detect origins of the

---

[8] Weber: *"Kritische Studien auf dem Gebiete der kulturwissenschaftlichen Logik,"* Gesammelte Aufsätze (1951).

[9] Nietzsche: *"Historia abscondita,"* Fröhliche Wissenschaft.

romantic movement in classicism, what we realize is, according to Bergson, simply a creation of the retroactive power of romanticism. Had there been no Rousseau, no Chateaubriand, no Victor Hugo, not only should we have been unable, according to him, to detect anything like romantic elements in classicism, but there would not have been anything romantic to detect. Bergson compares the features that a later generation finds in the earlier to the forms an artist may see in drifting cloud-masses. Romanticism creates germinal forms for itself within classicism, as the artist finds his shapes in the formless or sees his own visions in the clouds. We notice these early indications of what is coming in history only because we already know the way things actually have gone; those indications are in reality no more than antedated consequences.[1] In his characteristic way, Bergson makes a mystery out of the correct observation that without the romantic movement no one would have noticed romantic features in classicism. In fact, what we call the "romantic" features in classicism would have been there whatever happened, only they would not have been defined as such or clearly distinguished from the other features. The truth is that romanticism makes possible a differentiation that could not otherwise have been made; but any view that hypostasizes a historiographical concept by treating it as if it were a historical reality is incorrect and untenable. If one calls romantic what had previously been regarded as classicism, one is simply introducing a new category, at most discovering a new aspect, not a new reality. In T. S. Eliot the idea of the present playing a constitutive role in respect to the past is more exactly and more acceptably formulated; however, his treatment of the philosophy of history is also founded upon the Bergsonian concept of time. He also is concerned with the changes that historical structures undergo in the light of subsequent events, that is, with the organic connection of the historical process as a whole; but the changes that he notices do not affect the concrete objects, the actual works of art them-

[1] Bergson: *La Pensée et le mouvant* (1934), pp. 23–4.

selves, but only their interrelations, their *post facto* arrangement and evaluation by history. According to Eliot, the appearance of a truely original and creative new work alters the whole mutual relationship of the existing monuments of art, yet these remain unaffected in their own being; what changes is no more than their connections, proportions, and rank.[2] In all these observations the point of cardinal importance for the theory of art history is that through the rise of a new conception of art earlier works take on new values, and that this may involve depreciation as well as appreciation. Frans Hals, Rubens, and Chardin now appear to have anticipated the painterly attitude of Manet, Delacroix, and Cézanne; the former grow in stature with the emergence of these new masters. On the other hand, Perugino loses value directly one thinks of Raphael; alongside of Michelangelo, Signorelli seems pedantic and monotonous; they are suddenly reduced to the rank of mere "precursors." From the standpoint of impressionism, the late style of Titian, Rubens, and Velasquez takes on a new dimension; on the other hand, set beside the works of Rembrandt, the whole of seventeenth-century *chiaroscuro* painting looks to us like a mannerism.

No work of art has a definite and complete significance from the very start, none an unchangeable and final meaning. Rembrandt was not the same painter for Delacroix as for Van Gogh, and the fate of Phidias lay, as has been remarked, in the hands of Michelangelo, even though the latter probably never saw a single one of the works that we today link with the Greek master.[3] The significance of Greek sculpture for the Renaissance, baroque, or classicist periods derives as much from the history of those periods as from the history of classical antiquity; its varying significance is as much the creation of subsequent ages as of contemporaries. And this is the case with all art; it is a precipitate of all that is capable of becoming an artistic experience for

[2] T. S. Eliot: "Tradition and the Individual Talent," in *Selected Essays* (1934), p. 15.
[3] Malraux: *Les Voix du silence*, p. 66.

any subsequent generation or century. Therefore no history of art can ever be regarded as final; each is but the description of an open, unfinished, ever-alterable process of development, a process whose elements can give rise to the most various effects. Art owes its peculiar power of survival, but also its liability to be misunderstood, to this factor of spontaneity.

Reflections and theories about the interpenetration of past and present center mainly round the complex, many-leveled character of all the later phases of a historical development. Such reflections fasten again and again upon the problem of the coincidence of phenomena strikingly disparate in their origins, the problem of what Wilhelm Pinder called "the uncontemporary features of the contemporary" (*die Ungleichzeitigkeit des Gleichzeitigen*), but which might better be designated as "the contemporary existence of older and younger." The ambiguity of any historical situation is most evident when one considers the symbiosis of the different generations, and it was this that suggested to Pinder his explanation of the simultaneity of the various tendencies found together in any given epoch.

Contemporary artistic achievements are obviously not all on the same level of stylistic development. Not only in the different arts, but also within the same species of art, we find more or less "contemporary," more and less "advanced" works, as if some had run on ahead of their time and others were lagging behind. Since the eighteenth century, one could hardly have failed to notice, with the growing social differentiation of the public interested in art, that literature, painting, and music have not remained upon the same level of development, that in one of these branches formal problems have been solved which have as yet hardly presented themselves in the other branches. Music is more backward than literature, and within music more and less conservative phenomena are to be found —it is a remarkable fact of artistic evolution that Johann Sebastian Bach, the greatest master of his century, should have been one of the most conservative artists of modern times.

Nothing is more natural than to explain the diversity of attitudes and aims by reference to the different generations to be found at work in any given situation; nothing more understandable than that Johann Sebastian and young Johann Christian should take very different lines with the same musical problems. They do not live in the same spiritual world, any more than the old Titian and the young Tintoretto painted in the same Venice; nor was it the same Europe for Heine, to whom the July Revolution seemed an epoch-making event, and for the eighty-one year old Goethe, to whom it was an inconsiderable trifle not worth considering. In such cases, difference of generation is certainly not the only reason for difference of attitude, but it is at least one circumstance deserving the historian's attention, the more so because it can be verified definitely, measured and linked up with other concrete facts. But with this advantage are bound up the indubitable disadvantages incurred by the use of the concept of "generation" in history. "Generation" is really a biological concept that loses a good deal of its precision, when applied to spiritual and social phenomena. On the one hand, a person's spiritual "age" depends on many circumstances besides the actual number of his years; and, on the other, belonging to the same generation is certainly not the only, often not even the most important, criterion for determining spiritual affinities. There are many stronger sources of solidarity than the age-group, many that exert a much greater power over men, both in rational and in irrational ways. It is possible to observe differences of principle within the same age-group, as well as essential agreements extraneous to and even in conflict with the prevailing disposition of an age-group.

But Pinder is above all concerned to correct the error that, as he sees it, derives from the assumption of a "one-dimensionality" of historical time. So what he is above all eager to show is that the subject of historical attitudes and achievements, as of current tastes and artistic production, are not some "ageless normal humans"; on the contrary, real men of various ages participate in the various artistic possibilities open to them at the time, and these possibilities mean different things to them according to their age.[4] His relativistic conception of time also evidently stems from Bergson's distinction of objective and subjective, external and internal time. However, while Pinder too emphasizes the subjectively conditioned and individually differentiated character of historical time, he is not, like Bergson, interested in the incompatibility of the physicist's time-concept and our inner experience, but is concerned about the unsatisfactory nature of the anonymous type of history which substitutes figures for men and turns complex historical happenings into "a sequence of unambiguous, one-dimensional presents."[5] He is perfectly right in asserting that "there are no such simple presents" because every historical moment is experienced, interpreted, and utilized by men of various ages. Even so, the analysis of an "actual historical situation" remains inadequate. Pinder's "three-part polyphony" of the generations is, as he himself concedes, an oversimplification of the facts: after all, a new generation is born every minute.[6] And however many "parts" one assumed, an exposition based upon that concept would still be a dangerous simplification, for the differences do not really manifest themselves on a single plane only, but on various planes and in various directions. Pinder's objections to "anonymous" art history, especially to its one-dimensional time-concept, which assumes the predominance of one single trend at least within each branch of art, are absolutely justified; but his assumption that an art history based on age-groups can do complete justice to the complexity of a situation is untenable. The inadequacy of Pinder's theory is shown by his criticism of "anonymous art history" solely for its having a one-dimensional concept of time, at the same time that it upholds its doctrine of the periodicity of evolution, and that in a still more dubious form than Wölfflin's. He speaks of the

[4] Pinder, op. cit., pp. 14–15.
[5] Ibid., p. 15.
[6] Ibid., p. 30.

"rhythm of the generations" founded upon "the grouping of decisive births," and does not hesitate to employ such highly dubious notions as "nature's broods" (*Würfe der Natur*), "rhythmical pauses for breath" in the evolution, and "problems set by destiny" for a certain epoch.[7]

He does allude to the possibility that a historical situation may manifest not only the polyphony of the different age-groups, but also some such thing as the "infection" of contemporary generations by one or another of them. However, instead of tracing the origin of this "infection" by research into the role of such socio-historical forces as imitation, opposition, competition, tradition, and convention, he remains imprisoned in his biological preconceptions and inquires whether the forces governing the generations, if it be admitted that there are any, will not "in the end turn out to be the meeting of some individual entelechies of generations."[8] But on these lines Pinder, though he is continually talking about groups and classes, can find no way out of the blind alley of his unsociological view of history, and so his achievement consists simply in having recognized the fact that each historical moment displays a crossing of "uncontemporary" lines of development, and that a historical situation has different meanings and contents for those acting in it according to their different age-groups. The nonbiological causes of differentiation are almost wholly neglected by him.

In an age fragmented by social and spiritual conflicts, one can do no more than note the atomized pattern of artistic endeavor; we should give up the idea of finding behind the various more progressive or more reactionary phenomena any "unitary agent" of evolution.[9] Dvořák's notion of the freedom from contradiction of all spiritual activities is just as untenable a fiction as the romantics' unitary *Volksgeist*, Hegel's sovereign

---

[7] Ibid., pp. 25–7.
[8] Ibid., pp. 97–8.
[9] Dagobert Frey: *"Zur wissenschaftlichen Lage der Kunstgeschichte"* in *Kunstwissenschaftliche Grundfragen* (1946), p. 45.

Weltgeist, Wölfflin's autonomously evolving "seeing" (*Sehen*), or Pinder's conception of generation. None of these categories does justice to the manifold differentiation of a concrete historical moment. "A historical period, even a short one," writes Henri Focillon, "exhibits a number of floors, or if you prefer it, of strata. History is not like the Hegelian 'becoming'; it is not to be likened to a sort of river bearing along events and their residues, all at the same speed and in the same direction. What we call history consists precisely in the differences between currents. We must think of something like overlying geological strata, their varying slopes often broken by abrupt faults which permit us to discern at the very same place and time various geological ages, and in such a way that we envisage the various periods at one and the same time as past, present and future . . . What is a year? For the astronomer, a certain definite quantity, for the historian, something that is for ever varying. Events do not repeat themselves with the punctuality of saints'-days. A year as it is experienced by individuals or groups manifests the manifold variety of the subjects experiencing it. The rhythm of inspiration and expiration is now sluggish, now febrile, runs now in short waves, now in long. At one time it seems empty, at another full of events." [1] Yet even this description is not wholly satisfactory. It is not enough to observe that artistic trends and achievements always present a broken horizon to us and rest upon a deposit of many and various historical strata; one must also recognize that like historical conditions are taken up in various ways and developed in various directions. There is not simply a kind of geological stratification or a confluence of different tributaries, but a dynamic interaction among individual forces differentiated both in respect to origin, stratum, and direction and also in their function in relation to the other factors. If exponents of a new culture come to the fore and introduce a new mode of thought or trend of taste, this is not equivalent to the disposition of a new stratum upon older ones, but effects a changed

[1] Focillon: *L'An Mil* (1952), pp. 7–8.

relationship of all social strata to one another. The new is not simply a continuation or completion of the old; it brings about a new situation. Thus, one can never speak of the simple recurrence of a previous style. And that is why artistic terms such as naturalism or abstraction, impressionism or expressionism, which one is accustomed to apply indifferently when speaking of the various ages, never really mean the same thing. Every attitude, every style, every form, undergoes the most complete transformation in the course of its history, a transformation both of meaning and of function.

7. *THE SOCIOLOGICAL APPROACH*

The history of art has no single method of research equally applicable to all its problems and equally successful in all fields; it takes up various sorts of problem, attempts to solve these in various ways; its answers to the questions that arise are sometimes satisfying, sometimes less so. Its first aim must be to place the work or group of works which is the subject of the investigation in its original historical nexus by discovering such facts as date and place of origin, identity of the artist or artists, school or movement within which the work or works originate, social position and influence of the purchaser, and terms governing the execution of the work. Next, it aims to determine the traditions and conventions, the current standard of technique, the range of occurring subjects, and the prevalent rules of taste on which the artist relied. Then it endeavors to ascertain the extent of acceptibility and effectiveness of the works in question, their importance as representative of the artistic aims of the time, their place in respect to the competing spiritual tendencies of the age in which they occur. The fulfilment of these tasks consists in part of the establishment of concrete, definitely verifiable facts, in part of a drawing of inferences, which are much less firmly based. Thus the art historian is faced, on the one hand, by questions that can be answered from the unequivocal evidence of documents and other sources and, on the other hand, by problems for whose solution he must rely on his flair for what is characteristic of a historical style or an individual artist. In a word, the work of an art historian consists in both ascertainment of facts and criticism of style, in the establishing of a historical nexus on the basis of external data and in the supplementing or development of the ascertained facts on grounds of internal evidence. These are two different procedures which ought to be for ever complementing one another, but in practice they often run into conflict, and are usually esteemed differently.

In any art history that lays claim to be scientific, facts known or ascertainable must in all circumstances rank before judgments based on stylistic grounds and extrapolations based on the history of forms. One has a perfect right "to criticize even documentary sources by certain qualitative standards"[2] or even "to correct sources";[3] but if the sources stand up to criticism, one has no right to twist what one finds there, whatever the critical approach may make of it. It is however possible to hold that by itself mere ascertainment of facts is not art history—that history begins only, as Dvořák said well, when we have got an ordered inventory of the extant works. That is not to say that "science begins where the facts come to an end" (Ortega y Gasset), but that with the establishment of the facts science by no means comes to an end. Until the origin and chronological and geographical connections of a large number of works are definitely known, we would scarcely speak of a style or of placing anonymous and undated works in their proper stylistic position. Yet, no aggregation of definitely dated and attributed works, however large, entails their inclusion

---

[2] Richard Hamann: *"Die Methode der Kunstgeschichte," Monatshefte für Kunstwissenschaft* (1916), IX, 104.
[3] Frankl: *Die Entwicklungsphasen der neueren Baukunst* (1914), p. 8.

under the concept of a style or affords a hard and fast criterion for the inclusion among them, on grounds of style, of anonymous or doubtfully dated works. In other words, no workable concept of a style can be derived from a single work or a few works; and however many works one may know, the origin and attribution of each anonymous work remains a problem.

However, criticism of style does not depend upon mere intuition; it relies, rather, upon certain typical relationships that, though they are certainly not historical laws, are useful for suggesting psychological analogies. Thus, for example, from formal similarity between works one infers chronological or geographical contiguity; [4] or one assumes that a more primitive, more clumsy, more rigidly conventional mode of expression is earlier than a more versatile and more masterful one. This assumption is usually confirmed. [5] But that this is no law governing the course of evolution is clear when we observe that the simple and undifferentiated by no means always comes before the complex and many-sided, and that the historical sequence always hangs upon a number of particular, quite incalculable circumstances. For example, neolithic art gives one the impression of being far more primitive than palaeolithic. If anyone objects that in this case we are dealing with two different cultural epochs and that the gulf between them invalidates the argument, one may well reply that even within palaeolithic art itself the later products often have a less developed appearance than the earlier. And if this example is thought to be unconvincing, on account of the gaps in our prehistoric material, we have only to think of Egyptian art, in which the monuments of the Middle Kingdom have often a much more archaic character than those produced in the first great period of Egypt's cultural history.

If there are no universally valid rules on which to establish style-criticism, and the data have run out, what is to be done about this situation?

[4] Hamann, op. cit., pp. 103 ff.
[5] Ibid.

A good part of the work of that criticism consists in exact description and analysis of the works of art, attentive characterization of them in terms of their subject-matter and formal features. Such exact conceptual ascertainment of their contents and the means of expression employed anticipates to a certain extent the definition of the style they exhibit. Not so very long ago it was customary, especially in the countries of Western Europe, to include the whole course of art from the end of the Middle Ages to the end of the seventeenth century under the heading "Age of the Renaissance." Then people gradually began to distinguish Early Renaissance from High Renaissance, Renaissance from baroque, and finally mannerism from Renaissance on the one hand and baroque on the other. Today we do not only see the distinct outline of a certain original, unmistakable style where formerly men could see nothing but some late forms of the Renaissance or early forms of the baroque; we also distinguish several clearly perceptible phases of the newly discovered style. No doubt any description of this sort, which analyzes forms and distinguishes particular stylistic features, goes beyond the strictly empirical; it already contains ordering concepts, which are formed *pari passu* as the observation goes forward, yet are not derived from it. It was not the discovery of new "facts" which led to the distinguishing of the various styles between 1500 and 1700, but rather the birth of a new sensitiveness, which certainly was not so much the result of researches into the past as of fresh experiences in the present. Without some preconceptions about style, no distinctions of style can be made, and yet the concepts assumed for working purposes have to be tested by the facts over and over again if they are to continue to be employed. Here too we have to dissolve the provisional synthesis again and again, as required by dialetic method, to correct it and apply it in a new form that does better justice to the facts. In examining such a concept as that of an art-style, one can never either get back to a mere set of naked facts, nor yet forward to an ultimate form of the concept which will not be liable to further revision.

256

The process from synthesis to analysis and back again is an endless one.

In art history, both factual research and style-criticism are directed above all toward determining the position occupied by each particular work of art in the whole process of evolution. Both are concerned with questions of dating and attribution. But all this does not even touch upon the strictly historical problem, that of the actual genesis of the works; the question of where any particular art-form comes from and how changes in it are to be explained remains unanswered. Yet, once the question of genesis is raised, objections are heard at once, for genetic explanation involves not merely disregarding, but often even destroying, the specific character of the object. Knowing where anything originates is not the same as knowing its real nature; in fact, if one's whole attention is turned upon the genetic composition of an object, one easily loses sight of its formal structure. The special quality of violet color is in no way clarified when we have learned that it is a mixture of red and blue. Rather, its essential quality is destroyed if it is analyzed into these elements. There is no trace of red or blue in our visual experience of violet; they simply cease to exist once they have been mixed. In contrast with them, the violet quality is something novel and completely irreducible. The work of art is similarly underivable and irreducible; it is not contained in its elements. Even if these were completely ascertained, its most essential quality would be missing; for what makes anything a work of art is just the circumstance that its genetically derivable components, all of which might occur in other combinations, in fact occur in this particular, unique, unrepeatable complex.

When one looks at the matter from this angle, one can well understand why Wölfflin, with his doctrine of immanence of artistic evolution and autonomy of artistic vision, avoids all genetic explanations, that is, all derivation of his "visual forms" from anything extrinsic to the aesthetic sphere, and why he maintains that the "basic concepts of art history" are formal principles, changing indeed in the course of history, but en-

257

tirely intrinsic to art. With his general outlook, he is bound to deny the existence, or at any rate the relevance, of any formal elements that might be inaccessible to the aesthetic experience. It is comprehensible that in order to do justice to the history of art without destroying the uniqueness and unity of the work of art, one should seek to portray this history as an autonomous process of formal change. But there is no reason why one must at all times be attending to this formal uniqueness of the object. If the art historian is to understand the phenomenon of stylistic change, he cannot avoid taking the leap from the self-contained work of art into the manifold world of practical reality. There is simply no other explanation of stylistic change but a sociological or psychological explanation; any art history that wants to go beyond simple analysis of the material is obliged to relate the unique work of art to psychic dispositions and collective aspirations. No doubt, such psycho-sociological motivation operates on quite a different level from that of purely aesthetic relations, and in discussing it, one inevitably loses contact with the source of the original aesthetic experience; but the question is whether this was not already in a way abandoned when the merely formal analysis of the works started—whether any and every departure from the structural unity of the work is not inevitably a "leap," a straying into a new and foreign field.

But why should one reject a scientific method simply because it explains one phenomenon by another? Is it not of the essence of science not to be content with things as they are, but to seek to derive one from another and, above all, to derive the complex from something simpler? No one reproaches the chemist for analyzing water into its elements, although these do not resemble water in the least. Why, then, must the unity of the work of art be preserved at all costs? Certainly, something is lost when its complexity is analyzed, something that the chemical compound never possessed; but that quality is indispensable only for aesthetic experience, for direct personal contact, whether of a productive or a receptive kind with the work. Once the sphere of direct experience is left behind—and that occurs with the very first step in the direction of analysis or criticism—the unity of the work, inapprehensible conceptually, begins to disappear. But the fear that to explain a spiritual creation, artistic or other, genetically is to destroy its inmost structure beyond repair is just a bogy of the philosophers. Such an explanation temporarily puts the phenomenon's intrinsic character "in brackets," to use Husserl's phrase; it does not abolish it. When we elucidate *Hamlet* with the help of a psychic mechanism like the Oedipus complex, or Rembrandt's pictures with such psycho-sociological concepts as Protestant subjectivity and middle-class intimacy, these works lose much of their unique artistic character; but provided that one is aware of the loss and accepts the genetic explanation with the proper reserve, nothing prevents one finding one's way back to the original configuration of the work. In any case, genetic explanation of forms leaves the true problem of art history unsolved.

When Burckhardt made merry at the expense of professional "attributors," he certainly was not objecting to their penchant for "facts," but to their lack of feeling for synthesis, their incapacity to survey an epoch or sense the currents that flow through history. Every important historian of art since Winckelmann has had such a synthesis in view; each has seen in art a mirror of the spiritual evolution of the peoples, and has sought to solve the central problems of art history by way of a comprehensive vision. Burckhardt himself is undoubtedly among the historians who have contributed most to the solution of these problems; but that reconciliation of the different fields of culture which Dvořák found lacking in Schnaase—who, he said, wanted a "transmission belt" to couple his researches in art to his cultural history—is lacking in Burckhardt too and, in fact, in Dvořák himself. He too makes the theological and philosophical thought of the Middle Ages a mere backdrop for the Gothic; at most it suggests for him analogies to the course of artistic production. But if these two sets of phenomena are treated as running parallel, it is not clear how they can ever come into contact, how the communication of ideas from one level to the other can take place—in a word, how the "transmission belt" works. Dvořák starts from the assumption, which for him has the significance of an axiom, that the ideas are always and in all respects the same, that their recurrence on the different levels of culture does not need any explanation—that *they* are the "transmission belt." [6] The possibility that a philosophical idea and an artistic idea might have no more in common than, for example, economic competition and spiritual rivalry, or mechanical technology and artistic technique, seems never to have entered his head.

The exponents of the history of ideas readily fall into the error of giving philosophical thought precedence over artistic forms just because the former gives clearest expression to their "ideas." And if in Dvořák's exposition of the Gothic, philosophy and theology get a rather excessive prominence, in Erwin Panofsky's *Gothic Architecture and Scholasticism*,[7] the last notable essay of a wider cultural interpretation of stylistic change, the place of philosophy as canon for the understanding of the contemporary art is even more strongly stressed. Yet there are no grounds at all for thinking that in philosophy is to be found the true origin, or at least the paradigmatic form, of that medieval world-view which is also expressed in art; or that the philosophy has any more direct connection with the vital problems and the other cultural endeavors of the time than the art. Medieval art has at least as much connection with feudal forms of lordship, with the ideas and emotions of chivalry, with the rebirth of towns and the urban middle-class, with the political structure of the Church, with the elements of technological knowledge, with the monastic discipline of work, with the organization of the mason's lodge and the guild, as it has with the *modus operandi* of scholastic philosophy. Medieval art

[6] Cf. Dvořák: *Idealismus und Naturalismus in der gotischen Skulptur und Malerei* (1918).
[7] Panofsky: *Gothic Architecture and Scholasticism* (1951).

may have taken many a problem and motif from the philosophical literature, but its relation to philosophy was not that of a secondary spiritual form to a primary one. The philosophical ideas were no more for it than raw material—an alien and refractory mass awaiting form—as were the other contents of the artist's immediate experience.

The idea that the different fields of spiritual endeavor are connected by wide corridors, whereas all other vital activities are sundered by unbridgeable gulfs is nothing but an idealistic fiction. People are too inclined to forget that an idea expressed in the abstract conceptual forms of philosophy and one expressed in the concrete sensuous forms of art is never "the same" idea; even if one feels inclined to speak of ideas common to philosophy and art, the two modes of expression are so utterly different as not to be related very easily. The gulf between a philosophical idea and its artistic expression is at least as great, and presupposes the existence of as many intermediary stages, as are to be found between an epoch's economic organizations and its cultural ideals. To speak of such thought-processes as "manifestation," "demonstration," "subordination," and "conclusion" in a manner intended to apply to both art and philosophy leads to nothing but unconvincing analogies and confusing equivocations.

The fact that philosophy and theology proved such copious sources of medieval art, which does often seem to be no more than an illustration of ideas and doctrines developed in the philosophical and theological literature, does not imply that the formal characteristics of the art are directly derived from the methods of scientific thought then current. Medieval art and science may in fact have certain formal features in common—desire for completeness, acceptance of the principle of hierarchy, liking for symbolism, and so on—but if one takes these parallelisms too literally and treats these formal correspondences as direct, causal relationships, they cease to be particularly illuminating. The most important features on the one side often correspond to only minor features on the other, the most striking phenomena come to be treated as a sort of metaphor; actual methods of working are watered down into mere associations of ideas. To connect the rigorous formalism of medieval art with feudal lordship and the authoritarian culture radiating from the Church may not do much to explain the special artistic quality of the works in question, but it does establish a significant, if indirect, relationship between two quite differently organized cultural structures, thus making intelligible the attraction of this type of art for those who were contemporary with it in some degree. On the other hand, to assert that the successive phases of Gothic architecture are just the expression in art of the *sic, non,* and *respondeo dicendum* of the scholastic thought-pattern is simply to describe certain artistic occurrences in a metaphorical, equivocal manner, which at best has no explanatory force. That a taste for horizontalism in architecture gives place to a taste for verticalism has nothing to do with logical negation, but derives from a fresh world-view and a new power of vision arising out of it. The mixed, horizontal-vertical style corresponds not to a logical operation, but again to a new artistic vision. The fact is, moreover, that in logic thesis, antithesis and synthesis arise *out* of one another, not one *after* the other like the phases of an art-style. When one is on the search for such analogies and neglects this vital difference, one falls irremediably into the Hegelian mode of pairing systematic relations of logic with unsystematic relations of history, the rock on which Hegel's whole philosophy suffers shipwreck, for he has to maintain that the logical and the historical order are ultimately identical, history merely realizing in concrete form what is entailed in the idea of logic.

A similar love of analogies and taste for making out direct contacts between analogous cultural phenomena is displayed by those who seek to apply to history the theory of the alleged "mutual illumination of the arts." This theory proceeds from the axiom that it makes no important difference whether one chooses to express one's experience in words or notes, lines or colors, thus not only ignoring the constitutive role in art of the means of expression, but assuming an identity of experience underlying the various art-forms, whereas in reality the experience itself, and not just the artistic form it ultimately takes, is moulded by the available means of expression. Dagobert Frey in his exposition of this doctrine declares among other things that the decisive difference between the ancient and all subsequent music is to be ascribed to their respective formal principles of monody and polyphony. "By contrast to the purely temporal succession of monody," he asserts, "polyphony signifies the introducing of a second dimension . . . Hearing together [in music] corresponds to seeing together [in painting and sculpture]." [8] "In the same way and almost at the same time as in the visual arts," he continues, "simultaneous representation in music took the place of successive representation." [9] "The melody as a harmonic structure no longer has a linear character, but by reason of its immanent, vertical relationship is two-dimensional, spatial . . ." [1] This passage is full of metaphors and equivocations. The words one-dimensionality and two-dimensionality, linearity and spatiality, simultaneity and successiveness, here employed as the basis of the alleged parallelism, are used, in the different arts, to signify such utterly different perceptions that their transposition from the visual arts into music and *vice versa* must appear precarious from the very start. To speak of horizontal and vertical structure in music as if it were optical simultaneity or succession is certainly misleading. One might perhaps speak unequivocally of greater or less "complexity" in each of the different arts. But in that case simultaneity in music would mean the very opposite of what it does in painting, for the sound-structure is complicated by voices being heard simultaneously, whereas the optical impression is simplified by the restriction of the picture

[8] Frey: *Gotik und Renaissance* (1929), p. 227.
[9] Ibid., pp. 240–1.
[1] Ibid., p. 248.

to a single scene at a certain place and time; this latter produces the simplicity and clarity of the Renaissance, the former the complexity of the baroque.

A synthesis of the several different lines of development which the cultural historian traces can be effected in various ways: the historical process as a whole can be subordinated to a single principle and oriented toward a single goal, as by Hegel; it can be made to illustrate a single unbroken chain of causality, as by Marx; the several cultural structures can be exhibited as functions of one another, as most perspicuously by Max Weber; or, finally, a parallelism between the various processes of cultural history can be worked out, as by Dvořák. This last formula has the advantage that it can be extended in a way that may prove to be of the greatest importance for historical synthesis. For the historical events in two fields of culture may appear closely connected although no causal nexus between them can be established; or, on the contrary, they may lack any inner connection in spite of an indubitable causal nexus. For example, one cannot fail to recognize a relationship of style between fifteenth-century economic rationalism and rationalism in art, although it is hard to discern any direct causal relation between the two sets of phenomena. But there is no connection of any importance for the history of style between the Thirty Years' War and seventeenth-century German art, in spite of the direct effect that the war had on the future of German culture as a whole. The fact that a certain effect occurred does not tell us much about those communications of ideas which Dvořák described as the "transmission belt" between the various historical processes. An occurrence is significant and historically suggestive only when one knows why it could and did take place, why it became historically relevant instead of having merely external and practical consequences. The excavation of Pompeii had, as is well known, a profound effect on artistic developments in the eighteenth century; the true task of the art historian, however, is not simply to ascertain this effect, but to answer the question of how it could occur in the circumstances of the case. Why did the excavation of Herculaneum, which preceded it, remain without any noticeable consequences? One must try to find some common denominator between the various historical processes, if one is to remove their contacts from the sphere of mere chance and render significant the influences or borrowings that link them. From a historical point of view, common origin of two phenomena may be more suggestive and of more importance than direct causal nexus. By itself, the excavation of Pompeii reveals no more than the prevalence of a certain fashion, but the contemporary reaction against absolute monarchy, courtly culture, and aristocratic forms of life reveals both the new interest in excavations, with a new understanding of a culture so different from the rococo, and the change to neo-classicism.

Society is a soil in which the various cultural processes go on in intimate contact with one another. On the social level they do not necessarily manifest their whole content or the whole wealth of their interrelations, but they do manifest those features which can be most satisfactorily reduced to a "common denominator." Cultural structures are social structures, vehicles of the self-perpetuating activity of the society and of the mutual understanding of its members; from this point of view they are always comparable, always interpretable in common terms. In the course of their development they may take on features that do not derive from their social origin and are inaccessible from this point of view. However this may be, they still remain symptoms of that same social being, expressions of the same social interests, answers sometimes positive sometimes negative to the same questionings and challenges. If, then, there is any "transmission belt" linking one field of culture with another and making their connections seem less accidental, this is where one must look for it.

When Riegl made it clear that the disappearance of sculpture in the round from the art of the early Middle Ages was not just a sign of degeneracy, but a sign of the new "optical" approach that took the place of the "haptic" sense of form typical of the ancient world, the principle of explanation thus introduced was an epoch-making novelty in art history. This new way of looking at things made it possible to discover an inner connection where chance or arbitrariness had formerly reigned. But Riegl was content to assert the inner logic and necessity of his theory of artistic intention, and did not go on to enquire what was really the origin of this new form of sensuous experience, this new perception of space, this new subjectivism and illusionism. Why should men at the end of classical antiquity begin to rely on optical rather than tactual impressions? Why at the beginning of the seventeenth century should they begin to see in a recessional instead of a planimetric way? Why should they suddenly be attracted by open, atectonic forms instead of closed, well-knit forms? Questions of this sort have never been answered satisfactorily, hardly ever have been correctly formulated, by the art historians. Are they unanswerable, perhaps even insusceptible of formulation, as the exponents of the "pure history of forms" implicitly assume? Or is the only possible answer to point to analogies among the various fields of culture, each with its own ideal foundation, as the exponents of "art history as history of ideas" assume? No one will wish to assert that an artistic form can be extracted from some extrinsic and alien fact as demonstrably as an egg from a hen—though we need not hold that in such matters history begins only with an egg! Even Wölfflin, at least when pressed, does not deny that along with the immanent formative factors other externally existent causes of a sociological kind play a role in the development of art. A parting of the ways occurs only when the historian is compelled to determine which of the two causal series is the decisive one, or at least which is the more decisive of the two, which is the independent variable or at least shows the greater spontaneity in its variations—in a word, to determine at what point in this web of mutual dependence a first step was taken, a first sign of change of view or of taste was recognizable.

If one begins to track a given stylistic form to its real origin, one has first of all to consider its public. And the first thing to note is that not only "not everything is possible at all times," but also that even at the same time not everything is equally possible for the various social strata, economic classes, professional groups, or educational levels. Whenever there is social differentiation, several variants of what is currently possible come to be realized. There are always various criteria of tastes and standards of quality corresponding with the various groups of persons interested in art, and the first stimulus for a change of style always originates—even if not exclusively—in the emergence of new classes of interested persons. In the case of each radical change of style—from Greek geometrism to archaism and from classicism to Hellenism, from Greco-Roman to Christian art, from the Middle Ages to the Renaissance, the baroque, and the rococo, from neo-classicism to romanticism, from romanticism to naturalism and impressionism, and from these to post-impressionist developments—the new outlook is always connected with a social upheaval or a change in the social composition of the public interested in art. And moreover, without getting deeply involved in questions of the ultimate truth of historical materialism, we can take a further step: we can confidently assert that, whatever the true cause of these stylistic changes, they could scarcely have won general acceptance without appropriate social and economic changes. The victory of Greek archaism over the art-forms of the Homeric age is unthinkable apart from the corresponding victory of aristocracy over feudal monarchy; equally unthinkable is the development from classical rigorous formalism to Hellenistic naturalism and subjectivism apart from the transformation of the patrician city state with patriarchal slave economy into the Hellenistic capitalist world economy, with cosmopolitan middle classes. Unthinkable, again, is the transition from medieval symbolism to the artistic rationalism of the Renaissance without the change from feudal economy and lordship to the bourgeois social order of the towns; the transition to the refinements of mannerism and the emotionalism of the baroque

267

without the new rise of the aristocracy, the economic and social crisis of the Reformation, and the emergence of absolute monarchy; the triumphal march of romanticism without the triumph of the French Revolution and the bourgeoisie, emancipation of the individual, the notion of free competition, and its application to spiritual as well as material production. Now, the word "unthinkable" should not be taken to mean that the above stylistic changes were possible only in these and in no other historical circumstances; the meaning is simply that the relation of the stylistic form to the socio-economic form seems so striking that we can hardly picture it as occurring under other conditions.

Objections to social history of art as a method of interpretation result mostly from attributing to it aims that it neither can nor will carry out. Only the very crudest type of social history would seek to represent a particular type of art as the homogeneous, conclusive, and direct expression of a particular form of society. The art of a historically complex age can never be homogeneous, if only because the society of such an epoch is not homogeneous; it can never be more than the expression of a social stratum, of a group of persons with some common interests; it will exhibit simultaneously just as many different stylistic tendencies as there are different cultural levels within the relevant society. "Inner contradictions" need not, as has been assumed, occur within the same class; they are none the less among the most potent impulses making for change. Art can express the structure of a given society either positively or negatively, can assent to it or reject it, promote some features and oppose others, serve as propaganda weapon, defence mechanism, or safety-valve. It is essential to realize that art's dependence upon society can take the most varied forms, and that apparent opposition is often no more than "negative imitation." There never is complete accord between art and society, or between the different arts within the same society, if only because no historical period can start afresh with its own art; it always starts with a burden, so to speak, of inherited forms, each of which has its own history and tradition, which fit it or unfit it, in various degrees, to take part in the social struggle.

No sociology that goes beyond the most naïve form of materialism will view art simply as a direct reflection of economic and social conditions. Any critic of the social interpretation of spiritual developments is perfectly right to object to the simple equation of feudalism with formalism, of absolutism with classicism, or of capitalism with individualism. The earliest formulations of historical materialism of any consequence were ready to concede that conditions of production did not manifest themselves in culture directly and literally, that only through a long chain of intermediaries did they find expression in scientific doctrines, moral principles, and creations of art; on the way from "being" to "conscious being" these gradually become more spiritual and more remote from their material origin. Thus the degeneration of the manorial economy and the beginnings of the new town-based monetary economy do not straightway bring about Gothic naturalism; what they do is to loosen ancestral obligations, alter outmoded legal concepts, weaken traditional principles of morality and custom, make hitherto unquestioned dogma seem empty, favor a nominalistic view of the individual, and promote St. Thomas's idea that God has joy in all things—because even the least of them has its own unique value—so that in the end they cease to be mere symbols and begin to be interesting in themselves and worthy of representation in art as true and substantial. And however much one might prolong this series, it would still be an arbitrarily shortened, enormously simplified account of the real process, which leads through numberless intermediate steps from the serf's leaving the soil for the town to the naturalism of a late Gothic altar-piece.

Plekhanov once remarked that social conditions could never explain the form of the minuet. Henri Focillon, following the same line of thought, said that the most intensive study of social conditions of the period would never enable us to infer the lines of the Laon Cathedral towers. Such attempts at explanation are foreign to the socio-historical interpretation of art. To explain the form of the minuet or of the towers of Laon in Plekhanov's and Focillon's sense would be a sort of conjuring trick that no scholarly historian would undertake. Social history of art merely asserts—and this is the only sort of assertion which it can seek to substantiate—that art-forms are not only forms of individual consciousness, optically or orally conditioned, but also expressions of a socially conditioned world-view. The musical form of the minuet is not "entailed" by the social conditions of the eighteenth century, but the pre-revolutionary world with its refinement, elegance and etiquette, its inclination toward the charming and the playful, was one of the pre-suppositions for the emergence of this kind of art. Eighteenth-century society is in a way implied in the minuet, but the minuet is not implied in the social forms of that society. Each art-form is original and creative, not to be deduced from either the material or the intellectual conditions of the time. If we knew nothing but the social structure of a public, we could neither "picture" nor reconstruct its art, for socially conditioned though it be, the essential unpredictability of the artist's creative gifts renders futile all prediction in the field of art. In this field there can be only correlations, empirically observable links between what goes before and what follows, and such formulations can always be modified or upset; and can never guarantee the recurrence of like effects. But while not allowing of the formulation of laws, such observed links prove very suggestive, somewhat in the way that certain brain operations prove successful in the treatment of some mental disorders without anybody's understanding why; problematic as are the limits of indication and effectiveness of such operations, their success rests upon a definite correlation of surgical and psychiatric data.

There is nothing that could be called a universal law of the social history of art. This is not only because there are no rules of artistic creation; besides the irreducibility of art to rules, there is the additional fact that art as a social agency is implicated in a process that never repeats itself and constantly throws up new combinations. In consequence, it is always possible for the social significance of a style to change, even to take on a function the very opposite of the function that it fulfilled previously. One need only mention the metamorphoses to be observed if one traces the social role of classicism or romanticism through the centuries. Just as there is no social criterion of artistic quality, so there is no social function that a style fulfils unequivocally; it can be employed in the service of various political and social aims. Yet it is not a completely neutral instrument; but the concept of a style is vaguer than the systematic concepts of sociology and takes its particular social significance on each occasion from the totality of historical forces at work. Thus, a certain social stratum may be inclined to adopt a style simply to be different from its opponents, or to give up a style as compromised through employment by an antagonistic group; but equally, it may employ certain means of expression and influence because its opponents have employed them successfully or because they have become common property and the most effective means of communication. Classicism, which in seventeenth-century France was the representative style of absolute monarchy and the court aristocracy, became, if in a modified form, the official style of the Revolution, primarily because it could be regarded as negation of the standards of taste, protest against the frivolity, of the rococo. As in the course of the eighteenth century the aristocracy, partly in consequence of its social contacts with the bourgeoisie, had come to take more and more pleasure in the intimate effects of the painterly style, so now the opposition in its struggle against the rococo culture of the nobility and the higher bourgeoisie went back to the stylistic ideals of the former ruling class, which, courtly and aristocratic though it was, seemed to be cast in a more heroic mould. Yet, in spite of this changed significance and revaluation of a style, it would be wrong to assert that the artistic aims of the absolute monarchy, the courtly aristocracy, or the revolutionary middle class were independent of and uninfluenced by social and political considerations. Numerous as are the instances of change in social significance of a style, they certainly do not prove that artistic styles are socially unimportant and without effect. Flaubert, Maupassant, and the brothers Goncourt employ naturalism in their guerrilla warfare against bourgeois democracy, although this naturalism was the idiom of the hated bourgeoisie and came into existence partly through bourgeois opposition to the reactionary tendencies of romanticism. Romanticism in its turn is even more ambivalent and kaleidoscopic than naturalism. There is a romanticism of socially progressive and a romanticism of conservative strata: consider the romanticism of the Hellenistic bourgeoisie, of medieval chivalry, of the late Gothic, of the hispanophile French nobility, the romanticism of the reaction against revolutionary France and of those classes which were determined to maintain at any cost the spiritual heritage of the Revolution, especially its emancipation of the individual. The romantic movement that gripped all Europe in the age of the Restoration had in one country a predominantly revolutionary character, but in another was rather counter-revolutionary; even within the same country, it sometimes played a liberating role, inspiring the individual with a sense of self-reliance, sometimes an obscurantist role, clouding and confusing the minds of men. We recognize that there were hints of modern romanticism long before the outbreak of the Revolution, but this fact is seen in its proper light only when we realize that the romantic movement would never have had its profound and widespread effect without the achievements of the Revolution, and that it was from the very beginning a symptom of the social crisis that led to the Revolution.

The socio-historical treatment of art can claim to be scientific in spite of the fact that no hard and fast laws governing the relation between social form and art-form can be established. For although the social function of the attitudes typical of a style changes, so that these become linked with various

class-interests and ways of life, they are still not socially indifferent attitudes, not compatible with any and every social
position. There is one romanticism of the medieval knight and
another of the modern bourgeois, but there is no peasant romanticism. And though one can speak of the artistic rationalism
of the fifteenth-century bourgeois and that of the seventeenth-
century aristocracy, a rationalism associated with the knightly
ideal of life seems inconceivable. A more concrete example:
the dramatic unities were introduced into French tragedy for
the most part with a view to making more lifelike what went on
on the stage; later, however, they lost this realistic significance
and became the vehicle of the most extreme stylization; but
all the time they represent an essentially rationalistic view of
life which would be quite incompatible with the genius of the
medieval, as with that of the romantic, drama. To return to the
case of naturalism, it is not a monopoly of politically progressive and liberal circles, as socialist art theory will have it; yet a
type of society whose interests are bound up with the conservation of socially backward conditions will wherever possible
support those tendencies in art which are inclined to idealize
existing conditions. None the less, the leaders of this kind of
society may on occasion find it advisable to employ naturalistic methods in art, as Gros, for example, who began to paint
naturalistic battle-pieces when the misery of the Napoleonic
campaigns could no longer be covered up. It was no doubt a
romantic kind of naturalism that was there expressed, the language of the post-revolutionary middle and upper bourgeoisie,
whose favor he had to court. This is not a case of inner contradictions within a class, in the Marxist sense, but of the adaptability of a social stratum that possesses its own preferred weapons and tactics, but often has to adopt those of opponents or
future allies in order to maintain itself—as, for example, the
knightly armies adopted infantry tactics when the age of gun-
powder came, the knights giving up, for the sake of survival
and the common victory, the chance of winning individual
fame. Certainly, the weapons employed may change from time

to time and pass from the hands of one group to those of another, but in the face of the spectacle of the dramatic social struggles in which we see art continually implicated, to deny that its tasks and methods are practically conditioned is obstinate blindness.

One thing more needs to be said. To recognize that economic conditions often have a decisive influence in shaping spiritual structures is not equivalent to the denial of the bright immaculate supermundane ideals and the willing acceptance of all dark material forces, nor does it mean ascribing to these latter a higher value than to all ideal principles. It does not even necessarily imply that the material factor in history is more real than the ideal factor. It is simply to assert that we never find any human spiritual endeavor unless there is some tension with the material conditions of living. If we give proper weight to this fact, we should concede Marx's thesis about the relation of being and conscious being. This thesis by no means excludes the possibility that ideal factors may react upon material conditions. The objection that the human spirit often runs counter to all economic incentives, and can emancipate itself from them by an act of will is not fatal to historical materialism. For the kernel of that doctrine is the assertion that spiritual achievements originate in a dialectical relationship to economic conditions of production; it does not suppose that they are mere copies of the economic conditions. In some cases the dialectical contest may actually end with the outward triumph of the ideal, giving rise to idealistic constructions that seem for the time being able to override the material limitations upon man's spirit. But the important question is to what extent a certain idealistic point of view is tied to particular external circumstances, to what extent it presupposes particular external, material conditions in society. As a king is no less of a social figure than a beggar, so idealism has its roots in social conditions no less than materialism has. The individual's subjective feeling of independence cannot be taken too seriously in comparison with the objective facts that have been estab-

274

lished by historical materialism. The real objection to this doctrine is that it has not been content to note the dialectical
development arising from the opposition of material and ideal
factors, but has replaced the untenable doctrine of the absoluteness of spirit by the equally untenable absoluteness of
matter, one metaphysic by another.

The employment of the sociological method in the history
of art does not necessarily presuppose this extreme form of
historical materialism. It need not imply a claim to give a
strictly sociological explanation of the talent of the individual
artist, with all his particular impulses and inclinations. It is
merely that we are guided by the principle that one individual's opposition to some collective tendency of the time, no less
than another individual's acceptance of it, is partly a product
of social forces. The artist no doubt produces what he will and
as he will, but the question of what elements go to make up his
"will" always remains. The artist, to be sure, has the last word,
but the role of those who have the last but one is not to be un-
derrated, especially as their word can normally be detected in
the utterance of the artist. The weakest of the objections raised
against the sociological point of view is that the creators of the
great works of art were extraordinary persons in that they were
"great solitaries." We are unduly narrowing the concept of
"the social" if we take it to exclude solitariness. Even W. B.
Yeats inappropriately restricts the field of social efficacy with
his dictum: "A work of art is the social act of a solitary man,"
for he sets up an opposition between the social product and its
lonely creator, ignoring the fact that loneliness is a social category, and that as an individual experience it can exist only in a
society. One can certainly be alone in all sorts of circumstances,
but one can only *feel lonely* in a world in which others somehow or other partake. For reasons that psychoanalysis is able
to explain in part, the artist is more estranged from his society
than most other men, but it is not obvious that in consequence
of this estrangement artistic activity must be more intractable
to the sociologist than any other occupation or obsession. If one

allows that some social preconditions of criminality can be found, it seems incomprehensible that one should not admit similar social conditions of artistic production. The spiritual world of the artist may be incomparably more complex than that of the criminal, but as far as the relation between individual freedom and social causation goes, there seems to be no difference of principle between the creation of a work of art and the commission of a crime.

The work of art is indeed something incommensurable on account of the good fortune its creator enjoys and the happiness it bestows on others. That is why those who have had most experience of that happiness have wanted to base the interpretation of art upon principles that should be unique and peculiar to it; no method that has proved useful for anything else seems good enough. This is the only explanation for such assertions as: "Social history of art is as senseless as an art history of society would be." [2] But the cleverness of the formulation should not blind us to the unsatisfactory substance of the thought. The fact that sociological concepts do not enable us to comprehend the *essence* of art is not to say that art cannot be elucidated by sociological concepts any more than can society by aesthetic concepts. The relationship between art and society cannot be thus simply reversed. Society is anything but an aesthetic phenomenon, whereas art is an eminently social achievement; whatever else it may be, it is among other things a product of social forces and a source of social effects. About the forces operative in art and the effects that proceed from it much that is noteworthy can be said without presuming to fathom its intrinsic being or fearing to dispel its magic.

[2] G. Previtali: *"Una 'Storia sociale dell'arte,'"* *Paragone*, No. 71 (November 1955), p. 53.

V

Educational Strata in
the History of Art:
Folk Art and Popular Art

1. *THE ART OF THE PEOPLE,*
THE MASSES, AND THE EDUCATED

IN THIS CHAPTER "folk art" signifies the poetical, musical, and pictorial activities of those strata of the
population which are uneducated and not urbanized or indus-
trialized. It is of the essence of this art that those who keep it
in being are not only passively receptive, but normally are creative participants in the artistic activities, and yet do not stand
out as individuals or claim any personal authorship of the productions. "Popular art" on the other hand is to be understood
as artistic or quasi-artistic production for the demand of a half-
educated public, generally urban and inclined to mass-behavior.
In folk art, producers and consumers are hardly distinguished,
and the boundary between them is always fluid; in the case of
popular art, we find on the contrary an artistically uncreative,
completely passive public, and professional production of artistic goods strictly in response to the demand for them. It is
indeed a striking fact that folk art, especially folk-poetry,
emerges from the ranks of those who enjoy it, whereas popular
songs—the street-ballads and popular "hits"—derive from pro-
fessionals belonging to and spiritually dependent upon the upper classes.[1] But really the most important distinction between
the two types of art lies in the different character of their publics. The people who maintain the folk-song are the unlettered,
though not necessarily illiterate, inhabitants of the countryside,
the villages, the little market-towns; the readers and consumers

[1] John Meier: *Kunstlieder im Volksmunde* (1908).

of murder-stories, picture papers, sentimental novels, and oleo-graphs, are the lower classes of the cities, who are less clearly separated from the educated than the country-folk are.

As there are usually at least as many different trends in art at any one time as there are cultural strata, art history should take more account than it has generally taken of the particular demands and aims of groups differing by education. If it did so, it would have to portray the development of art by the use of cross-sections, and that would make people realize that in art there are always several different traditions running par-allel, and would dispose of the dogma that everything con-temporary must be organically connected. However, to describe the lines of artistic development according to whether they are attributable to the spiritual élite, the urban masses, or the country-folk, and thus to distinguish the history of sophisticated art from that of popular art and folk art, would be to perform only the first and easier half of the art historian's task; he would have to go on to investigate how level of education and class situation are related, what dialectical contradictions are found within the same educational stratum, and how the tensions be-tween class standpoint and educational standpoint may be re-solved. His task should only be considered accomplished when he has shown that the influence of education is not at all a simple function of economic and social conditions, but increases or diminishes in importance in accord with the total historical situation. For the significance and value of education vary re-markably; in the Middle Ages, for example, it enjoyed enor-mous prestige and yet was not so indispensable for success in art as it became in later centuries.

However, an exposition of the history of art by cultural strata would be wholly appropriate only for the post-Renais-sance, or perhaps for the post-revolutionary period—*i.e.*, for the period during which the strata of the art-public became more sharply separated and more definitely independent in their requirements. The art historian might indeed, and should, take note of earlier phenomena, such as that of the ancient mime as folklike art in contrast to the official Athenian theater, or that of the medieval ballad, which sank to the status of folk-poetry in contrast to the heroic poetry of the warlike nobility. He could in particular refer to the numerous pictorial and sculptural productions of the Middle Ages—mainly devotional objects—which are of a rather modest character and obviously were produced by and for a lower stratum, yet without one's being able as a rule to label them folk art or popular art in the sense defined above, or even clearly to distinguish what in them is owing to lower class status and what to individual lack of skill. At this early stage of development we can perhaps speak of a folk art alongside the sophisticated art of the clergy and courts, but hardly of a "popular" art. Only at the end of the Middle Ages can one discern the beginnings of the production of an art that was not expected to interest either the educated élite or the country-folk, but met the demand of a fairly prosperous, although not wealthy, urban middle class. Before that time, there could be no question of producing pictures or sculpture as wares to suit a popular taste: no section of society except the upper classes was in a position to purchase such things. The woodcuts of the transition period between the Middle Ages and the Renaissance were the first art-products to be bought to some extent by the less well-to-do townsfolk.

The negative features that distinguish folk art and popular art from the higher art of the educated, the expert, and the connoisseur seem at first sight more striking and more important than the positive features which these different types of art have in common. Serious, authentic, responsible art, which necessarily involves a wrestling with the problems of life and an effort to capture the meaning of human existence, art which confronts us with a demand to "change our way of living," has little in common either with folk art, which is often hardly more than play and adornment, or with popular art, which is never more than entertainment and a means of passing the time. When one thinks of the creations of Michelangelo or Rembrandt, Bach or Beethoven, Flaubert or Baudelaire, one feels reluctant to reckon as art either the playful and clumsy ornaments and songs of peasants or the literature and music of the modern entertainment industry with its coquetry and flattery of the common man. And though folk art may perhaps retain some of the prestige it derived from the romantics, one feels disinclined to name in the same breath the *Merry Widow* and Mozart's *Figaro*, Böcklin's *Isle of the Dead* and El Greco's *Burial of the Count of Orgaz*. Anyone who has known the shattering experience of being involved with a real work of art easily becomes intolerant of all exploitation of cheap effects and is very ready to maintain that there is only *one* art, indivisible and incapable of being diluted, and beside which all else is devoid of significance or value.

The true character of art is not to be understood from either folk art or popular art; it reveals its nature only upon the highest level of creative activity. Looking out from that level, we seem to descry unbridgeable gulfs in every direction. One can find no common denominator in Mozart and Lehar. And yet the extremes are linked by numerous intermediate phenomena; there are degrees of realization of aesthetic values. Works of art do not originate in the thin air of a spirit-world; artistic production is something dynamic and dialectical, an act bound up with the whole of life, an activity rooted in practice. And so its contacts and connections with non-artistic and quasi-artistic spheres of activity are of the most manifold kind. The success of the enterprise is always in doubt, the work always liable to be spoilt or falsified; still, even in this precarious situation the artist may be lucky enough to reach his goal by a kind of light-heartedness, the light-heartedness of the showman. Great art nearly always includes certain elements of the lower sorts of art. The most sublime work aims to please and interest, and so employs some of the means and methods characteristic of a lower level. The romantics exaggerated the childlike innocence of the artist, who goes to work in a way that is by no means so naïve and spontaneous as they liked to pretend. But there is also always a certain element of playfulness about his work, and as there is something of the child, so there is always something of the simple jester about him. In art, the most desperate wrestling with the meaning of life and the most ruthless self-criticism often go along with the most frivolous urge to entertain and the most sentimental self-satisfaction.

Every work of art contains more and less successful portions; there are sublime works, yet perhaps not a single really "perfect" work of art. The predestined, unalterable and unsurpassable artistic form, in the meaning of Flaubert's *mot juste*, is as bold a philosophical fiction as the alleged divine inspiration by which the artist lays hold of the archetypes of being. A sense of perfection is not a necessary ingredient of the aesthetic experience. Works of great art may often have a certain likeness to folk art or to popular art; they reach down to these levels, or emerge out of them, without suffering any harm. Just as the art-song which later becomes a folk-song may be garbled, but also improved, in the process, so a work that simply aims to entertain may fall to the lowest depths, but also may rise to heights of almost magical charm.

The farther one goes back in history, the more difficult it becomes to determine with certainty which strata of the public the artist was addressing. Even with Shakespeare, the boundary between his poetry and his clowning, between his tidbits for the boxes and his strong meat for the pit, is as hard to draw as the boundary between serious art and folk art in the Middle Ages. In the theater the fare offered for the entertainment of the public seems at all times to have been of a somewhat mixed character. None the less, the difference in degree between the artistic means employed often becomes a radical difference of quality. Thus, to take one of the most typical cases, a survey of the graphic art of Dürer and that of his followers who popularized and vulgarized his work reveals at first only a very gradual decline; but in the end, in the broadsheets of the eighteenth century, we see, as has been clearly demonstrated, the emergence of a mass art fundamentally different in character from what has gone before.[2]

2. FOLK ART, PEASANT ART, PROVINCIAL ART

Art history turns upon the individual, since it is from the individual that the general stylistic trends, for all their persistence, derive their most significant traits. Within the inner and outer—psychological and sociological—limits, the creative role of personality is certainly the decisive factor. Without it art would lose not only its peculiar quality, but also one of the moments in that dialectic that keeps it in a condition of historical change. The principal feature of folk art and popular art, however, is that in them the influence of the individual is reduced to a minimum, so that both the productive and the receptive forces in the development are representatives of a group, and vehicles of common aesthetic taste, in a far stricter sense than is ever the case with the more sophisticated forms of art. For although the originator of a folk-song may be a more or less definitely ascertainable individual, his creative activity is very largely conditioned, not only by the models that he discovers and adopts from the music and poetry of the higher social levels, but also by his dependence upon the taste of his group. He is in fact the spokesman of a community, and in this sense it is perfectly correct to describe folk art as a collective activity. The folk-song is indeed an individual achievement down to its smallest detail, but even its most complex forms are so contrived that any member of the community can feel the song as his own. Even if it is going rather too far to say with Hans Naumann that the folk-song indeed

[2] Wilhelm Fränger: *"Deutsche Vorlagen zu russischen Volksbilderbogen des 18. Jahrhunderts," Jahrbuch für historische Volkskunde,* II (1926), 163.

derives from a certain individual, but that "any other individual could just as well have written it," [3] it is at any rate a fact
that though talent is individual, the spiritual interests and the
content of experience expressed in it are common, that a song
is a folk-song only when it has become a common possession. [4]
Again, in popular art as in folk art, we can speak of an individual's influence only within very narrow limits. The producers
of art for the masses express their personal taste, where that
might diverge from the general taste, much less than the real
artist expresses his; while the members of the public to which
they address themselves are distinguished primarily by lack of
any personal taste.

Neither the public of folk art nor that of popular art is
able or willing to treat art as art, or judge it by formal standards.
Their attitude to art rests upon relationships quite extraneous
to it, is connected far more directly with the common interests,
hopes, and fears of the group than is the case with connoisseurs
of art. The latter are inclined to feel every artistic achievement
as the victory of the artist over some great technical difficulty,
to evaluate everything from this point of view, and to be more
thrilled by a technical victory than most people are over the
triumph of their favorite hero of romance in some perilous
situation. The readers of mass literature know nothing of the
author's difficulties, and the authors of this literature positively
pride themselves on never having felt any. This indifference
to matters of form is by itself sufficient to explain how styles
in folk art and popular art change more slowly and by fewer
gradations than those in serious art. Folk art, it is true, reflects
the changes in the art of the educated with a much greater
time-lag and much fewer nuances than does the art of the urban
mass public; but just as folk art follows only to a small extent
the changes that are going on in the higher forms of art, and
shows a rather sluggish development, so also the popular art of
the urban masses makes a very narrow, even if not very pains-

[3] Hans Naumann: *Primitive Gemeinschaftskultur* (1921), p. 6.
[4] Cf. Meier: *Das deutsche Volkslied: I. Balladen* (1935), Pt. I, p. 7.

taking, selection out of the various subjects and forms offered to it from above. Thus this type of art too develops more slowly, that is, exhibits fewer transitional forms, than the art of the educated and the connoisseurs, which shows its pulsating life most strikingly in a continuous differentiation of forms that to the consumers and producers of mass art seems meaningless and unintelligible.

However, the individuality of serious art and the impersonality of the more popular types are not quite mutually exclusive or entirely without intermediates and transitions. Even the most individual, the most stubbornly original of artists moves within the bounds of a style, a tradition, a system of conventions; he cannot always do what he wants to do—indeed, he cannot always want to do what in a general way he might like to do. He too shares the basic principles of his art with others, and produces his works for a fairly homogeneous public —at any rate he is governed in his work by the idea of such a public. And at the other extreme, only the most primitive forms of folk art can be regarded as "communal art"; at a very early stage it is transformed either into the art of a class or into a mode of expression in which only the more talented can make themselves understood. All art is, as Croce says of poetry, at once personal and impersonal; all art expresses both the unique and the typical.[5] Folk art is not the creation of a "people" in the sense of some homogeneous psychic force, as the romantics imagined. The "folk soul" is no more than a personification of the functional unity that connects the various manifestations of a community. This unity is not an independent entity; it is at most a consciousness or indefinite feeling of belonging together. The folk soul is no more than a psychological construction, the fictitious subject of various compatible but not organically coherent modes of behavior. One can give a meaning to the concept, but should not ascribe to it spiritual activity or feeling or thought or power of artistic creation. Artistic production which would be truly collective is a completely un-

[5] Benedetto Croce: *Poesia "popolare" e poesia "d'arte"* (1930), p. 6.

imaginable process, part of the myth of the "genius of the folk," which, as Dilthey observed, is just as useless as a historical explanation of spiritual phenomena as the concept of "vital force" is for the purposes of physiology.[6]

The romantic theory of folk art rests on a mistake; it fails to recognize that though several individuals *in succession* may take a hand in the composition of a folk-song, they cannot possibly all compose it *at the same time*—that a folk-song is the continually modified result of a process of mutual adaptation, not at all like a unanimous resolution by an executive committee. Folk art, like a historical style in art or thought, is at once the creation of individuals and the possession of the many; as no work of art completely expresses all the aspects of a style, so also no version of a folk-song can be regarded as the only authentic one; every version is admissible and relevant. What gives folk-songs their collective character is that they pass on from mouth to mouth, not some property of being sung simultaneously and in the same manner by large numbers of people.

Romanticism ignored the concrete features of folk art, and for the sake of emphasizing its supposedly universal and archetypal character, transformed it into a phenomenon vague in conception and mysterious in origin. No products of the human spirit have been so deeply dyed with the concepts of the romantic philosophy of art and history as the folk-epic, the folk-song, and the folk-tale, all of which were less a discovery than an invention of the romantic era. It took a long and painful effort for historical research to free itself from the notion of a people collectively improvising things in what was imagined to be the spiritual atmosphere of prehistoric times, and to recognize that every product of folk art, every folk-song, and every theme in a song had its own author and its own hour and place of birth.[7] The romantics took their stand upon the conception that folk-poetry, unlike the literature of the educated, must be al-

---

[6] Wilhelm Dilthey: *Einleitung in die Geisteswissenschaften* (1922), pp. 31 ff.

[7] Cf. G. Doncieux: *Le Romancéro populaire* (1904), p. ix.

most wholly the outcome of deep-seated drives, must owe almost nothing to external influences; that it derived its finest features, in modern psychological terms, from a collective unconscious. This plant-like, organic growth of folk art was for the romantics the prototype of the mysterious act of creation, from which all that was profound and spiritually significant seemed to them to flow. Here contacts between romanticism and psychoanalysis are most strikingly evident. The psychoanalytic interpretation of spiritual structures finds its richest source of material in folk art, and the romantic type of folk-lore finds nowhere in modern academic studies so favorable a reception and so definite a confirmation as it gets from psychoanalysis. The identification of the country-folk with their singers and artists is indeed more complete than that of the educated with their own spiritual leaders. That high degree of solidarity is what renders possible the wide currency of the works and gives them a communal quality. But folk art is especially favored as a subject for psychoanalytic interpretation for another reason: it reflects an incipient stage of sublimation, so that the original drives are more clearly discerned in it than in most other cultural structures. The psychological primitiveness of folk art manifests itself not merely in its lack of all prudishness, but also in the episodic and rhapsodic manner of expression and in the incoherence of its concepts and images, which gives us a very direct insight into the workings of the unconscious. It is evident that, as in ordinary life, so in art the leveling out of contradictions and the plastering over of cracks is largely the effect of our efforts to erase unwelcome traces of unconscious lines of thought.

The romantics' excessively sharp distinction between folk-poetry and art-poetry, and especially their doctrine that folk art, as organic growth propagated by unbroken living tradition, is something absolutely different from the conscious and experimental art-production of the educated, or "overeducated" —all this is, in the main, still to be found in Riegl. He too makes so sharp a distinction between folk art as "grown" and fine art as "intended" that there is no place for the art of the country-folk in an art history based on his conception of "artistic intention" and the peculiar rationality of art.[8]

Riegl concentrates upon the visual arts of the country-folk, and defines folk art as the home crafts and home industry of peasants who make and adorn for themselves objects of common use. Thus at the outset he excludes from folk art all products of skilled handicraft practiced as a trade, ignoring the whole field of peasant house-building and the manufacture of furniture, pictures, and other forms of image for the church. His concept of folk art is a purely economic one, based mainly on the circumstance that in this field producers and consumers are identical, production being for use and not for sale on the open market. No doubt this point of view explains some of the most important features of folk art, not only its amateurish character and clumsiness, but also its conservatism and traditionalism, its retention of traditional motifs and forms—in fact all those traits which mark its independence of fluctuating market conditions, competition, and advertisement, of artificially induced and rapidly changing fashions. Though in his investigations, Riegl considers only the decorative arts, his principle of explanation applies equally to folk-poetry and folk-music; it certainly is characteristic of these that they do not have to seek the favors of their audience. But Riegl neglects the fact that an appreciable part of the products he has in mind is not produced *by*, but only *for*, the country-folk. This is peculiarly the case with the visual arts, and it is extraordinary that Riegl should have overlooked the fact. It is a serious general defect of his theory that he only takes account of conditions of production and does not pay sufficient attention to the circumstances of consumption. Had his point of view been less one-sided, he would have recognized that country-folk exert a greater and more pervasive influence upon art not as producers, but as consumers.

[8] Alois Riegl: *Volkskunst, Hausfleiss und Hausindustrie* (1894).

289

For the social structure of art, the social status of those for whom it is intended is in general more important than that of its producers. However different the provenance of the artists, the works tend to bear the stamp of the class for which they are produced. Artistic themes may make their way upwards from the country-folk, or—far more commonly—downwards to the country-folk from the upper strata, but the public to which the producers address themselves is really decisive for their social character. The artists of the upper classes are recruited from all sections of society, only to a very small extent from the governing class itself. Country-folk take an infinitely greater share in the production of their own art, and it is practically speaking only here that we find, especially in the visual arts, production for own use. Most figural representations however, the woodcuts and copper engravings that country-folk buy, the devotional pictures and figures of saints that adorn their houses, the furnishings of country churches and places of pilgrimage, derive in the main from men who produce them as a trade, who, though mostly having their origins in the country-folk, can hardly be reckoned as belonging to it still.

It is remarkable that Riegl, recognizing and appraising, even perhaps exaggerating, the importance of the economic conditions of folk art, should have so misconceived the sociological nature of this art and have been so blinded by the romantic dogma of the unitary folk-spirit as to assert that folk art is "that sum of traditional art-forms which are the common property of all members of the people (*Volk*) and not of any one class such as the property-owners." [9] His sociological views were evidently uninfluenced by his economic insight. He failed to notice that a phenomenon such as folk art presupposes social differentiation and is incompatible with the concept of a unitary culture or psychic attitude pervading a whole nation. One can speak of folk art only where there are already differences of class and education; if there is no social and spiritual élite, there is no sense in introducing the concept of folk art, for it has

[9] Ibid.

significance only by contrast with the art of educated strata
and with sources of production which are not "folklike." Folk
art is not communal art, but the art of a class and of a status,
like the art of the upper class. A peasant society that knows no
differences of education (even though from the point of view
of government it may no longer be quite uniform), like that of
the neolithic age or the Germanic tribes of the time of Migrations, produces peasant art, but not folk art. Riegl, and in
folk-song research above all Béla Bartók, fail to see the distinction, having too narrow a conception of "folk." What may have
misled them is the fact that modern folk art is almost entirely
the work of peasants; one ought however to admit that, even if
all folk art is peasant art, not all peasant art can be folk art. So
long as the carriers of the culture are peasants, as in the New
Stone Age or the age of the Migrations, one should speak of
peasant culture and of peasant art; one should speak of folk
art only where alongside of the "art of the folk" (who no doubt
consist mainly of peasant farmers) there is also an "art of the
élite." If we were to insist on applying this term in an age
such as that of the Migrations, in which the social differentiation implied in the concept of folk art had not yet taken place,
the entire artistic production would have to be denominated
"folk art"—but that would simply be to confuse the sense of the
term. We certainly cannot think of the products of that age
as "primitive communal art": although the educational strata
are not yet differentiated, the assumed uniform psychic attitude
to life, which might provide the basis for a communal culture,
has long ago vanished.

It is indeed very questionable whether there ever was
any "communal culture," whether the conception of culture does
not necessarily imply the differentiation of society by social
stratum and status. Upon any level of evolution on which it is
admissible to use the word "poetry," man must have outgrown,
psychologically and sociologically, the state of "communality"
in Naumann's sense of the word. It is unthinkable that man
should have composed poetry before being conscious of himself

as an individual or distinguishing himself from others, or at least trying to distinguish himself. Individuality may be pushed into the background, as in folk art, but it is one of the preconditions of artistic activity of any sort. Naumann smuggles the romantic concept of the folk-spirit back into anthropology in the guise of primitive communal spirit, although he admits that folk-poetry is not a direct continuation of the primeval communal poetry and that "the folk" derived its heritage from this poetry by way of conscious art-poetry—so that in his view a song deliberately composed might be nearer to primitive communal poetry than a folk-song.[1] But however one may define the paradisal state of communally poetizing man, the origins of art and poetry are not to be found in a state of things in which man had no sense of history and was wholly immersed in nature. The desire for art and the capacity to produce art are historically conditioned forces that could only become effective in a historical situation.[2]

Nor is folk art to be identified with provincial art any more than with peasant art. One of the most striking features of folk art is its contrast to the art of the towns and cultural centers; but though it is essentially a non-urban art, it is not an art that would like to be urban but cannot. Provincial art is continuously dependent upon the taste of the big town, and so never escapes from a certain sense of inferiority; but folk art, though itself dependent upon the art produced in the towns, courts, and monasteries, never emulates it consciously, intentionally, or slavishly. Though a second-hand art, it is not inspired by fashion or any desire to produce works indistinguishable from those it imitates. Again, though it does not attempt to keep up with the art of the cultural centers, it has no particular desire to maintain its own traditions at all costs, is ready to give these up when something new catches its attention. The country-folk do not aim

---

[1] Naumann, op. cit., pp. 6–7.
[2] Cf. Alfred Götze: *"Begriff und Wesen des Volksliedes," Germanistisch-romanistische Monatshefte*, IV (1912), p. 78; C. Brouwer: *Das Volkslied* (1930), p. 116.

to have an art of their own different in principle from that of the rest of society. "There never was a conscious, that is a deliberately produced folk art," is the verdict of a well-known exponent of folk-lore.[3] The fact that most folk-songs are not in dialect, but in the language of the educated,[4] shows how devoid of vanity and self-conceit country-folk are in this matter. Dialect songs are usually the product of professional poets, who think that they should make an effort to find their way down to the people; whereas real country-folk, when they make up a poem, are not trying to be "natural," but are putting on their Sunday clothes, emotionally and linguistically.[5]

The provincial public is a far more complicated social structure than that which the Germans designate by the word *Volk* (and which we have referred to as "the country-folk"). The regionally differentiated Egyptian provincial art, for example, which tried somewhat laboriously to keep up with the artistic activity of the royal courts and temple precincts, was neither folk art nor peasant art; its exponents were in part the minor feudal lords who had gradually separated themselves from the court, in part the middle-class provincial bureaucracy, whose taste may indeed have been influenced by the older peasant art, but consciously rejected that art.[6] In the same way, certain regional trends that cropped up along with the official Byzantine art appear to have had little in common with folk art. Similarly, the art-products of the Rajput School, active in India around 1700, are examples of provincial art, not folk art.[7] On the other hand, late Roman provincial art has a thoroughly "peasant" character and seems to be the sole example of this type of art which was influential in its day and significant in art history.

[3] R. Forrer: *Von alter und ältester Bauernkunst* (1906), p. 6.

[4] Cf. Eduard Wechssler: *Begriff und Wesen des Volksliedes*(1913), p. 13.

[5] Heinrich Morf: *Das französische Volkslied: Aus Dichtung und Sprache der Romanen,* II (1911), p. 90.

[6] Cf. Arnold Hauser: *The Social History of Art* (1951), I, 62–4.

[7] Cf. M. Harmon: "Primitive and Folk Art," in *Standard Dictionary of Folklore,* ed. M. Leach (1950), p. 896. *Benjamin Rowland: The Art and Architecture of India* (1953), pp. 202 ff.

It would however be a mistake to speak of it as the spiritual product of the peasantry's "closeness to nature and rootedness in the soil." [8] The historical role of this provincial peasant art has nothing to do with the "country-folk's eternal youth," much to do with the age and decadence of the ancient urban culture.

3. RECEPTION THEORY AND PRODUCTION THEORY

The thesis that folk art consists of "cultural goods that have drifted downward" is a commonplace that hardly anyone now thinks of doubting. In this view, art-forms and art-styles, subjects and motifs, conceptual and emotional patterns find their way down from the upper levels of culture; and thus folk art has become cruder, grosser and wilder during this process of precipitation. According to the prevailing opinion, country-folk are essentially unproductive; they produce scarcely anything themselves, but only reproduce. "Country-folk cannot compose, only adjust or at most vary; they do not create, only select." [9] Folk-songs for the most part are nothing but plagiarism.[1] The folk-poet is the typical amateur who recalls all manner of examples when he sets himself to "make poetry." He cannot free himself from the songs that stick in his memory, so that particular lines, phrases, and images turn up in his poems almost word for word as he heard them. But he does not even *try* to free himself from his models; he has no ambition to be original. He need not fear competition, requires no advertisement, and that circumstance gives his whole performance a "medieval" air—which constitutes the allegedly "Gothic" character of folk art.

The doctrine of "sunken cultural goods" entails a certain

[8] F. A. Scheltema: *Die deutsche Volkskunst* (1938), p. 19.
[9] W. Tappert: *Wandernde Melodien* (1868), p. 38.
[1] Gabriel Vicaire: *Etudes sur la poésie populaire* (1902), p. 80.

explanation of the backward character of folk art. This always limps behind the art of the élite, with an appreciable time-lag, so that trends in style and taste intrinsically akin are found on these two different levels to be separated by a considerable interval of time. This interval has been estimated at about one hundred years, and the whole theory has been illustrated by instructive examples from the products of the visual arts.[2]

Now whether this chronology be correct or not, the backwardness of folk art is undeniable. In the older periods of art history, such as the medieval, this backwardness is often the only indication we have of the folk origin of certain objects.

The art of the élite, when popularized and ruralized, loses not only its appropriateness to the times, but even as a rule its aesthetic quality. Its themes are treated in a banal fashion, its devices take on a clumsy appearance, and the final result often gives the impression of being the parody of an ill-understood original. Country-folk do not judge art by aesthetic standards; folk art is regarded as "art" only by the educated; those who created it are not conscious of having produced anything outside of the ordinary round of daily habit and practical need. Country-folk lack both the conception of art as a special affair of its own and the capacity to distinguish the better from the worse. Any collector of folk-songs knows from his own experience that the country-man, when asked to sing, unpacks his whole repertoire and gives his best genuine folk-songs, humorous pieces, and popular "hits" of the town, all jumbled together.[3]

But this lack of aesthetic judgment among country-folk does not in the least imply that what they produce is inferior. They create as the child does, innocently, irresponsibly, uncritically, but not necessarily without talent. Faguet's dictum *"La littérature et l'art ne sont populaires qu'à condition d'être médiocres"* [4] has its appeal as roundly destructive of romantic

[2] Meier: *Kunstlieder im Volksmunde*, p. xiv.
[3] Cf. Henri Davenson: *Le Livre des chansons* (1946), pp. 26–7.
[4] Emile Faguet: *Politiques et moralistes*, I, 167.

illusions. It would be truer however to say that folk-taste is indeed entirely uncertain and unreliable, but luckily in their production of art country-folk are not wholly governed by their own taste. If we admit this, we must not fall again into the mystifications of the romantics, who ascribed to the individual all manner of powers, capacities, and endeavors of which he was wholly unaware and about which he could do nothing, and which therefore must have been inspired by some higher intelligence. The fact that country-folk, out of mere endeavor to make something or out of uncertainty how to go on with it, grasp at ready-made traditional forms that they do not really understand how to use by no means implies that these forms have, so to speak, fallen into their lap. Tradition in the end derives from individual achievements going on all through folk art—whether, with the "receptionists," notably Tappert, Forrer, Meier, and Naumann, one regards the process as a clumsier repetition of forms once developed in a more refined version, or with the "productionists," *i.e.*, the romantics from Jacob Grimm to Joseph Pommer, one considers it a process of original creation.

One of the unconfirmed assumptions of the "production theory" is that of Pommer, who claims that we know at once whether a song is a folk-song or an art-song; and that it is inconceivable for a song that did not originate among the country-folk to have the artistic merits that we value in a folk-song. The fact that the most highly qualified experts have so frequently been mistaken on this very point shows how fallible romantic intuitions are. As a matter of fact, the history of modern folk-song research consists very largely of discoveries that prove folk-songs to be generally no more than "art-songs as sung by the country-folk" (*Kunstlieder im Volksmunde*). The objection that this has not been proved for all folk-songs is irrelevant; it suffices to have been proved that every type of folk-song had its origin in a composition of conscious art and that the hypothesis of its being thus taken over is not incompatible with the characteristic features of folk-poetry or folk-song.

Incontestable as the basic thesis of the "reception theory" may be, we can accept the theory only with certain reservations. Above all, the extreme contrast that it makes between what is "elevated" and what has "sunk," between "educated" and "uneducated," between art for connoisseurs and art for the people, must be modified. As almost always in history, we do not find unbridgeable gulfs, but rather a road with passes, bridges, and side-tracks. An attempt to explain and simplify difficult, not easily apprepreciated works of art often sets in on the very highest level. Not only do disciples and imitators try to introduce the works of a difficult artist in wider circles; the master himself, be he ever so self-willed and ruthless, often makes certain concessions to the public which set in motion a process of gradual popularization. All the schools, courses, museums, exhibitions, books, newspapers, and journals thereupon take up the process, and through their teachers, critics, and publicists mediate between the masters and the public; the latter purchases its initiation to a higher level at the cost of a certain condescension to it on the part of the masters.

The romantics were the first to call attention to the fluidity of the boundary between folk-poetry and art-poetry. Achim von Arnim maintained in his correspondence with Jacob Grimm that there is no absolute "nature-poetry" because, he said, "there is no moment without its history." [5] "History" meant for him the sphere of transitions and mediations in which difference of degree is suddenly transformed into difference of kind—where rigid concepts such as up and down, spontaneous and artificial, folk-poetry and art-poetry are only to be used with caution. With the beginning of history, which is the very stuff of human life, the state of mere nature is at an end; from then on there are only combinations of nature and art. When we realize this, neither the production theory nor the reception theory provides us with a wholly satisfying conception of folk art. The latter no less than the former draws too sharp a

[5] Letter of July 14, 1811, quoted by R. Steig: *Achim von Arnim und Jacob Grimm* (1904), p. 134.

297

boundary between spontaneity and receptivity; its conceptions are too unrealistic and romantic, for it too subscribes to the myth of creative power, only inverting the sign and ascribing all true creativity to the educated élite.

The essential defect of the reception theory lies in its neglect of the fact that the taking over of art-forms and themes into folk art always depends upon the realization of certain conditions. The reception never takes place mechanically, but manifests certain principles of selection in which the country-folk give effect to their own taste and their own characteristic feeling for form. It is not sufficient to assert that they derive their art from the higher social classes; one must also endeavor to show in what manner and on what principles this borrowing takes place. The reception theory only looks at the negative side of a process whose positive side may at first seem insignificant, but cannot be neglected. The real task of the art critic then is to acknowledge the fact of transformation, to reveal the principles according to which the material is transformed in becoming folk art. It is not easy to define the formal criteria of this art, but still the folklike flavor of a work— whether genuine or spurious, original or imitated, organic or artificial—is unmistakable. The question is what features a work of art which springs from the educated must have in order to please the country-man and be accepted by him, and what his contribution in taking over and transforming the work amounts to. Indubitable as is this contribution, it is none the less most doubtful whether the special character of folk art has a prehistoric origin, as is often asserted. Love of the geometrical in peasant art may well be a neolithic trait, but we have seen that folk art is not simply equivalent to peasant art. Nor can the historical continuity of this geometrism be proved even for peasant art. Bartók, who equates folk-music with "peasant or village music" and holds that peasants are incapable of inventing melodies, does not only ascribe to them an urge to transform in a certain definite way musical themes they have picked up; [6] he also goes so far as to assert that the uniform style of Hungarian village-songs is based upon "an ancient incomplete pentatonic scale that their forefathers brought with them from Asia." [7] But he offers no proof of this alleged unbroken historical continuity. When folk art is given a pre-historic origin, the motive is generally to maintain its primeval character as asserted by the romantics, not just to extend the historical limits within which this or that folk art is actually found. The important thing, however, is to insist that it is always found within definite limits. That it has a special character does not imply that this has remained unaltered throughout the whole course of history. [8]

The influence of folk art upon the more sophisticated forms of art presents us with a special problem. There is not the slightest doubt that folk-song has from time to time had a decisive influence upon sophisticated poetry and music, so that we should be justified in saying that cultural goods "rise" as well as "sink." Folk melodies were used, especially by Haydn, Mozart, Beethoven, and Schubert, as themes for variation [9] no less frequently than subjects of folk-poetry were used by the romantic poets. But apart from the fact that art-music in such cases is only taking back something that folk-music had originally borrowed from it, these borrowings, like most other extraneous influences upon art, are not in themselves creative, but simply provide an occasion for inner renewal. Folk-poetry or folk-music had its effects, much as antiquity had upon the Renaissance or medieval art upon romanticism, only because the preconditions of these effects were already present and because men read their own feelings, thoughts, and images into

[6] Béla Bartók: *"Der Einfluss der Volksmusik auf die heutige Kunstmusik," Melos* (1920); "Hungarian Peasant Music," *The Musical Quarterly,* XIX (1933), 286.

[7] Bartók: *Die Volksmusik der Magyaren und der benachbarten Völker* (1935), p. 1.

[8] Cf. Meier: *Das deutsche Volkslied,* p. 7.

[9] Walter Wiora: *"Volkslied," Deutsche Philologie im Aufbau,* ed. W. Stammler (1954) column 40.

the sources of inspiration before they actually began to draw upon them. Folk art, from which the renascence movements in music seem to originate, is in reality only something upon which the will of renewal fastens; this will to renewal and even its general direction was already there. Bartók's discovery and re-valuation of Hungarian folk-music was also just the expression of his own artistic intentions, arising out of his reaction against late romanticism and his own version of impressionism. Both the selection he made from the village-songs and the interpre-tation he put upon the material in the course of his composition are altogether personal and creative; people now hear Hun-garian folk-music with his ears. Thus in the case of art that "rises to a higher plane," as in the reverse case, a sharp line between reception and production is hard to draw. And wherever it be drawn, the mere fact that sophisticated art gets stimulation from folk art proves nothing regarding the aesthetic value of the productions from which these stimuli proceed. To the real artist the most varied stimuli can prove equally fruitful, and the same stimuli and experiences work out very differently in artists of different rank. Liszt's and Bartók's Hungarian styles have no more than the label in common.

4. *IMPROVIZATION AND SCHEMATIZATION*

The most obvious difference between folk-song and art-song is the former's wide diffusion. Sophisticated art too is ad-dressed to the tastes and interests of a more or less unitary group, but it appeals rather to the individual member of that unity, and attaches itself to such experiences, feelings, and moods as mark the individual off from others and heighten his sense of personality. Folk art on the contrary makes contact only with those emotional contents which either are intrinsically common to all or can be immediately assimilated by all mem-

bers of the community. The essential condition of existence
of the folk-song is its currency, that is, its suitability to be accepted at once by all members of the group. The collective
character of folk art consists in its being ownerless, in that no
one would think of laying an individual claim to its authorship.

The works of folk art are not indeed necessarily anonymous,
but are always impersonal; they may be original in one point
or another, but they do not strive for originality. Their authors
may often possess special talent, but they do not try to make
their works seem different from what their neighbors might
have produced. Folk art is not an individual wrestling with the
problems of life, as sophisticated art is. Everything in folk art
proceeds within the bounds of fixed conventions, whereas in the
art of the educated even the most conventional of forms become
a medium of personal expression. This peculiarity of folk art
however does not derive from any particularly intense sense of
solidarity or community, which as a matter of fact is seldom
found among peasants, nor from an exceptional lack of ambition and vanity, but solely from the special function that art fulfils in the life of the country-folk. Because these works are not
as a rule either a source of gain or a field of competition, and
in consequence lack the tinge of fierce subjectivity which marks
the art of the educated, they are not felt as the expression of a
personality, although they are in some respects attributable to
a particular person. One can see how fond the country-man is
of putting his name and the date on objects of this sort—the
date not of their manufacture, but of their coming into his
possession—without showing any interest in portraits or other
forms of personality cult.[1] However, in this respect there are
historical differences between the different national communi-
ties, and conditions may produce, along with the individualism
of the upper classes, a corresponding feeling for personality
among the country-folk. In many parts of the world the peasants

---

[1] A. Haberlandt: *"Gedanken über Volkskunst," Die bildenden
Künste,* II (1919), 230. Karl Spiess: *Bauernkunst, ihre Art und ihr
Sinn* (1925), p. 70.

still live in the spiritual climate of the Middle Ages; in some lands their way of life already approximates that of the industrial worker.

For the romantics, improvisation was an essential feature of folk art; it was the counterpart of the inspiration of the poet by the grace of God, and, like that, evidence for the instinctive nature of artistic creation. Herder had already asserted that "natural poetry," in contrast to learned poetry, was a spontaneous, unconscious, and naïve manifestation of the folk, who sing like birds and grow and flower like plants. For the romantics themselves the most valuable things in art-poetry were those which seemed to them to manifest the spontaneity and naïveté of folk-poetry. But even they were aware of the limitations of this point of view. Charles Lamb distinguishes in principle two different attitudes to art: "The poet dreams being awake—he is not possessed by his subject but has dominion over it." Malraux is enunciating a variant of this idea, when he says of the art of the child: *"Si l'enfant est souvent artiste, il n'est pas un artiste, car son talent le possède, et lui ne le possède pas."* In contrast to the conscious and critical artist, the creators of folk art evidently belong in the same category as the child, the primitive, and the psychopath; all of these are vehicles, not masters, of their natural talent.

But it would be a mistake to regard improvisation by a folk-singer as altogether genuine and as completely naïve and spontaneous. That it is not, for it consists largely of fixed formulae, traditional motifs, typical phrases, standing epithets, similes and images, continual repetitions and self-quotations, stereotyped introductions and conclusions; these give it its special character. The most artistic of heroic epics and the simplest folk-song move in set forms and utilize a ready-made stock of devices. Poetical forms do not become conventional after having been improvised;[2] generally speaking, they can be improvised only because the poet has firm conventions to fall back upon. The method of the singers of the Khirgiz seems to have been

[2] H. M. Chadwick: *The Growth of Literature* (1925–39), III, 669.

that of the Homeric poems also: [3] "they are composed like a mosaic of a vast number of little pieces of recitation, descriptions of certain typical events and situations such as birth and childhood of a hero, price of his weapons, his preparation for battle, speech of the heroes before the fight, death of the hero and so on." [4]

Folk-poetry constantly employs formulae, but is not therefore static or incapable of development. The elements of the style and the particular devices of the performance occur over and over again, but the structure of the piece as a whole is in a process of perpetual change and flux. The folk-song never outgrows this state of fluidity. It has no permanent form; each of its versions represents a transition. In consequence, folk-poetry may be regarded as the ideal subject for research in the history of styles, as the discontinuity in the stream of development which each work of a great master brings about is absent here. One can only set to the life and growth of a folk-song artificial limits. Folk art is not so much a product as an activity; Steinthal has already noted that folk-poetry is a *nomen actionis*, that is to say, a phenomenon very similar to that of language. There is no one authentic version of a folk-song; one is just as authoritative as another. In this respect it contrasts strongly with the concept of a work of art set up by classical aesthetics. If one is going to revise that concept, it will be necessary to diminish the distance between folk art and sophisticated art in two respects at least. For on the one hand even the most perfect work of art retains something of a contingent, provisional, and changeable character, akin to the waxing and waning forms of folk art; the most satisfactory solution is only one of many that were possible, and not always the best thing the artist could have done. And on the other hand, though the work of art seems to get its unique authentic shape from the hand of the artist, every new interpretation changes its meaning and con-

[3] George Thomson: *Studies in Ancient Greek Society,* I (1949), 527–40.
[4] Meier: *Werden und Leben des Volksepos* (1909), p. 13.

tent. The different generations write, paint, or compose "upon" the works of the masters in the same sort of way that country-folk work "upon" their own songs and tales. In fact, as the centuries go by, a work of art can be said to disintegrate and be reconstituted in the same way that the folk-song gets worn out and remodeled. The writing down of folk-songs, for lack of which, it is said, they get lost, slows the process, but does not stop it.

The country-folk's collective contribution consists precisely in such breaking down and disintegration of the alien products of higher culture. But only the most radical exponent of the reception theory will see in this process something wholly negative. In fact, "singing a tune to death" (*Zersingen*) can be the source of quite positive values; it provides the formal elements that turn an art-song into a folk-song. The jerky, rhapsodic, disconnected structure of folk-poetry is only the most obvious of these elements. The terse phrasing of folk-song and folk-ballad, which corresponds in some respects to the geometrical stylization of visual folk art, may perhaps, though it need not, be linked with the phenomenon of "singing to death." Disintegration of the form could give rise to prolixity as easily as to terseness.

The principle of disintegration is common to the concepts of "dis-organization" and of "tectonization" by which the formal characteristics of folk art have been described—correctly, though not completely.[5] These concepts aim to emphasize the "dissolution of the organic life" of nature, but also the schematization of natural forms and their transmutation into something essentially ornamental. Their authors were impressed by the fact that country-folk, who live in extreme closeness to nature, do not manifest any particular love of nature. This fact expresses not only something fundamental in the psychology of country-folk, but also one of the most important factors determining their attitude toward art. The lower classes mani-

[5] Kurt Freyer: *"Zum Problem der Volkskunst," Monatshefte für Kunstwissenschaft,* IX (1916), 223 ff.; Fränger: op. cit.

fest complete indifference, if not distaste, toward anything related to the circumstances of their everyday life, their daily cares and worries. This explains both their interest in descriptions of upper-class life and their dislike of straightforward naturalism. This phenomenon exhibits very clearly the influence of economic and social conditions upon principles of style and criteria of taste. Such conditions explain why folk art confines itself to the production and decoration of articles of use and avoids any depicting of human and animal forms that would require a higher degree of imitative skill.

Pictures of human form penetrate to the lower social strata only after the invention of the various techniques of printing reproductions, and not until the eighteenth century do they figure in anything that could be called folk art. The conditions described by Balzac in *Illusions perdues*, in which the huts of the peasants are decorated with prints of the stories of the Wandering Jew, Robert the Devil, Fair Magelone, and so on produced in Mme Séchard's printing works relate to the early nineteenth century.[6] Such prints, as well as the illustrated chapbooks, are forms of art in which country-folk participate solely as consumers, for which they have to depend entirely upon the productions of specialized professional artists and craftsmen. If one leaves the well-to-do yeomen out of account, one can hardly put late enough the date when the country-folk first began to purchase objects of art. Even the so-called "folk-books" were not sold at a price that ordinary country-people could pay. One need only look at the imposing folio form of the first specimens of the fifteenth and sixteenth centuries in order to realize that these books, like the manuscripts of an earlier period, were destined for a refined and wealthy public. This public may have included the upper ranks of the towns-folk relatively soon, the middle sort of townsfolk somewhat later; but there cannot for a long time have been any question of the country-folk buying books. For that, the first essential was

[6] Honoré de Balzac: *Illusions perdues*, III: *Les Souffrances de l'inventeur*.

a cheapening of production by reduction of the size to octavo and the employment of the same woodblocks somewhat mechanically to illustrate various different texts.[7]

Apart from the graphic arts, there are of course other sorts of artistic activity in which the country-folk participate merely as consumers because these require a set of craftsmen who have a certain contact with the educated classes and a well-organized system of production. In some lines, for example painting on glass, the producers may have originally been villagers, but even in so minor a field a rationally organized division of labor is so essential for economic success that such production is hardly compatible with the circumstances of country life and work. Anyhow, the principles of taste by which production is governed are such that the products may properly be counted as folk art. With other products, such as flags, signboards, wrought ironwork, and the decorative carving of roundabouts, ships, and wagons, the relation of the producers to the country-folk varies, but the fact that they are the productions of skilled craftsmen does not of itself prevent their having a folklike character.

5. *THE BEGINNINGS OF FOLK ART*

However favorable one's attitude may be on the question of the independence, value, and influence of folk art, one has to decide yet another question. Can one say that folk art has a history of its own, or is this true only with reservations? It must be evident enough that an art history based on the conception of educational strata cannot consist of a portrayal of three uninterrupted, parallel lines of development. Certain stylistic peculiarities may persist for a longer time and in purer form in

[7] Cf. W. Liepe: *"Volksbuch," Reallexikon der deutschen Literaturgeschichte,* ed. P. Merkler and W. Stammler, III (1928–9), 484.

folk art than in the art of the educated, but as the historical changes in folk art depend in the main upon external influences—the effects of the filtering down of cultural goods—the reasons for change lie outside of folk art itself, and the course it takes, seen by itself, often appears illogical and capricious. An independent history of folk art would in any case be impossible owing to the serious gaps in our material. The country-folk seem always to have made some attempt to satisfy their desire for art, but their productions have been less well preserved than those of the upper classes or of the Church; and the folk-origin of what has been preserved cannot always be ascertained. In the earlier periods of history one can never be certain whether one is dealing with the work of a bungler, of a backward provincial artist, or of a folk artist. In consequence of these gaps and uncertainties, the course of development in folk art looks much more irregular than in the other forms of art, in spite of the persistence of some stylistic trends. Cultural catastrophes that shatter the whole existence of the upper classes and completely change their style of life generally leave the lower classes almost untouched and permit the country-folk to carry on their own cultural traditions, even if in rather modest forms. Still, tough and resistant as these traditions may be, they are by no means imperishable or unchangeable.

The circumstance that works of folk art often can only be placed with some difficulty within the stylistic categories of the art historian, that they often cannot be dated or can be dated only very roughly, that, as has been observed, they do not fit into "the rhythm of early, middle and late stages"[8]—all this does not mean that they have no history. It is untrue that there is no development in folk art, that it always remains at the stage of "archaic style."[9] Measured by higher cultural standards, its forms may appear "uncomplicated," "elementary," "easily satisfied," but these features manifest themselves within a gen-

[8] H. Karlinger: *Deutsche Volkskunst* (1938), p. 9.
[9] Paul Frankl: *System der Kunstwissenschaft* (1938), p. 876.

eral historical framework and are subject to historical changes. If the rhythm of the history of styles is here less definitely articulated, that is only because folk art is not autonomous, but mostly takes over the results of historical development in a ready-made form, jumping over some stages of the process. What Eduard Wechssler says of German and French folk-songs —that "nothing would be more erroneous than to suppose that they remain unchanged for centuries" [1]—holds of folk art generally. One gets an impression of unhistorical timelessness as a result of the slowness of this art's development, but even a slow development has a temporal quality.

Again, folk art is often said to be "devoid of style," *i.e.*, without consistency of style. It certainly has no regard for stylistic unity. The furnishings of a family farmhouse show the most various stylistic elements, remnants of Gothic mixed with Jacobean decoration, Georgian and Victorian furniture. Such mixture of styles is partly the result of constant, seemingly uncritical borrowing from the art of the upper classes, partly the result of the conservatism with which country-folk in general stick to what they have once accepted; so that the old is retained alongside the new, and various stylistic elements are put together in a purely superficial fashion. Bartók observed this mingling, and points out that folk-music, while aiming at a unitary style, often manifests different levels of style.[2] To be sure, lack of balance among the stylistic elements of the work is most conspicuously noticeable in folk art, but is not unknown elsewhere; on any fairly advanced level of artistic development we may find an incomplete harmony of elements drawn from different periods. In this respect also, folk art represents the extreme case in a series of gradual transitions.

At the very outset of any history of folk art it needs to be stated that the alleged primeval character of its creations, like their alleged timelessness, is pure legend. Folk art may be of immemorial antiquity, but the thesis that history begins with

[1] Wechssler: *Begriff und Wesen des Volksliedes*, p. 39.
[2] Bartók: "Hungarian Peasant Music," loc. cit., p. 270.

folk art, that all national literatures, for example, begin with a period of folk-poetry,[3] has not been and cannot be proved. One of the best known ways of falsifying history is to represent as the earliest and most original those cultural forms which seem best to fit in with the preconceptions of one's own philosophy. Nothing therefore could be more natural than that in an age of counter-revolution and romanticism, folk art with its conservatism and irrationalism should have been declared to be the mother-tongue of mankind.

The earliest examples of art we have belong to the art of painting. The earliest known specimens of poetry belong to a far later age, and permit no definite inference as to the origins of poetry. As for the origins of visual art, known to us in the palaeolithic cave-paintings, the most striking thing about them is their remarkably naturalistic and almost exclusively "representational" character—features which do not accord with the principles or the range of interest of any folk art that we know. Only in neolithic times do we find art-forms that remind us of later folk art. Here also we meet for the first time an artistic activity directed to the manufacture of implements for the house—which must have had its origin in home craft. The style of this art, of which we can form some idea chiefly from the pottery of the epoch, shows the first signs of that "disorganization" and schematization of forms which characterizes folk art generally. For the persistence of this style in the folk art of the subsequent periods, which does actually keep certain individual motifs of neolithic ornament, we have no satisfactory explanation. The rationalism that replaces the planless mode of life of hunters and food-gatherers by the organized economy of cattle-breeders and tillers of the soil at best explains the change from naturalism to stylization,[4] but the persistence of the new style remains a problem. Just as Bartók attributes certain features of Hungarian folk-music to an Asiatic origin, so also in other fields of folk art, for example, Romanian peasant art, scholars

[3] R. von Liliencron: *Historische Volkslieder,* I, xiii.
[4] Hauser: op. cit., I, 32.

have claimed to find thousand-year-old motifs and to connect these with neolithic ornament, but that is all pure conjecture.[5] Neolithic culture was a peasant culture, so the predominantly peasant origin of later folk art would explain the similarity to a certain extent, but to assume historical continuity of the geometrical style, which in this case would have to extend over a period of some 5,000 or 6,000 years, seems scarcely compatible with all the changes that took place during this time. The explanation is evidently not to be found either in an uninterrupted tradition or in a permanent, immutable psychic disposition, but in similarity of living conditions. Throughout all the historical events that have radically altered the structure of society in general there is no social stratum whose forms of life have changed so little as those of the peasantry, just as there is no branch of production whose methods have been so little affected by technical invention and the metamorphoses of capital as peasant agriculture.

Although the neolithic geometrical style of decoration dominates all artistic production between 5000 and 500 B.C., yielding ground only with the beginnings of Greek naturalism and classicism, no continuity of development can be shown before the Bronze Age. From then on, geometrical art changes its character in many respects. Progressive social differentiation, the emergence of more clearly defined conditions of lordship, the growing prominence of a military upper class, the beginnings of feudal organization, and the rise of kingship give the art of the metal-working ages, concentrating as it did mainly upon the production of weapons and personal ornament, the stamp of an upper-class art. This was no doubt strongly influenced by the forms of neolithic peasant art, but lay entirely in the hands of specialized craftsmen and professional artists, and cannot have had much to do with the persistence of neolithic forms in folk art. In Egypt and Mesopotamia the peasantry, isolated in settlements that went back to neolithic times, followed its own way of life more or less independently of

[5] Alexander Tzigara Samurcas: *L'Art du peuple roumain* (1925).

310

the towns. The peasants evidently went on making their pots and implements, doing their basketry, and weaving in the old style, but peasant art gradually lost all influence upon the art-production of the towns. However, the spirit of the old formalism is traceable until the very latest phases of Ancient-Oriental urban culture, and disappears from the art of the leading social strata only when Greek culture is at its height, then going underground for centuries.

Greek geometrism, which flourished between 900 and 700 B.C., manifests striking analogies with the style of neolithic decoration. It shows not only the same abstract, disorganized, devitalized treatment of natural forms, but also a similar style of ornament, derived from the techniques of plaiting and weaving. In contrast to the Ionian culture, the culture of the Greek mainland at this period was of an essentially peasant type. But the geometrism of the Dipylon vases cannot be described simply as peasant art or folk art, not only because the technical skill with which the vases are made shows that they were the work of trained and practiced craftsmen, but also because the mannered, even precious, style of the painting implies cultivated taste and purchasers of refinement, not mere peasants. Greek vase-painting developed thereafter into one of the most highly sophisticated industries in the country. In its classical period it had nothing more to do with the simple peasantry, but one may reasonably suppose that Greek country-folk still went on practicing the potter's art within the bounds of their own homes and never let the geometrical tradition die out.

Folk art seems to have had no further definitely ascertainable influence upon the art of the upper classes until the age of the Migrations. But in that age the effects of artistic tendencies which began at the bottom are perhaps more marked than in any other phase of Western history. In fact they set in motion a completely new tradition in art. Usually nothing but romantic enthusiasm for the "state of nature" is at work when writers assert that all renewal after the decline of an urban civilization comes from the "youthful," unspoilt, unsophisticated country-folk. And it is indeed sheer fancy that makes the Dipylon, upon the breakdown of Mycenaean culture, the "origin of all Hellenic art," [6] for whether that style be folklike or not, "Hellenic" art certainly does not begin here, but with the later, "archaic" style. This geometrism still has an unmistakable prehistoric and oriental look about it, whereas the new, Western character of Greek art consists in substantiality, statuesque massiveness, and naturalism, all of which put in an appearance after the end of geometrism. Far different is the relation of the geometrical style of the Migrations to medieval and modern art.

Christian art is distinguished from ancient classical art by two essential attributes: it generally depicts either an epic sequence of events or else a state of mind; and its formal structure has as a rule a certain independence that gives it abstract decorative beauty of line. So far as the epic treatment goes, the connection of post-classical art with Roman art is clear. One need only compare a work such as Trajan's Column with the creations of the earlier classical art on the one hand, and with the treatment of biblical history in the Middle Ages on the other, to recognize that the revolutionary change initiating a new artistic conception occurred in pagan Rome. Certainly, history painting originated there. Now, epical and psychological treatment in the visual arts had its origin, not exactly in folk art, but in a popular type of art. We know what a tremendous role painting, as a means of informing people about current events, played in the public life of the post-Augustan age. It became—in contrast to sculpture, which was and has remained the classical art par excellence—the art of the Roman masses, an art that would speak to all in a language intelligible to all. In fact it developed a kind of mass production. Posters with pictorial representations were displayed in triumphal processions as reportage of the detail of the past campaigns, in the courts of law to depict an offence or explain the innocence of the accused, in temples as gifts and as votive offerings; the picture was news, leading article, court exhibit, advertisement,

[6] Spiess: op. cit., p. 282.

documentation, illustrated paper, and film drama. This vogue for graphic art testifies to the same love of pictures, the same pleasure in a form of expression that is direct, uncomplicated, easily grasped, the same childish desire for the illustrative, as that to which film, television, and the illustrated magazine now owe their popularity. The art connoisseurs of imperial Rome undoubtedly feared in their day a degradation of public taste as a result of the spread of this love of pictures into serious art just as educated people of today fear degradation from the overwhelming influence of film and radio. But crude and vulgar as the beginnings of the new art may have been, they carried in them the germ of later Christian art. Without their epic treatment, the transformation of the monumental art of antiquity into the art of the illuminated manuscripts, the wall paintings, and the church porches of the Middle Ages would have been inconceivable.

As in classical antiquity we find no—or scarcely any—representations of epic material, so also the other element of Christian art, decorative form and abstract beauty of line, plays no important part in classical times. This factor first emerges in the age of Migrations, and thereafter is never absent from Western art. The calligraphy of the Irish miniatures, the complicated play of line in the expressionism of late Romanesque art, the billowing lines of Gothic forms, the decorative composition of Renaissance painting, the virtuosity of drawing of mannerism, the baroque, and the rococo, all exhibit traces and recollections of the decorative art developed in the time of the Migrations. So the second feature of the new artistic tendency also had a popular origin. For though the art of the Migrations cannot strictly speaking be called folk art, it was a peasant art that formally as well as historically had points of contact with folk art. At any rate, it had its roots in folk art, whether its invention be ascribed to the Germanic tribes themselves—that is to say, to their Sarmatian teachers—or traced back to Roman provincial art. According to Georg Dehio, the art of the Migrations was a hybrid that must have arisen in the ethnographic melting-pot of the Roman legions. The earliest finds were indeed made on German and Scandinavian soil, but the later finds in Italy, in Dehio's opinion, demolish the theory of the Germanic origin of this art, for the products obviously did not travel from North to South, but *vice versa*. They reached the provinces of the Empire as trade goods and as utensils for the peasant inhabitants, either by purchase or as the booty of the Germanic soldiers, and were subsequently imitated and improved upon by the Germanic peoples themselves.[7] Incidentally the purely formal analysis of the art of the Migrations points to a Roman provincial origin. We find in late Roman provincial art the same reduction of natural forms to their bare outlines and the same neglect of spatial relationships —that is, the same translation of spatial depth into flat and linear terms as in the subsequent art of the migratory period. In both cases we find the loss of feeling for plastic form and the gain in painterly effects which Franz Wickhoff holds to be typical of the latest phase of classical art.[8]

A "democratization" of classical art had already set in at the end of the Roman republic. With the social rise of simple country-folk in considerable numbers, the penetration of Roman society by foreigners and barbarians, the degeneration of the upper classes, and the loss of feeling for classical values, provincialism spread in art as elsewhere.[9] The influence of provincial art upon the art of the upper classes did not of course make itself felt spontaneously or suddenly. It was rather a case of two parallel and gradual processes: the classical sense of form was inwardly disintegrating and becoming increasingly receptive to the revival and the vogue of provincial art. Therein

[7] Georg Dehio: *Geschichte der deutschen Kunst*, I (1930), 4th ed., pp. 24–5.

[8] Franz Wickhoff: *Römische Kunst: Die Wiener Genesis* (1912). Dehio: op. cit.; Arnold Schober: *"Zur Entstehung und Bedeutung der provinzialrömischen Kunst,"* *Jahreshefte des Oesterreichischen Archäologischen Institutes*, XXVI (1930), 14, 48, 49.

[9] Schober: loc. cit., p. 49.

Roman art was harking back to an old Italic tradition, which as heritage of the Etruscans and of the early Republic had always been one of the factors in classical Roman art, though for a while it was submerged by Hellenistic fashions; that tradition, like late Roman provincial art, also had its roots in a peasant culture.[1] Interesting as these connections may be, they explain the negative features of the new style rather than its positive features. They explain the loss of understanding for spatial relations, plastic form, and painterly values, but they do not explain the complicated, wildly exuberant decorative style of the new art, to which nothing in the classical or pre-classical periods is at all analogous.

6. *ON THE HISTORY OF FOLK-POETRY*

No kind of art is more clearly folklike in character than the drama of the Middle Ages. This in essentials, though by no means in its entirety, derives from the Greek mime. In classical antiquity, folk influences upon the theater went very deep; this was not only the case with the mime—the purest form of folk-theater, which became a literary fashion for a time and then resumed its original folklike character—but also with high tragedy, which grew out of dances rooted in folk-belief and folkways. And although the religious element in these dances is only in part attributable to a folklike origin, the delight in pretending, in dressing-up, in imitation, is thoroughly folklike and popular. This sort of mimic-dramatic folk-poetry—which gave rise to the literary mime, the Theocritean idyll, Greek New Comedy, and the entire comic drama of the Romans—flourished alongside tragedy, and certainly came into being long

[1] Ibid., pp. 50 ff.

315

before the birth of tragedy out of worship and dance.[2] The theater was and remained essentially folk art, simply because large numbers of people could enjoy its performances, so that it was able to provide a fairly cheap form of entertainment. The official state theater at Athens, however, just because there was free entry, was much less in accord with the artistic requirements of the common people than was the mime, which they had to pay to see. The fact is that only a theater that the public has to maintain and which therefore depends on keeping its goodwill, really belongs to it.

As the feeling for classical forms gradually died, the mimes, with their unpretentious and partially improvised scenes, penetrated into the city, and everywhere dominated the theater in the last period of the ancient world. They were probably the last manifestation of antiquity to give way to the new Christian morality and the new taste for Christian religious subjects. And the mimic actors survived the mime. When the West had been conquered by the barbarians, and the theaters lay in ruins along with the basilicas, baths, triumphal arches, and the rest, the mimic actors went back to being the jugglers, acrobats, and conjurers they had been originally. And when even the last remnants of the ancient culture had died out, they were still roaming around the Germanic lands. They gave their shows in taverns, in the streets and market-places, and at festivities both of the country-folk or of the lords. The Church opposed their art as coarse, impudent, and frivolous, but they were too numerous, lively, and popular to be stamped out or to leave the religious theater unaffected by their influence. The clergy had to borrow their resources for the mysteries and miracle plays, found itself obliged to make the biblical stories more attractive to the public by including a burlesque element. The medieval drama cannot be regarded simply as a continuation of the mimes, as was formerly supposed, but the dependence of the Christian religious play upon them cannot be doubted. It should not, however, be overlooked that the mime,

[2] Hermann Reich: *Der Mimus* (1903), pp. 19 ff.

while influencing the higher forms of drama, was in turn influenced by them and had to make considerable concession in order to get on to a proper stage from the plank between two casks.[3]

In the Middle Ages two sorts of theater remained, just as in the ancient world. There was the unliterary theater of the mimic actors, uninterested in any "higher values," and there was the religious drama that developed out of the liturgy and remained dependent upon the Church. In the former, the people were simply spectators, but in the latter they were also the actors. And so it came about that the religious plays, in spite of their literary origin and their link with the clergy, are "folk art" in a deeper sense than the mime and other performances of the sort that employed professional actors; these required immensely more sleight of hand, mimicry, acrobatic, musical, and other skill than did participation in the religious plays. In the latter we find amateurs, in the former professional artists, even if their art was on a somewhat low level; they can still properly be called folk-artists in spite of their making a regular trade of it. These folk-artists—not the authors of the religious plays—were the direct forerunners of the originators and performers of the Italian *commedia dell'arte,* the French *farce,* the Spanish *entremesa,* the German *Posse* and the English "interlude." The question then remains of how and when the leap from mimic productions to true drama took place. The mime, it has been well said, "belongs to the domaine of the *artiste* . . . The distinction arises because what one would call mime or mimicry is capable of development, and can turn into drama. A man, for example, who mimics a drunken man in a comic fashion is not much different from a man who pretends to swallow knives. But the drunken man can be made to talk to himself or to a second actor and to play a little scene in which his drunkenness leads him into a fight; out of this performance farce

---

[3] Cf. E. Wüst: *"Der Mimus,"* in Pauly-Wissowa: *Realenzyklopädie der Klassischen Altertumswissenschaft,* XV/2 (1932), pp. 1727–64. A. Kutscher: *Elemente des Theaters* (1932), pp. 92–3.

and comedy can develop, whereas the knife-swallower can never do more than show off his own skill . . ." [4]

This is an excellent illustration of the fact that the origin of an artistic device is quite irrelevant to the question of its value or usefulness, and of the way a motif or formal element emerging on the lowest levels of art can prove productive on a higher plane. It is questionable whether one should draw at all so sharp a distinction between the happy improvisations of an entertainer and the professional poet's ideas—which are the fruit of a long training, although he often does not know how he comes by them. Is the mimicking of an animal in a dance, which certainly has not much to do with art, so utterly different from the imitation of a man, say, a drunken man, that we have to envisage the transition from the one to the other as a sort of "leap"? Must we not rather, on the whole, admit that a direct line leads from the animal masks of primitive peoples to the stock personages of the mime, and from these to Shakespeare's clowns and Molière's slyboots? In Shakespeare, at any rate, apart from the clowns and fools, the Falstaffs and Malvolios, the Porter in *Macbeth* and the tradesmen in *A Midsummer Night's Dream,* an immense amount comes straight from the medieval theater, and is undisguised miming.

Shakespeare wrote his plays for an extraordinarily large and various public, and achieved more general popularity than any other great dramatist before or since. His public, however, was sociologically far more akin to the mass audience of the modern cinema than to the "folk" of folk art. And like Shakespeare's audience, that of the medieval folk-plays cannot have been altogether homogeneous.

The type of poetry which the romantics took as showing most clearly the characteristic marks of folk-poetry, namely, epic, is the one that has the least contact with the common people. On the basis of F. A. Wolf's theory of the heroic lay,

[4] Paul Ernst: *Der Zusammenbruch des deutschen Idealismus* (1931), 3rd ed., p. 106.

318

the folk-epic was taken as an equivalent of the heroic epic, and the epic declared to be the product of an anonymous "folk." Only after a great deal of unprejudiced research did it become clear that the original forms of heroic poetry have no sort of communal character, but on the contrary a quite un-folklike, aristocratic, and chivalric quality. And even if we allow that the gaps between the different social strata—at least in respect of education—were not always so great as they later became, so that for a time the same epic material could be enjoyed by lords and common people, still the gulf between upper and lower classes was never quite bridged, and the popularity of heroic poetry was always limited to short periods and particular social circumstances. The heroic lays, out of which the epic was developed, whether by a process of infla-tion or of integration, were the most undisguised and uncom-promising class poetry ever created by a master class. They had nothing to do with "folk," were pure art-poetry, and poetry of a nobility. If there had once been communal poetry, its day was long past when these songs were composed. The medieval lays were the product of the Migrations, and must have originated in the social upheavals of that time, especially in connection with the rise of the new warrior nobility after the successful invasion of the West. Not only were the heroic lays governed by the interests and principles of taste of a privileged, exclusive stratum of society; they were also, unlike any folk-poetry, the product of a well-trained class of poets carrying on their pro-fession in the service of a military class.

The origin of epic in the heroic songs and panegyrics of a warlike nobility can quite easily be shown; the real problem is the way in which part of this heroic and aristocratic poetry reached the common people, became popular, and rose again in the social scale—the problem, in fact, of the causes and ef-fects of their transmission from one social stratum to another.

When Charlemagne had "the old barbarian songs" re-corded, the heroic lays no longer suited the taste of the upper class; the refined and the educated were now demanding learned, classical poetry. The succeeding generations were altogether averse to the old, raw poetry of heroes; they favored biblical and other religious subjects. The lordship of the new aristocracy was already so firmly established that it did not need to emphasize and exalt its own heroic virtues. The heroic poetry was gradually driven from the court and from the castles of the lords, but it must have continued to exist somewhere and in some form or other in order to start on its new career in the courtly-chivalric epic of the twelfth and thirteenth centuries. In this interim period it must have obviously lived upon the favor of the lower classes. The old epic material passed from the educated and honored courtly singers, who now had other themes to treat of, into the hands of the less educated, roaming folk-singers, and so, during the centuries that elapsed between the heroic age and the courtly-chivalric age, this material did become popular. Even so, it never became "folk-poetry" in the strict sense of the word. The poems may in their new form have been mainly addressed to the common people, but they were only occasionally sung by them, and then only in snatches. They remained the possession of professional poets, to whom the changes of form and content which the poems underwent are to be ascribed. Thus in no phase of the development is there any of that "organic growth" that the romantics discerned in heroic poetry; nowhere is the conception of collective activity, of continuous, unconscious, instinctive creation—as opposed to the intermittent, deliberate production of the individual poet—less appropriate; for these epics, even in their most popular form, treated of a far too extensive and complicated material for them to have been sung, let alone further developed, by ordinary people.[5] The heroic songs never became folk-songs.[6] They may have become folk-ballads, but they were always an affair for specialists. In their debased form they no longer retained anything of the elevated

[5] Meier: *Das deutsche Volkslied*, I, 1. p. 10.
[6] Hermann Schneider: *Germanische Heldensage*, I (1928), 36.

style and solemnity of the old heroic lays,[7] but still they remained minstrels' poetry.

The concept of the minstrel, certainly, is far too equivocal to be of much use in this connection. People have become accustomed to lump together under the name of minstrelsy anything that the Middle Ages produced in the way of poems, songs, dances, plays, or even acrobatics. Since the time of the romantics, court-poets, folk-singers, wandering scholars, mimics, itinerant musicians, and conjurers have all tended to be called simply "minstrels." In the age in which the stories of heroes were popular there was, no doubt, a certain mingling of categories; but the poets and singers who recited these stories to a varying public, sometimes of feudal lords and knights, sometimes of burghers or of peasants, now in the manor, now in taverns or market-places, were at no time identical with the *jongleur* in the sense of juggler and trickster.[8] The minstrel as composer of the folk-epic—or more properly, of the folk-ballads based upon the heroic lay—stood somewhere between the respected courtly poets of chivalry and the despised vagabond, and equally, somewhere between the art-poet and the folk-poet. With the former he shared a certain measure of education, with the latter the advantages of anonymity.

Andreas Heusler claims that the fact that the author of so fine a poem as the *Nibelungenlied* remains unknown to us shows that he was a minstrel. For wherever in the Middle Ages the author of a poem was a courtier, a knight, or a cleric, his name, so Heusler asserts, was named and held in honor, whereas a minstrel did not dare to put his own name to his work and none held him worthy of mention or remembrance.[9] But recently this explanation has been rejected as too simple, for it seems to have been ascertained that the author of the anonymous

[7] W. P. Ker: *Epic and Romance* (1908), p. 125.

[8] Naumann: "Spielmannsdichtung," *Reallexikon der deutschen Literaturgeschichte*, III (1928–9), 253–65.

[9] Andreas Heusler: *Nibelungensage und Nibelungenlied* (1929), 3rd ed., p. 105.

Nibelungenlied was the imperial chaplain Konrad von Passau,[1] a personage who certainly had no reason to suppress his name. So the naming or anonymity of an epic poet in the Middle Ages was now held to be due more to the kind of material he treated than to his social position. In this view, poems whose subjects were derived from Germanic sagas of heroes were expected to be kept anonymous because they were regarded and valued not as poetry, but as history, as records of olden times, whereas other poems based on the sagas of the Round Table and the romances of Arthur were looked on as mere fictions, and so could be ascribed to an individual poet.[2] The strange thing about this theory is that the authors of the courtly-chivalric epics were just as little independent and just as strict followers of tradition, *i.e.*, as much or as little "creative," as the authors of the heroic epics or the folk-epics—and this was common knowledge at the time. The romantic-nationalistic background of this theory is unmistakable; it manifests a special point of view resulting from local conditions in Germany and from that historical idealism which imagines spiritual achievements more dignified if anonymous than if they are connected with a name under which an individual might seek distinction. Indeed, the exponents of this theory expressly declare that the romantic doctrine ascribing heroic epics to the "folk" rather than to individuals, defective as it may be, is shown by recent research to be truer in essentials than modern psychological and sociological theories.[3]

The most fruitful and characteristic species of folk-poetry is undoubtedly the lyric song. This category includes not only the most abundant, but also the most valuable creations of folk art. The song is a fairly simple and flexible form, and in it the

[1] Dietrich Kralik: *Wer war der Dichter des Nibelungenliedes?* (1954), pp. 11 ff.

[2] Otto Höfler: *"Die Anonymität des Nibelungenliedes,"* Deutsche Vierteljahrsschrift für Literaturwissenschaft und Geistegeschichte (1955), XXIX, No. 2, pp. 171 ff.

[3] Ibid., p. 211.

folk-poet finds the greatest freedom and variety of self-expression. At the same time, it is the species that has always provided the principal object of controversy between the advocates of the reception theory and those of the production theory; for in no form of folk-poetry are the traces of borrowing so evident and so incontestable as here; in no other form is the genuine artistic talent of the common folk so strikingly manifest. Folk-songs exhibit both the most naïve borrowings and the most charming poetic inventions. Even so radical an exponent of the reception theory as Naumann thinks that we can see in what he postulates as the archetypes of lyric—primitive work-songs, short love-verses, wedding-songs, funeral dirges, war-songs, religious chants, charms, and so on—the product of collective, spontaneous, truly original creation. He emphasizes indeed that the actual examples of folk-songs known to us are connected only indirectly, that is *via* the art-lyric, with the postulated though no longer accessible forms of poetry mentioned above; still, he calls them "primitive communal poetry" and regards them as the nearest thing we have to the collective improvisations in which all folk-poetry, according to the romantics, originates.[4]

Folk-song, judging by the examples we actually have, is very young. No known song goes back beyond the troubadour lyric, which is not only the most abundant, but seems to have been the original source of these songs. For the age in which this par excellence courtly and chivalric poetry was at its height was followed, especially in France and Germany, by the first great blossoming of the folk-song. There is no evidence of any folk-song in the West before 1400.[5] One need only think of the *pastourelles* so widespread in European folk-poetry in order to realize how unfolklike, how refined—one might almost say, decadent—these first beginnings of the folk-song are. In these songs, which describe a country scene and normally consist of a dialogue between an enamored knight and an unyielding

[4] Naumann: *Primitive Gemeinschaftskultur*, p. 6.
[5] Wechssler: *Begriff und Wesen des Volksliedes*, pp. 39–40.

323

shepherdess, there is hardly a feature that cannot be traced back to models in the precious-chivalric, courtly literary fashion.[6]

In spite of all this, the revival of romantic tendencies in modern folk-lore has brought with it fresh doubts as to whether folk-song can really be derived from the courtly love-poetry. The features common to the earliest lyrics of the different nations, so the argument runs, point to the existence of a widespread, pre-national lyric poetry of a folklike character.[7] This notion recalls an ancient controversy that raged, in the main, around the question of whether the identical motifs, which one finds in the folk-tales of the most various peoples, arose spontaneously in different regions or were diffused by migration and borrowing. The generation of scholars to which Max Müller, Theodor Benfey, and Gaston Paris belonged ascribed the commonest of these motifs to an oriental origin. A later school, whose interests were primarily anthropological, headed by E. Tylor and Andrew Lang, maintained against them the view that the similarities are to be attributed to similarity of human dispositions as the same themes appear in the fairy-tales of peoples inhabiting the most remote and geographically isolated regions. Opposed as these schools are in principle, the one thesis is as one-sided and "romantic" as the other. The anthropological explanation, basing itself upon the similarity and constancy of human nature, reflects one aspect; the diffusion theory, treating individuals and folk as an indifferent substratum of "tendencies," "influences," and "reactions," reflects another aspect of the same historicist philosophy. In both views, a supposedly higher reality or more fundamental order prevails over the ephemeral individual. Neither party recognized that similar cultural structures can arise independently of one another—that is, without any external contacts—but that this need not

[6] Cf. Groeber: *Die altfranzösischen Romanzen und Pastourellen* (1872), p. 19. Alfred Jeanroy: *Les Origines de la poésie lyrique en France* (1925), pp. 18–23.

[7] T. Frings: *Minnesinger und Troubadours* (1949). Erich Seemann: *"Volkslied," Deutsche Philologie im Aufriss* (1954), II, 21.

imply an identity of human nature through all its manifold variants. Similarity of cultural structures is for the most part a result of the fact that the individuals who originate them live under similar social conditions in spite of ethnic differences. Some cultural structures migrate, are borrowed, are imitated with variations; others arise independently of one another in the same form in various places; most are mixed forms in which borrowings and spontaneous inventions are mingled. It should be borne in mind that borrowing, no less than spontaneous invention of the identical, implies a certain similarity of inclinations; why else should the foreign mode of expression be taken over? We have therefore always to assume a certain constancy of human nature. But the "universally human" is not a great deal of use as an explanation in the history of culture; it is one of the presuppositions, but leaves just where it was the problem of why some cultural forms recur while others change.

In any case, the solution of the problem of how and to what extent different cultural regions are in contact with one another by way of transmission of fairy-tale motifs would provide no answer to some of the main questions of research in this field. We should still need to know about the mutual relations between folk-tales and literary tales to know what influence written literature has upon the country-folk's treasury of stories, how much in folk-tales goes back to sagas, histories, romances, literary short stories, and so on, how much is genuine folk-product, and indeed whether there are any genuine, original folk-tales independent of the literature of the educated. No general answer can be given to this last question, either one way or the other. Of the animal fables, for example, it can be said with a fair degree of confidence that they did not come from folk into literature, but *vice versa*. No fables seem to be older than the *Roman de Renard*; the French, Finnish, and Ukrainian stories of this type are all more recent, and undoubtedly derive from literary models.[8] It is claimed, however, that even today there are still to be found, among primitive peoples,

[8] Bédier-Hazard: *Histoire de la littérature française*, I (1923), p. 29.

folk-tales in their original state alongside literary tales told by country-folk.[9] But whatever the origin of a tale or of a motif, there is constant displacement of the material "upwards" and "downwards"; literary stories become current among the country-folk, and folk-tales are taken up and worked up by poets— and even these may originally have been "literary stories retold by country-folk." It is the same state of affairs as in folk-poetry generally; themes, motifs, and forms wander back and forth, but their origin is always attributable to a certain place, time and author.[1] In any case, it is not essential to the folklike character of a tale that the story-teller be a peasant or a rural craftsman, any more than that folk-epic be recited by the country-folk. Both in West and East, fairy-tales were not related only at courts of kings and princes by learned and skilful story-tellers; there were always also professional story-tellers of a lower order who, like the medieval minstrels, entertained the ordinary country-folk from the resources of their art. We are told for instance of such a story-teller in Denmark who, as late as 1917, traveled from farm to farm.[2]

7. THE BLOSSOMING AND DECAY OF FOLK ART

Middle Latin clerical poetry must have had a good deal to do with the origins of troubadour poetry, and so indirectly of folk-poetry.[3] Even greater and more direct must have been the influence of the Church upon the music of folk-song. Most Western folk-songs are composed in the modern tonality and differentiate between major and minor; but some songs still preserve traces of the early medieval structure. Gregorian

[9] Friedrich von der Leyen: *"Zum Problem der Form beim Märchen,"* *Wölfflin-Festschrift* (1924), p. 44.

[1] Joseph Bédier: *Les Fabliaux* (1925), p. 64.

[2] F. von der Leyen: *Volkstum und Dichtung* (1933), p. 26.

[3] Hauser: op. cit., I, 223.

chant, which was well known to everybody, must have been one of the principal sources of the melodies connected with the text of the songs, often serving unchanged as musical support for several different texts. Many of the folk-songs still sung in the West undoubtedly go back to the twelfth or thirteenth century.[4] It may be that they have their origin in a folklike musical tradition that was independent of Church music—but there is not the slightest evidence for such a hypothesis. As time went on, the art of the troubadours became another musical source of folk-song, and if at times it was influenced by folk-music, it was only taking back what it had originally lent. In later centuries this process of give and take became a well-known phenomenon of musical history. In no other form of art have the country-folk so richly repaid their borrowings as in music.

At the time of the Reformation, the influence of Church music upon folk-music was even greater, especially in Protestant countries; nothing is more characteristic of the age than the fact that Protestant hymns were called "spiritual folk-songs."[5] And so it is understandable that the myth of communal culture is taken up again at this point by romantic-minded writers and applied to the Reformation era in spite of the far-reaching social and educational differentiation that had taken place by that time.[6] They failed to see the difference between the popular unity realized at such times, which was simply that of a united political front, and the unity of a primitive culture.[7] For although the Reformation in many ways signalized the beginning of a culture that was more folklike and had more generally accepted standards than that of medieval chivalric society, still this cannot properly be described as a "folk-culture." The picture of "the poor soldier and the rich merchant's son,

[4] Davenson: op. cit., pp. 19–20, 112.
[5] J. von Pulikowski: *Geschichte der Begriffes Volkslied im musikalischen Schrifttum* (1933), p. 273.
[6] Hans Joachim Moser: *Geschichte der deutschen Musik* (1930), 5th ed., p. 219.
[7] Cf. Pulikowski: op. cit., pp. 294–5.

the student and the artisan, all having approximately the same sentiments and speaking the same language, so that for all his high artistic skill any straightforward utterance of a great artist was immediately intelligible to the great mass of the people"[8] is just a naïve expression of the author's yearnings. The gulf between folk-song and art-song had perhaps been narrowed, and the production of folk art doubtless had been enriched through the leveling of social status; that leveling, however, only signified a drawing-together of neighboring ranks in the social order, with new and more direct points of contact between nobility and upper middle class, between the middle and the petty bourgeoisie, between middle class and country-folk; it did not signify a reversal of the process of social differentiation. The contrary was happening; the number of ranks was increasing and the ordinary country-folk was getting farther removed from the spiritual élite, *i.e.*, separated from them by a larger number of steps or degrees than ever before. The Renaissance produced a bourgeois art, and even a kind of petty bourgeois art as well; but it also gave rise to highly specific tastes and requirements in art, and to a far more refined type of connoisseur than existed in medieval or ancient times.

The baroque merely continued and accelerated this contradictory, two-faced development. The Counter-Reformation gave birth both to an emotional, readily intelligible and a generally accepted type of art. The theatrical, rhetorical style of the age not only made concessions to bad taste, but also often added to the most elevated works of art a feature here and there in order to make them attractive to the broad masses as well as to the select circle of connoisseurs. The Reformation had been hostile to art; the Counter-Reformation, for purposes of Catholic propaganda, called into being a popularizing type of art produced upon a hitherto undreamed-of scale. In this way the baroque waged war not only against the intellectualism and frivolity of mannerism, but also against the paganism of the whole Renaissance period. For although the greater part of

[8] Moser, loc. cit.

328

the works of art produced in the Renaissance had biblical stories as their subject, or some pretension of a religious motive, the modern devotional picture really takes shape in the age of the baroque. Above all, those tearful features so characteristic of the popular religious art of the next two centuries now make their appearance. The baroque, in spite of the extraordinary refinement of means of expression in the art of its great masters, transforms the abstract formalism of the Renaissance and the complicated symbolism of mannerism into a simple, conventional, often insipid sort of allegory in which the cross, the crown of thorns, skulls, lilies, downcast or upturned eyes, hands folded or wrung, become the small change of art. The large-scale production of votive pictures begins in the seventeenth century, and at the same time pilgrimages become more and more popular. Numerous popular places of grace come into fashion, and the decoration of their churches and chapels bears the character of folk art. Prints of various kinds, namely, broadsheets with picture and text, now begin to have a wider distribution. The coarse, popular woodcut becomes differentiated from the more refined copper engraving, though it is only in the eighteenth century that the production of prints for country-folk assumes more considerable proportions and is taken over by small tradesmen also.[9]

Not until the eighteenth century do we find what is ordinarily called "folk art." From that century derive not merely most of the folk-songs known to us and still sung, but also almost the whole repertoire of decorative forms of modern folk art. In that century originate most of the patterns in weaving, embroidery, and lace-making, the ornamentation of plates and jugs, the types of furniture and domestic utensil which we associate with the concept of folk art. From that century too dates the well-established set of subjects of the prints that were now very generally distributed: popular wisdom, proverbs, precepts, the allegories of the Ages of Man, of

[9] Fränger: Review of *L'Imagerie populaire* by P. L. Duchartre and R. Saulnier, in *Jahrbuch für historische Volkskunde*, II (1926), 196–7.

the Tree of Love, of the Topsy-turvy World, the legend of the Wandering Jew, and so on. The nineteenth century then adds to this repertoire the tales of sensation and horror, figures and scenes from famous criminal cases and from current history. From that time on, each generation contributes something to the stock material of the modern film and magazine.

It has been said that there is no more folk art because there is no longer anything that could be called "folk," [1] and this is in fact true of the West and especially of the Anglo-Saxon lands, for in them not only the masses in the industrial towns, but also those employed in agriculture have now hardly anything in common with those who kept the former folk art alive. Complete isolation from the cultural centers is by no means a precondition of folk art; without a certain amount of contact the appropriation of cultural goods by the country-folk would be impossible, but the immediate neighborhood of the town is a great danger for it. The circulation of urban culture through modern transportation, film, radio, television, the illustrated paper, and the daily press brings about not merely the utter democratization, but also a uniformity of culture in the face of which the artistic forms of expression native to the country-folk cannot survive. There is no longer any folk art in the Western countries because urban mass culture spreads and changes so quickly that the country-folk never get a chance to develop their own traditions or to transmute what they receive in accordance with those traditions. In these countries nothing can prevent the extinction of folk art and its replacement by the mass art of the big town. The country-folk now sing the "hits" of the town and forget their own songs; they copy needlework invented in the town and neglect the beautiful old patterns; they buy the most horrible mass-produced pottery to substitute for their own charmingly decorated plates and jugs. In the civilized countries there are each year fewer people who can sing the old folk-songs. In Hungary during the nineteenth century the old folk-music was already being replaced

[1] André Malraux: *Les Voix du silence*, p. 512.

by the so-called "gipsy music." But that was taken over and interpreted by the country-folk with a certain freedom and independence; the hits and the croonings that pervade the countryside nowadays are repeated quite mechanically and found so much more attractive than the old-fashioned, naïve, unsophisticated village songs that no attempt is made to adapt them to the native musical idiom.[2]

The expectation that the big town itself might become a soil in which a new folk art could grow shows no sign of being fulfilled.[3] Neither the American Negro music nor the songs of the modern industrial worker have any of the marks of a folk art. They have neither the impersonal style nor the extraordinary flexibility of the songs that were current in the village; they are also addressed to a public that is not in the least folk-like in spite of the continual influx from the country into the town. The urban proletariat is not, like the peasantry, uneducated, but half-educated or miseducated; far from being attached to any traditions, it displays a positive aversion to all tradition. The ephemeral character of all artistic activities connected with the urban worker is enough to forbid our describing such things as folk art.

8. *THE CONCEPT OF POPULAR ART: STANDARDIZATION AND COMMERCIALIZATION*

The popular art of today is mass art in a double sense: it offers the same artistic entertainment to all sections of an enormous public, and it turns out uniform products on an enormous scale. The mass public is a product of the democratization of society, the mass production a result of the new mechanized methods of manufacture which technical progress

[2] Cf. Bartók: "Hungarian Peasant Music," loc. cit., pp. 278, 286–7; *Die Volksmusik der Magyaren*, p. 4.

[3] Cf. Louis Harap: *Social Roots of the Arts* (1949), pp. 130–3.

331

has made possible. The democratization of art and culture has been going on since the beginning of the nineteenth century. The serial novel, the boulevard theater, lithography, and so on were unmistakable symptoms of a development that was to lead on to the cinema, the radio, and the magazine; they ushered in the technical age in art. In a sense, no doubt, the technical quality of art is as old as art itself. Every artistic expression depends upon some process, every art is tied to an apparatus of technical or instrumental devices, be the instrument brush or film camera, etching-needle or power-loom. This dependence is of the very essence of artistic form, is inseparable from the translation of spiritual contents into sensuous forms. The wheel of the neolithic potter was a "machine"; between it and the technical apparatus of the modern artist the difference is of degree.

The process of technicalizing the artist's activity has gone on continuously, but not without some perceptible leaps related to the changes in current economic and technological conditions. The most fateful change occurred with the invention of methods of graphic reproduction at the beginning of the modern era; for with these the work of art lost the "aura" that goes with the unrepeatable, irreplaceable uniqueness of a painted picture or a sculptured statue.[4] The work of art became reproducible mechanically, and the way opened to the present state of things, in which the same film can be shown simultaneously in thousands of cinemas to hundreds of thousands of spectators. The sensation of the artist's direct touch was thereby lost. Yet one must avoid making an inscrutable myth out of the artist's "autograph" and the "aura" of the work of art. Uniqueness is only an essential and indispensable feature of the artist's creation in those cases in which it formed part of his conception from the very start. A copy of Rembrandt's *Night Watch* may be artistically quite worthless, but the various

---

[4] Walter Benjamin: *"L'Œuvre d'art à l'époque de sa reproduction mécanisée,"* Zeitschrift für Sozialforschung (1936), V, No. 1, pp. 40–6.

copies of an etching hardly differ in artistic value: the value in the picture depends upon the unmistakable and inimitable handling of the brush, whereas in the etching it is unimpaired by the process of multiplication. The technical process is always an integral part of the artistic idea, a precondition, not a subsequent addition.

But as for the turning of art-products into "commodities," which is said to have resulted from their mass-production, one must first make some distinctions of principle which have not much to do with the mere fact of multiplication as such. A picture that is unique of its kind can be produced as a ware or a saleable good and be considered from this point of view just as well as the copies of an etching or the photographic reproductions of a work of art. But whereas the worth of a painting cannot by any means be reflected in the form of a price, an etching can be more or less "correctly" priced; it is possible to assess it as "priceless" only if it is the last copy extant. The photographic reproduction of a picture, in contrast to both the picture and the etching, is a commodity pure and simple, and like the gramophone record, a mere reproduction without any individual value. It is a substitute for a wholly unreproducible original, and as such aesthetically worthless. Thus it differs from the copy of a film in essential respects, for a film consists of nothing but copies, so to say copies without an original (for the negative is also only a mechanical reproduction), or of copies whose original "exists" only in the sense in which the idea of a picture, apart from the actual picture, might be said to exist.

The artistic value of a work does not depend upon the nature of the technical means the artist employs, but simply and solely upon the way he employs them. Just as it is not true that the change from working with one's hands to working with a machine inevitably brings deterioration of the workman's spiritual capacities, neither is it true that the employment of modern techniques in art necessarily means a lowering of quality. "More brains," writes the editor of a technical journal,

333

"are needed to keep the machine functioning than to handle a shovel." [5] In art, it is true, the relation between simple tool and true machine is somewhat different than it is with physical work in general, but it can scarcely be denied that the film, which eliminates all personal contacts, has its masters no less than the living theater, in which person speaks to person. The film excludes certain dramatic effects, but makes new sorts of aesthetic achievement possible. Yet a certain lowering of standards does inevitably follow from large-scale production. Even in so splendid a literary age as eighteenth-century England, quality, of the novel in particular, suffered from the excessive pressure of demand. But whatever the drawbacks of technical progress may be, the course of history cannot be reversed. Only a blind romanticism can suppose that technical devices that are not just economically advantageous, but also so deeply rooted in the daily habits and needs of men, could simply be given up. This technical development cannot be delayed even in matters in which it brings no great practical benefit, for it seems that to the man of today it often comes more natural to use a machine than to use his hands. Our present cultural task is to master the machine instead of being enslaved by it, to use it in truth as an instrument instead of worshipping it as a fetish.

Every art-form involves an element of standardization, is more or less conventional. Every art-form is governed by certain stylistic principles proper to its nature, appropriate to the vision which it offers and to the public to whom it it offered; it necessarily employs standard formulas of expression and stereotyped arrangements of its material. Not only do the tango and the mambo, the fugue and the minuet, equally entail standardizations of musical means of expression; even the forms of classical-romantic music can be reduced to certain schemata, which restrict the freedom of the composer from the very outset, but on the other hand enable him to get a foothold on something settled and unproblematical, and so to avoid para-

[5] Quoted by Stuart Chase: *Men and Machines* (1929), p. 173.

lyzing indecision. The conventional and the stereotyped obviously play a much greater part in the necessarily impersonal mass production of art than in the art of the masters, but really the difference is just that the standardization in the one case takes more rigid, in the other more flexible, forms. The form of the minuet is more flexible than that of the tango; that is to say, it *became* more flexible in the hands of masters such as Haydn and Mozart, but in itself it is no less conventional than the dance-forms of today. In genuine, serious art, the validity of conventions simply means that the artist can make a start somewhere without hesitation or doubt upon organizing his often overwhelming material; it does not set him free from all risk. The artist walks a tight-rope over an abyss; to succeed in his performance requires a certain rashness, indeed sometimes a wild exuberance, of which the producer of popular art, employing conventions as crutches, has no conception.

Genuine works of art are distinguished from such productions not by the strictness of the formal principles they acknowledge, but on the contrary by the freedom with which these are observed and interpreted. By contrast, the rules according to which mass art has to be produced are strict, rigid, and inexorable. There are certain well-worn lines whose popularity has already been proved, by the use of which the success of a novel, a film, or a dance-song seems to be assured; the producers stick to these with extreme dogmatism until they break down and give way to a new formula. The current rules are so powerful and the permissible models so faithfully followed that for their sake considerable inconveniences will be accepted, as for instance by the jazz-arranger who, as has been wittily remarked, simplifies Mozart because he is too difficult and complicated, but is also quite prepared to make him more difficult and complicated, where he is thought to be too simple to fit the required schema.[6]

Two factors have been singled out as the essential pre-

---

[6] M. Horkheimer and T. W. Adorno: *Dialektik der Aufklärung* (1947), p. 152.

conditions of industrial mass production: the manufacture of standardized and interchangeable parts, and the assembling of these parts with a relatively small amount of labor.[7] This is also the method employed, with certain modifications, in the mass production of art. Still, revolutionary as are its effects at the present time, as an artistic procedure it is not new. As we have seen, the Khirgiz folk singers, and the Homeric rhapsodes too, operated with ready-made formulae, utilizing these in their songs in a somewhat mechanical manner. What is decisive for the value of this method is not that it employs formulae, but that the repetition of such elements may be expressive or not.

The commercial practices of the entertainment industry certainly constitute one of the most ominous aspects of the present cultural crisis; but really it is not so much the commercialization of art-production that is so novel and important for contemporary interpretation; it is rather the present alienation and detachment of higher art, which, since the romantics, has claimed to exist for the artist alone, and takes or pretends to take no account of the public. This ostensible lack of regard for the public is no doubt usually a cloak to cover the artists' desperate competition for public favor; but the ideal of an art that is disinterested, makes no concessions, is inevitably misunderstood by the present generation and appreciated only by future generations, is none the less a genuine ideal and basic for the world-view of the romantic. Before the day of romanticism, every art-product was recognized as being a commodity to a greater or lesser extent; every work of art had its price, though this was not necessarily paid down in hard cash. The artist accepted it, in one form or other, without any false shame, and scarcely ever had any feeling that he was giving way when he complied with his patron's wishes. He realized that his true value was not enhanced by keeping up a semblance of inde-

[7] Chase: op. cit., p. 95.

336

pendence; it was only the romantic's bad conscience that attached such extraordinary value to that semblance. In a word, the new, queer feature about the modern artist's relation to his profession is his unnatural, inhibited attitude toward everything material and practical, not the fact that he plies his art as a trade.

Since the romantics, the artist has the feeling of being faced, not by a friendly patron or a circle of well-known, well-disposed individuals interested in art, but by an indefinite, indifferent, and often hostile public. He stares out at an expressionless mask and tries to imagine behind it a more sympathetic audience somewhere in the far future. Such imaginings are vain, unfruitful, and dangerous. The alienation of the idealist from the present entails no less of a risk than the materialist's readiness to compromise; the former is in danger of developing a private language and becoming unintelligible, the latter of becoming in the end unable to speak anything but the impersonal, colorless language of the masses. Present-day art moves between these two dangers; in such a situation, in which neither of the extremes can be accepted with equanimity, no artist, be he ever so uncompromising, should ignore the requirements of popular art.

What marks the commercialization of art in the age of mass culture is not just the effort to produce saleable, if possible the most profitable, works of art—apart from the romantics and their circle that was common enough in former times—but rather the notion of finding a formula by which the same type of thing may be sold to the same type of public on the biggest possible scale. The business man is often accused of sticking to the same model as long as possible because, as is well known, it is precisely the saleability of the same product over a long period which makes a business really profitable. But oddly enough, he is also accused of artificially inducing a demand for new types, that is, for a change of fashion, so as to increase consumption. As Georg Simmel describes it: "Articles are not first produced, then become fashionable; articles are produced to create a fashion." [8] In practice, no doubt, both methods are employed, as best suits the situation. Certainly, modern mass production plays upon people's wants in a manner that often runs counter to the natural development of their taste; sometimes it creates a new demand, sometimes it artificially keeps an old demand in being.

The question then arises as to whether the phenomenon of the mass, that is, spiritual monotony and lack of independence on the part of the public, is the effect of the artificial standardization of modern art production; or whether the masses themselves are to be blamed for the low quality of the art served up to them. Does the public really get what it wants, or is it conditioned to want what is set before it? No doubt, the entertainment industry does little or nothing to educate the man in the street in independent thinking, to improve his taste or strengthen the sense of his own personality, but even if it wanted to do so, this would not be easy. It is certainly easier to manipulate puppets than personalities, but in any case the masses do not consist of personalities. To charge publishers, film producers, and record manufacturers with carrying on a planned conspiracy to keep their public from growing up spiritually seems rather fantastic.

The structure of modern industrial society, the mechanical regularity of city life, the inevitable, if largely unintentional and unconscious, adaptation of the individual to the common forms of behavior disposes men to be mass-minded; and this disposition is being continuously intensified by means of press, radio, cinema, advertisements, posters, in fact everything that the eye sees and the ear hears. The facts to be noted, the issues to be decided, the solutions to be accepted are all served up to the people in a form to be swallowed whole. In general they have no choice and are quite content to have none. The mistake is to suppose that the masses thought or felt differently in the days when there were not quite so many of them. They

[8] Georg Simmel: *Philosophische Kultur* (1911), p. 34.

never were any more capable of judging, never had a more independent or more reliable taste, never had any objection to having their spiritual nutriment predigested for them. If the art products that they formerly accepted were of somewhat better quality than at present, that was only because such products were not in the first instance made for them. Art for general consumption is always on a lower level than art produced for the educated. But however small the change in this respect, however unimportant quantity always is as compared with quality in matters of art and culture, the consequences of the fact that ever greater masses of people are coming into the market as consumers of art are quite incalculable. The products of mass culture not only ruin people's taste, make them unwilling to think for themselves, educate them in conformity; they also open the eyes of the majority for the first time to fields of life which they never came in contact with before. Often they are confirmed in their prejudices, but still a way is opened for criticism and opposition. Whenever the circle of consumers of art has been widened, the immediate result has been to debase the level of artistic production. The most instructive example is that of the dissolution of the courtly-aristocratic culture and the rise of a bourgeois culture at the end of the rococo; while the rise of the middle classes about the middle of the nineteenth century affords another example. Today, in consequence of the emergence of the lower middle class and certain sections of the industrial workers as consumers of art, a phenomenon well known in past history is recurring. Though the present situation may not be very encouraging, it is, to judge from history, not a hopeless one; the middle class also took time to improve its taste.

Today's mass-produced art has, like all art, an ideological origin and aim, which, thanks to the refinement of modern propaganda methods, it no doubt subserves more successfully than was ever possible before. Yet to maintain that the producers are engaged in a devilish conspiracy against all that is spiritual is a silly example of vulgarized Marxism. The captains

339

of the entertainment industry naturally only want to earn money, choosing for that end bad art rather than good, in the first place because they generally have no notion of the difference, and secondly because bad art is easier to produce and to sell. That is not to say that they take no part in the ideological struggle. We know that ideologies function apart from all intention or consciousness, and that they can be active without there being any conspiracy or definite plan or campaign. But the publishers of best-sellers and the film manufacturers of Hollywood are by no means among the most loyal exponents of their class ideology; they might more reasonably be accused of lacking conviction than of being unbending fanatics. They address themselves to all and sundry, want to satisfy everybody, not to hurt anybody's feelings; they must keep their customers. The ideological principles that they follow are thus rather of a negative than of a positive kind; the essential thing is that certain subjects are not to be treated or even touched upon. These are primarily: healthy sex relations, class war and the workers' movement, any criticism directed against the existing order of society or the authorities, anything involving religious doubts or opposition to the Church. The avoidance of these themes obviously signifies a tacit acceptance of existing conditions, but the positive propaganda, generally speaking, amounts to no more than a somewhat hesitant assurance that this world is the best of all possible worlds.

The assertion often made that the products of mass culture are put out by the entertainment industry not to satisfy, but to exploit, people's cultural needs is no doubt essentially true; and it is no less true that the poor quality of these products is due to a historical coincidence—of democratization of culture with competitive capitalism. The conclusion, however, which some have thought fit to draw from this critical situation, that "we must remove either exploitation or democracy if culture is to recover its health," [9] is not convincing. Tension between the spir-

[9] Dwight Macdonald: "A Theory of 'Popular Culture,'" *Politics* (1944), p. 23.

itual élite and the rest of society is not a phenomenon of today or yesterday; a certain opposition to higher artistic culture has at all times characterized popular art. It would be a utopian dream to expect that this tension should suddenly cease and give birth to a communal art that would interest and satisfy everybody. There are indeed ways and means of raising the level of popular art, and progress in that direction would certainly require sweeping economic and social changes, but not necessarily the disappearance of either capitalism or democracy. The mere abolition of barriers between classes and of external hindrances to the operation of natural selection would scarcely provide any automatic solution of this problem. The hope that the opening of the gates of culture to the people would produce a flood of new talent has not been fulfilled, and is hardly likely to be fulfilled, at least in the way it was formerly conceived.[1] Talented persons do not march through open gates of culture of their own accord; good taste, the power of discriminating good from bad in art and consciously choosing the good, is not something that can be left to the spontaneous feelings, the "uncorrupted" healthy instincts of people, masses, proletariat, or what you will. Good taste is not the root, but the fruit of aesthetic culture.

It is therefore but an empty argument to disclaim responsibility for the present state of popular art with the phrase that the public gets what it wants. Public taste is not a primary datum; it is what it has become. It is by no means just the public that decides what it would like; its likes are in part determined by what is offered it. That pattern is of course a circle, but one that can be broken. To break it would, however, cost time and money, and as is well known, publishers and film-producers are not philanthropists. They are not even, as business men go, especially enterprising; mere assurances that education of the public is bound to pay in the long run [2] would not be likely to induce them to risk upsetting a safe market.

[1] Cf. D. W. Brogan: "The Problem of High Culture," *Diogenes*, No. 5 (1954), pp. 3 ff.
[2] Gilbert Seldes: *The Big Audience* (1950).

341

9. *FLIGHT FROM REALITY*

The history of modern popular art begins about the middle of the nineteenth century with the rise of the idea that art is relaxation, the prevalence of a desire to find in art a means of distraction rather than of concentration, entertainment rather than education or deepened understanding. Before that time there were, as there have always been, more and less successful, more and less ambitious, more and less complex forms of art; but now there emerges for the first time the notion of an art which does not present any difficulties or problems, but is immediately intelligible. Everything comprised today under the headings of "light music," "light reading," "decoration for the home" was before then practically non-existent. Of course, entertaining books were written—often a good deal more entertaining than the books of today—tuneful, rhythmical, easily memorized music was composed, "pretty," agreeable pictures were painted; but their agreeableness was only a by-product, a means to an end, not an end in itself. Art has always wanted to please, usually to entertain as well; but the people to be pleased and the level on which they are to be entertained have varied from time to time.

It has been well said that to feel pleased means "being in accord with the prevailing circumstances." [3] Cervantes, Voltaire, and Swift wrote extremely amusing books; Rubens and Watteau painted pictures that are a sheer treat to the eyes; Mozart composed the most charming music; but it would not have occurred to any of them to turn out works designed to make people blindly contented; the serious side of life, a feeling for the precariousness of human existence was never quite absent from their major works. They amused themselves and others by depicting the strange twists and turns of life without any idea of escaping from reality; they poked fun at the ab-

[3] Horkheimer-Adorno: op. cit., p. 172.

surdities and the awkward situations one finds in the world, but they never thought of pretending such things did not exist.

However, feeling happy is a relatively harmless way of ignoring or falsifying reality; sentimentality is very much worse. The people who weep most at the fate of the unfortunate hero of romance or film are precisely those who seldom feel any compassion in real life. Sentimentality fulfils essentially a surrogate function of this sort in the life of society. There is no generation so content to wallow in emotional stories and melodramatic situations as one that has been frustrated in the expression of its normal emotional life. Feelings banned from real life, and which in everyday reality wither or degenerate, find a refuge and fulfilment in the sentimental backstairs novel and the operetta. The writers of former ages, and especially those of the otherwise sober eighteenth century, by no means despised heart-stirring effects, but they invariably appealed to the reader's reason as well as to his heart, recalling him, often somewhat rudely, from wish-dreams and utopian fantasies to a sense of reality. They were acquainted with and respected the secrets of the heart, they did not make a mystery of them. By contrast, the modern best-seller depicts emotion not as something normal and inevitable, not as a natural and in its way valuable element of human life, balanced by reason and a sense of decency and self-respect, but as something quite exceptional, the outcome of a sort of perpetual crisis, always with a tinge of the solemn, the extravagant, and the morbid. Sentimentality is sentiment repressed. Feelings for which there is no room in the life of society, being something one must not give way to, are exaggerated, over-valued, raised to the level of the ideal and the unreal, divorced from life and from all need to stand the test of time.

The great attraction of the successful film and novel of today lies in the escape from reality it offers, through identification of the reader or spectator with the hero. Of course, such identification and vicarious participation in the hero's fate, his struggles and successes, has at all times played an important role

343

in the enjoyment of art; indeed art in general can be described as a satisfaction of man's desire for another self and a better life. Yet never before was there such a blind wallowing in wish-fantasies of that kind as there is today. The first beginnings of this unrestrained self-deception through art go back to the romantics. With them, the identification of the reader with the hero takes a form calculated to eliminate all distinction between poetry and reality, author and public, the personage of fiction and the sympathetic follower of the story. The romantic poet makes the reader his confidant, so that anybody can feel himself to be a poet in a way, and sets up between reader and hero a degree of intimacy which allows anybody not only to participate in the hero's fate, but actually to imagine himself in the privileged position of a fictitious character. The reader sees and judges the characters by reference to his own aims, hopes, and interests. He does not merely put himself in their place; he also sees them in situations that are quite inappropriate to them and have meaning only for him. Certainly the heroes of great poetry of all times were in a sense ideal figures, the expression of people's wishes, models to which they looked up, often not without envy; but the reader would never have thought of measuring himself by their standards or of claiming to behave as they did. It was obvious to him from the start that the hero of an epic, a romance, or a tragedy moved in a different circle from his own. But since the romantics, all the bounds that once enclosed that ideal, remote, and forbidden life have been broken down; in the popular literature of today they have vanished so utterly that the modern reader sees the heroes of his favorite novels as no more and no less than the fulfilment of his own frustrated or muddled life, the realization of all he has missed.

However, only a very simple psychology would explain this identification entirely in terms of wish-fantasies and wish-fulfilment. Few readers or cinema-goers really hope for a "happy ending" in Hollywood style, though they play with such ideas as a part of their enjoyment. The illegitimate relationship that they develop toward their heroes is one of self-dramatization and self-pity quite as much as self-deception. Usually they do not expect overmuch of life, but they measure their own successes and failures, their own resources and possibilities, by a standard that is fundamentally unreal and unsatisfactory. Self-deceiving romanticism is at the bottom both of the mass-public's optimism and of its pessimism, so that sorrow for all the good things they have irrevocably missed or wasted is as powerful a source of tears shed in the cinema as is the weak hope that perhaps they have not missed everything after all.

The moral harm done by the cinema is a favorite topic of the cultural critics of our day; they are always talking about the bad example the conduct of film heroes sets the ordinary man. They scarcely seem to consider that no bad example is so harmful as the life-fantasy that the hero's romantic fate implants and instils in spectators, who feel that it relieves them of responsibility for the tasks of their own unromantic lives. Madame Bovary is the prototype of the novel-reader who by means of this kind of life-fantasy concludes a comforting, if ultimately untenable, pact with life. She is the classical example of the romantic born too late who claims extraterritoriality in life without having earned it in any way, missing modest happiness through constantly expecting happiness on the grand scale—expecting a first prize that he never draws.

Which is the lesser evil, to read too much or too little? The answer is not so simple as it appears to the believer in progress. That people read the amount they do is by no means clear gain. The danger of the insatiable hunger for romance, which today is mainly fed by cinema and radio, first made itself felt at the beginning of the nineteenth century, and was recognized in its full extent by Coleridge. "For as to the devotees of the circulating libraries," he writes, "I dare not compliment their pass-time, or rather kill-time, with the name of reading. Call it rather a sort of beggarly day-dreaming, during which the mind of the dreamer furnishes for itself nothing but laziness, and a little mawkish sensibility . . . We should therefore transfer this species of amusement from the genus reading, to that comprehensive class characterized by the power of reconciling the two contrary yet co-existing propensities of human nature, namely, indulgence of sloth, and hatred of vacancy." [4]

Boredom is a product of our restless, sensation-hungry, urban way of life. The peasant does not feel bored; he goes to sleep—which of course is not necessarily more admirable. But he is at least innocent of that unhealthy dread of doing nothing, that vague urge to do something or other which Coleridge refers to and which is unknown outside the atmosphere of the modern big town. The demand for art of the urban masses is just hunger for more raw material, a hunger that must be satisfied in order to prevent from running idle a machine that cannot be stopped. The art that satisfies this hunger is no more than an indifferent fuel, a miserable stopgap. The feeling that something is wanting may be genuine, but people have no idea what really is wanting. They must read a novel, see a film, hear dance-music, have the wireless singing, crooning, or at least humming, because they don't know what else to do with themselves. Well, perhaps they get something out of it, but all that has little to do with the enjoyment of art. With the emergence in the course of the eighteenth and nineteenth centuries of the modern public, reading, from being a somewhat rare pleasure, became a passion. Only in our own day has the enjoyment of art from being a passion become a mere habit, that is, the satisfaction of a want that one is only aware of when it is *not* being satisfied.

But serious as the situation may be, it is no worse than that in which popular art found itself in former times. Excessive pessimism about the present is usually just the reverse side of an excessively favorable estimation of the past. Obviously the abrupt democratization of culture, the breath-taking speed

[4] Samuel Taylor Coleridge: *Biographia Literaria,* § XXII.

of technical change, and the ruthless sway of the profit-principle in the field of art have produced phenomena of a novel type; the assertion, however, that there has been nothing in the past at all analogous to our present mass culture rests upon a superficial view of things. Those who lament modern art-production, supposing that there has never been anything comparable with the mechanization and commercialization of our popular art, with its dependence upon the ideology of the ruling class and its evident inferiority to the art of the educated, see the past in too rosy a light. There has always been more than one level of artistic culture, and the wider the social basis of a particular type of art, the greater has always been the risk of its becoming degenerate or altogether dependent upon extraneous interests. Folk art has generally been a poor imitation, and whatever the addition of its own special values, it has seldom been in proportion to the loss of artistic quality suffered in the process. The popular art of the half-educated masses, however, has never possessed any independent value at all; the only function in the evolution of art which it might be said to have fulfilled has been that of providing a counterweight to certain extremely esoteric tendencies.

Popular art and folk art, in spite of their apparent kinship, have scarcely any points of contact. The notion one often encounters that the art of the modern masses is in the main a continuation of the former folk art has no better foundation than the attribute of "popularity" which they both share—though the sense of this word is different in the two cases. Folk art and popular art are, logically speaking, at most coordinate species, deriving from a common origin, but certainly not from one another. Folk art is naïve, crude, clumsy, and old-fashioned, popular art often skilful and technically apt, though vulgar, subject to superficial and rapid change, but incapable of achieving either more radical transformation or finer discrimination. Genuine art is used up, disintegrated, and simplified by folk art; it is watered down, botched and bowdlerized by popular art. In former periods the gap that sepa-

347

rated the country-folk from the lower strata in the towns was not so great as it is today, so that it is not always clear whether some particular work is a product of the half-educated middle class or the uneducated country-folk; whereas today the art of the urban masses is impossible to confuse with folk art, being utterly incompatible with it. Indeed, nothing is less attractive than folk art to the modern half-educated crowd that apes the ways of life and modes of culture of the upper class; what the educated value and enjoy in folk art escapes the half-educated altogether.

identify ourselves with heroes in fantasies

10. THE ORIGINS OF POPULAR ART

The modern mass public emerged in the great centers of industry; the first impulse toward its formation came in the Industrial Revolution. It achieved its present decisive role as a factor in social and cultural history through the rise of large-scale industry at the turn of last century, and through the development of technical devices for disseminating cultural products which ensured the participation of the masses in the enjoyment of culture to an undreamed-of extent. Popular art in the sense of mass culture came into being, strictly speaking, at that time, but its prehistory goes a long way back. For ever since there was a flow of the lower strata to the towns, bringing about a contact of the country-folk and the upper classes—that is, ever since the latter days of the Ancient Oriental cultures—there have been tendencies toward the development of a popular art. We know that in the Middle Kingdom in Egypt the trading class, and in the New Kingdom even the lower ranks of civil servants, were prosperous enough to purchase objects of art of a modest size; these objects, however, do not seem to have differed much in style or taste from those in the possession of the upper classes. But whether the urban middle class in its turn influenced the taste of the cultural élite, whether in particular the great change in taste which occurred in the time of Akhenaton was connected with the social changes accompanying the rise of the middle class, is hard to say.[5] There certainly was no sign of any attempt to produce art for a larger public or of its degenerating as the result of diffusion.

We encounter popular art in the stricter sense—that is, art produced for a half-educated stratum somewhere between the petty bourgeoisie and the urbanized peasantry—in Hellenistic times at the earliest. Even so, there were no works of visual art, except for some small genre figures, beyond what were produced either at home or by artists working for the court, nobility, and higher bourgeoisie. But by this period at the latest the mime has become a type of general popular entertainment similar to the entertainments of our own mass culture. Simultaneously, literary drama was assimilated to that of the middle and lower classes. The possibility of such a development could be discerned in the time of Euripides, but it was not fully realized until the rise of the New Comedy. The emotionalism and naturalism that then found expression in drama gradually came to penetrate all forms of art, with sculpture, for example, developing on the one hand in the direction of emotional violence and on the other toward the pretty and agreeable. But it is still hardly appropriate to speak of "mass art" in spite of enormous production, illustrated above all by the large number of terracotta figurines which has survived. These statuettes were certainly fairly cheap; their purchasers must for the most part have belonged to the middle classes; and there is no doubt that, for all their attractiveness, they must have been turned out more or less mechanically;[6] but they were still so intimately connected with the standards of classical art as to show no signs of a degeneration of taste. Even if the makers of the Tanagra figurines in particular were aiming at pleasant effects of a schematic kind, which make one think of

[5] Hauser: op. cit., I, 61.
[6] T. B. L. Webster: *Greek Terracottas* (1950), p. 29.

the standardization of modern mass production, the standard of taste remained so high that one could hardly guess what these tendencies will lead to.

Throughout the Middle Ages the theater remained the most fertile branch of popular art. The wandering players' public comprised all the lower classes, so that we can properly regard the mime and its descendants indifferently as a rural, an urban, or quasi-urban form of entertainment. In the theater the boundaries between the different social strata are always somewhat blurred, and in the case of the medieval theater, even the more elevated, religious drama implied a mixing of the different social categories. The art of the minstrel, in the age when heroic poetry was decaying, was in a similar border-line position. The oldest literary forms that manifest a differentiation within the lower classes, a separating off of the townsfolk as a special art public from the country-folk, are the *fabliau* and the short story of the Italian Renaissance. In these we can see a decidedly "bourgeois" literature, certainly a good deal more solid than the popular literature of today, but none the less betraying an unmistakable tendency to standardization and a preference for entertainment pure and simple.

At any rate, it is in literature that we can first discriminate a public for popular art from the public for folk art; the diffusion of the habit of reading for oneself provides the most striking criterion of this. For the country-folk—peasant farmer, land-worker, rural craftsman, farm-servants generally—do not read much even today, and before the Reformation they can have been reading only in exceptional cases. The so-called "folk-books," as we saw, filtered down very slowly from the upper classes, and reached the country-folk proper only at a fairly late date.

The literary types which lie upon the border-line between folk-poetry and popular literature are above all the folk-ballad and the street- and broadside-ballad, which were always addressed to a public socially inferior to that of the "folk-books," and which therefore can more properly be regarded as "popular." The loose sheets on which the words of the broadside-ballads and street songs were printed and circulated are "literature" of a sort, and so had only a limited public; but at the same time they were being sung by minstrels, itinerant singers, and musicians, and in this way taught to the audiences. In France of today music and text of street songs are still offered for sale by the singers themselves, but in general their function as teachers of songs has now been taken over by the gramophone record.

In the visual arts there was scarcely a trace of popular trends before the fifteenth century. The country-folk had of course long had their own forms of decoration, but only the upper classes could actually order and buy works of pictorial art until the woodcut came on the scene. These woodcuts began to be purchased by the lower classes; their diffusion downward was a slow process, but one that undoubtedly commenced as soon as this mode of reproduction was invented. It is certainly difficult to determine exactly the classes of people who were interested in them, and before the eighteenth century it would hardly be possible to discriminate between what was bought by petty townsfolk and what was bought by the peasantry. It is in Italy that one can first discern a public for works of visual art among the lower, though not the lowest, class of townsfolk; the production of a workshop like that of the painter Neri di Bicci certainly amounted to a sort of manufacture of popular art.[7] There were already signs of mass production, although the market, owing to the rather costly nature of the product, was still limited to those who were fairly well off. But these products, for all their conventionality and insipidity, maintained a level of taste and execution which is not to be found in the mass production of today.

In the baroque, too, this level was on the whole preserved, despite a growing crudity of taste in the works designed for the larger sections of the public. The Counter-Reformation in fact marks the birth of an art addressed not only to country-

[7] Hauser: op. cit., I, 309.

351

folk, but also, and to a much greater extent, to the lower classes in the towns. Many of the most essential features of popular art have their origin here. The cult of suffering and of exuberant emotion, of the bliss of martyrdom and of ecstatic states, the readiness to abandon oneself to the irrational, the inconceivable, the unfathomable, are universal and ubiquitous features of baroque art; with them, modern emotionalism and self-dramatizing subjectivism finds its way into visual art and prepares the way for the later romantics. From a Rubens or a Bernini we still get completely spontaneous, deeply expressive works; but when the requirements that called forth their art were fulfilled by the average *routinier,* we get a virtuosity in heart-rending flattery according to a recipe essentially that of modern mass art. The iconography of Catholic Church art adopts step by step those motifs which give the modern devotional image its petty bourgeois character. Christ carrying the Cross, Christ as a gardener, the penitent Magdalen, the good Samaritan, doubting Thomas, Christ at Emmaus—such scenes now come to occupy the center of artistic interest—all of them heart-rending, tearful, many of them scenes of a particularly intimate character.

The first epoch in the history of painting to be dominated as a whole by bourgeois taste was that of the seventeenth century in Holland. But it is not easy, from the works that we possess, to draw definite conclusions regarding the degree of understanding of art manifested by the different groups of citizens. Business speculation, the search for objects of investment, and the fashion of collecting were as fundamental features of the art-production of that age as any interest in the work of art for itself. All classes of the people, in so far as they had any capital at all, the peasantry not excluded, took part in this speculating in pictures and building up of art collections. The extraordinary quantity of pictures produced might lead one to speak of mass-production, but the quality of these remained relatively high because people usually bought them, not to suit their own taste, but for their market value, which tended to be determined by the connoisseur.[8] The only points about these pictures which are suggestive of the later popular art are their small size, their everyday subjects, and their often somewhat ostentatious naturalistic technique.

11. *THE POPULAR ART OF THE MODERN BOURGEOISIE*

With the breakdown of the old system of patronage in the eighteenth century, the elimination of court and aristocracy as regular purchasers of art, and the consequent dependence of the artist upon the open market, the prehistory of popular art comes to an end. Its history proper begins in England and is concerned in the main with literature, in the first instance with the upper and middle strata of the bourgeoisie. The new hunger for reading matter, the ever-growing demand with which the better authors cannot keep pace, and the stirrings of novel, pre-romantic criteria of taste produce a gradual lowering of the artistic level and a coarsening of the cultured form of literature, and that even in the works of the best authors. Fine sentiments are now accorded naïve and uncritical admiration, a fashion from which henceforth only a few artists can shake themselves free; literature becomes what it has on the whole remained to our own day, an analysis of feelings. The love-romance turns into the *"éducation sentimentale"* of the hero or heroine, strips them of all heroic character, and assimilates them to the reader's own ways of life, thus taking the first steps on the road of triviality and ending up in products that are a sheer travesty of their kind.

If one looks backward from the modern best-seller, the most important discovery of the eighteenth century was the horror-story. That already combined the most essential ele-

[8] Ibid., p. 466.

353

ments of the modern sensation-literature: love, secrets, crime, cruelty, and disaster. Many of these motifs are already to be found in the old romances of chivalry and adventure; others derive from the picaresque novel and the folk-ballad; but most have a pseudo-historical source connected with the pre-romantics' interest in the Middle Ages. The horror-story's immediate progeny were the tales of highwaymen and violence of the early nineteenth century. These were succeeded by a somewhat tamer sort of adventure stories, which in their turn were displaced, toward the end of the century, partly by the love-romance and partly by the detective story. This course of development finds its parallel, and to a certain extent its model, in the popular theater, which manifests a continuous evolution from the sentimental domestic drama of Lillo and Diderot, via melodrama, vaudeville, and the *pièce bien faite,* to the sensational film of our own day. The serial novel and the boulevard theater are the first outright examples of popular art in the modern sense. Their public comprises all sections of society with the exception of the real country-folk, and is dominated more and more by a half-educated social stratum whose artistic requirements are rather modest. In its beginnings, popular literature included the works of such authors as Balzac and Dickens, but the process of deterioration was so headlong that very soon its classical representatives were Georges Ohnet and Marie Corelli. It began with the wish-dreams of Rastignac and ended with Cinderella-stories of the private secretary who had such pretty legs and was at the same time so virtuous that her boss was left with no choice but to marry her.

In no form of art can the steady degeneration of taste be so readily observed and traced as in the operetta—a form that undoubtedly, from the beginning, contained in itself the seeds of later decay, but which, at least at first, could attract the talent of such a master as Offenbach. The operetta in the course of its journey from Paris to Vienna and Budapest was transformed from a piquant satire upon society into a vapid and mendacious idyll in which unreality and bad taste are

354

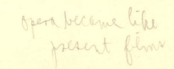

about equally balanced. But *The Merry Widow* and *The Csárdás Princess* are not at all at the end of the road; only with the blaring, crashing tunes and the extravagant proportions of the modern spectacular revue and big musical film does the ideal of operetta really come into its own. And it is still one of the essentials that it should not only blare, but also murmur, that the sentimental love-song, derived from the eighteenth-century romances, should retain its proper place among these bewildering, ear-splitting attractions. The recipe is not new; not only the desire for colossal effects, the overpowering of the senses by noise and glare, by ostentation on the most extravagant scale, but also that special mixture of sensuousness and intimacy, brutality and sentimentality, without which few films can now succeed—all these can be traced a long way back. But the criteria of taste have been getting steadily lower all the time. Of course there is nothing novel about "bad taste," and a thoroughgoing history of bad taste— of stereotyped clichés, wily appeals to extraneous interests and feelings, the strategy of operating on the tear-glands, methods of extorting the public's sympathy—would help us to understand the influence of these tricks, not only upon popular art, but also upon the art of the genuine masters. Few periods in the history of art have been able to steer clear of them altogether, and hardly any periods did not bring forth, along with masterpieces, works that are inferior, tasteless, amateurish, or totally botched and bungled. But what really distinguishes the art production of the present day from all that went before it is the sureness and skill with which carefully cultivated rubbish and elaborately organized trash are turned out.

The history of bad taste in the modern sense begins towards the end of the eighteenth century with the pictures of Greuze. We find here for the first time an irruption of literature into painting, not simply in the sense of pictures having a content that could be formulated in poetical or philosophical terms—for before the impressionists that was the normal thing —but manifesting itself in the production of works with a

355

purely literary content and almost no pictorial value at all. Then begins the history of that banal painting of wish-fantasies and anecdotes, sometimes moralizing and sometimes lascivious, but always pretending to be something different from what it really is. This mendacity comes from the ideology of a public which, owing to its heterogeneous make-up, is torn between liberal aspirations and dogmatic prejudices, romantic revolutionary fancies and conservative practice, ideas about moral freedom and cowardly conformism, and which remains in a state of vacillation.

The next turn in the history of this ideologically unclear and fundamentally discordant type of art occurs with the rise of the bourgeoisie to a position of absolute power, in France of the Second Empire and in Britain of the Victorian Age. The untruthfulness and contradictions in this art now become associated with a parvenu mode of life, with a grandeur, luxury, and culture which are simply copied from other people, which subordinate the whole production of art to extraneous considerations of prestige. The ideas and sentiments that it is to express are as false as the material in which they are expressed. Nobility becomes a moral cliché, chastity a play of equivocations, decency a mere façade, just as the marble is only plaster, the stone mortar, and the gold gilding. Only the plush and the silk on the sofas and door-curtains are genuine.

The international character of the new official taste is nowhere so uniformly and so pompously displayed as in painting. Gérôme, Bouguereau, Cabanel, and Regnault in France; Leighton, Poynter, Alma Tadema, and Herkomer in England; Markart, Böcklin, Klinger, and Stuck in the German-speaking lands: with all their differences and distinct spheres of activity they are one and all exponents of the same agreeable fashion, effected by poor or at most indifferent painting; their "literary" manner, if nothing else, derives from the art of Greuze. Instead of conveying something genuinely visual, they try to express in a visual medium experiences that are essentially non-visual. They aim to save themselves and their public the mental effort that the reduction of reality to optical terms involves; their skill consists in arousing feelings of self-satisfaction in the most effortless way possible. They paint pictures to make the spectator feel proud of his rather modest historical knowledge, of the history that has been served up to him, of his national heroes, of the great representatives of humanity, of all that is grandiose, pompous, and ostentatious; the French are to be made to feel proud of being the heirs of the Revolution and of Napoleon, and the rest, if nothing else, of belonging to the heroic race that originated all this grandeur and magnificence. They paint lovely little idylls, "full of feeling," which enable the spectator to bask in the cosiness of his childlike innocence. They paint anecdotes designed to make life with all its cares and trials appear a harmless game. They paint nudes carefully kept just upon the border-line between pornography and a seemingly healthy, sensuous paganism. And, in compensation for their lack of any genuine personal relationship to reality, they exhibit in their pictures an obtrusive, ostentatious, painfully minute "truth to nature." Because they cannot convince, they have to bluff. They are responsible not only for the type of picture which is most generally acceptable even today, but also for the stereotypes upon which must be based both the descriptions of nature by a successful author and the creation of "atmosphere" by an ambitious film director.

12. *THE CINEMA*

The final and decisive step in the origination of modern mass-produced art was taken with the mingling of the petty bourgeoisie and the working-class, and the evolution of a social type that moves between those classes and is estranged from both, a type that today fills the cinemas and buys the largest number of television sets, the newest records, and the worst colored prints. Of all arts, the film satisfies the demands of such people most completely, as it is also the most characteristic product of mass culture. No form of art offers such variety all at once; none is able to satisfy so many different demands at the same time. But none requires such large investments and is so utterly dependent upon immediate material success.

The film developed into a popular art out of a kind of folk art. In its beginnings it was, however, not an art for the masses, but was supported by that rather small group of people who are attracted to any novel form of entertainment. The film made no claim to be "art"; that is: producers and spectators of the early films were no more conscious of taking part in an artistic activity than are country-people singing their songs or decorating objects of household use. These films, which as a matter of fact were no more than little sketches from life, a locomotive starting up or a horse in a race, and somewhat later short and more or less amusing everyday scenes, were certainly not looked on as artistic representations, but as simple reproductions of reality. The situations pictured in these films were expressed in simple, naïve, generally intelligible terms, as in folk art, and little or no professional skill was required of their producers. They were not intended to be original, but merely understood; originality and subtlety of expression came later. Even today the film resembles folk art in that in it the tension between good quality and popularity is not so marked as in the other forms of art, so that the chances for success of a good film are greater than those for a good novel or painting. For apart from the films, every progressive art today employs a language of its own, which in some measure is intelligible only to the initiated. The learning of this language involves an extensive and lengthy preparation that cannot easily be short-ened or undergone at an advanced age. The language of the film, on the contrary, is something that the last generation could learn without the slightest education or the slightest trouble. And it is still, so to say, intellectual common property, although the "filmic" modes of expression—especially since the invention of the talking film and its wholesale appropriation

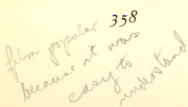

film popular because it was easy to understand

of the technique of the stage—are gradually decaying and being confined to certain special, so-called "artistic" purposes. The next generation will hardly understand all the means of expression which were created in the heroic age of the film, and the cleavage, which in other branches of art divides connoisseurs from laymen, will be evident in film audiences also.

Only a rather young art can be generally intelligible without necessarily being superficial; a more highly developed form of art requires for its understanding some familiarity with earlier stages, which, though superseded, have left their traces. The history of modern art consists largely in the separating of elements that previously were more or less intimately connected; thus, in literature, poetry becomes divorced from recreation, pure music from occasional music, pictorial decoration from creative visual interpretation of reality. The only form of art in which this divorce has hardly made itself felt, or at any rate did not until lately make itself felt, is the film. In no other art would it have been possible for such novel and valuable achievements as the films of Eisenstein, Pudovkin, or René Clair to be great popular successes as well.

To understand an art means to realize the connection between its formal and material elements and to feel this connection as perfectly self-evident. An art lacks meaning when its formal elements fulfil no function in expressing content; it appears to be devoid of meaning when this function is not recognized and the form consequently strikes one as arbitrary or bizarre. As long as an art is young and relatively lacking in tradition, that is, as long as it manifests no well-established, rigid formulas, content and means of expression are connected in a natural, unproblematic manner. The forms arise out of the contents, or at least it seems that a direct and apparently inevitable path led from the subject-matter to the form of its expression. But it is characteristic for all evolution in art that forms, becoming detached autonomous structures applicable to diverse contents, become at the time more abstract and empty, and in the end are intelligible only to the educated and the connoisseur. In the case of the film, this process of the detachment of forms has only just begun. Many cinema-goers belong to the generation that experienced the rise of this new formal language of the film; for them its modes of expression are self-evident. But the process of estrangement has begun and can hardly be halted.

The film has ceased to be a "folk art," insofar as it ever was, and is now on the one hand a popular art of the masses and on the other an artistically ambitious mode of expression of educated and aesthetically trained people interested in its formal peculiarities—though it is being employed less and less in this latter role. Even in the best days of the silent film, that is to say, in many of the most successful Russian and French films, one could already detect a rather too self-conscious and complacent utilization of the so-called "filmic" effects; a formalism developed in which the former unity of form and content, mode and object of representation, optical means and narrative motif, became lost. As long as artists were concerned about exploring the formal possibilities of the new art and employing them upon the subject in hand, the original course could be maintained; as soon, however, as they began to practice formal devices for their own sakes, these devices became the monopoly of an *avant-garde,* which was bound sooner or later to lose contact with the general cinema-going public. The once so beloved "effects" with changing camera-angles, distances, and speeds, the tricks of cutting and copying techniques, fade-outs, and flashbacks, are already beginning to seem rather artificial and disturbing. Script-writers, directors and cameramen are now simply concerned to tell a story clearly, rapidly, and excitingly, employing to this end the methods of the stage rather than the special techniques of the camera and the screen.

The film developed step by step into an art for the masses, a fate for which it was predestined by the technical and economic conditions of its production. In consequence of the methods of its manufacture, reproduction, and distribution, it was from the start peculiarly fitted to become an article of mass consumption, and the entertainment industry took full advantage of its possibilities. It can employ picture and speech, music and color, unlimited space and unlimited time, an unrestricted number of persons and inexhaustible stores of properties, to produce complete illusion in the minds of the public without the least mental exertion on its part—and so all these resources, and more than could have been imagined, have been put at its disposal.

Every art reduces reality to a particular plane of perception, translates the variety of experience into a more or less homogeneous formal language. Through this indirectness of expression, art makes the most intense impression upon those who encounter it, requiring of them, however, that they should be able and willing to translate their own experiences into a more condensed and more difficult language. Enjoyment of art is directly proportional to the spectator's talent for understanding mere suggestions or hints, for filling out the artist's elliptical mode of expression. From this point of view, what distinguishes the film from the other arts is that it works on a sort of "hey presto, here it comes!" principle. It serves up one complete picture after another in such a way that the spectator sees and hears only what is of itself visible and audible, and has no more to do than make mental associations—the elements of which are actually supplied to him one after another. Whereas art in general requires an intensified activity of thought or imagination, film actually shows the picture to be imagined, or at any rate leads the spectator on from one image to another, saving him the trouble of using his own mental powers. It has justly been called a *biblia pauperum*— "a picture-book of life for those who cannot read." [9]

And yet the film possesses a formal principle of its own; it is photography in motion, and as such offers us a really novel point of view. But this fact—that it has its proper prin-

[9] Bernhard Diebold: *"Film und Drama," Die Neue Runschau*, XLIII (1932), 404.

361

ciple—does not entail either its being bound to be very fruitful artistically, or its taking rise from the solution of an artistic problem. The basic idea of the film—that of portraying events and experiences in the form of moving pictures—arose as a mere by-product of a discovery that was on the whole rather accidental. Someone hit upon the notion that a series of instantaneous photographs taken of an occurrence might be shown as a continuous sequence; the point of the device lay in the possibility of recording and reproducing movements. In this case an art did clearly arise out of the special nature of a technique, as Semper would have it. Certainly, the technique was there before the artistic problems that became soluble by means of this technique; it was in fact fully developed before anyone really knew what to do with it.[1] It may be true that the course of evolution more commonly runs in the reverse direction, from the awareness of an artistic problem to the invention of a technique; but the film shows that we have become accustomed to regard too uncritically the history of art as a history of problems, and the principles of art as mere solutions of problems. The story of the origin of the film should be a warning to us of the role played by chance—or what in the context of artistic problems and solutions has to be called "chance"—in the history of spiritual creations. The film, however, is only the most striking, not the sole, instance of a technical novelty giving birth both to a new artistic form and to a new artistic problem—evidence that the history of art is not always logical. Here we find solutions without any foregoing problem; solutions, found accidentally, disclose problems never hitherto formulated; a technique often proves fruitful beyond all expectation. The evolution of art does not proceed at all simply from a problem to its solution or from a requirement to a technical process; often, as with the film, it goes in the opposite direction.

The essentially photographic character of the film entails

[1] B. Balázs: *Der sichtbare Mensch* (1924); *Der Geist des Films* (1930).

362

that it must preserve some portions of reality unchanged and allow the "voice of nature" to be heard more directly than is the case with the other arts. For however "naturalistic" these may be in their choice of means, they can never do more than imitate natural objects, never employ them in a raw, original, unmodified state. In representing the things, they produce a new form of object; they are disintegrating the objects of common experience and establishing new connections among their elements. The film is the only art that takes over considerable pieces of reality unaltered; it interprets them, of course, but the interpretation remains a photographic one. A landscape photographed or street photographed, a face or gesture photographed, remain very much what they are in themselves. One example will show how thoroughly scenery and properties retain their "natural" character on the screen and how different reality on the stage is from reality in the film: an accurately operating clock would be intolerable on the stage, but it is one of the commonest and least noticed properties in the film. The truth of the matter is that all sensible objects in the film, actor as well as scenery, facial expressions as well as landscapes, are simply stage properties.

In spite of its fundamental naturalism, the film works with fixed types, schematic characters, and accepted psychological formulas. All the famous film actors, Chaplin, Mary Pickford, Douglas Fairbanks, Greta Garbo, and the rest, specialized in certain very particular types of role. Each of them was less a great character-actor than a rare specimen of animal; their individual physiognomies, their types of body, gaits, and gestures, were far more important for the tasks assigned to them than any power of creating characters. Goethe's remark about the theater: "All in all, the bodily appearance of the actor matters most, a handsome man, a beautiful woman . . ." is all very well, but in the film an actor's value is often no more than that of a splendid animal.

The film director Pudovkin, who maintained that the film uses men only as raw material, treating such "human material,"

363

as he called it, on exactly the same footing as landscapes or intimate objects, emphasized at the same time how much more important is physical type in a film actor than spiritual individuality. As a matter of fact, Kuleshov had already shown experimentally the comparatively slight importance of expressive power in film acting. To prove his thesis, he linked by cutting one and the same close-up of an earnest, but not otherwise notable, face of a man with various motifs, showing thereby that the same facial expression, according as it was cut next to a laid dining-table, a naked breast, or a severed head, was taken by the spectator to express hunger, sex-desire, or fear and disgust.[2] But if this is really so and the expression of emotions can be effected by the same sort of mechanical means as that of spatial and temporal relations, the professional film actor should, as the Russians maintain, be fully replaceable by the amateur; and in that way a point of contact, if no more, could be established between film and folk art.

Pudovkin somewhere mentions that the thoroughly natural, convincing, and indeed thrilling impression of a bomb explosion which occurs in one of his films was not achieved simply by photographing an exploding bomb—that would have given an utterly confused and ineffective picture; he had to collect the filmic components of the occurrence to be represented from the most various, even the most disparate fields of natural phenomena, and then bring them into a wholly artificial relation with one another. The film is thus a "fabrication," not only for the reason that it is more intimately bound up with a certain technical apparatus than any other art form. It is not simply the case that, as in the other arts, the instrument intrudes itself as vehicle almost unnoticed between the artist and his work, between the person enjoying and the source of his enjoyment. A special feature of the film is that the achievement of the desired impression is the outcome of a process completely "reified," externalized, and mechanized, devoid of all relation

[2] V. I. Pudovkin: *Film Technique* (1935), pp. 139–40; *Film Acting* (1935), pp. 65–78.

to the original experience in the mind of the artist. The estrangement of the artist from his own merely inward and personal experiences, inevitable concomitant though it be of any *ex*-pression, of any communication which is to be intelligible to others, is here found in a degree previously unknown. Equally, the film achieves the complete materialization of the spectator's inner experience; no other institution has been so effective as the cinema in moulding all the various self-expressive behavior of modern man to certain fixed formulas, certain impersonal and mechanically repeated schemes. The girl of today does not only dress and make up, but also speaks and smiles just like her admired and envied film star. It is no longer a question of that indispensable identification—always at a certain distance—of the reader or spectator with an author's ideal creations; it is the complete abandonment of his own personality and the transformation of his own being into a "thing" or "commodity," that same transformation which the film industry has already effected with the actors, the story, the images and dreams of the author. Here the salesman does not have to conquer the customer; the public is there waiting to be hooked.

All art is essentially a tension between subject and object, inner experience and form, original vision and enduring work. This tension arises both in the creative process of embodying the artist's vision and in the receptive process of inner debate between the objective meaning of the work and the spectator's personal world-view. Unembodied, merely private visions of the artist and unconnected, non-committal imaginings of the spectator are without this vital tension and are irrelevant to art. Seen from this point of view, the enjoyment of most cinema-goers is tension-less and irrelevant. The works of art there exhibited are not encountered by persons with individual experience of life and spiritual aspirations of their own; the film just impinges, so to say, upon sets of recording apparatus, each of which can do no more than play back what has been spoken into them.

VI

Conflicting Forces
in the History of Arts:
Originality and the Conventions

1. *THE LANGUAGE OF ART*

IF ONE HAD TO GIVE a general criterion of what constitutes art, one might think of saying: originality. But there is no such criterion. One can hardly make any statement about art without having to admit, in some context or other, the very opposite. The work of art is at once form and content, an affirmation and a deception, play and revelation, natural and artificial, purposeful and purposeless, within history and outside of history, personal and superpersonal. Still, none of these characteristics seems to have such universal significance as that of originality; a work of art must express its own novel and particular view of the world if it is to have any value in itself, indeed, if it is to have aesthetic quality at all. For every kind of art, novelty is not only a justification for its production, but also a constituent of its being. Yet no work, however great its originality, can be novel in all respects, in every one of its elements and aspects. Every work of art that has originated in a historical context—that is, all art that we know of—manifests conventional as well as original features. It must employ known and tried means of expression to some extent, not only in order to be understood, but even to "get at the things." In order to be able and to want to represent an object, the artist must have seen how people *do* represent such objects.

The leap from nature to art, from the conjuration to the imitation of nature, from invocation to conscious fiction, is something we cannot reconstruct. It is evident however that once this leap has been taken, there is no more room for unrestricted originality, for then the history of the learning, transmission, and development of forms begins. We have no idea how an artist might portray reality in the absence of any previous attempts to portray it; we can only say that all artistic representation known to us must have been based upon earlier endeavors, for they all employ a number of means of expression which, taken by themselves, could not have been intelligible to anybody. Man's first attempt at a work of art, were we to come upon it, we should not recognize as such; we should take it for something different from what it was intended to be. For art is neither the primeval speech of humanity, anterior to all other modes of expression, nor yet a world-language, intelligible at all times by everyone. But it *is* certainly a "language," necessarily spoken and understood by many different persons. If art were free from all preconditions, if it merely relied on some *ad hoc* means of expression, different from case to case—it would be useless as a vehicle of communication and mutual understanding.

Since then, in accord with its character as language, art replaces things by signs, and as there are always fewer signs than things, art cannot avoid schematizing and conventionalizing to a certain extent. Even the most spontaneous and truthful art does not employ one special sign for each impression or idea, but utilizes a sort of dictionary in which there is often only a single expression for several different concepts. Every period, every generation—in a sense every artist—has its own dictionary and employs its own means of representation whenever, for example, a tree, a mountain, a hand, or an ear is to be depicted. These are variations upon the conventional forms that arise out of the limitations confronting the different arts, and offer a resistance to the naturalistic endeavors of the individual artist. In painting, these forms arise out of the two-dimensional surface upon which the artist has to give an impression of space and solidity; in the theater they derive from the limited time of the performance and the restricted space of the stage, within the framework of which a plot consisting of a number of different episodes has to be played out; in the film they result from speech being either lacking or necessarily brief, so that the most important task of the author and director is that of translating the plot into non-linguistic forms. The fact that the work of art succeeds in effecting the required illusion in spite of these limitations is primarily due to the willingness of the reader or spectator to submit to the representational conventions, to treat them as "rules of the game," of unquestionable validity. The pretences that the persons in the play are "thinking aloud" when they are alone on the stage, that their "whispers" are audible in the last row of the gallery, but not on the stage itself, that they converse about some matters merely for the information of the audience—these are all presuppositions of the theater to which people usually feel no objection. Without tacit agreement between stage and auditorium to admit such conventions, there would be no theater, without "willing suspension of disbelief"[1] on the part of spectator or reader, no art. A child's demand to hear exactly the same stories again and again, excluding all possibility of surprise or the creation of new elements of illusion, exhibits this self-suggestion in its purest form.

Spontaneity by itself cannot produce anything communicable or comprehensible. A work of art that consisted entirely of original, strictly creative elements would be unintelligible; it becomes intelligible only through a certain sacrifice of originality. The living, pre-rational experience of the individual must first undergo a certain rationalization and conventionalization if it is to emerge from the purely private sphere and carry some of its meaning into the world of interpersonal relations. As a matter of fact, the struggle against conventions in art is not only a way of sacrificing intelligibility for a gain in immediacy; as Nietzsche remarked, it is often inspired by a positive desire *not* to be understood.[2] Movements in art such as

---

[1] Konrad Lange: *Das Wesen der Kunst* (1901).
[2] Friedrich Nietzsche: *Menschliches Allzumenschliches*, II, 122.

mannerism and romanticism set themselves against the conventions of the foregoing periods, not because those conventions were too esoteric or not perspicuous, but because they had become all too perspicuous and called forth no effort. Mannerists and romanticists are seeking not for simpler, but for more complicated, modes of expression; they become more intelligible and more enjoyable for their contemporaries in proportion as their own means of expression become more a matter of convention and formula. One must not, however, picture the process of communication as one in which the conventional forms are somehow applied subsequently, like an external framework, to the spontaneous core of the work; rather, we must regard every work and every part of a work as embodying the result of a conflict between originality and convention, between the novel and the traditional. It is not a case of spontaneous living experience being made communicable and becoming vicarious through the employment of conventional forms; the original experiences themselves move as it were upon rails that have been already laid down by convention. The notion of an experience that would be completely spontaneous, uninfluenced by any schema, unconventional in all respects, is no more than a limiting concept; actual experience is always infinitely far removed from this romantic ideal of absolute immediacy.

Every artist speaks the language of his predecessors, and some time elapses before he begins to speak with his own voice. To assert, however, that he always begins by imitating another artist and that every early work is a kind of pastiche [4] is to simplify the matter unduly. In the present connection it is not of importance to observe that the young Rembrandt acquired the style of Lastman, Greco in his Italian period the style of the Venetians, Raphael the technical accomplishments of the Florentine masters of his time; the important fact is that even those artists who from the very start were far more independent than they were—the young titans and rebels, the youthful prodigies

[3] André Malraux: *Les Voix du silence,* pp. 279, 310, 313.

372

and the self-taught—expressed themselves at first in the formal language of an older generation. The important, indeed the crucial, fact for an understanding of the role of convention in the history of art is that in order to reach a formulation of its own aims and ideals, even an opposition has to employ the means of expression characteristic of the style it opposes. In this respect a revolutionary artist is no more independent of the past than the feeblest follower of tradition.

André Malraux observes that it is beyond our power to imagine what would have become of any great artist if he had been acquainted only with the works of nature, and not with any works of art.[4] He is evidently recalling Wölfflin's dictum that a picture always owes a great deal more to other pictures than to the artist's observation of nature.[5] But Malraux gives us a new variant of Wölfflin's idea, suggesting that art is not merely the rival of nature, but the very source of artistic inspiration and the principal content of the work that is to be created. He puts this point in his remark that the artist is concerned only with his work; the musician is not concerned with the nightingale, but with music, the poet not with sunsets, but with the beauty of verses, and one who is a painter loves not landscapes, but pictures.[6] Throughout he emphasizes the autonomy of art, the inbreeding and self-generation of artistic conventions. Were this not so, every painter would have to invent painting afresh, every composer invent music, every dramatist the theater. Konrad Fiedler, with his phrase about art not originating in the dark womb of the soul, but in the act of its birth, anticipated this line of thought to some extent. "One must not think of the artistic process," he writes, "as if a work of art were fetched up from the depths of a formless world of sensations and impressions; one must think of the artist . . . on his way toward a novel goal, suddenly finding himself in a world from which he can make a start . . . There he finds

[4] Ibid., p. 280.
[5] Heinrich Wölfflin: *Kunstgeschichtliche Grundbegriffe* (1929), p. 243.
[6] Malraux: op. cit., p. 276.

already achieved what he is aiming at; with all his seeking and his aspiration, he does not feel himself a stranger any longer; he gains a sense of security because he sees that the urge alive in him aspires a thousand others; he sees himself as infinitely helped because, whereas he formerly stammered, he has suddenly found a language in which he can speak his mind." [7]

According to all this, the linguistic character of conventions does not merely answer the question how art, literature, the theater, and so on persist as institutions, as substrata of the spiritual development of mankind; it also actually purports to explain how an inner vision achieves communicable form. But to characterize the function of art as a "language" not only answers, but also raises, questions; in fact it raises the most difficult question with which the persistence of art-forms confronts us. Linguistic forms—meanings of words, idioms, and metaphors—are products of thought, serve for the communication of thoughts. But once they reach a state of finality and have been used by various subjects in various situations, they tend to be employed in a mechanical, often imprecise, or even positively confusing fashion; by providing a "well-worn track" for thought, they tempt the thinker to develop his thought along particular given lines and in accord with more or less rigid models. Language is not only the "clothing of thought," is not only formed by the content of thought which is to be expressed; it reacts upon that content and even forms it before, strictly speaking, it is conceived. It is not simply the case that language shapes itself according to what one wants to say in it; mostly one only wants to say what the current means of expression permit one to say. However, those who criticize the stereotyped and rigid character of linguistic expression are usually not content with noting the mutual dependence of language and thought, form and content, convention and experience; they also maintain that the means of expression exert not merely a restricting, but also a positively degrading, influence upon the content of thought. The danger that they believe they must

[7] Konrad Fiedler: *Schriften über Kunst* (1914), II, 171.

and can combat is one of impoverishment, loss of the intrinsic color and vigor of the personality through constant employment of superficial, threadbare, lifeless forms of language. One may recall the passion and eloquence with which Bergson, for example, wrote of this peril to lively and creative thinking, thus giving new life and influence to the old romantic suspicion of all mediating factors in culture. For the cultural criticism of the romantics had originated in an experience of the contrast between creative inner life and dead external forms, and found its most poignant expression in its conception of words killing the idea, forms killing the soul, rules killing the spirit. Now the same fear of the soul-destroying effect of anything formal became the spring of a new cultural criticism, and provided the driving force in the war that the disciples of Bergsonian spiritualism and vitalism waged and, to a certain extent, are still waging against conventions. According to Bergson's philosophy, speech is the mask of thought, just as, according to Marx's sociology, science, being ideologically conditioned, is the distortion of truth, and just as, according to Freud's psychology, the apparent life of the soul is a concealment of its real motivation. All these concepts—the romantic-idealist concept of form, the historical-materialist concept of ideology, the psychoanalytic concept of rationalization—derive from a certain type of psychology—a "psychology of exposure"—which sees in all concrete culture a degradation of spiritual content. Its leading idea of "spiritual alienation" dominates the entire thinking of the late romantic and post-romantic era. According to this psychology, health is to be found only along a road that leads away from objective forms and ossified conventions back to spontaneity, immediacy, and authenticity of soul. Yet neither the diagnosis nor the therapy recommended is altogether convincing. The Kantian philosophy offers a much more realistic account of the trouble and a much more promising attempt to remedy it.[8] According to Kant, we do not have to unveil a spiritual "thing-in-

[8] Cf. Maurice Blanchot: *Comment la littérature est-elle possible?* (1942).

itself," but to recognize that the forms within which all thinking, feeling, and acting move are limitations upon, and also
enabling conditions for, the functioning of the mind. When we
can see only with spectacles, it is not only senseless to dis-
course upon the distorting effect of spectacles, but also useless
to spend much time speculating what seeing without spectacles
would be like. However narrow may be the limits which art's
conventional means of expression set for the portrayal of actual
living experience, it is through them alone that a way is opened
up to what would otherwise be utterly inaccessible. Obviously
the sign is not the thing itself, yet we know of the thing only
through the sign.

No doubt there is a difference of principle which confronts us when we distinguish the various sorts of sign. Some
signs are essentially imitative, and others have purely symbolic value; the former depend upon similarity, the latter upon
convention. In practice, however, they are always mingled; the
most faithful portrayal of nature employs schematic, suggestive
forms here and there, and the imitative signs themselves have
some of the aspects of a cypher-language. Giotto, for example,
depicts natural phenomena such as mountains, trees, and ani-
mals in a wholly conventional manner, whereas his treatment
of the human figure is far more naturalistic. But with the later
masters, too, whether the leaves of a tree or the folds of a robe
receive a more or less summary treatment has nothing to do
with the extent to which naturalistic technique had been developed up to then; sometimes it seems to them natural, sometimes unnatural, to represent all the details. In the composition
of its elements no work of art is wholly homogeneous; a purely
naturalistic art exists as little as a purely stylized art—if we
except simple geometrical ornament. The standard of what
constitutes truth to nature is never altogether uniform or unequivocal. The extent to which this incoherency in the means of
expression is accepted or positively overlooked is a matter of
the current convention; and this may best be defined as the

willingness of the spectator to tolerate certain inconsistencies in the artistic rendering of reality.

However, a regularly recurring and no longer disturbing deviation from reality becomes a true convention only when it is no longer the result of incapacity, but has "made a virtue of necessity," so to speak. A convention generally originates in some technical difficulty, arises out of inability to master this; but certainly it cannot be wholly explained in terms of lack of artistic skill. The frontality of Egyptian art, that paradigm of all conventions, obviously originated in the difficulty of drawing foreshortened aspects; but the circumstance that it remained current long after the primitive state of technique in which it arose had been overcome shows that in the course of history it had taken on a significance of its own, had been transformed from a mere expedient into a symbolic form, from an improvisation into an institution.

2. *THE INCOHERENCE OF THE WORK OF ART*

It is a classicist dogma that the work of art is a completely unitary organic whole, permeated in all its parts by the same formal principles. In reality it is no more than a clearly delimited complex consisting of elements that only within this complex and in relation to one another possess aesthetic meaning and value. To talk of the characters, the plot, or the situations of a novel or drama as if they were independent phenomena, to ascribe to them an existence going beyond the work of art and explicable apart from it is as senseless as it would be to appraise various factors in a picture, such as composition, perspective, and coloring, otherwise than in relation to one another. Taken apart from the work as a whole, each of these components would have another meaning. When Balzac speaks of his characters as persons of the *Comédie humaine,* or even as individuals of his own private acquaintance, and no longer just as figures in the *Illusions perdues, Père Goriot* or *Cousine Bette,* when for example he discusses with his friends whom he shall marry Eugénie Grandet to, or when Ibsen talks about his Nora's childhood, how she was spoiled, how she got her name and so on—all this is upon a plane of reality beyond the boundaries of the works in question and has nothing to do with them as such.

E. M. Forster in his essay on the novel distinguishes "flat" and "round" characters, according as the writer delineates homogeneous personages dominated by one particular characteristic, or such as are many-sided, full of inconsistencies, and incalculable.[9] But strictly speaking, in a work of literature, however large in scale or rich in content it may be, there are never anything but "flat" characters. Reduction of the concrete "roundness" of characters is of the essence of communicability by means of descriptive writing, just as two-dimensionality is the essence of the painter's way of depicting things. Only he who is willing to accept them as "flat—as in fact they are—who does not take what he finds in the work as an invitation to supplement and elaborate it, will be able to understand a novel or a drama and to appraise it as a work of art. To answer the question: "How many children had Lady Macbeth?" is not to deepen in any way Shakespeare's "flat" characterization of the heroine; it is simply to move on to a plane wholly irrelevant to the drama.

But the fact that what counts artistically is only that which actually occurs within the limits of the work and figures among the elements of the complex does not at all imply that the work of art is always a completely integrated whole. The thesis that none of its components could be omitted or anything added without destroying or at least impairing the effect of the whole applies only to the productions of the strictest classicism. Many of the greatest masters seem to have cared little for formal

[9] E. M. Forster: *Aspects of the Novel* (1927).

378

unity and integration in their works; they were more concerned about imparting life, vigor, and completeness to particular details, and often gave an impression of formal unity by means of a subsequent and somewhat external co-ordination of the parts. To illustrate the piecemeal structure of these creations, it is enough to recall Cervantes's masterpiece, in which so important a personage as Sancho Panza owes his existence to an afterthought of the author; or Dostoevsky's *Idiot,* of which eight different drafts were made without the character of Rogoschin, the most important and successful figure in the whole story, ever having occurred to the author. If we knew more about Shakespeare's method of working and of the process by which his individual works came into being, we should undoubtedly find there many more striking examples of the role played in the creation of works of art by improvisation, caprice, and chance.

At any rate, one gets that impression from the general incoherence of Shakespeare's works, the recent interest in which, especially in connection with his character-drawing, has led to the development of a fresh point of view in criticism. It has been recognized that Shakespeare owes his greatness as a portrayer of character neither to any special "knowledge of human nature" nor to any mysterious power of infusing into his characters some power of independent spontaneous life.[1] The critics have come to see that the contradictory character of these personages derives neither from psychological observation nor from any special interest in psychological complexity, but simply from the endeavor to make individual scenes as lively and dramatic as possible by means of paradoxical exaggeration and extravagant contrasts. Shakespeare increases the intensity of the individual episodes at the expense of the total effect;[2] that is the explanation of the inconsistent attitudes of his characters and the incoherent structure of his plots. This

[1] T. S. Eliot: *Selected Essays* (1932), p. 188. E. E. Stoll: *Shakespeare Studies* (1942).

[2] L. L. Schücking: *Character Problems in Shakespeare's Plays* (1922), pp. 114 ff.

method of his is evidently connected with the persistence in his time of a living tradition of medieval "additive" composition, and thus is the more readily understandable. But it is a remarkable fact that drama in general, even in the rigorous form of the Greek or French tragedy, exhibits an "atomistic" type of structure similar to that of opera or oratorio, with their great arias and *tutti*, and relying on the particular effect of each individual scene. In fact, the successful drama is not only a work of art, but also an "artifice" that heaps trick upon trick and effect upon effect, and thus by its repeatedly interrupted, "isolating" manner of representing the individual scenes is sharply distinguished from the "continuous" representation of epic. The crucial importance of contrast and conflict in drama is obviously in connection with this atomizing method, and follows from the principle of maximum effectiveness on the stage, which in turn is altogether dependent upon the scenic structure of the piece. However, the dramatic conflict is continually taking on new forms in accord with the current stage conventions; in general, it reflects the history of these conventions.

Greek tragedy relies upon the contrast between the character and the actions of the hero, between his moral greatness and his mad, ruthless, self-destructive deeds. Here however the dramatic contrast does not develop into an actual conflict: the hero is the innocent victim of his destiny, and sins against the divine order only after his destruction is already certain. The drama revolves around a tragic blindness, not a "tragic guilt"; the plot consists in the revelation of the madness that led to the hero's destruction, in the opening of his eyes when he is already on the edge of the abyss that is to swallow him. The elimination of any question of guilt and the satisfaction of the audience with the mere spectacle of the hero breaking down under the blows of fate are among the most important presuppositions of this type of drama. It is only because blame and justification, and thus all psychological motivation and development of character, are so irrelevant—everything depend-

ing upon the experience of a single sudden overwhelming revelation of destiny—that the convention of the "dramatic
unities" provides an adequate framework for the tragic events.

In French classical tragedy, unlike Greek, the dramatic
contrast consists in the tension between two attitudes of soul—
inclination and duty, love and honor, passion and reason—and
develops into a true moral conflict. The plot exhibits the inner
struggles of the hero, the victory of the principle of duty or
reason, and the acknowledgment of this victory by the hero
himself. The hero is guilty, becomes aware of his guilt, and
must pay the penalty. The development and solution of the
conflict takes the form of a series of rational debates with a
logical conclusion. The philosophical basis of this conception is
a belief in the possibility of a rational discussion and decision
of questions of guilt. This permits the action to be reduced to
a bare dialogue, and the unities to be retained as the firm external structure of the logical operation that is here proceeding.
In French classical tragedy nothing can be expressed for which
this formal framework is too narrow; but the framework can
remain narrow as it is only because the rationalism of the age
has clothed it with symbolic meaning.

In the modern naturalistic drama, psychology take the
place that logic held in the *tragédie classique.* The dramatic
struggle now takes place between opposed psycho-physical
dispositions—hereditary defects, irresistible habits, unconscious
drives, and ambivalent sentiments; the decisive act is no more
than the result of a process that runs its course in accord with
the laws of nature, and could be described in scientific terms.
Here laws of nature play the role reserved for fate in Greek
tragedy. Once again the hero is guiltless; he is the victim of his
psycho-physical constitution, his heredity, his social milieu, the
circumstances of his life. However, in spite of this recurrence to
a negative attitude upon the question of guilt, the substitution
of laws of nature for destiny brings with it a formal difference
that sharply distinguishes modern from Greek tragedy. Modern
drama, regarding man as a function of his environment, in-

evitably abolishes the unities; further, it requires the identification of the ideal time of the drama with the actual time of the performance, and of the ideal space of the drama with the actual space on the stage. The fiction of the "invisible fourth wall" between stage and auditorium, or in other words of a performance "without spectators," is the core of the system of conventions of the modern theater. The whole relation of the audience to the action on the stage is radically altered, the actor now avoids addressing himself to the spectators in any way—that is the meaning of the "fourth wall"—because the drama has lost its avowed, formerly quite explicit, character of *play.* The increased illusionism of the presentation makes the willingness of the public to put up with the usual conventions of the theater—curtain, raised stage, intervals, and so on—seem all the more remarkable.

With Shakespeare, as with the Greeks, there is a notable contrast between characters and their actual behavior; the hero is nobler and greater than his deeds would suggest.[3] On the other hand, in Shakespeare's personages inner contradictions come to light which make one think of the heterogeneous combination of traits we find in the figures of modern drama. Shakespeare indeed refrains, unlike the modern dramatist, from giving an explanation of these contradictions.[4] Undoubtedly, in Greek tragedy also the contrast between the moral greatness of the characters and the moral dubiousness of their deeds remains unexplained. But in that case no explanation was required: the work of destiny, which is and is to remain a mystery, is most strikingly displayed in the unintelligibility of that contrast. The real misfortune that befalls the hero and leads to his undoing is the act that is "out of character" for him. On the other hand, the inner contradictions in Shakespeare's characters

[3] Stoll: op. cit., pp. 94 f. Stoll too compares Shakespearean drama with Greek tragedy and with the modern naturalistic drama; but the questions he is concerned with only partially overlap those of the present work.

[4] For what follows, compare the works of L. L. Schücking, E. E. Stoll, Wilson Knight, L. C. Knights, and M. C. Bradbrook on Shakespeare.

work themselves out in a way totally different from that of the characters in a modern play. Shakespeare is content simply to exhibit the phenomena of contrast: for his particular purposes he needs no more than a play of conflicting forces and the theatrical effects of contrast. He does not even attempt to make the manifold contradictions of his characters psychologically plausible and intelligible; they are to remain surprisingly and overwhelmingly strange. It is not psychological mechanisms that interest him and his public, but paradoxical states of affairs and bizarre situations. And it is not the complexity, the incalculability, the unfathomability of the human soul which impresses him and which he seeks to impress upon others, but the violence of a strong passion, the power of an unbridled personality, the outbreaks of a temperament that rages like some natural force, destroys everything within its reach, and leaves a path strewn with wreckage. The more contradictory the behavior of his characters in different parts of the play, and the more glaring and surprising the colors in which they are painted, the greater the impression they will make—which is what he wants to achieve. From his point of view, psychological preparation, explanation, reconciliation of inconsistencies, would only diminish the dramatic effect. The modern naturalistic dramatist wants to show how the hero becomes what he is, how he comes to do the deed that is his downfall; he wants to show how the hero reconciles himself to his deed, and how in spite of it he deserves pardon and respect. Shakespeare on the contrary wants to make him beyond all understanding, fathoming, or interpretation; the more incommensurable he is, the greater the theatrical effect in the eyes of the Elizabethan public.

All the "psychology" in epic and dramatic literature serves only to accomplish an identification of the spectator or reader with the personages represented. Only if one can understand a character and see the motives for his behavior can one put oneself in his place and participate in his fate. Such psychology brings about a community of spirit in which the hero comes to seem more human and the reader or spectator more poetical and heroic than they really are. Shakespeare and his public do not want any such identification; they feel that the gulf separating a tragic hero from an ordinary member of the audience is unbridgeable; Shakespeare and the other Elizabethan dramatists make their heroes so full of contradictions, irrational and paradoxical as they are, precisely in order to widen that gulf. This paradoxical character of the personages becomes, in accord with the unromantic outlook of the age, a universal convention of the theater. The representation of space and time on the stage becomes atomistic like the psychology of the characters; just as their behavior is lacking in consistency, so does the plot lack spatial and temporal continuity. The same lack of continuity manifests itself also in the style of the scenery, which combines realism of stage properties with the barest schematic indication of locality. And finally the whole expresses the rhapsodical character of the manneristic sense of life, which at this critical hour of Western culture was dominated by the thought of the equivocal character of human existence and the dual nature of man.

3. *SENTIMENTS AND CONVENTIONS*

Sentiments can be just as conventional as characters, situations, or plots. Sentiments have their history, their heyday and decline, manifest themselves in forms which may or may not be widespread and well-recognized. The various epochs of human history differ not so much through one's being more sensitive or more spontaneous in its sentiments than another, but rather through the varying fashions that decreed the "showing" or not-showing of certain emotions. The sentimentalism of the eighteenth century is no more spontaneous or more "natural" than the puritanism of the seventeenth century or the rationalism of the eighteenth. The troubadour's pining away and the romantic's enthusiasm are just as much literary conventions as the heroism of the ancient epic or the philanthropy of the Victorian novel. In the days of Rousseau and Richardson a man of feeling was always being moved to tears; in other times only the hypocrites are. In Homer the heroes weep if anybody angers them, but they kill off, with a spear in the thigh, another half-dozen opponents without turning a hair.

Nothing makes one realize more clearly the conventionality of artistic forms than the fact that most works of art are strikingly lacking in the one element generally supposed to be the most indispensable, namely in feeling that is genuine, intensive, and sincere. Certainly we can find no support for the assertion that only what is sincerely felt is artistically effective and aesthetically valuable; as a matter of fact, utterly insincere emotional attitudes can produce valuable, even splendid works. One might even perhaps maintain that successful artistic creation requires a certain emotional detachment rather than any very strong emotional attachment to the object to be represented. Already we find Diderot remarking in his *Paradoxe sur le comédien* that, as a rule, the more genuinely and intensively the artist feels what he is to portray, the weaker his expression of it is likely to be. An eye wet with tears does not see clearly, a mouth quivering with emotion is hard to control; on the whole, the amateur is more genuine and has deeper emotions than the real artist. And though it certainly is not always true that the deepest emotions give rise to the worst poems, still there is no guarantee that, given sincere feelings, any more convincing representation will emerge than with insincere feelings.

Sincerity is a moral, not an aesthetic quality. There is a saying that the same person may be a nice man and a bad musician: the natural coincidence of sincerity and artistic capacity is but a philosophical dream modeled upon the *kalos kagathos* and postulating as a metaphysical presupposition the unity of all cultural values. The first difficulty this idea has to face is that one cannot discover any criterion of what in art is genuine, in the sense of expressing real and not fictitious emotions. Certainly no direct evidence of the sincerity of the artist can be derived from the works themselves. But even if one were to allow that in art anything that gives the impression of being sincere is sincere, the problem would still not be solved by any means, as attitudes demonstrably and admittedly insincere, artificial and affected, can give rise to outstandingly valuable creations, as mannerism and rococo show. But the difficulty confronting us here really arises apart from all question of sincerity. For genuine or not, emotions as such have no relevance to artistic merit; indeed, they are no more a special feature of art than most of the other aspects and manifestations of the human spirit. Eduard Hanslick, who makes the irrelevance of the emotions accompanying a piece of music into a basic principle of his aesthetics, supports his thesis with a remark of Handel's contemporary Boyé, who declared with an ingenuousness astonishing for the age in which he lived that the text of Gluck's famous aria: *"J'ai perdu mon Eurydice, rien n'égale mon malheur*, might just as well have been: *"J'ai trouvé mon Eurydice, rien n'égale mon bonheur."* [5]

What anyone feels or does not feel concerns him as a man, not as an artist. For the artist, emotions are just raw material in the same way as are characters he observes or a type of society he studies. He does not need to have felt any particular emotion in order to represent it, any more than he has to be a murderer—or even a "sublimated murderer"—in order to depict a murderer. He only has to produce the image of these emotions in himself; and it may be an actual precondition of this that the emotion itself should be absent. At any rate, imagined emotions can achieve thoroughly original and convincing expression in art, whereas genuine emotions often clothe themselves in the most impersonal and indifferent of forms. In short, it is sometimes the emotions, sometimes the forms that are conventional.

The tension between original sentiments and conventional

[5] Eduard Hanslick: *The Beautiful in Music* (1891), p. 48.

forms on the one hand, and between original forms and conventional sentiments on the other is a most powerful stimulus
to artistic development; it is one of the mechanisms through
which the dialectic of art history manifests itself most frequently
and most strikingly. If a change in sentiment, inclination, and
mood always went hand in hand with a renewal of forms, instead of—as we actually find—forms outlasting the vitality of
the psychic dispositions appropriate to them and novel experiences emerging before appropriate forms of expression are
available, the task of art history would no doubt be much simpler, but also much less fascinating than it is. Art history derives its special character and its philosophical significance
precisely from this stratified nature of the development, the
persistence of certain forms and the anticipation of others, the
varying tempo of conventionalization in the various levels of
artistic production, the resistances that have to be overcome
before an older, now empty, form is abandoned or a novel
sense of life finds its appropriate expression.

No mode of expression, however personal and vital it may
once have been, can retain its spontaneous character for more
than a certain length of time, and equally no form, however
rigid, began its life as a convention. Even the sonnet and the
pastoral were the invention of individual poets, and became
conventionalized only as more and more poets adopted them
and applied them to appropriate and inappropriate material
indifferently. Such a process no doubt has its dangers, but an
art-form does not necessarily lose artistic value through being
conventionalized; it may actually gain in expressiveness and
adaptability. The dramatic monologue, for example, was originally a remarkably awkward and unattractive solution of the
difficulty that arose when matters had to be related which for
some reason or other could not be discussed in the dialogue.
But it gradually developed into an artistically fruitful convention, partly through people having got used to this device and
being no longer disturbed by its artificiality, but partly because

the dramatists discovered in it the possibility of novel dramatic effects. The series of opponents of the monologue begins with Abbé d'Aubignac in the seventeenth century [6] and grows steadily until the close of the naturalistic period in drama. This rock of offence was finally eliminated only by Ibsen, who writes in triumph to Georg Brandes in a letter of June 26, 1869, that in his new play *The League of Youth* there is not a single monologue or aside. Meanwhile the monologue not only had its defenders from time to time, but gradually took on a new significance and achieved an artistic value of its own. Otto Ludwig terms it "that which really gives life to the drama, the truly dramatic," [7] and Jacob Grimm even sees in it "the climax of dramatic art." [8] A. W. Schlegel and Hebbel note the "dialogical-dialectical" character of the monologue, and emphasize that the inner struggles therein expressed are no less dramatic, are indeed often more dramatic, than a conflict between two different persons. Other thinkers more closely connected with naturalism would like to keep the monologue, although not as a whole or in its naïve form, yet in part or with modifications; maintaining that there is a difference of principle between the primitive form, which was only devised to help the dramatist work out the plot or delineate the characters, and the sophisticated form of "inner dialogue," which is not a simplification but an enrichment of dramatic technique. Even Strindberg finds excuses for retention of the monologue, and that not only in his expressionistic period, but also at the time when he was writing *Miss Julie,* and was at the height of his naturalistic phase. Indeed even Alfred Kerr, the most radical of exponents of naturalism in the drama, justifies the monologue to a certain extent. "Where I have nine improbabilities already, I may as well have a tenth," [9] he writes; and in noting that the modern dramatist replaces monologue by pantomime, he tacitly

[6] François Hédelin D'Aubignac: *Practique du théâtre* (1657).
[7] Otto Ludwig: *Dramaturgische Aphorismen.*
[8] Jacob Grimm: *"Ueber den Personenwechsel in der Rede," Kleine Schriften,* III, 292.
[9] Alfred Kerr: *Das neue Drama,* p. 299.

concedes that its elimination leaves a gap that simply cannot be filled by dialogue.

4. THE CONVENTIONS OF THE THEATER

No other form of art has retained so many of its conventions unchanged over so long a time as the theater because no other has so strong an intrinsic propensity to conventionalism. "Every art," writes Sarcey, "employs certain tricks (*tricheries*) that derive from its material conditions. But in the theater they are more numerous than elsewhere."[1] These tricks are more or less equivalent to what is generally understood by "conventions," but they do not at all simply correspond with the technical conditions and inadequacies, from a naturalistic point of view, of the stage. The borderline marking the extent to which the theater abandons truth to nature and permits deviations from our ordinary experience, or in other words, the line between the acceptable and that which breaks the spell, is less sharply and clearly drawn than is usually the case in art. It is remarkable that nobody minds the actors drinking out of empty glasses or fighting with tin swords, whereas people object strongly if a shot is heard a fraction of a second too soon or too late, or if a piece of scenery, painted in a naïve manner that is nevertheless quite accepted, begins to shake. The drama is in the main idealized existence, but the stage operates to some extent with things of our most common experience, living actors, real properties, real space and time. Perhaps the fictions that distinguish the doings on the stage from the spectator's world are as numerous and arbitrary as they are just because the reality of the stage is so obviously tangible and crude. However that may be, we can compile, in the case of the drama, a list of fictions—and extremely persistent fictions at that—longer than for any other form of art.

[1] Francisque Sarcey: *Quarante ans de théâtre*, I (1900), 198.

389

The first concession that every theater-goer has to make is to accept the fiction that Mr. Smith or Mr. Robinson is Julius Caesar or Shylock for the duration of the evening—often in spite of the fact that his figure is obviously unsuited to the part. This change of personality is one of the fundamentals of drama: willingness to believe in the "part" being played is one of the conventions without which there would be no theater.

The most striking deviations of the theater from reality are the platform-like character of the stage and the fact that the action takes place within the framework of the proscenium. But nothing is so odd about this isolated imaginary space as its open front turned toward the audience, *i.e.*, the "fourth wall," which is missing from the scenery, but which the spectator has none the less to imagine as existing.

Anyone who reads an epic follows the poet's story in a way more or less left to him to choose. He may conjure up little or no imagery or he may, as long as he remains within the framework of the story, imagine the scene of the action in as bright and as rich colors as he will—he is not tied to any scenery. The spectator in the theater has no such freedom. He is required to take the bare boards of the stage now for the parquet of a drawing-room, now for a grassy meadow, now for the blood-soaked earth of a battlefield. The leaps that he has to accomplish in fancy are always so great that the difference between the bare platform of the Elizabethan stage and the artifices of the modern revolving stage seems slight by comparison. The unrealities of the stage-setting require such a radical adjustment of outlook on the part of the spectator that, for example, he is scarcely aware of the changes of spatial scale which occur from scene to scene; he finds it natural that the study in the second act should be the same size as the battlefield of the first. In his readiness to fall in with the fictions of the scenery, he goes so far as to treat the stage, if the plot demands it, as a general meeting-place and *rendezvous;* he finds it in no way disturbing that the "hall" of the seventeenth, the "anteroom" of the eighteenth, or the "drawing-room" of the

nineteenth century should be accessible to anybody whose presence the situation happens to require, just like the "street" of
Roman comedy—that everything, in short, should take place
publicly, and the dramatist should have his personages, like
puppets, always on the end of a string. The way in which the
drama separates its persons is no less arbitrary than the way
in which it assembles them. The stage is a dovecote with parti-
tions which, whenever the plot requires it, are sound-proof and
impenetrable. When really necessary, actors standing a few
feet apart are unaware of one another's presence; the one is
blind to what the other is doing and deaf to what he is saying.

The fiction that only some occurrences are audible or visible to the audience is connected with the licence with which
the author can push his persons about, bring them on and take
them off again, arrange for a regular traffic on the stage, provided only that he maintains connections and avoids collisions.
Together these conventions form a unitary system that is simply
a consequence of the economy of space which the stage demands. To the requirements of this economy even the most
self-willed of dramatists has to yield. In a piece so naturalistic
in character as Tolstoy's *Living Corpse,* the guests in the house
have to be asked, for example, to leave the room when their
presence would upset the further course of the plot.

Time on the stage is treated almost as arbitrarily as space.
Often it appears to stand still—that is the real sense of the
"unity of time"; equally often it rushes ahead with incredible
speed. And though it can be accelerated even with the curtain
up, a lowering of the curtain is used to give the impression that
between the two scenes hours, days, or even years have elapsed
—and then after these gaps in time the continuous time-lapse
begins over again.

Yet another feature that is altogether capricious and artificial is the loudness and ostentation of the theatrical voice
and gesture, their self-consciousness and exaggeration. The
mere fact that there is so much talk and that it is assumed that
everything can be said in words is already fiction enough;

391

this love of talk and the urge to find someone to talk to are quite unnatural and forced. Not only do the characters talk about everything that is on their minds, but they are always ready to discuss their lot and argue about it. The fact is that people go to the theater to hear clever speeches and powerful tirades, quick repartee and witty epigrams; they enjoy the swarm of words as one form of the duel that is the core of every dramatic performance.

Among the fictions which the dramatist employs in order to characterize his personages as completely and unmistakably as possible, the monologue and the aside have an important place. They are almost the only resources available to the dramatist in the place of direct description of the characters by the story-teller. Without them the old comedy of intrigue, for example, with its many complications, would be unintelligible to the public. "He hasn't an inkling!"—"What innocence!"—"The villain is trying to trick me!"—"I can't control myself any longer!"—no one talks to himself like that, certainly not in the presence of others, but all this is part of the exhibitionist method, which is quite indispensable to the theater. "Acting" as such, performing emotional somersaults in front of people, necessarily betrays a knowledge of the presence of the audience; monologue and aside are only the most obvious forms of this complicity of actor and audience. There is no great difference of principle between the self-introduction of the medieval *dramatis personae* ("Now I come here, the devil Beelzebub"), the opening monologue of Richard III, and the description of a character before he comes on the stage.

Conversations and consultations of hero and heroine with their *confidants*, confessions before an old friend or before the famous aged nurse or lady-companion, fall in the same category as the monologue, in fact are no more than monologue disguised. The *confidant* is a technical expedient which, like the reports of messengers or the reading of letters aloud, helps the dramatist to overcome the limitations of dialogue.

392

Two of the most important tasks of the dramatist, exposition and *dénouement,* are often performed in a purely conventional manner. The audience is prepared to accept the fact that in order to get the piece going the characters tell each other things they must all have known already, and is prepared to admit the winding-up of a really careful and well-thought-out plot by means of a more or less playful, sketchy, and hasty finale—a finale that cuts the dramatic knot instead of untying it. All this goes to show that in the theater the providing of entertainment and of simple but forceful effects is, as a rule, more important than any other consideration.

Apart from these artifices, which were universal up to the beginnings of modern naturalism, there is another set of dramatic conventions which has been accepted only within certain historical and geographical limits. One of the most notable of these is verse, which, as a means of poetical stylization and idealization, was long considered the only appropriate form for the "elevated" type of drama, whereas for the drama of low life, even in the early days of the mime, verse seemed as inappropriate as buskins, mask, or megaphone would have seemed. However, the public of the "Comédie française" still enjoys, not merely verse, but even what one might call residual traces of the megaphone. Another Greek device for widening the gulf between tragedy and everyday life which maintained itself for a long time was that of assigning female parts to male actors. This convention also was early broken through by the mime, but in the literary theater it persisted until Shakespeare's time. On the other hand, the convention of giving several parts in the same piece to one actor was confined to classical antiquity, which, however, contrived to make a virtue of concentration out of the necessity of a small cast. By assigning to the same actor different roles that were inwardly akin and expressive of the same mood, it succeeded in producing an intensified dramatic effect unique in the history of the theater. In Sophocles' tragedy, the actor who played Antigone also played Teiresias

393

and the Messenger who reports the catastrophe, thus permitting
—as Gustav Freytag acutely remarks [2]—the voice of the dead
heroine to be heard again from Hades. The actor who played
Orestes also took the part of Clytemnestra, and the identity of
the actor in these two parts would make the spectator even
more powerfully aware of the tie of blood that had been so
impiously torn asunder.

To the public of the *tragédie classique* it seemed quite natural that Greek and Roman heroes should wear seventeenth-
century costume on the stage. For the spectators of medieval
drama it did not dispel the illusion in the least that the actors
remained on the stage after they had played their parts in the
piece. Chinese and Japanese audiences are not at all disturbed
by the presence of stage assistants; in fact, in the Far East
nothing is done to disguise the artificiality of a stage-play and
the spuriousness of scenery and properties. A black workman's
overall is enough to indicate the invisibility of the stage-hand,
and he moves freely about the stage during the action, pushes
the furniture in and out, fetches properties and takes them
away again, or smokes a cigarette and reads his paper in the
corner. Equally unembarrassed is the dresser in his concern
with the costume of the actors during the performance; in full
view of the audience he helps put on or take off a kimono,
fastens a girdle that has come undone, or tidies the actors' hair
while they are playing. A few chairs are enough to indicate
a boat in which two lovers are gliding down a stream between
flowery banks; behind them two supers make rowing movements in the air with bamboo poles.

Strange as these conventions are to us, Western opera with
its exclusion of normal speech makes no less of a challenge to
the audience's sense of reality; and the speechlessness of the
former silent film entailed in its day, in spite of the naturalism
of the optical means employed, as great an interference with
the laws of empirical reality. The sub-titles were indeed a
partial substitute for the dialogue, but from the point of view

[2] Gustav Freytag: *Die Technik des Dramas,* pp. 131–3.

of the illusion they were much on a par with the texts issuing from the mouths of figures in medieval pictures. The enjoyment of a film depends on conventions that in many ways demand more of the spectator than is demanded by the fictions of the theater. Instead of objects in the round and living bodies he sees no more than flat, two-dimensional, colorless or unnaturally colored pictures. As a piece of photographed actuality the film may be more realistic, but considered as a shadow reproduction of life it is more unreal than the theater, which at least employs men of flesh and blood. Here we find at every turn an extraordinary mixture of naturalistic and antinaturalistic elements. The situation is the more complicated as the film often appears to use the same technical means in order now to approach nearer to, now to get farther away from reality. The rapid movement of the action, the unrestricted shifting of the point of view, the linking up of anything with anything, on the one hand betoken a victory over that disturbing isolation of single phenomena which is a general feature of all art; but on the other hand the leaps and gaps in the pictures stand in the sharpest contrast to the continuity with which things happen in our world. To give an illustration, we may be standing at the outset of a film with a visitor before the closed door of a house. The visitor rings, and all of a sudden we find ourselves inside the door. The parlor-maid opens, we accompany the visitor in, and before we have had time to look around we are standing before the lady of the house inside the apartment. The visitor looks hard at her, and suddenly we see her as a child, as the visitor is supposed to have known her many years before. The room is transformed into a nursery; on the floor two children— presumably the lady and the visitor—are playing as they used to play once upon a time.

Now this whole procedure, when compared with a scene acted on the stage, seems completely unreal, even fantastic; but once we are sufficiently familiar with the conventions of cutting, and are ready to relate the jerky character of the action to the jerkiness of our mental associations, the sequence of the pictures appears absolutely convincing, indeed most illuminating.

5. *ON THE LANGUAGE OF THE FILM*

Most of the means of representation peculiar to the film derive from the technique of cutting, or *montage;* these are in fact the principal source of the conventional forms of expression which the film employs.

If a person in a film notices something, and immediately thereafter some object appears magnified, the spectator automatically identifies the object with what the actor has just noticed. Or, if there is talk of an unknown person, and thereupon somebody new comes in, it is obvious to the spectator that this is the person who just has been mentioned. In the same way, he identifies localities and other circumstances of the plot.

If we first see the aiming of a gun and then a figure collapsing, we automatically assume a causal connection between the two phenomena. In that case cause is shown before effect, but the sequence can just as well be reversed; *e.g.,* we see a car skid and then a damaged tire; it is at once clear that the tire is the cause of the accident.

Events simultaneously in progress can be represented by alternating montage of the different phases of the events. This mode of jumping backward and forward from one to the other was employed in the earliest sensational films, which in their stereotyped final scenes represent the marvelous rescue of the threatened hero by showing, now a picture of the ever-increasing danger, now one of the approaching rescuer, the point of view changing with ever-increasing rapidity. But in handling a naturalistic drama the director can neither let things come to a sudden standstill nor allow a repetition of particular stretches

of time; he may not show the same movement—say the opening of a door, twice in succession—first in total and then in one
or more close-ups. If he wants to supplement the total by
close-ups, these must carry on the action shown in the total.
Again, he must be equally careful to avoid making the picture "jump," and also, in representing an event by means of
several shots, to avoid repeating the same section of the event.
Just as in the latter case he has to bear in mind that during an
interpolated shot of something else the original action has been
going forward, so in the former case he must remember, each
time he leaves out a piece of the action, to put in a corresponding piece or shot of something else. If, for example, a person
goes from the window to the door, but his doing so is uninter-
esting and takes too long, the director cannot simply cut out a
piece of the film and let him "jump" from window to door; he
can however "cut in" another detail of the same scene or another view of the scenery, and so shorten the distance shown.
By means of this cutting-in of intermediate shots, even very
long sections of the action in progress can be left out and replaced by other episodes. There is no fixed relation between
the duration of what is left out of the principal scene and that
of the scenes inserted, but none the less a certain proportion-
ality between these two durations can be discovered. As has
been noted, we judge the duration of what has been left out by
the distance of the place of the interpolated scene from that
of the principal scene; the farther they are separated, the longer
the gap in the main action appears to be.[3]

In every film there are shots whose temporal connection
with the rest of the action is indefinite or a matter of indifference, and which often stand outside of the dramatic time. A
close-up may for example serve merely as explanation or sup-
plementation of a total view. When, say, someone comes on the
scene and the next picture shows a scar on his face, the two
shots are not in any sort of temporal relation to one another;

[3] B. Balázs: *Der sichtbare Mensch oder die Kultur des Films* (1924),
p. 125.

397

the action has not gone forward at all from the one picture to the other. Landscapes and pictures giving atmosphere between sections of the main action are for the most part nothing but caesuras, having neither any duration of their own nor any temporal connection with the events of the film. Parables again have no dramatic duration.

Close-ups generally take place outside empirical space, just as they are outside the dramatic time. In the case of film-parables such as Eisenstein's parallel between the shooting of workmen and the slaughter of oxen, the picture intended as a parable has indeed its own spatial quality, but it is on a different level of reality from the principal scene, and so seems in a way to be out of space.

Such abandonment of the sphere of space and time throws a good deal of light on the nature of film-parables, which have a rather unfortunate tendency to become allegorical, and are by no means one of the film's more fruitful forms of expression. Where the language of the film is really creative, it does not confine itself to such mere translating of conceptual associations into visual forms. Anyone who has seen Chaplin's *Gold Rush* will remember the delightful scene in which the starving Charlie is about to eat the shoes he has boiled, when his eye falls upon his comrade in misfortune, who suddenly appears to him as a fat hen flapping its wings—picturing the cannibalistic associations that arise in the tortured mind of the little man. But amusing as the scene is, it amounts to no more than the simple illustration of an idea, and owes its effect to Chaplin's acting. It is something unique and unrepeatable—in other words, contains nothing that could be the germ of a fruitful artistic convention. By contrast, the following effects, achieved partly by moving, partly by shifting the camera, are of the essence of the film, altogether visual, models of what an artistic convention can achieve: We see the faces of a man and a woman—in close-up. They are sad and don't talk much. Finally the woman turns to go. The camera is moved gradually back from the man, and as more and more of his figure comes into view, we see

398

shadows of long vertical bars on his clothes. We now know that the woman has been visiting the man in prison. Or again: We see a man running along a street. He comes to a station, rushes on to the platform, and suddenly stops. We see no more than his set, disappointed face. Then we see strips of light and shadow moving across his face at ever-increasing speed. Anyone familiar with the conventions of the film knows what has happened; the man hoped to catch somebody before the train left, but arrived too late. Such devices can be used again and again without losing much of their value; they belong to the repertory of a formal language that anybody can use, which each novel idea may but does not necessarily enrich.

6. *FICTIONS REGARDING TRUTH TO NATURE IN THE VISUAL ARTS*

Every art is governed by a certain norm of what is natural, but none is in immediate contact with nature. Each has its own conventions, and even if these, as in the visual arts, are shorter-lived and seemingly less arbitrary than those of the theater, they set definitely perceptible limits to all striving after "truth to nature." In visual art, truth to the optical impression is not even always the governing principle of the representation; often the conceptual picture prevails over the visual. It is not just children and primitives who depict, to some extent, what they know about the things rather than what they actually see; in all Ancient-Oriental, archaic Greek, and medieval art, visual impressions are subjected to conceptual correction. And in their case, conventionalism of form is by no means confined to the noetic elements in the representation. The rejection of shadows in the painting of Eastern Asia, the frontality of Egyptian art, the canonic proportions of Greek classicism, the neglect of space in early medieval art, the central perspective of the Renaissance, the chiaroscuro of the baroque, the dissolution of outlines by impressionism—all these are sheer conventions that do not, or do not in the main, arise from any observation of nature, but are on the whole violently imposed upon the picture formed from nature.

In palaeolithic art, conventional elements are relatively few, though not absent; but as soon as the neolithic civilization begins to take more definite forms, as soon as more rigorous conventions and more enduring historical traditions come into play, art-forms also become increasingly conventionalized. Taking on a ritual and symbolical meaning, they allude now rather to the object of the representation; they can, indeed they often must, reject all impression of undue "closeness" to nature. The work of art gradually becomes less of a representation and more of an expression of the object; the signs, however, through which an object is "expressed" are in a higher degree a matter of convention than are the standards by which the imitative value of a representation is judged. But representation and communication, impression and expression, copy and sign, can no longer be rigorously distinguished, and become limiting concepts, which in the history of art are realized only in combination. The frontality of the Egyptians, the archaic severity of the early Greeks, and the ceremonial formalism of the Byzantines are expressive, symbolical means of representation that have to assert themselves against a progressive tendency toward naturalism, and give way to the principle of truth to nature as the way of life they express loses its meaning. The gold ground of Byzantine painting, as is well known, is not to be regarded as something merely negative or as simply signifying absence of space; but when from being an expedient of inadequate technique it becomes a convention having expressive content of its own, it finds itself in tension with increasingly naturalistic demands, and in the end has to give way to them.

The Middle Ages with their dependence upon the authoritarian culture of the Church are an epoch par excellence of conventional art-forms. The art of the Ancient Orient may be more conservative and more monotonous, that of Versailles more rigid and narrower, but no other period developed so complete and comprehensive a system of artistic conventions as the Christian Middle Ages. Every feature signifies something over and above the natural object it directly depicts, and the relation to this something else is based upon firm conventions. Natural phenomena are seldom wholly neglected, but there is hardly ever complete equilibrium between sign and copy, meaning and appearance, spirit and bodily form. The picture contains both more and less than could be seen of the object in reality. It shows what the artist "knows" as well as what he sees, and it by no means shows all that he sees. Nothing illustrates more clearly the position of art as intermediary between two worlds than the representation in the Rossano Gospels of the scene in which Judas brings back the pieces of silver to give to the high priest. In this picture one of the front pillars of the baldachin under which the high priest is sitting is partially covered by his figure, although he must be supposed to be sitting *behind* the pillar. Obviously, the artist considered it more important to show the disdainful gesture of the high priest clearly than to trouble about giving things their correct position in space. It would not have occurred to him to question the convention that allowed him to disregard, or even distort, mere everyday experience for the sake of rendering clearly and unambiguously a scene of biblical history or theme of dogma. To the medieval mind the unnatural seemed credible, not in spite of its incompatibility with experience, but because it was in accord with an order of things beside which all else was insignificant. The unnatural relations of size, which accorded with the spiritual importance and supernatural place of the figures, were not felt to contradict experience—with which they simply had no contact; the "reversed perspective" did not compete with the normal, but exhibited relationships that could not have been expressed otherwise. Again, schematic drawing was not felt as inadequate, but on the contrary as the only appropriate way of depicting beings without individuality.

The Renaissance is far from being the end of conventionalism in art, as one might like to think. Above all, central perspective, especially as employed by the Quattrocento, is just as fictitious an arrangement of space-relations as is the medieval juxtaposition of spatial components. It is simply the fiction of an age that rationalized and systematized space, subordinating everything to a unitary point of view in accord with the unitary explanation of the world which it aimed to substitute for the philosophical dualism of the Middle Ages. The perspective of Uccello, Mantegna, or Piero della Francesca is no more "correct" than Ambrogio Lorenzetti's spatial conception; it simply corresponds to more scientific conventions. And like the representation of space, all the other elements of a Renaissance picture—the composition, the coloring, the treatment of light, the representation of the human body and so on—are given a scientific twist, being subjected to artistic conventions permeated by science. The unitary, systematic character of the world-view becomes an artistic ideal. The effect is to give an illusion of a harmony that seemed to the next, mannerist generation so utterly spurious that its discontent produced the first conscious revolt in history against the prevailing artistic conventions. This epoch-making turn of events, the real beginning of modern art, was the outcome of an experience that the world is not at all so well-ordered, meaningful, and "beautiful" as the Renaissance masters, following the conventions of their aristocratic culture, portrayed it; that it is, on the contrary, an insoluble riddle, an equivocal tragi-comedy, a sensual-spiritual, rational-irrational, divine and demonic middle realm. In line with this experience, the mannerists, in all that they take as subject of their art, stress contradictions, double meanings, the inseparable unity of reality and dream, of the common and the fantastic, of the intoxicating and the sobering. And so their revolt ends in new conventions, indeed in some of the most artificial conventions ever set up. Nothing is more characteristic of the mechanical nature of these conventions than the fact that in literature, for example, the play upon words is regarded as the one essential feature of all poetical effectiveness.

402

The baroque starts by invoking a reaction against this conventionalism, and calls into being a new art emotionally more spontaneous and freer from intellectual assumptions. In time, however, it creates its own stereotyped forms, and in its turn develops an extremely artificial and conventionalized mode of expression. And this process repeats itself with every change of style. The rococo is the result of the rejection of the courtly and academic conventions of the baroque, and is the most conventional of styles. Neo-classicism, which started as a movement for artistic liberation, parallel to the French Revolution, led to the most stubborn and persistent academicism we know of.

The romantics organized a regular crusade against artistic conventions. They fought against everything they considered stereotyped, regular, and authoritarian in the field of art; every well-established form they found to be commonplace, a cliché, a mechanical debasement of the available means of expression. Only since the romantics, with their suspicion of all norms whatever, has the concept of convention taken on that pejorative sense which it now ordinarily has. Only with the romantic campaign against all conventionalization of forms does the cultural crisis heralded by mannerism manifest itself in its full proportions and bring about a radical revaluation of our historic culture. Mannerism, indeed, had as yet no word for the evil it was combating; the word "convention" does not occur in the modern sense until the eighteenth century. We do find the expression *"fictions du théâtre"* in Corneille,[4] but he does not understand these "fictions" at all in the sense that the word "convention" later acquired, as referring to the result of the somewhat superficial, formal culture of the rococo. The interesting thing is that the conception emerges only as the golden age of conventions is drawing to a close; it would seem that people did not become conscious of them until they became something of a problem.

But the conventions connected with the culture of the *ancien régime* had already begun to decay long before the tran-

[4] J. Lemaître: *Corneille et la poétique d'Aristote* (1888), p. 67.

403

sition to romanticism. Romanticism was in fact only a symptom of the general crisis of conventionalism, a result of the industrial and political revolution that was the most obvious expression of that crisis. Mme de Staël was one of the first to notice the close connection between social and artistic revolution in her time. *"La nature des conventions,"* she writes, *"est inséparable de l'aristocratie des rangs dans le gouvernement, vous ne pouvez soutenir l'une sans l'autre."* [5] The artistic conventions of the *tragédie classique,* which Lessing, in line with the "enlightened" ideas of his time, had sought to explain in terms of political and social circumstance, did certainly perish along with the ideology of the *ancien régime,* but Mme de Staël failed to observe that the conventionalization of art-forms is not peculiar to aristocracies, that every fairly well-established order of society develops its own conventions. The generation of the romantics was certainly no exception to this; in fact, it produced one of the most crippling conventions of all time, the principle of originality-at-all-costs. For from then on the achievements of all the former generations weighed down the young artist, who could express his own artistic personality only by making tremendous efforts to escape from everything that had been done before.[6] Nor did this convention of unconventionality suffice: the romantics developed a whole new dictionary of permissible means of expression, which in time became just as well-worn as the pre-romantic one. The only difference was that they used the new dictionary with a bad conscience, and all the time felt themselves guilty of a plagiarism. But they "plagiarized" none the less.[7]

Modern naturalism in its turn merely substitutes one convention for another, refers to a "dictionary" quite as often as to nature. And impressionism itself is just as artificial and arbitrary a system of ephemeral conventions as any former style. Arbitrary and not dictated by nature is the impressionist paint-

[5] Mme de Staël: *De la littérature* (1800).
[6] Jean Paulhan: *Les Fleurs de Tarbes* (1941), pp. 33–4, 49.
[7] Ibid., passim.

ers' exaggerated brightness of color, their dissolution of shapes into patches of paint, their blurring of outlines, their elimination of mass and depth, their disregard of composition and frame, their long-distance views and their techniques of improvisation, their separation of the visual from all other kinds of experience, their exclusion of everything conceptual from their view of the world. Impressionism too is a change of taste rather than a break with conventionalism. If after Monet, Pissarro, and Cézanne no one can paint a landscape as landscapes were painted earlier, that is not because those painters discovered a new "truth" or a new technique inherently more appropriate to natural phenomena; it is only because their combinations of form and color set up a convention from which the next generation cannot free itself. They did not give a truer rendering of nature; they gave currency to a new fictitious equivalent of truth to nature.

7. *SPONTANEITY AND CONVENTION*

The romantics insisted that only what was free from conventions, formulas, and commonplaces should count as art or poetry; and they branded as commonplace every attribute once used, every impression already described, every familiar accent. No writer dared to write a sentence without asking himself whether it was sufficiently striking, extraordinary, novel. Their experience that a desperate desire to be original is likely to lead to crass conventionalism only increased their fear of the cliché. Instead of realizing the inevitability of the conventions belonging to every formal language and contenting themselves with being as original as possible within those limits, they tried to escape from conventions altogether, and got all the more hopelessly enmeshed in them.

All expression must in a sense "atomize" what in living ex-

405

perience is given as an integral undifferentiated unity, must break it up into features, attribute to it various predicates. Art is concerned with preserving the unity and coherence of living experience as much as possible, in spite of the dissolution that sets in with the process of expression. This contradiction lies at the core of art; it is the source of art's dual nature, at once rational-irrational and sensual-spiritual. Both the rational and the sensuous elements in art, both its abstract formal principles and its optical or acoustic means of expression, set up a "distance" between the subject and the object of experience; the creation of art involves both intending this distance and intending its annihilation. Art is not content with irrational experience, but desires also the rationalizing and organizing of experiences; it is not content with the spiritual, but also wants the embodiment; can dispense neither with the body it builds for the spirit nor with the spirit for which it builds a body.

"Whereof one cannot speak, thereof one must be silent," wrote Ludwig Wittgenstein.[8] For science, in distinction from all other spiritual endeavors, there is indeed nothing about which one would necessarily have to be silent. Because all that is is in principle knowable, and because all that is knowable is scientifically expressible, science faces no formal problem analogous to the problem of the limits of artistic expression. In science it may be true that "what we can't say we can't say, and we can't whistle either."[9] What science knows, it can speak about; in art on the contrary, by no means all that can be experienced can be directly expressed, and the artist must often "whistle" for want of speech. That is, he must express himself in an indirect, incomplete, inexact manner, by means of conventional, stereotyped signs that dilute his experience. It is a mistake, however, to think that no one who employs conventional and stereotyped means can ever get beyond the conventional, or that originality must fade out wherever conventions come into

[8] Ludwig Wittgenstein: *Logisch-Philosophische Abhandlung* (1921).
[9] A. J. Ayer: "The Vienna Circle," in *The Revolution in Philosophy*, ed. Gilbert Ryle (1956), p. 75.

play. For though we see everything in a distorting perspective and express it in a distorting medium, yet we can note the deficiencies of the medium and to some extent correct them. We possess means whose distorting effect not only varies from case to case, but is also related to different portions and aspects of reality, means, too, which distort differently when employed by different individuals. The conventionality of the means of expression may introduce an unbridgeable element of distance from reality, but the keenness of the individual eye makes itself apparent even so. Artistic originality shows itself both in opposition and in submission to the conventions, and can show itself only within the bounds of established conventions.

A system, procedure, or game in which one has to follow definite, settled rules manifests to the superficial onlooker only negative features, those which appear to restrict the free movement of the players, but the person who plays the game does not feel embarrassed by the rules, and moves freely within the limits set. No soccer-player reflects that he may not hold the ball with his hands; no chess-player finds any special difficulty because bishops can only move diagonally and castles not jump like a knight; in these restrictions, as far as he is aware of them at all, he recognizes the preconditions of the whole game and of the exercise of his own skill. And just as a player's skill is called forth only by the skill of his opponent, so every artistic achievement is the result of a sort of argument between the intentions and creative talent of the artist and the available conditions, means of expression, and conventions.

"La rutina y la improvisación son dos enemigos mortales del arte" is the motto on a memorial tablet to the conductor Erich Kleiber in Buenos Aires. This is true enough, but it is also true that without a certain minimum of routine and improvisation no art is possible. Both must play their part in the work of art, and they must complement one another. A purely conventional art in which all spontaneity and originality was lacking would be completely insipid; but an art in which everything had to be original would be not only impossible in

practice, but even unthinkable—for where everything is original, nothing is original. Conventions indeed provide not only the conditions of existence for artistic achievement, but also the standards by which these are evaluated. The originality of an artist is most notable where a number of artists submit to the same conventions. Both the dependence of Raphael and his originality are most clearly seen when he is set alongside the masters by whom he was most deeply influenced.

Although romanticism was right in maintaining that every convention brings with it signs of torpor and death, that each in the end must cease to mediate expression and effect an impression, yet every novel, spontaneous, unconventional form has about it something embryonic, not worked out, incomplete. A style in art is only capable of development as long as its conventions are lively and elastic enough to absorb the novel, the spontaneous, the unconventional; and a novel artistic idea can be formed only if there is tradition and convention for it to link on to. Though it is this dependence which makes an artistic idea communicable, it is the originality of the idea which makes it worth communicating. The history of art is a process in which striving for the novel and the personal gradually stretches the limits of the conventions and from time to time bursts them. There is no change of style for which this formula does not hold. The straight-line development of a style is necessarily a progressive conventionalization of forms, but every new stylistic idea interrupts this process to a certain extent.

When one seeks to do justice to the historical role of conventions in art, and also to the resistance they provoke, it is hard to avoid going too far in the one direction or the other. Undoubtedly Carl Philipp Emanuel Bach was a more original composer than his father, Haydn's music a greater novelty in its time than Mozart's, Debussy's idiom more revolutionary than Verdi's. Perugino, Dosso Dossi, Lorenzo Lotto, and Pontormo are more peculiar and original in a sense than Raphael or

Titian. But who would be misled into ranking them higher on that account? And who would venture to decide whether convention or revolt was more important to such artists as Giotto, Leonardo, Michelangelo, El Greco, and Breughel? Or who would dare to say how much Mozart owed to convention, Beethoven to revolt against convention? Can we hear their music, when we try to answer that question, as they and their contemporaries heard it? Do we not rather hear it with the ears of a generation contemporary with Bartók and Schönberg which grew up on the music of Wagner, Debussy, and Mahler?

It has recently become customary to play the musical works of a former age on the instruments for which they were composed; in performances of the works of Bach and his contemporaries, for example, the piano is being replaced more and more by the harpsichord. No doubt that brings out certain features of the works better, but it would be false to assume that by this means we hear Bach just as his audiences heard him. That is unlikely; the harpsichord notoriously sounds different since the invention of the pianoforte; it is actually no longer the same instrument. As the introduction of new musical instruments alters our mode of hearing, so does it alter the tone-quality of the old instruments. To an ear accustomed to the pianoforte, the harpsichord sounds colder, weaker and less mellow that it must have sounded to Bach and his contemporaries. The pianoforte introduced a new standard of loudness and timbre, so that for us today the modern instrument is more in accord with the spirit of Bach than the harpsichord, as being an elaborate instrument on which the most lively dynamic and coloristic effects are obtainable—as the harpsichord was for Bach's age. Historicism, conceiving the authentic too literally, and ignoring the power of convention to change the meaning of the authentic, inevitably ends by falsifying history. One gains a much deeper understanding of the works of a past age by translating what was once lively and novel into a language that sounds lively and novel today. It is certainly wrong to play

Mozart just as "dynamically" as Beethoven, but it is equally wrong to make of him simply a charming, light-hearted "rococo" artist. He was for his contemporaries, as Bach probably was for his, a "romantic" in Proust's sense.[1]

But just as we are not in a position to judge the tonal effects that Bach's compositions had upon his contemporaries, so also we are unable to perceive in all their original effectiveness the quality of the colors used by the old masters. With each new step in the history of coloring, one gets farther away from an adequate understanding of them. One need only think of the revaluation of color by the impressionists to realize what a leap such an understanding would require. The restoration of the old pictures, aiming to restore their coloristic effect in its original freshness, may increase the distance that separates us from them, just as employment of the harpsichord in a way increases our distance from Bach. Everyone would prefer to see genuine color rather than opaque varnish, but one should not suppose that these colors speak a language intelligible in itself to people who approach them with ever-varying coloristic standards. In the variability of the measure by which the intensity of sensuous effects is felt and in the variability of the conventional criteria of taste by which aristic means are selected and deployed lie the sources of that misinterpretation from which the art of former centuries is never altogether free. We shall never learn so much about the intentions of its creators, the objective content of their works, and the importance their contemporaries ascribed to them, as to be able, when appraising it, to estimate precisely the changes that our sense-organs, our sensitivity, and out taste have undergone in the course of the time that has elapsed. What is the use of knowing how the instruments really sounded, how the colors really looked, if our ears and eyes are so formed as to devalue their

---

[1] *"Seuls les romantiques savent lire les ouvrages classiques, parce qu'ils les lisent comme ils ont été écrits, romantiquement."* Pastiches et mélanges (1919), p. 267.

sensory effect, and we still do not hear or see the works as they were meant to be heard and seen! But why—one might well ask, with those who distrust the historicist approach—should we wish to see and hear the works in any other but the way in which they most surely delight and move us?

Index

xiii